God Bless America

God Bless America

The Origins of Over 1,500 Patriotic Words and Phrases

Robert Hendrickson

Skyhorse Publishing

Skyhorse Publishing books may be purchased in bulk at special discounts for sales promotion, corporate gifts, fund-raising, or educational purposes. Special editions can also be created to specifications.For details, contact the Special Sales Department, Skyhorse Publishing, 307 West 36th Street, 11th Floor, New York, NY 10018 or info@skyhorsepublishing.com.

Skyhorse® and Skyhorse Publishing® are registered trademarks of Skyhorse Publishing, Inc.®, a Delaware corporation.

www.skyhorsepublishing.com

10 9 8 7 6 5 4 3 2 1

Library of Congress Cataloging-in-Publication Data is available on file.

ISBN: 978-1-62087-597-1

Printed in the United States of America

Publisher's Note

In compiling this book, we have tried to include as many interesting selections as possible, if only to make this one of the most entertaining and exceptional works on the subject. The source material, *Encyclopedia of Word and Phrase Origins* by renowned etymologist Robert Hendrickson, provided thousands of meticulously researched definitions, histories, and anecdotes. We've certainly strived to preserve the integrity of that work with this new, polished package, focusing fully on the richness of the American language and its peoples. Yet in the final analysis any selection from such a vast semantic treasure house must be highly subjective. Perhaps we have erred in devoting too much space to fascinating but speculative stories about word origins and American history, but we don't think so, for the wildest theories often later turn out to be the correct ones. The only limitations we have imposed are those of importance and interest. We hope you enjoy this trip through American linguistic history as much as we have.

Abbreviations for the Most Frequently Cited Authorities

BARTLETT—John Bartlett, *Dictionary of Americanisms* (1877)

BARLETT'S QUOTATIONS—John Bartlett, *Familiar Quotations* (1882 and 1955)

BREWER—Rev. Ebenezer Cobham Brewer, *Brewer's Dictionary of Fact and Fable* (1870)

DARE—Frederic Cassidy, ed. *Dictionary of American Regional English,* Vol. 1, 1986; Vol. 2 (1991); Vol. 3 (1996); Vol. 4 (2002)

FARMER AND HENLEY—John S. Farmer and W E. Henley, *Slang and Its Analogues* (1890–1904)

FOWLER—H. W. Fowler, *Modern English Usage* (1957)

GRANVILLE—Wilfred Granville, *A Dictionary of Sailor's Slang* (1962)

GROSE—Captain Francis Grose, *Dictionary of the Vulgar Tongue* (1785, 1788, 1796, 1811, 1823 editions)

LIGHTER—J. E. Lighter, ed., *Random House Historical Dictionary of American Slang,* Vol. 1 (1994); Vol. 2 (2000)

MATHEWS—Mitford M. Mathews, A *Dictionary of Americanisms* (1951)

MENCKEN—H. L. Mencken, *The American Language* (1936)

O.E.D.—*The Oxford English Dictionary* and Supplements

ONIONS—C. T. Onions, *The Oxford Dictionary of English Etymology* (1966)

PARTRIDGE—Eric Partridge, *A Dictionary of Slang and Unconventional English* (1937; 8th ed., 1984)

PARTRIDGE'S ORIGINS—Eric Partridge, *Origins,* A *Short Etymological Dictionary of Modern English* (1958)

PEPYS—Henry Wheatley, ed., *The Diary of Samuel Pepys* (1954)

RANDOM HOUSE—*The Random House Dictionary of the English Language* (1966)

ROSTEN—Leo Rosten, *The Joys of Yiddish* (1968)

SHIPLEY—Joseph T. Shipley, *Dictionary of Word Origins* (1967)

SKEAT—W. W. Skeat, *An Etymological Dictionary of the English Language* (1963)

STEVENSON—Burton Stevenson, *Home Book of Quotations* (1947)

STEWART—George R. Stewart, *American Place Names* (1971)

WALSH—W. S. Walsh, *Handbook of Literary Curiosities* (1892)

WEBSTER'S—*Webster's Third New International Dictionary of the English Language* (1981)

WEEKLEY—Ernest Weekley, *Etymological Dictionary of Modern English* (1967)

WENTWORTH AND FLEXNER—Harold Wentworth and Stuart Berg Flexner, *Dictionary of American Slang* (1975)

WESEEN—Maurice H. Weseen, *The Dictionary of American Slang* (1934)

WRIGHT—Joseph Wright, *English Dialect Dictionary* (1900)

Many different works by the same authors, and additional works by other writers, are cited in the text.

A

aa. *Aa* for rough porous lava, similar to coal clinkers, is an Americanism used chiefly in Hawaii, but it has currency on the mainland, too, especially among geologists, or where there has been recent volcanic activity, mainly because there is no comparable English term to describe the jagged rocks. The word *aa* is first recorded in 1859, but is much older, coming from the Hawaiian *'a'a,* meaning the same, which, in turn comes from the Hawaiian *a,* for "fiery, burning."

Abe's cabe. American slang for a five-dollar bill. So-called from the face of Abe, Abraham Lincoln, on the front of the bill, and from *cabe,* a shortening and rhyming pronunciation of *cabbage,* which in slang means any currency (green). Coined in the 1930s among jazz musicians, the term is still in limited use today. *See also benjamin.*

abide. To endure, stand, or tolerate, usually in the negotiation sense, as in "I can't abide him." Mark Twain used this expression, which has been considered standard American English since at least the early 1930s.

Abraham Lincoln. Old Abe's nicknames include, among others, *Honest Abe, The Railsplitter, The Liberator, The Emancipator, Uncle Abe, Father Abraham, The Chainbreaker,* and *The Giver of Freedom.* He was called many derogatory names, too, notably the sarcastic *Spot Lincoln,* because he had supported the anti-Mexican War resolution in 1847, demanding that President Polk identify the exact spot where Polk claimed Mexico had already started a war on American soil. During the

Civil War Lincon was called *Ape* in the South, the word mocking his appearance and playing on *Abe. Tycoon,* in its sense of military leader, was also applied to him at that time.

absquatulate. A historical Americanism coined in the early 19th century and meaning to depart in a clandestine, surreptitious, or hurried manner, as in "He absquatulated with all the funds." The word is a fanciful classical formation based on *ab* and *squat,* meaning the reverse of "to squat." The *Rocky Mountain News* (1862) gives the following example: "Rumour has it that a gay bachelor, who has figured in Chicago for nearly a year, has skedaddled, absquatulated, vamosed, and cleared out."

ace; aces. *Aces* has been American slang for "the best" at least since the first years of the last century, deriving from *aces,* the highest cards in poker and other card games. But *ace* for an expert combat flier who has shot down five or more enemy planes appears to have been borrowed from the French *as,* "ace," during World War I. From there *ace* was extended to include an expert at anything. The card name *ace* comes ultimately from the Greek *as,* one. An *ace* in tennis, badminton, and handball, among other games, is a placement made on a service of the ball, while an *ace* in golf is a hole in one. The trademarked *Ace bandage,* used to bind athletic injuries, uses *ace* meaning "best," too. *Ace* figures in a large number of expressions. *To ace* a test is to receive an A on it, and *ace it* means "to complefte anything easily and successfully." *To be aces with* is to be highly regarded ("He's aces with the fans."), and *to ace out* is to cheat or defraud ("He aced me out of my share.") *Easy aces* in auction bridge denotes aces equally divided between opponents; it became the name of a 1940s-1950s radio program featuring a husband

and wife team called *The Easy Aces.* Another old *ace* term is *to stand ace high,* to be highly esteemed.

aces all around. Everything is going well, splendidly, first rate, like being dealt all aces in a poker or other card game. Someone might ask "How are you doing?" and get the reply "Aces all around." The expression was heard in Washington, D.C. (2006) but is doubtless much older.

acid test. This expression dates back to frontier days in America, when peddlers determined the gold content of objects by scratching them and applying nitric acid. Since gold, which is chemically inactive, resists acids that corrode other metals, the (nitric) *acid test* distinguished it from copper, iron, or similar substances someone might be trying to palm off on the peddlers. People were so dishonest, or peddlers so paranoid, that the term quickly became part of the language, coming to mean a severe test of reliability.

Acoma. A Native American tribe of New Mexico and Arizona. The tribe's name means "people of the white rock" in their language, in reference to the pueblos in which they lived. Acoma is also the name of a central New Mexico pueblo that has been called "the oldest continuously inhabited city in the United States." The name is pronounced either *eh-ko-ma* or *ah-ko-ma.*

act your age. Perhaps *act your age!* originated as a reproof to children, but it is directed at both children and adults today, meaning either don't act more immature than you are, or don't try to keep up with the younger generation. The expression originated in the U.S., probably during the late 19th century, as did the synonymous *be your age!*

African American. *African American,* a term many blacks and whites prefer as the name for blacks today, is not of recent origin and wasn't coined in the North, as some people believe. African American did become common in the late 1980s but was first used in the American South some 140 years ago. Even before its birth, terms like *Africo-American* (1835) and *Afro-American* (1830s) were used in the names of black churches.

after someone with a sharp stick. To be determined to have satisfaction or revenge. John Bartlett called this phrase a common Americanism in 1848 and it is still occasionally heard today.

aggie fortis. An Americanism meaning anything very strong to drink. As one old-timer put it ". . . this man's whiskey ain't Red Eye, it ain't Chain Lightnin' either, it's regular Aggie forty [sic], and there isn't a man living who can stand a glass and keep his senses." *Aggie fortis* derives from *aqua fortis,* strong water, the Latin name for nitric acid.

ain't got sense enough to poke acorns down a peckerwood hole. An old rural Americanism said of someone pitifully stupid. A *peckerwood* is a woodpecker but can also mean a poor southern white. *See* CRACKER; REDNECK.

ain't hay. *Hay* has meant a small amount of money in American slang since at least the late 1930s, which is about the same time that this expression is first recorded. Little more is known about the very common *and that ain't hay* for "a lot of money," a saying that I would suspect is older than currently supposed.

ain't he (she) a caution. Isn't he or she remarkable, unusual, or, especially, funny; an old term still heard infrequently. Could be a variation of *ain't he a corker,* once frequently heard among Irish Americans.

ain't no place in heaven, ain't no place in hell. Nowhere for one to go, limbo. The expression is from an old African-American folk song quoted in William Faulkner's *Sanctuary* (1931): "One day mo! Ain't no place fer you in heaven! Ain't no place fer you in hell! Ain't no place fer you in white folk's jail! Whar you gwine to?"

airtights. Canned food was called *"airtights"* by cowboys in the American West during the latter part of the 19th century. Canned beef was *meat biscuit* or *beef biscuit.*

aisle. *Aisle* strictly means a section of a church or auditorium, deriving from the Latin *ala,* "wing," and that is how the word has been used by the British until relatively recently. But Americans have long used *aisle* to mean a passageway in a church, auditorium, or elsewhere, and this usage is becoming universal.

alamo. The name of several poplar trees, including the cottonwood; from the Spanish *alamo* meaning the same. The Alamo is also the name of a Franciscan mission in San Antonio, Texas, besieged by 6,000 Mexican troops in 1836 during the Texan war for independence. The siege lasted 13 days and ended with all 187 of the defenders being killed. "Remember the Alamo!" became the Texan battle cry of the war. The most recent use of the Alamo's name is San Antonio's Alamodome sports stadium constructed in 1992 at a cost of $130 million.

Alaska. *seward's folly, seward's icebox,* Seward's iceberg, Icebergia, and Walrussia were all epithets for the 600,000 square miles now known as Alaska. All of these denunciations today honor one of the great visionaries of American history, William Henry Seward. Seward's most important work in Andrew Johnson's administration was the purchase of Alaska, then known as Russian America, from the Russians in 1867. Negotiating with Russian Ambassador Baron Stoeckl, the shrewd lawyer managed to talk the Russians down from their asking price of $10 million to $7.2 million, and got them to throw in a profitable fur-trading corporation. The treaty was negotiated and drafted in the course of a single night and because Alaska was purchased almost solely due to his determination—he even managed to have the treaty signed before the House voted the necessary appropriation—it was widely called *"Seward's folly"* by irate politicians and journalists. Seward himself named the new territory Alaska, from the Aleut *A-la-as-ka,* "the great country."

Albany beef. Sturgeon was once so plentiful in New York's Hudson River that it was humorously called *Albany beef.* The term is first recorded in 1791 and was in use through the 19th century; sturgeon caviar was so cheap in those days that it was part of the free lunch served in bars. Cod was similarly called *Cape Cod turkey* in Massachusetts.

alewife. One early traveler in America, John Josselyn, seems to have thought that this plentiful fish was called the *alewife* because it had "a bigger bellie" than the herring, a belly like a wife who drank a lot of ale. More likely the word is a mispronunciation of some forgotten American Indian word.

Alexander Hamilton. Sometimes used as a term for one's signature, similar to the use of *john hancock* or *john henry.* The term, of course, comes from the name of American statesman Alexander Hamilton (1757–1804).

Alibi Ike. Someone who is always making excuses or inventing alibis is called "Alibi Ike." The designation was invented by Ring Lardner in his short story "Alibi Ike" (1914) as a nickname for outfielder Frank X. Farrell, so named because he had excuses for everything. When Farrell drops an easy fly ball, he claims his glove "wasn't broke in yet"; when questioned about last year's batting average he replies, "I had malaria most of the season"; when he hits a triple he says he "ought to had a home run, only the ball wasn't lively," or "the wind brought it back," or he "tripped on a lump o' dirt roundin' first base"; when he takes a called third strike, he claims he "lost count" or he would have swung at and hit it. The author, who had a "phonographic ear" for American dialect, created a type for all time with Alibi Ike, and the expression became American slang as soon as the story was published. In an introduction to the yarn the incomparable Lardner noted, "The author acknowledges his indebtedness to Chief Justice Taft for some of the slang employed."

all aboard! This common train conductor's call is an Americanism, first recorded in 1837, and is nautical in origin. Wrote Joshua T. Smith in his *Journal in America* (1837): "They [the Americans] describe a situation by the compass 'talk of the voyage' of being 'all aboard' & etc.; this doubtless arises from *all* their ancestors having come hither over ocean & having in the voyage acquired nautical language." The call *all aboard!* was used on riverboats here before it was used on trains.

all-American. Walter Chauncey Camp, "the Father of American Football" who formulated many of the game's rules, picked the first all-American football team in 1889 along with Caspar Whitney, a publisher of *This Week's Sport Magazine*. But the idea and designation was Whitney's and he, not Camp, should be credited with introducing *all-American* to the American lexicon of sports and other endeavors.

all chiefs and no Indians. Many businesses have experienced trouble because they had all chiefs and no Indians, that is, too many officers who want to do nothing but give orders to others. The origin of this common worker's complaint has been traced to about 1940 in Australia, where the expression was first *all chiefs and no Indians, like the University Regiment.* Yet the first half of the expression has an American ring, and one suspects that some determined word sleuth might turn up an earlier printed use in the United States.

all dressed up and no place to go. Said to have originated in a 1915 song by U.S. comedian Raymond Hitchcock. The words are still heard today but nowhere nearly as often as they once were.

alley-oop. This interjection may have been coined by American soldiers during World War I, for it sounds like the French *allez* ("you go") plus a French pronunciation of the English *up*—hence *allez oop,* "up you go." During the 1920s *allez-oop* (often spelled *alley-oop)* was a common interjection said upon lifting something. The expression became so popular that a caveman comic strip character was named Alley Oop. Soon *alley-oop* became a basketball term for a high pass made to a player near the basket, who then leaps to catch the ball and, in midair, stuffs it in the basket. In the late 1950s, San Francisco 49er quarterback Y. A. Tittle invented a lob pass called the *alley-oop* which was thrown over the heads of defenders to tall, former basketball player R. C. Owens.

all good Americans go to Paris when they die. *See mutual admiration society.*

all hands and the cook. *All hands and the cook on deck!* was a cry probably first heard on New England whalers in the early 19th century when everyone aboard was called topside to cut in on a whale, work that had to be done quickly. Fishermen also used the expression, and still do, and it had currency among American cowboys to indicate a dangerous situation—when, for example, even the cook was needed to keep the herd under control.

all hat and no cattle. A Texan phrase describing someone who acts rich or important but has no substance, such as a person who pretends to be a cattle baron, even dressing the part: "He's all hat and no cattle."

all his bullet holes is in the front of him. A colorful phrase describing a brave man, not a coward, coined by cowboys in late 19th-century America.

all I know is what I read in the papers. This saying has become a popular American expression since Oklahoman Will Rogers coined it in his *Letters of a Self-Made Diplomat to His President* (1927). It has various applications but is commonly used to mean "I'm not an expert, just an ordinary person, and what I've told you is true to the best of my knowledge." It implies one may be wrong because one's sources are not infallible.

all oak and iron bound. A 19th-century Americanism meaning in the best of health and spirits, as in "He's feeling all oak and iron bound." The comparison is to a well-made barrel. Oak alone is a hard, strong, durable material.

all quiet on the Potomac. Sylva Clapin explained this phrase in *A New Dictionary of Americanisms* (1902): "A phrase now become famous and used in jest or ironically as indicative of a period of undisturbed rest, quiet enjoyment, or peaceful possession. It originated with Mr. [Simon] Cameron, Secretary of War during the Rebellion [Civil War], who made such a frequent use of it, in his war collections, that it became at last stereotyped on the nation's mind." E.L. Beers published a poem in *Harper's Weekly* (Nov. 30, 1861) extending the expression: " 'All quiet along the Potomac,' they say, / 'Except now and then, a stray picket / is shot, as he walks on his beat to and fro./ By a rifleman hid in the thicket.' " General George McClellan is also said to have invented the phrase. *See all quiet on the western front.*

all quiet on the western front. Although it may owe something to the Civil War slogan *all quiet on the potomac,* this phrase became well known in World War I because it was often used in communiques from the western front, a 600-mile battle line that ran from Switzerland to the English Channel and was in reality far from quiet just with the moans of the wounded and dying. The most famous use of the words is in the title of Erich Maria Remarque's great antiwar novel, *All Quiet on the Western Front* (1929).

all systems go. All preparations have been made and the operation is ready to start. Widely used today, the expression originated with American ground controllers during the launching of rockets into space in the early 1970s.

all vines an' no taters. An Americanism of the 19th century used to describe something or someone very showy but of no substance. "He'll never amount to nothin'. He's all vines and no taters." Probably suggested by sweet potato plants, which produce a lot of vines and, if grown incorrectly, can yield few sweet potatoes.

almanac.

> "Early to bed and early to rise
> Makes a man healthy, wealthy and wise."

The above is just one sample of the shrewd maxims and proverbs, almost all of which became part of America's business ethic, that Benjamin Franklin wrote or collected in his *Poor Richard's Almanac.* This was by no means the first almanac issued in America, that distinction belonging to *An Almanack for New England for the Year 1639,* issued by William Pierce, a shipowner who hoped to attract more paying English passengers to the colonies and whose almanac was (except for a broadside) the first work printed in America. *Poor Richard's* was written and published by Franklin at Philadelphia from 1733 to 1758 and no doubt takes its name from the earlier English *Poor Robins Almanac,* first published in 1663 by Robert ("Robin") and William Winstanley. Almanacs, which take their name from a medieval Latin word for a calendar with astronomical data, were issued as early as 1150, before the invention of printing, and were compendiums of information, jokes, and proverbs.

aloha. Both a greeting and farewell, the Hawaiian *aloha* means, simply and sweetly, "love." It has been called "the world's loveliest greeting or farewell." Hawaii is of course the *aloha state,* its unofficial anthem "Aloha Oe" (Farewell to Thee) written by Queen Liliuokalani. *Mi loa aloha* means "I love you" in Hawaiian.

"Aloha Oe." The Hawaiian queen Liliuokalani (1838–1917) is the only ruler known to have written a national anthem. A prolific songwriter, she wrote the words to "Aloha Oe" ("Farewell to Thee"), today Hawaii's unofficial state song.

aloha shirt. Although these colorful Hawaiian shirts with bright prints of hula girls, surfers, pineapples, and other Hawaiian subjects date back to the 1920s, they were made famous by manufacturer Ellery Chun (1909–2000), who first mass-produced them. The shirts were made in small Honolulu tailor shops until Mr. Chun, a native Hawaiian and Yale graduate, manufactured them in quantity and coined their name in 1933. They sold for 95 cents apiece during the Great Depression. *See aloha.*

aloha state. *See aloha,* above, for this nickname for Hawaii, which is also called the Crossroads of the Pacific and the Paradise of the Pacific.

also-ran. The joy may be in playing, not winning, but *an also-ran* means a loser, someone who competed but didn't come near winning. The term is an Americanism first recorded (as *also ran*) with political reference in 1904, and derives from horse racing. The newspaper racing results once listed win, place, and show horses before listing, under the heading "Also Ran," all other horses that finished out of the money.

amalgamationist. "Blending of the two races by amalgamation is just what is needed for the perfection of both," a white Boston clergyman wrote in 1845. Few American abolitionists were proponents of amalgamation, but many were called amalgamationists by proslaveryites in the two decades or so before the Civil War. This Americanism for one who favors a social and genetic mixture of whites and blacks is first recorded in 1838, when Harriet Martineau complained that people were calling her an amalgamationist when she didn't know what the word meant.

ambulance chaser. It is said that ambulance chasers in days past had cards like the following:

SAMUEL SHARP

THE HONEST LAWYER

CAN GET YOU

$5,000	$10,000
for a leg	for a liver

Ambulance chaser is a thoroughly American term that originally described (and still does) a lawyer who seeks out victims immediately after an accident and tries to persuade them to let him represent them in a suit for damages. The expression probably originated in New York City during the late 1890s, a time when disreputable lawyers frequently commissioned ambulance drivers and policemen to inform them of accidents and sometimes rode with victims to the hospital to proffer their services.

Ameche. Though not much used anymore, *Ameche* has been American slang for "telephone" since 1939, when actor Don Ameche played the lead role in *The Story of Alexander Graham Bell,* the inventor of the telephone.

amen corner. A group of fervent believers or ardent followers is called an amen corner, after the similarly named place near the pulpit in churches occupied by those who lead the responsive "amens" to the preacher's prayers. The term may come from the Amen Corner of London's Paternoster Row, but it is an almost exclusively American expression today. Also, a name coined by sportswriter Herbert Wind (1916–2005) for "the treacherous stretch of the Augusta National [golf] course on the 11th, 12th and 13th holes," as his *New York Times* obituary (June 1, 2005) put it. The name had been suggested to him by the spiritual "Shoutin' in the Amen Corner," a jazz record he had bought when in college.

America. Many writers have assumed that the Italian navigator Amerigo Vespucci (whom Ralph Waldo Emerson called "a thief" and "pickle dealer at Seville") was a con man who never explored the New World and doesn't deserve to be mentioned in the same breath with Christopher Columbus, much less have his name honored in the continent's name. Deeper investigation reveals that Vespucci, born in Florence in

1454, did indeed sail to the New World with the expedition of Alonso de Ojeda in 1499, parting with him even before land was sighted in the West Indies. Vespucci, sailing in his own ship, then discovered and explored the mouth of the Amazon, subsequently sailing along the northern shores of South America. Returning to Spain in 1500, he entered the service of the Portuguese and the following year explored 6,000 miles along the southern coast of South America. He was eventually made Spain's pilot major and died at the age of 58 of malaria contracted on one of his voyages. Vespucci not only explored unknown regions but also invented a system of computing exact longitude and arrived at a figure computing the earth's equatorial circumference only 50 miles short of the correct measurement. It was, however, not his many solid accomplishments but a mistake made by a German mapmaker that led America to be named after him—and this is probably why his reputation suffers even today. Vespucci (who had Latinized his name to Americus Vespucci) wrote many letters about his voyages, including one to the notorious Italian ruler Lorenzo de' Medici in which he described "the New World." But several of his letters were rewritten and sensationalized by an unknown author, who published these forgeries as *Four Voyages* in 1507. One of the forged letters was read by the brilliant young German cartographer Martin Waldseemuller, who was so impressed with the account that he included a map of the New World in an appendix to his book *Cosmographiae Introductio,* boldly labeling the land "America." Wrote Waldseemuller in his Latin text, which also included the forged letter: "By now, since these parts have been more extensively explored and and another 4th part has been discovered by Americus Vespucius (as will appear from what follows); I see no reason why it should not be called Amerigo, after Americus, the discoverer, or indeed America, since both Europe and Asia have a feminine form from the names of women." Waldseemuller's map roughly represented South America and when cartographers finally added North America, they retained the original name; the great geographer Gerhardus Mercator finally gave the name "America" to all of the Western Hemisphere. Vespucci never tried to have the New World named after him or to belittle his friend Columbus, who once called him "a very worthy man." The appellation *America* gained in usage because Columbus refused all his life to admit that he had discovered a new continent, wanting instead to believe that he had come upon an unexplored region in Asia. Spain stubbornly refused to call the New World anything but *Columbia* until the 18th century, but to no avail. Today Columbus is credited for his precedence only in story and song ("Columbia, the Gem of the Ocean"), while Amerigo Vespucci is honored by hundreds of phrases ranging from *American know-how* to *American cheese*.

American. The first person recorded to have used this term for a citizen of the U.S. or of the earlier British colonies was New England religious leader Cotton Mather in his *Magnolia Christie Americana* (1702).

american. The Japanese have taken to many things American, but not our coffee, which they find weak. Preferring espresso or other strong brews, they call any weak coffee *american.* This seems to be the case in many countries. In Spanish-speaking places, for example, an espresso mixed with extra water is called a *cafe-americano*.

the American dream. The American dream is almost impossible to define, meaning as it does so many different things to so many different people. These words go back at least to de Tocqueville's *Democracy in America* (1835) and are usually associated with the dreams of people new to these shores of freedom, material prosperity, and hope for the future.

American English. There are thousands of Americanisms that are different from English expressions, although these have dwindled with the spread of movies, television, and increased foreign travel. A good example of such differences is found in a story about *tuna fish*. The highest word rate ever paid to a professional author is the $15,000 producer Darryl Zanuck gave American novelist James Jones for correcting a line of dialogue in the film *The Longest Day*. Jones and his wife, Gloria, were sitting on the beach when they changed the line "I can't eat that bloody old box of tunny fish" to "I can't stand this damned old tuna fish." If they had translated *box* they would have substituted *can*.

American Indian language words. English words that come to us from American Indian languages include: chocolate, tomato, potato, llama, puma, totem, papoose, squaw, caucus, Tammany, mugwump, podunk, chinook, chautauqua, tomahawk, wampum, mackinaw, moccasin, sachem, pot latch, manitou, kayak, hogan, teepee, toboggan, wigwam, igloo, porgy, menhaden, quahog, catalpa, catawba, hickory, pecan, persimmon, pokeweed, scuppernong (grapes), sequoia, squash, tamarack, hominy, hooch, firewater, pone, bayou, pemmican, succotash, cayuse, wapiti, chipmunk, caribou, moose, muskrat, opossum, raccoon, skunk, terrapin, and woodchuck.

Americanism. In 1781 Dr. John Witherspoon, president of the College of New Jersey (now Princeton), wrote a series of essays on "the general state of the English language in America." He listed a number of "chief improprieties" such as Americans using "mad" for "angry," etc., and coined the word *Americanism* to define them.

America's Cup. This racing trophy was originally called the Hundred Guinea Cup when it was offered by the British Royal Yacht Squadron to the winner of an international yacht race around the Isle of Wight. The U.S. schooner *America* won the first race in 1875, defeating 14 British yachts, and the cup, still the greatest prize in yachting, was renamed in her honor. American yachts won the cup in every competition until

1983, when the Australians took it home to Perth, ending the longest winning streak in sport.

America the Beautiful; America. Katherine Lee Bates (1859–1929), was a professor at Wellesley College when she wrote the poem "America the Beautiful" (1893), which was made into the famous patriotic song of the same name. The lyrics have been set to music by 60 different composers. "America," another well-known patriotic song, was written in 1831 by Boston Baptist minister Samuel Frances Smith (1808–95) when he was a seminary student. It is sometimes called "My Country 'Tis of Thee," after its first line. *See god bless america.*

Americium. A chemical element that was discovered in 1944 by U.S. scientist Glenn T. Seaborg, who named it in honor of America. The element Seaborgium is named after him.

Ameslan. *Ameslan* is the acronym for American Sign *Language*, the shorter term being first recorded in 1974. American Sign Language, a system of communication by manual signs used by the deaf, is more efficient than finger spelling and closer to being a natural language. Finger spelling is just "a means of transposing any alphabetized language into a gestural mode."

AMEX. American Express.

Amurrican. Linguist Raven I. McDavid Jr. told of how his conservative professors, literally interpreting the pronunciations indicated in *Merriam-Webster's Collegiate Dictionary,* fifth edition, criticized his educated South Carolinian pronunciation of the word *American.* McDavid pointed out that there are at least five pronunciations, one as good as any other, these including the second syllable with the vowel of *hurry,* with the vowel of *hat,* with the vowel of *hit,* with the vowel of *hate,* and with the vowel of *put.* There is no all-American pronunciation of *American.*

Similarly, many Americans voted against what H. L. Mencken sarcastically called "the caressing rayon voice" of the politician Wendell Willkie because the Hoosier pronounced "American" as Am*ur*rican.

Amy Dardin case; Amy's case. An obsolete term for procrastination. Virginia widow Amy Dardin of Mecklenburg County submitted to Congress her claim to be compensated by the federal government for a horse impressed during the American Revolution, sending a bill every year from 1796 to at least 1815; some sources say she kept dunning Congress for 50 years before the procrastinating government paid.

and how! Indicating "intensive emphasis of what someone else has just said," *and how!* is a long-popular catchphrase first recorded in 1924. The Americanism possibly derives from the German *und wie!* or the Italian *e come!,* meaning the same thing, and once very common among Americans of German and Italian extraction, respectively.

and then some! *And then some!* is an Americanism dating back to about 1910. But its roots probably go deeper than this in history, some investigators believing it is an elaboration of the Scots *and some,* meaning "and much more so," which is recorded about two centuries earlier. One British professor claimed he found a parallel expression in the *Aeneid* (Book viii, line 487)!

Andy Warhol. According to the *New York Times* (September 20, 2006) the artist's name should be Andy Warhola—the final "a" in his name was omitted early in his career by a typesetter. The artist was nicknamed Raggedy Andy "because he delivered his early commercial artwork in brown paper bags."

Angeleno. Anyone residing in Los Angeles, California; this Spanish term dates back to the mid-19th century.

Anglo. A term for an English-speaking white person, an Anglo-American, that originated among Spanish speakers in the Southwest in the early 19th century and is now common throughout the United States. Unlike *gringo,* it is not always a derogatory term. *Anglo* can also mean the English language: "He doesn't speak Anglo."

antifogmatic. An antifogmatic is any alcoholic drink taken in the morning to brace one against the fog or dampness outside, or taken with that as the excuse. This amusing Americanism is first recorded in 1789.

ant killer. A humorous term for the foot, especially a big foot. The term is an Americanism dating back to the mid-19th century.

antsy. Originating in the early 1950s, *antsy* means jittery, restless, nervous. The expression derives from the earlier phrase *to have ants in one's pants,* which dates back to World War II America and is recorded in humorist H. Allen Smith's book *Putty Knife* (1943): "She dilates her nostrils a lot, the way Valentino used to do it in the silent movies to indicate that he had ants in his pants." The quotation shows that *to have ants in one's pants* can suggest lust, but to my knowledge *antsy* never has this sexual meaning.

anxious seat. Front seats at religious revivalist meetings in the American West during the 19th century were called anxious seats, because their occupants were so eager to be saved.

Anytime Annie. American slang for a woman who is always willing to have sex. Heard by author, who can find no recorded source for the name.

anyways. Anyway, anyhow, in any case. "Anyways I've got my opinion," Mark Twain wrote in "The Celebrated Jumping Frog of Calaveras County" (1865). The Americanism can also mean to any degree at all: "Is he anyways hurt?"; or at any time: "Come visit anyways from May to October."

A-O.K. An accidental coinage, *A-O.K.* was not used by American astronaut Alan Shepard while making the first suborbital space flight, as was widely reported. The term is actually the result of a mistake by NASA public relations officer Colonel "Shorty" Powers, who thought he heard Shepard say "A-O.K." when the astronaut, in fact, uttered a rousing "O.K." Powers liked the sound of *A-O.K.* so much that he reported it several times to newsmen before he learned of his mistake. By then it was too late, for the term became part of the language practically overnight. Speech purists insist that *A-O.K.* is a repetition, increasing O.K. 50 percent in size, but in spoken communication redundancy is not necessarily bad—in fact, it is often essential to clarity and understanding, especially in emergencies. And in everyday conversation A-O.K. usually means "better than O.K.," "great," "near perfect"—not, repeat *not,* just "all right." *See o.k.*

Appalachia. The Appalachian Indian tribe gave its name to this mountainous region in the southeastern U.S., though the naming was a mistake. As Roderick Peattie put it in *The Great Smokies and Blue Ridge* (1943): "[The Spanish explorer] De Soto left no memorial or trace, except for the name Appalachian itself (from the Appalachi tribe of Muskhogeans on the Gulf Coast), misapplied by him to the fair mountains he traversed so long ago." It is interesting to note that Washington Irving once suggested (in the *Knickerbocker Magazine,* August 1839) that the name *United States of Appalachia* be substituted for the *United States of America.*

apple; apple hawk; apple orchard. *Apple* for a baseball dates back to the early 1920s; before that the ball had been called a "pea," a term heard no more. A good fielder was called an *apple hawk* at the time, this term obsolete now, and the ball park was called an *apple orchard,* an expression still occasionally used. *Apple* itself comes from the Old English *appel* for the fruit. An *apple* can also be a derogatory name given to certain American Indians by other American Indians who believe their values are too much like those of whites; that is, they are, like an apple, red on the outside and white on the inside. This term is based on the American black derisive name *Oreo* for a black person whose values are believed to be too much like those of whites. An Oreo is a trademarked chocolate cookie with creamy white filling.

apple-pie order. One old story holds that New England housewives were so meticulous and tidy when making their apple pies—carefully cutting thin slices of apples, methodically arranging them in rows inside the pie, making sure that the pinches joining the top and bottom crusts were perfectly even, etc.—that the expression *apple-pie order* arose for prim and precise orderliness. A variant on the yarn has an early American housewife baking seven pies every Monday and arranging them neatly on shelves, one for every day of the week in strict order. Nice stories, but the term *apple-pie order* is probably British in origin, dating back to at least the early 17th century. It may be a corruption of the French *nappes-pliees,* folded linen (neatly folded) or cap-a-pie, "from head to foot." Yet no use of either *nappes-pliees* order or cap-a-pie order appears in English. "Alpha beta order" has also been suggested, but seems unlikely. The true source of the term must still be considered a mystery, the matter far from in apple-pie order.

applesauce. The expression *applesauce* for disguised flattery dates to the early 20th century and may derive from "the boarding-house trick of serving plenty of this cheap comestible when richer fare is scanty," according to a magazine of the time. The term also came to mean lies and exaggerations. As a word for a sauce made from stewed, sweetened apples, *applesauce* is an Americanism dating back at least to the mid-18th century. *Applesauce* as a term for insincere flattery may also have been invented by American cartoonist Thomas Aloysius Dorgan

(1877–1929), "Tad" having been the most prolific word coiner of his day. No one knows for sure.

apple slump. Apple slump, a popular New England dessert, takes on another meaning in Louisa May Alcott's story "Transcendental Wild Oats" (1876), an account of her father Bronson Alcott's failed utopian community, Fruitlands, 32 years earlier: " 'Poor Fruitlands! The name was as great a failure as the rest!' continued Abel [Bronson Alcott], with a sigh, as a frostbitten apple fell from a leafless bough at his feet. But the sigh changed to a smile as his wife added, in a half-tender, half-satirical tone, 'Don't you think Apple Slump would be a better name for it, dear?' " The dessert is sometimes called *apple pandowdy* and *flummery*. So much did Harriet Beecher Stowe like the dish that she named her Concord, Massachusetts, house Apple Slump.

Appomattox. The name for a Virginia river that in turn gave its name to a sleepy town it meandered through in south-central Virginia, a hamlet more properly called *Appomattox Court House,* where all Confederate dreams died at the end of the Civil War when General Lee surrendered there. *Appomattox* itself later became a synonym for surrender or for victory, or for reconciliation, depending on who pronounced it. But perhaps Carl Sandburg defined the word best in *Abraham Lincoln: The War Years:* "For a vast living host the word Appomattox had magic and beauty. They sang the syllables 'Ap-po-mattox' as a happy little carol of harvest and fields of peace and the sun going down with no shots in the night to follow."

Arbor Day. "Tree Day" is the exact meaning of *Arbor Day,* for *arbor* is a Latin word for "tree." Arbor Day was first celebrated in 1872, when Nebraskan J. Sterling Morton and his supporters persuaded their state to set aside April 10th for tree planting, to compensate for all the trees

Americans had destroyed over the years in clearing the land for settlements. More than a million trees were planted on that first Arbor Day alone, and today the holiday is celebrated in every state.

Archie Bunker. Among the most recent of eponymous words, an *Archie Bunker* means a bigoted lower-middle-class American. The words recall the bigoted lead character of the long-running television show *All in the Family.*

archy. Perhaps the only and certainly the most humorous cockroach in American literature. He was invented by satirist Don Marquis (1878–1937) for the author's newspaper columns, along with archy's friend mehitabel the cat, both of their names uncapitalized. The inspired cockroach writes free verse because he can't work a typewriter shift key. The cat's motto is *toujours gai*, "always gay, merry." Their adventures were first collected in 1927.

are you a man or a mouse? American slang probably dating back to the early days of the century, *Are you a man or a mouse?* is used to disparage or spur on a timorous person. The reply is often: "A man; my wife's afraid of mice."

are you kidding? "You must be joking, you can't be serious." The Americanism *no kidding* probably suggested the longer exclamation, first recorded in about 1945.

Arizona. Our 48th state, admitted to the Union in 1912, is nicknamed "the Grand Canyon State." *Arizona* derives from the Papago Indian word *Arizonac,* "the place of the small spring."

Arizona nightingale. A humorous Americanism for a braying burro or mule that dates back to the late 19th century.

Arizona strawberries. American cowboys and lumberjacks used this term as a humorous synonym for beans, also employing the variations *Arkansas strawberries, Mexican strawberries,* and *prairie strawberries.* Dried beans *were* pink in color like strawberries. One wit noted that the only way these beans could be digested was for the consumer to break wild horses.

Arizona tenor. A person suffering from tuberculosis and the coughing that accompanies it; many people with the illness were drawn to the dry Arizona climate.

Arkansas. Originally spelled *Arkansaw,* our 25th state, nicknamed "the Wonder State," was admitted to the Union in 1925. *Arkansas* is the Sioux word for "land of the south wind people."

Arkansawyer. A nickname for a native of Arkansas, often used by Arkansas residents themselves, because the original spelling of the state's name was Arkansaw. *Arkansawyers* have suffered their share of insults in the language, including *Arkansas asphalt* (a log road); *Arkansas chicken* or *T-bone* (salt pork); *Arkansas fire extinguisher* (a chamberpot); *Arkansas lizard* (any insect louse); *Arkansas travels* (the runs, diarrhea); and *Arkansas wedding cake* (corn bread).

armadillo; Texas turkey. *Armadillo* is the Spanish diminutive of "the armed one" and is related to words like armor, this obviously in reference to the little porkilotherm's being encased in bony armor and by its habit of rolling itself, when threatened, into an impregnable ball. The Mexican native, which cannot survive north of Texas, was a source of food to Americans during the Great Depression, when it was known as the "Hoover hog" or "Texas turkey." Darwin was fascinated by the little armadillo and its ancient prehistoric predecessor, the glyptodont, which was about the size of a Volkswagen Beetle. A children's poem has it that a peccadillo of the armadillo is that it must be washed with Brillo.

armstrong. A high trumpet note, such as those played by American jazz great Louis "Satchmo" Armstrong (1900–71). "Satchmo," which he liked to be called, refers to his rather large mouth.

A-Rod. People who have little or no knowledge of baseball might have trouble with these initials. They are short for Alex Rodriguez, the famous Yankee baseball star.

arse; ass. *Arse* is generally used by the British for the buttocks. They use *ass* for the animal. Americans say *ass* for both the animal so called and the anatomical designation. In fact, the word *arse* in any sense is rarely heard in America, except possibly as a euphemism.

artsy-fartsy. A pompous, pretentious person who tries to appear more educated or knowing about something, especially art, literature, or music. Originally an American expression, perhaps patterned on *arty-crafty*, and first recorded in 1965.

as long as grass grows and water runs. A promise, meaning "forever," often made to Indian tribes in the American West regarding their rights to their lands and their freedom. But as a writer put it in *Colliers Magazine* (11/30/07): "The white invaders [settlers] pleaded for Statehood, and Statehood forever laid aside the promise to the red man that he should have freedom 'as long as grass grows and water runs.'"

assembly line. The term *assembly line* was first recorded in 1914 in connection with Henry Ford's car company, but the practice in America goes back at least to the 18th century, when muskets were made from several standard parts in one factory. Among automobile manufacturers, Henry Ford is generally credited with the idea for an assembly line, but Ford actually improved upon a method the Olds Motor Vehicle Company, maker of the Oldsmobile, used long before him in 1902, although he did introduce the electric conveyer belt.

ass in a sling. The *Dictionary of American Slang* says that *to have one's ass in a sling* means "to be or appear to be sad, rejected, or defeated." Originating in the South perhaps a century ago, the now national expression was probably suggested by someone with his arm in a sling, that image being greatly and humorously exaggerated. A good story claims that this *ass* is really a donkey, that the expression comes from a practice of blacksmiths rigging slings for donkeys, or asses, because they can't stand on three feet while being shoed. But the good story isn't a true story. Donkeys *can* stand on three feet, and so far as is known, no blacksmith ever shod a donkey in a sling.

as the crow flies. Meaning, "in a straight line," the expression dates back to at least 1800. *Corvus brachyrhynchos* of North America is a remarkable bird, far too clever for any *scarecrow*. These crows are said to hold conventions of 40 to 60 birds in which a leader they will follow is chosen. They can apparently be ruthless, too. Wrote the New England naturalist Alan Devoe: "The most extraordinary rites of a flock are the 'trials' they conduct. When a crow has broken the laws of crowdom, the flock gathers in judgment, parleying sometimes for hours while the offender waits some distance away. Suddenly the discussion ceases; there is a moment of silence. Then the flock either rises in unison and leaves, or dives in a mass upon the offender, pecks out his eyes, and pummels him to death."

Astor Place riots. The eminent American actor Edwin Forrest (1806–72) was a great rival of the older English tragedian William Macready, who at 78 played his last role, as Macbeth, and who died in 1873 at the age of 100. In 1849, both actors were appearing in New York, where each had ardent fans, the "common man" favoring Forrest and the elite supporting Macready. The rivalry degenerated into "a struggle between democracy and Anglomania," in one critic's words, and on May 10 a mob led by E. C. Z. Judson (writer Ned Buntline), possibly encouraged by Forrest, attacked the Astor Place Opera House, where Macready was playing Macbeth. In the Astor Place riots, 22 people were killed and 36 wounded, making this probably the worst such theater disaster of all time. Judson went to jail for a year for his part in the affair.

AT&T. American Telephone *and* Telegraph, formed in 1885, was called The Long Distance Company until it acquired the Bell Company four years later and began buying local phone companies. Today, as the result of a 1982 antitrust suit, it has divested itself of local phone companies and is back to long distance again (along with some new ventures and the manufacture of phone equipment).

Aunt Hagar's children. A once commonly heard reference for African Americans in general. So called after Hagar, Ishmael's mother (Gen. 21:9); Hagar was the Egyptian servant of Abraham's wife, Sarah, in the Old Testament.

automatic writing. *Automatic writing* is writing performed without the will or control of the writer, sometimes without the writer being conscious of the words written. The phenomenon first appeared in mid-19th-century America as a tool of spiritualism, and the writer was sometimes (but not always) hypnotized or drugged and aided by instruments including a planchette, "a little heart-shaped board running on wheels," that was supplemented by a Ouija board containing the alphabet and other signs.

automobile. "[Automobile] being half Greek and half Latin, is so near indecent that we print it with hesitation," a *New York Times* editor wrote in 1899. But *automobile* and *car* are the only survivors of the many names Americans gave to early *horseless carriages,* which included *dia-mot, motor buggy,* and even *stink chariot* (probably the work of an early environmentalist). A French construction of the 1880s, it was broken down to *auto* here by 1899.

Avenging Angel. A Colt revolver with a portion of its barrel sawed off was called an *Avenging Angel* in the early West. Avenging Angels were used by Brigham Young's Morman followers, one of whom was said to have killed hundreds with his.

AWOL. This commonly used abbreviation meaning "absent without leave" originated during the Civil War, according to H. L. Mencken (*The American Language,* supplement I, 1945): "[In the Confederate Army] unwarranted absences of short duration were often unpunished and in other cases offenders received such trivial sentences as repri-mand by a company officer, digging a stump, carrying a rail for a hour or two, wearing a placard inscribed with the letters AWOL."

ayuh. Yes; though the word has shades of meaning ranging from the affirmative to the sarcastic. Chiefly heard in Maine, *ayuh* is found throughout New England in variations such as *eyah, ayeh, eeyuh, ehyuh, aaay-yuh,* and even *ayup.* A touchstone of New England speech, it pos-sibly derives from the nautical *aye,* "yes," which in turn probably comes from the early English *yie,* "yes." Another theory has *ayuh* coming from the old Scottish-American *aye-yes* meaning the same.

B

baaad. *Bad,* when slowly pronounced *baaad,* has long been black slang for something or someone good, and recently this meaning has come into general usage to a limited extent. The variation is so old that it is found in the American Creole language Gullah three centuries ago, when *baaad* was used by slaves as an expression of admiration for another slave who successfully flaunted "Ole Massa's" rules.

babbitt. Congress deemed the invention of babbitt or babbitt metal so important to the development of the industrial age that it awarded inventor Isaac Babbitt (1799–1862) a $20,000 grant. Babbitt is a soft, silver-white alloy of copper, tin, and antimony used to reduce friction in machine bearings. It was discovered as a result of the inventor's experiments in turning out the first Britannia metal tableware ever produced in America. After the Taunton, Massachusetts goldsmith successfully manufactured Britannia in 1824, he experimented further with the same three metals and ultimately invented babbitt, which he used to line a patented journal box in 1839. The metal proved far better than any other substance used for reducing friction and is still widely used for machine bearings today. *Babbitt soap,* no longer marketed, also bore the inventor's name. Babbitt wasn't the prototype for Sinclair Lewis's ambitious, uncultured, and smugly satisfied American businessman in his novel of the same name, but the character's name was probably suggested by Lewis's early memories of advertisements for the soap.

Babe Ruth. George Herman Ruth wasn't the first athlete to be called Babe, but he is certainly the most famous to bear the name, which was bestowed upon him in 1914 by a Baltimore Orioles coach, who shouted, "Here's Jack's new Babe!" when Ruth (signed by Baltimore owner Jack Dunn) first entered the ballpark. Over his long career, Ruth earned many other nicknames—including *Jidge, Monk, Monkey,* and the *King of Swat*—but history will always remember him as *the Babe.* A variation on this is *Bambino,* the Italian for "baby," which for centuries has meant an image of the infant Jesus in swaddling clothes. No sports records are better known than the legendary *Sultan of Swat's* 60 home runs in one season and 714 throughout his career (though both records have been surpassed), and his "call" of a home run in the 1932 World Series is on every list of "most memorable sports events." There seems no reason to doubt that when all his records are broken, Babe Ruth will still be more famous than those who broke them. Ruth (1895–1948), the poor boy brought up in an orphanage who became the most renowned American athlete of all time, is one of the few people ever to become a folk hero while still alive (Joe Louis is another). Some of the stories about the Bambino bear repeating. For example, he began his baseball career as a catcher for St. Mary's School in Baltimore. He was an outstanding pitcher in the major leagues before switching to the outfield. He led the major leagues in strikeouts in 1923 with 93, being a strikeout king as well as home run king. He once hit a home run that literally went around the world, the ball landing in a freight car that was transported to a ship. And one could go on for pages from memory alone. The New York Yankees star, the Homer of Home Runs, has never been equaled for talent or color. His name will remain a synonym for the ultimate in sluggers even after someone else has hit 120 homers.

baby-kisser. Politicians have been baby-kissing since the first election, but the term doesn't seem to have been used before the U.S. presidential election of 1884. The words were applied to Benjamin Butler, who ran on the independent Greenback- Labor ticket and came in a poor third behind Democrat Grover Cleveland and Republican James Blaine. "As a baby-kisser," a contemporary newspaper observed, "Ben Butler is not a success." One theory has it that the idea for the term appears in the Eatanswill election episode of Dickens's *Pickwick Papers* (1837), although *baby-kisser* doesn't appear there.

Baby Ruth. The popular candy bar was probably named after BABE RUTH in 1921, when Ruth was already a legendary star. Soon after, Ruth challenged the naming, trying unsuccessfully to patent his own *Babe Ruth Home Run Bar,* and the candy-maker then claimed its *Baby Ruth* had been named after President Grover Cleveland's daughter Ruth, widely called Baby Ruth. Since Baby Ruth had died in 1904, 17 years before the candy bar was marketed, such a naming seems highly unlikely. The Baby Ruth candy bar probably was named for Babe Ruth, even though the candymaker doesn't support the story anymore. Ira Berkow's "A Babe Ruth Myth . . ." *(New York Times* 4/7/02) tells the story in greater detail.

baby-sitter. *Baby-sitter* offers a good example of what is called back-formation of a word. Usually nouns derive from verbs, as *diver* derived from *dive.* In the case of *baby-sitter,* however, this process was reversed. *Baby-sitter* is an Americanism first recorded in 1937, while the verb to *baby-sit* was born from it over 10 years later. The noun has come to mean one who takes care of children or anything else that requires attention.

Baby State. A nickname for Arizona because it was long the youngest state in the Union, admitted in 1912. It is also known as the Valentine State (it was admitted on St. Valentine's Day), the Grand Canyon State, the Sunset State, the Sandhill State, the Coyote State, and the Apache State.

back the wrong horse. When we support the wrong person, party or thing, or bet on the loser in any situation, we back the wrong horse. The term is an Americanism taken from the racetrack, and is still widely used although it is a century or more old.

bad ball hitter. A term of recent vintage, a *bad ball hitter* describes someone who makes bad judgments or evaluations. The Americanism refers to a batter in baseball who often swings at pitches that are not strikes and usually misses. There is no similar term in cricket or tennis. It should be noted that many batters have hit so-called bad-ball pitches for home runs, including career home run record-holder Hank Aaron, who frequently did so.

bad hair day. A term that originated in the United States for a day on which it is hard to do anything with one's hair, male or female. The expression dates back to about 1990 and by extension came to mean a day on which nothing seems to go right.

bad luck comes all in a lump. The belief that bad luck comes one after another, without relenting. A proverb possibly from the American West, dating back to the 19th century.

bad man; badman. A mainly historical term for an outlaw or professional gunfighter who had killed people. Many were brutes, bullies, and psychopaths, but several who carried the title were men who had killed others in arguments or in selfdefense. In The *Great American Outlaw* (1993), Frank Richard Prassel has this to say about the compound word *badman,* as opposed to *bad man:* "Indirectly [John]

Wayne gave popular language the very word. His film *The Angel and the Badman* (1946) fixed the compound in vernacular English with a contradictory meaning. A badman is not necessarily bad; *goodman* has no meaning. Films issued before 1946 consistently divided the term; those made later routinely adopted the compound. For the original it was of no significance; whenever John Wayne played a badman, as he did with some frequency, something was clearly wrong with the law. His mere appearance in the role of a criminal made justification for illegality pointless; it could be assumed."

bad medicine. Among American Indians, bad medicine meant a person's bad luck, his spirits working against him. Cowboys used the term *bad medicine* to describe any very dangerous person, such as a feared gunfighter.

badmouth. To speak ill of someone. Probably originating among African-American speakers and possibly deriving from a Vai or Mandingo expression, *to badmouth* was at first employed mostly by southern blacks but is now used nationwide. Its first recorded use in this sense came in 1941 when James Thurber used it in a *Saturday Evening Post* story: "He badmouthed everybody."

bag lady; old bag; bag. Short for "shopping bag lady," *bag lady* entered the language in the 1960s. It has nothing to do with the term *old bag*, for an ugly woman (which goes back to the 1920s), or BAGMAN, a term for someone (often a policeman) assigned to collect bribe or extortion money, an expression also dating back to the flapper age. *Bag* has many meanings in American slang, including "to be sacked (bagged) from a job"; "a prostitute" (from douche bags being associated with prostitutes); "a condom"; "to arrest"; "a base in baseball"; and "to be drunk" (to have a bag on). But *bag* here refers to the shopping bags, filled with their possessions, that the unfortunate women we call bag ladies carry with them as they wander—from doorway to alley to abandoned car to park bench—through American cities. The *lady* in their name is both ironic and kind.

bagman. In America *bagman* means a racketeer or anyone assigned to collect a bribe, extortion, or kidnapping money. In England, however, a bagman is simply a traveling salesman, a drummer who carries bags of samples. "In former times," one authority tells us, "these commercial travelers used to ride a horse with saddle bags sometimes so large as almost to conceal the rider."

bald eagle. This American eagle is so named because the feathers on the head of the adult are white, making it appear bald when seen from a distance. Said to be the most pictured bird in the world, the bald eagle appears on the Great Seal of the United States and on many U.S. coins and paper currency. There was some controversy over its choice for the great seal by the Second Continental Congress because it commonly steals fish from other hawks, but its majestic presence prevailed. It has also been called the bird of freedom, bird of Washington, calumet eagle, gray eagle, brown eagle, nun's eagle, whiteheaded eagle, and national bird.

bald-headed. An expression used for a hurried action taken without caution or much thinking: "He really went at it baldheaded." As Maximilian Schele de Vere put it in *Americanisms* (1871), the expression probably derives from "the eagerness with which men rush to do a thing without covering the head."

ballpark figure. An approximation based on an educated guess or a reasonable estimate is a ballpark figure. Only about 25 years old, the American expression obviously comes from baseball, *ballparks* being another name for the stadiums where baseball is played. The phrase probably derives from the 1962 coinage of *in the ballpark* for "something that is within bounds, negotiable, not out of reach"; *out of the ballpark* means just the opposite. Baseball stadiums were first called ballparks around 1900; before then they had been called ball grounds, baseball grounds, ball fields and baseball parks.

balls to the wall. Originally a military aircraft term, this expression dates back to about 1966 and means at full speed, to the extreme, all out, maximum effort. According to the *New Dictionary of American Slang* (1986), the phrase derives "from the thrusting of an aircraft throttle, topped by a ball, to the bulkhead of the cockpit to attain full speed." Usually considered vulgar or obscene, the expression is commonly heard in Washington, D.C., today.

ball the jack. To move or work swiftly. Originally an American railroad term ("That train is sure balling the jack.") of the 19th century, *ball the jack* came to mean "to move or work swiftly," as in "When he saw his boss coming he really balled the jack."

Baltimore; Baltimore oriole; Baltimore clipper. An early dictionary tells us that the Baltimore oriole is "so called from the colors of Or (orange) and Sable in the coat of arms belonging to Lord Baltimore." This oriole is not closely related to the orioles of Europe, belonging to the blackbird or meadowlark rather than the crow family. In fact, many American birds with the same names as European species are in reality birds of a different feather. (The American robin, for instance, is really a thrush, and other Old World avian words given new significances include partridge, blackbird, lark, and swallow.) But whatever its true species, the Baltimore oriole definitely takes its name from the Baltimore family, founders of Maryland, the bright colors of the male bird indeed corresponding to the orange and black in their heraldic arms. The city of Baltimore, Maryland also honors the barons Baltimore, as do the early 19th-century Baltimore clippers, more indirectly, the famous ships having been built in the city. The same can be said of baseball's Baltimore Orioles and football's Baltimore Colts. No particular Lord Baltimore has been singled out for the honor. George Calvert, the first baron Baltimore (ca. 1590–1632), prepared the charter for the proposed colony that became Maryland, but died before it could be accepted; the charter was granted to his son Cecilius, but the second baron Baltimore never even visited the province; and the third baron Baltimore, Cecilius's son Charles, governed the province from 1661 to 1684. A Catholic who ruled quite arbitrarily over his predominantly Protestant subjects, Charles returned to England and never came back, leaving little more than the family name behind.

Baltimore Ravens. Would you believe this football team is named after a poem? It is. The *Baltimore Ravens* honors Edgar Allan Poe's "The Raven," one of the most famous poems in American history, which Poe wrote in 1844 and sold to the *New York Mirror* for 35 bucks. Poe was intimately connected with Baltimore, where he spent his last weeks on earth, dying four days after he'd been found delirious outside a saloon-polling place where he may have been casting ballots for drinks. Few remember that Poe was also an accomplished athlete, possibly the greatest author-athlete in American literary history. He once swam seven and a half miles from Richmond to Warwick, Virginia, against a tide running 2-3 miles an hour. He long-jumped 21 feet while at West Point and was a swift runner. Fully six members of Princeton University's 1899 football team were named Poe, each of them a great-nephew of Edgar Allan Poe. To further honor the writer, the Ravens have named their three mascot ravens *Edgar, Allan,* and *Poe.*

Baltimore Whore. A humorous name given to the B-26 Marauder bomber by U.S. pilots during World War II. The *Baltimore Whore,* made in Baltimore, Maryland, was so called because it was very difficult to fly and was frequently cursed out with such names.

the Bambino. Taken from the Italian *bambino,* baby, this is a well-known nickname of American baseball great Babe (George Herman) Ruth (1895–1948), also known as the Sultan of Swat. But *bambino* has for centuries meant an image of the infant Jesus in swaddling clothes in art.

bangs. A bang-tailed horse is one whose tail is allowed to grow long, and then cut or "banged off" horizontally to form an even tassel-like end. Such fashioning of horses' tails was popular in the late 19th century and when several bang-tailed horses won major races the style attracted wide attention. Apparently, American hairstylists or women themselves named the similar women's hairstyle after the horse-tail style, adding *bangs* to the fashion lexicon.

banker. A North Carolina seacoast inhabitant. "This term of 'Banker' applies to a scattered population of wreckers and fishermen, who dwell on the long, low, narrow beaches . . . from Cape Fear to near Cape Henry."

bank holiday. *Bank holiday* was one of the first of many words and phrases coined during the New Deal in America's Great Depression. President Franklin Delano Roosevelt used it on March 6, 1933, two days after his inauguration. Providing for the reopening of sound banks in a period when most banks had failed and "runs" had abounded, F.D.R. declared a four-day bank holiday while Congress rushed to pass the Emergency Banking Act.

barbecue. Here's an English word that comes from the language of the extinct Haitian Taino tribe. The tribe smoked meat on a framework of sticks called a *barbacoa*—at least the name sounded like that to Spanish pirates who visited Haiti in the mid-17th century. *Barbacoa* came to mean the cooking of the meat itself and passed into English as the American *barbecue*. The Tainos also gave us the word potato, which was first their *batata*.

barbed wire. When in the 1850s farmers began fencing in their land with barbed wire—twisted strands of wire fence with sharp barbs at regular intervals—ranchers tore the fences down so their herds could pass. This led to barbed wire fence wars in the West, notably one that broke out in Texas in 1884, and helped end the reign of the cowboy by the close of the century.

Barbie doll. I've heard *Barbie doll* used as American slang for a conformist or a dehumanized person since the late 1960s, though the first recorded use of the term seems to have been in a 1973 issue of *Rolling Stone*. The term derives from the trade name of a very popular blue-eyed blond doll made for little girls. The doll's name, in turn, comes from the name of Barbara Millicent Roberts, daughter of Ruth Handler, who created the doll in 1959-Barbie's birthday is March 9 to be exact. Barbie and her husband Ken became grandparents in 2003.

bark. American pioneers were often excellent marksmen. At a distance of 100 yards or more, for example, an expert could *bark* a squirrel with a rifle shot, that is, hit the limb the squirrel was sitting on, the concussion killing the animal without wounding it. Some marksmen claim they can do this today.

bark up the wrong tree. Coon dogs, which could be almost any breed of dog or even mongrels in Colonial days, commonly chased raccoons through the underbrush and treed them, barking furiously at the base of the tree until their masters came to shoot the "gone coon." But the crafty nocturnal animal, called a rahaugum by John Smith, often escaped through the branches to another tree in the dark, leaving the dogs barking up the wrong tree, which is the origin of the American phrase. Skilled hunters who could *bark* a squirrel, that is, strike the bark on the lower side of the branch where it sat, killing it by the concussion, have nothing at all to do with the expression. The *bark* of a tree comes to us from the Anglo Saxon *beore,* while a dog's *bark* is related to the Old English *barki,* "windpipe." It's said that dogs in the wild state howl, whine, and growl, but that their barking is an acquired habit—anyway, debarking operations are available to silence dogs whose barks are worse than their bites and dogs that bark at the moon. *Barkable* is an unusual old word. One would take the adjective to be a modern affectation, but it dates back to at least the 13th century, a treatise of the time on estate management advising lords to have "discreet shepherds . . . with good barkable dogs."

barlow knife. Russel Barlow, who has been called "the patron saint of whittlers," invented the barlow knife over 200 years ago and it has been known to Americans under one name or another ever since. The *barlow,* a single-bladed pocket-, pen-, or jackknife, was the pride, joy and bartering power of many an American boy, and is mentioned in the works of Mark Twain, Joel Chandler Harris, and many other writers. It has also been called the Russel Barlow knife.

barn; barnstorming. The Old English *bere,* "barley," combined with *ern,* "storage," gives us the word *barn,* which was originally a place to store grain. Only in early America did the *barn* become a joint grain storage place and animal stable, American barns becoming so big that they spawned sayings like *You couldn't hit the broad side of a barn* and *as big as a barn.* Eventually we had car barns, furniture barns, and antique barns. *Barnstorming,* first applied in 1815 to a theatrical troupe's performances in upstate New York barns, has come to mean tours of rural areas by political candidates.

barnyard epithet. This widely used euphemism for plain old *bullshit* was coined by a *New York Times* editor as recently as 1970 in reporting the reply of David Dellinger, one of the Chicago Seven tried for conspiracy to disrupt the 1968 Democratic National Convention, to a police version of his actions ("Oh, bullshit!").

baseball. The name of America's national pastime is first recorded in 1744 as "base ball" in *The Little Pretty Pocket Book* as a synonym for the British game of rounders, a direct ancestor of the sport. Another early mention of the name is found in Jane Austen's *Northhanger Abbey* (1788) in which the heroine mentions that she played base ball as a child. Around the turn of the century, *base ball* became *baseball* in America.

basketball; basket. The game of basketball might be called boxball today if its inventor's intentions had been realized. Canadian James Naismith (1861–1939) invented the game while working at the International YMCA Training School in Springfield, Massachusetts, in late 1891. Though Naismith gave the game no name, his plan called for hanging an overhead wooden box at each end of the school's gym. Since the school's supply room had no boxes, Naismith agreed to use two half-bushel peach baskets instead. This suggested the name *basket ball* to him, even though the game was first played with a soccer ball, and he used it a month later, in January 1892, in an article for the school magazine describing the game. Soon *basket ball* was contracted to *basketball*. Incidentally, Naismith's peach baskets were not cut open at the end and his players had to climb on a ladder to retrieve each ball sunk in the basket. *Basket* for a score in basketball comes of course from the peach basket first used in the game. But *basket* wasn't the most common name for a score until about 1905—before that a score was most often termed a goal. In fact, the very first score in the first basketball game—made by one William R. Chase—was called a goal.

batting average; batting a thousand. *Batting average* has come to mean one's degree of achievement in any activity, but the term dates back to 1865 when it was used only in baseball. There it is the measure of a player's batting ability that is obtained by dividing the number of base hits made by the number of official times at bat and carrying out the result to three decimal places. *Batting a thousand* is doing something perfectly. No one knows when the common saying came into the general language from baseball, but it is based on the fact that 1.000 is the perfect average in baseball with a base hit every time at bat.

batting eyelids. To bat your eyelids is to flutter them, an American expression that goes back to the late 19th century. It has nothing to do with bats flapping in a cave, someone "gone batty," or even baseball bats. *Batting* in this case comes from the lexicon of falconry in Tudor times. According to a falconry book written in 1615: "Batting, or to bat, is when a Hawke flut- tereth with his wings either from the perch or the man's fist, striving, as it were, to fly away." The old word had long been used by sportsmen, and some American with a lot of *Sprachgefühl,* "feeling for language," found a fresh use for it in the 1880s.

bawl; bawl out. Dating back to the 15th century, *bawl* for a loud, rough cry probably derives from the Latin for *baulere,* "to bark like a dog." The word was also applied to the sounds of other animals, especially cows and bulls, which supports the theory that to *bawl out* originated as American ranch slang, suggested by the bawling or bellowing of angry bulls.

bay window. *Bay window* has been American slang for a "pot belly" since the 1890s.

Beaneater; Boston baked beans. Since at least the late 19th century, *Beaneater* has been a humorous nickname for a Bostonian, Boston being called *Beantown. Boston baked beans* have been regarded as the best of baked beans for a half century longer and are still so thought today. They are made basically with navy beans flavored with molasses and slowly cooked with pork. Baked beans have been the traditional Saturday night supper in New England since early times, the leftover traditionally being part of Sunday breakfast.

beanpole. Another Americanism for a tall, thin person, *beanpole* takes its name from the tall poles that support climbing bean plants.

bear flag. The white flag with a star and grizzly bear upon it that was adopted by Americans in California in 1846 when they defied Spanish authorities and proclaimed the California Republic. It has since become the California state flag.

a bear for work. In the early 19th century, as Americans pushed on into the wilderness, a number of native expressions arose comparing men with great strength or strong appetites or emotions to bears. *A bear for work* was born at this time.

beat it! Although most authorities say *beat it!* is American slang first recorded in 1905 for "get out of here, go away!", the expression is much older. The term was used by both Ben Jon- son and Shakespeare for "go" and is said to have been coined by Shakespeare. It may be a shortening of "beat the trail" or some similar expression, but no one is sure.

beat the living daylights out of you. To say "I'll let daylight into you!" to an enemy in days past was to threaten that you'd open him up, make a hole in him with a sword, knife, or gun. The expression, in the form of its variant "I'll make daylight shine through you," is recorded in America as early as 1774 and is probably much older. Sayings like "I'll fill him full of holes" replaced the older expression when modern weapons like machine guns made wholesale ventilation easier, but it lived on in the form of *I'll beat the living daylights out of you*—I'll beat you to a pulp, punish you unmercifully. Unlike the old swordsman's words, this makes no sense literally. It is merely the ghost of an imaginative phrase.

beautiful nuisance. A euphemistic Southern name for the kudzu vine, a scourge in the U.S. South where it was introduced as a valuable forage crop and soil conditioner but became a fast-growing weedy pest in southern gardens. *Kuzu* is the Japanese name for this Asiatic plant *(Pueraria thunbergiana)* of the pea family. The kudzu has had more publicity but the most pernicious weed in the South, and in all America, is the purple nutsedge *(Cyperus rotundas),* which can grow 39 inches long and does far more damage.

bee. *Spelling bee* is among the last survivors of a large number of *bees* relating to social gatherings (bees being busy, cooperative, social animals) "for performing some task in common." These are American in origin—the first one recorded is a 1769 *spinning bee* in Taunton, Massachusetts, though the term was in use before that. Later came *bees* prefixed by apple, building, candy, checker, chopping, drawing, housecleaning, husking, knitting, logging, paring, picking, political, quilting, raising, sewing, shingle, shooting, shouting, shucking, spinning, squirrel, stone, tailor, and wood. There were even *rattlesnake bees,* where "the venomous reptiles . . . were summarily excised by fire and lethal weapons"; *kissing bees,* parties for young people; *whipping bees,* where toughs beat someone; and *lynching bees.* The affairs, sometimes called "frolics," were often followed by parties.

Beehive State. *See* MORMON STATE.

been there, done that. A recent American phrase, first recorded in 1983, usually said by someone bored to death with something overly familiar to him or her.

beep. A term used for a New York City borough president. First recorded in 1980 and patterned on *veep* for the vice president of the United States.

belittle. Thomas Jefferson coined the word *belittle* in about 1780 and Noah Webster included it in his 1828 dictionary, but many critics denounced it as an incurably vulgar term, one going so far as to say "It has no visible chance of becoming English . . ." The condemnations went on for almost a century, but needless to say all the belittling of *belittle* failed to ban the word from the language.

bellyache. *Bellyache* had earlier meant "colic" in England, but in the sense of "to complain" it is an Americanism coined about midway through the 19th century and first recorded in 1881. As with so many coined words, no one knows its clever inventor's name.

belly cheater; belly robber; belly burglar. *Belly cheater* is an old American cowboy term for a cook, which may date back to the 19th century but is first recorded as U.S. Navy slang in the form of *belly robber,* specifically referring to a commissary steward. The term has also been used for an Army mess sergeant. Another (later) variant is *belly burglar.*

Belmont Stakes. Part of horse racing's Triple Crown, which was named for Belmont Park on New York's Long Island. Belmont Park, in turn, was named for millionaire August Belmont. The other races of the Triple Crown are the Kentucky Derby and the Preakness. All are for three-year-old thoroughbreds.

Ben Day. A New York printer named Benjamin Day (1831–1916) invented the Ben Day process of quick mechanical production of stippling, shading, or tints on line engravings. *Ben Dayed* means produced by the Ben Day photoengraving method. The process, which has been used since about 1879, eliminates the shading of a drawing by hand.

Benedict Arnold. QUISLING and a few others have endured, but most traitors have not been included in the dictionaries. *Benedict Arnold* is an exception. The term has been used for over 200 years in America, and is still a common one. Every schoolboy knows the story of how General Benedict Arnold plotted to deliver the garrison at West Point to Major John Andre, how the plot failed with Andre's capture and how Arnold fled to the British army. Less familiar are the facts that Arnold was a brilliant soldier and that his treason was provoked by shabby treatment at the hands of superiors several times during the course of the Revolutionary War.

Benjamin. Probably the least known of American currency notes. The *Benjamin,* a two-dollar bill, honored Judah Philip Benjamin (1811–84), Confederate secretary of war and secretary of state during the Civil War. The brilliant lawyer, statesman, and plantation owner was one of Jefferson Davis's best friends and was known in the North as "the brains of the Confederacy." He escaped to England after the Civil War and carved out another brilliant legal career. Today, *Benjamin,* or *Ben,*

is common slang for a $100 bill, named in honor of Ben Franklin, whose pictures is on the bill. *See also* ABE'S CABE.

the berries. *The berries* has been American talk for "the best, the greatest" since 1902, when it seems to have originated as college slang. *Berry* had been recorded a few years earlier as slang for a dollar and perhaps this use suggested the expression.

best-seller. *Best-seller,* for a book that sells many copies, is an Americanism first recorded in 1905. The Sears Roebuck Catalog was probably the "best-seller" of all time, though it was distributed free for more than three-quarters of a century. Over 5 billion copies may be a conservative estimate for its total distribution since 1896. In second place is the Bible.

bet one's bottom dollar. To be so sure about something that one will bet all one has on it, the last of one's money, as in "I'll bet my bottom dollar on it." Commonly heard throughout the U.S. today, the expression comes from the American West over a century and a half ago, when poker was often played with silver dollars. Someone completely sure of a hand would push his whole stack of silver dollars, including the one on the bottom, into the pot to cover a bet or a final raise.

big enchilada. A person who is the boss, the head man or woman, the big shot of any organization. The term is first recorded on one of the Watergate tapes in 1973, the speaker, John Ehrlichman, referring to Attorney General John Mitchell. In a letter from jail to author William Safire, Ehrlichman later claimed he had coined the expression, having "cooked my own enchiladas for years" as part of his "California upbringing." Possibly the term owes something to the phrase *the whole enchilada*—everything, the whole ball of wax—which had been around at least seven years longer, first recorded in 1966. Other food-stuffs associated with bossdom include *big banana, big cheese, big fish, big potato,* and *big vegetable,* among others. An *enchilada,* an American Spanish word, is a tortilla rolled and stuffed with cheese, meat, or beans and served with a hot chili sauce.

black humor. Humor that regards suffering as absurd, not pitiable, or that regards existence as ironically pointless yet comic. The expression was first recorded in 1963, though such humor has always been around; it is said to have been coined by American author Bruce Jay Friedman. Wrote Friedman in *Newsday* (1/1/96) regarding the coinage: "I don't really know if I invented it, or if a publisher came to me and said, 'How about doing an anthology and calling it *Black Humor?*' What I do remember is, they were going to pay me for a chance to read writers like Barthelme, Heller and Pynchon, so it was a terrific deal. Then I had to write an introduction (to *Black Humor,* 1963), so slapped together some justification for the collection: the stories had a certain edge to them—they often connected with social issues in very bold colors—whatever. The next thing I know, black humor is being taught in college courses and becomes imprinted in the language."

black ice. A term used in many U.S. places meaning both (1) smooth ice with a dark appearance that forms on ponds and lakes and (2) the dangerous, thin, transparent layer of ice that forms on black road surfaces, making it appear as if the road is ice-free.

black power. No one is sure of the origins of this slogan urging or demanding political and economic power for African-Americans. CORE, the Congress of Racial Equality, used it as a slogan in the 1960s but it was not new at the time. In his *Simple Takes a Wife* (1953) poet and novelist Langston Hughes wrote: "Black is powerful," which may be the source for the term.

Black Republican. Long an insulting nickname for a Republican in the South, the term was first used to describe a Republican favoring emancipation of the slaves. It came to be applied to any Republican and is still occasionally heard.

black-shoe navy. Rear Admiral Edgar Keats, USN (ret.), kindly provides the true origin of this controversial term. "During the 1920s and 30s," Admiral Keats writes, "naval aviators were permitted to wear green cloth uniforms in cold weather and lightweight khaki working uniforms during warm weather, in addition to service dress blue and white. Nonaviators did not have that option. When World War II approached it became apparent that battles could not be won in the tropics by officers constrained to heavy blues or impractical whites, so khaki, but not green, uniforms were made available to all officers. The khaki uniform was changed somewhat with stripes being removed from sleeves and the shoulder boards of whites being substituted. Above all, and fatefully, the orders from Naval Headquarters gave officers the option of continuing to wear the black shoes they had previously worn with the blue uniforms. Aviators, without exception, continued with their brown shoes, but many senior surface ship officers, flag and ship commanders, decreed that in their commands only black shoes would be worn. Thus junior and midgrade officers on surface ships had no choice but to wear black shoes. In the early years there was hardly a ripple of controver sy, but as time wore on the words "brown shoe" came to be used as a substitute for "naval aviator" and "black shoe" came to be a designation for an officer who was not a naval aviator. Some, but not all, may have used the words as epithets, probably because of surface officers' jealousy of the increased pay of aviators. Another explanation may be naval aviators looking down on those not qualified to fly airplanes. The words have over time become identifiers of an intramural split within the naval establishment that, until recently, has had adverse consequences for the overall navy. Had there been far-sighted leadership in the navy in the early years of the war either brown or black shoes would have been ordered for all officers and, with uniforms being truly uniform, these unfortunate words would never have gained currency."

Blade Runnerization. Science-fiction writer Philip Dick's novel *Do Androids Dream of Electric Sheep?* was made into the classic movie *Blade Runner.* According to an article in the *New York Times* by Brent Staples, "His film struck a number of chords in the real world, its vision of the polyglot, environmentally ruined Los Angeles spawned the phrase 'Blade Runnerization' among urban planners who recognized it as a frighteningly likely vision of things to come."

blame game. An expression said to be coined by President Ronald Reagan in a speech given on October 14, 1982: "The pounding economic hangover America is suffering from didn't come about overnight, and there's no single, instant cure. In recent weeks, a lot of people have been playing what I call the 'blame game.'"

bless the meat and damn the skin. Part of an old American grace said before a meal: "Bless the meat an' damn the skin, / Throw back your 'eads an' all pitch in."

blind as a one-eyed mule in a root cellar. Unable to see or to understand, completely blind to sight or reason. The American expression is probably from the mid-19th century.

bling bling. A new word meaning flashy jewelry.

blizzard. In its meaning of a severe snowstorm *blizzard* seems to be an Americanism dating back to about 1835. Its direct ancestor is probably the English dialect word *blisser*, meaning the same, but could be the German *blitz*, "lightning, flash." Before *blizzard* meant a storm in America it meant a violent blow of the fist or a crushing remark.

blockbuster. The powerful high-explosive bomb called a blockbuster dates back to the beginning of World War II, when the bombs and word seem to have been invented by U.S. ordnance. It was applied to anything big or powerful. In the early 1950s a *blockbuster* came to mean any real estate agent who convinced whites to sell their homes by creating fears that blacks were moving into their block or area. Like the bomb, they bust up blocks. An alternate meaning is anything or anyone who is successful, effective, extravagant, etc.

bloody back. A contemptuous name Americans gave the British red-coats during the Revolutionary War. A newspaper of the day recorded the taunts of one group: "The Mob still increased, and were outrageous . . . calling out 'Come, you Rascals, you bloody Backs, you Lobster Scoundrels; fire if you dare!'"

blow his, her, own horn. The term *blowhard,* for "a braggart," can be traced back to the American West in about 1855. To *blow your own horn,* or "to promote yourself," derives from a much older expression, *to blow your own trumpet,* which goes as far back as 1576. Such "horn-blowing" may have its origins in medieval times, when heralds blew their trumpets to announce the arrival of royalty but commoners such as street vendors had to blow their own horns.

bluebacks. Paper money used by the Confederates during the Civil War; also called *graybacks.* "During the Civil War . . . the original Blue Backs of the Confederacy (so-called in opposition to Green Backs of the Union) soon became known as Shucks, a name sufficiently significant of their evil repute . . . ," Maximillian Schele De Vere wrote in *Americanisms* (1871). Over a billion dollars' worth of bluebacks and graybacks were issued by the South during the Civil War; the bills were worth about 1.7 cents in gold for each Confederate dollar by the end of the hostilities.

blueberry. The blueberry, like the BLACKBERRY, is of course named for the color of its berries. Blueberries have been a favorite food for centuries and are among the most widely distributed fruits. Early colonists gathered the "blues," "whortleberries," and "bilberries," and made good use of them as the Indians had done since prehistoric times. But more than any other fruit, cultivated blueberries are children of the

20th century. It was in the early 1900s that Elizabeth C. White of Whitesbog, New Jersey (one of several pioneer women fruit growers), offered local prizes for highbush blueberries bearing the largest fruits. Hearing of her work, Dr. Frederick V. Coville, a U.S. Department of Agriculture plant breeder, began to work in cooperation with her starting in 1909, and crossed many wild plants she or her contestants had selected from the Pine Barrens of New Jersey, an area with an acid, sandy, but fertile soil. By the time Coville died in 1937 there were 30 large-fruited, named highbush varieties where there had been none, and today there are myriad varieties that have been selected from hundreds of thousands of fruited hybrid seedlings. From its status as a lowly fruit often confused with the huckleberry (even though, unlike the bony-seeded huckleberry, its 50 to 75 seeds are small and barely noticeable when eaten), White and Coville had elevated the blueberry to a position where it became the basis for an entirely new agricultural industry. *Vaccinium corymbosum,* the highbush or swamp blueberry, had gone through a revolution rather than an evolution and became a mass-produced fruit in less than 25 years.

blue-chip stocks. The most valuable counters in poker are the blue chips. Since the early 1900s Wall Street, borrowing the expression from another world of gambling, has called secure, relatively high-yielding stocks "blue-chip stocks." Among the earliest terms for worthless or speculative stocks is "cats and dogs," first recorded in 1879.

Bluegrass State. A nickname for Kentucky since Civil War days (*see* BLUEGRASS). Kentucky has also been called the Hemp State, the Rock-Ribbed State, and the Dark and Bloody Ground (the translation of an Indian name for ground on which bloody battles between Indian tribes were fought).

blue hen's chicken. One who is a good fighter, because blue hens are said to breed the best fighting cocks; the term also means someone high-spirited, aggressive, quick-tempered or high-class and was applied to soldiers from Delaware during the Revolutionary War, resulting in the nickname *blue hen's chicken* for a native of Delaware.

Blue Hen State. A nickname for Delaware (*see* BLUE HEN'S CHICKENS). Delaware has also been called the Diamond State, Uncle Sam's Pocket Handkerchief (due to its small size), and New Sweden, after the 1638 settlement of Swedes there in *Nye Sverige*.

blue lights. *Blue lights* became an Americanism for traitors during the War of 1812 when on December 12, 1813 pro-British Americans flashed blue lights to British ships off the coast as a signal that Commodore Stephen Decatur's two frigates would soon be sailing from their New London, Connecticut harbor. Acting on this information, the British blockaded the port.

Bluemouths. An Indian tribe residing west of the Choctaws. Not much is known about them, but the Choctaws told travelers that there was a large city where these blue-mouthed or blue-lipped people lived and that if a person tried to kill one of these people, he would become insane.

bluenose. The term *bluenose* to describe a person of rigid puritanical habits was first applied to lumbermen and fishermen of northern New England and referred to the color of their noses, the blue induced by long exposure to cold weather. Only later was the word applied to the aristocratic inhabitants of Boston's Back Bay area in the sense that we know it today, possibly in alluding to their apparently "frigid" manner. *Bluenose* is also used as an opprobrious nickname for Nova Scotians, but there the word probably derives from the name of a popular Nova Scotian potato.

blues; blue devils. *Blues,* for a state of depression or despair, is probably a shortening of the 18th-century expression *blue devils,* or low spirits. Surprisingly, Washington Irving first used the term in *Salmagundi* as far back as 1807: "[He] concluded his harangue with a sigh, and I saw that he was still under the influence of a whole legion of the blues." Later *blue devils* became the hallucinations associated with the D.T.s, or delirium tremens, and a *blue devil* is now drug users' slang for sodium amytal, suggested by the color of the capsule and the narcotic's effects. *Blue devils, blue, blue-eyed,* and *blue around the gills* all have meant drunk in one way or another, possibly because blue is the color of approaching death and they are all associated with the SEVEN STAGES OF DRUNKENNESS. This would also explain the linking of blues with depression. *The blues,* toward the end of the 19th century, gave their name to the melancholy jazz music called the blues, deriving in part from sad black prison and funeral songs of slavery and oppression.

blue-sky laws. These are American state laws regulating the sale of securities, especially laws designed to inhibit the promotion of fraudulent stocks. Kansas, in 1912, enacted the first law so described by the press as protection against unscrupulous land promoters. Behind the words is the idea that suckers will buy even the blue sky from con artists or that "blue-sky" land or securities lack substance, like cloudless blue skies.

bluff. Mathew's *A Dictionary of Americanisms* records *bluff*, origin unknown, as the term for a riverbank as early as 1687, referring to a "Bluffe" in South Carolina. According to Stuart Berg Flexner, in *I Hear America Talking* (1976), this is a historical curiosity, the very first of what would be a long list of Americanisms that the British termed "barbarous." In poker to bluff is to deceive an opponent about the strength of one's hand by betting heavily on it. This *bluff* probably derives from the German *bluffen,* "to frighten by menacing conduct." Early names for poker, recorded in 1838, were bluff and brag. From poker also comes the expression *to call one's bluff.*

Bluff City. A nickname for both Memphis, Tennessee, and Hannibal, Missouri. Both cities are located on bluffs overhanging water.

boardwalk. A sidewalk made of boards, common in many early Western towns though seen only in historical replicas today.

bobble. An Americanism meaning a mistake or error. The word, first recorded in 1805, is commonly used today for a mishandled chance in baseball.

bodega. *Bodega* is Spanish for "storehouse." Originally indicating a small Hispanic grocery store, often selling a large variety of items, including wine, the word is now often used to refer to any small grocery store. There are thousands of bodegas in the United States today.

bogus. Most theories about the word *bogus,* meaning "fake or spurious," relate it to some form of bogey, in its sense of an imaginary or false thing. One version claims the word can be traced to May 1827 when the Painesville, Ohio, *Telegraph* ran a story about a gang of counterfeiters whose fake coins were so perfect that they were compared to the work of some supernatural bogeyman. Another says the word comes from the name of a device called a bogus, used for counterfeiting coins in the same state in the same year, connecting this machine with "tan-tra-bogus," an old Vermont term for bogeyman. Complicating matters is the fact that the first use of *bogus* isn't recorded until 1838. Although it is certainly possible that the word was in use 10 years or so before it appeared in print, another derivation traces it to a counterfeiter who was operating at exactly the time *bogus* was first recorded. "The word *bogus,"* according to a *Boston Courier* of 1857, "is a corruption of the name Borghese, a man who, 20 years ago, did a tremendous business in supplying the Great West of America with counterfeit bills on fictitious banks. The western people came to shortening the name Borghese to *bogus,* and his bills were universally styled 'bogus currency.'" However, there is still another theory that suggests a direct passage from *boghus,* a gypsy word for counterfeit coin. More than one of these speculations has to be bogus.

bolo alert. *Bolo* is a recent acronym used by law enforcement agencies, including the FBI, to mean *be o*n the *l*ook *o*ut for, in reference to the whereabouts and intentions of a terrorist or any criminal.

boloney. Al Smith, governor of New York and unsuccessful presidential candidate in 1928, helped popularize this expression with his remark "No matter how you slice it, it's still baloney." But *boloney* for "bunk" dates back to at least the early 20th century, bologna sausage having been pronounced *boloney* as early as the 1870s, when there was a popular song "I Ate the Boloney." There are those who say that *boloney* for "bunk" has nothing to do with bologna sausage, however, tracing it to a corruption of the Spanish *pelone,* "testicles," and claiming that this meant "nonsense" or "bunk" just as "balls," "all balls," and "nerts" did. The word is also spelled *baloney.*

bomb. *Bomb,* in reference to theatrical productions, has completely opposite meanings in England and America. When a play bombs in America it is a complete flop—a *bomb.* When a play "goes off like a bomb" in England it is often a great success. The British use seems to be built on the explosive force of a real bomb, while the American usage is based upon the destruction a bomb creates. The word *bomb* derives ultimately from the Latin *bombus,* "a booming sound."

Bonac. Roughly 100 miles from Times Square in New York City, a community of Long Island fishermen called the Bonackers speak a dialect that retains the sound of Shakespeare's England and has rarely, if ever, been recorded in any language book. The Bonackers reside in East Hampton, a town they helped settle in the 17th century. The Bonackers were not among the affluent settlers; they were, in fact, often the servants of the settlers, and at first they built shacks along the Accabonac Creek, which led the richer citizens to disparagingly dub them Bonackers. It is said that up to 1,000 Bonackers live in the Hamptons today, many of them speaking the old English dialect called *Bonac* that retains much of the vocabulary and the same vowel sounds the original settlers employed. "We speak the King's English, only we come under an earlier king," the Bonackers say. Common words used among them are *bub, cattywumper* (crooked), *durst* (does not), and *finiskind* (A-OK). Anyone born outside the eastern end of Long Island is a *foreigner* from *away. See* GULLAH.

bonanza. *Bonanza,* for a rich body of gold or silver ore in a mine, or any rich strike, began life as a Spanish word meaning "fair weather at sea." Miners in California probably learned the word from seamen, who also used it to mean prosperity in general, and applied *bonanza* to any rich vein of ore.

bond paper. In the early 1800s a Boston, Massachusetts paper mill made a desirable all-rag paper that was widely used for printing bonds, bank notes, and legal documents. People began to call it *bond paper* when ordering it, and the expression soon was applied to any high-quality paper.

bonehead play; pulling a boner. The original *bonehead play* was made on September 9, 1908 by Fred Merkle, New York Giants first baseman. It was the last of the ninth, two out, and the Giants had Moose McCormick on third and Merkle on first. The next man up singled to center and McCormick scored the winning run, but Merkle ran into the dugout instead of touching second base. Johnny Evers of the Cubs got the ball and stepped on second, forcing out Merkle. The winning run was nullified and the game not counted in the standings. Merkle's play became all the more important later in the season when the Cubs and Giants finished tied for first place and the Cubs won the pennant in a playoff game. Though *boneheaded* had been used in the sense of "stupid" a few years earlier, it was a sportswriter's use of *bonehead play* in reference to Merkle's blunder that introduced the phrase to the language, along with the related *to pull a boner.*

boner. *See* BONEHEAD PLAY.

bonnet squash. This common vegetable sponge *(Luffa cylindrica)* was so named in the American South because women made bonnets out of its fibrous matter. Wrote Joel Chandler Harris in *On the Plantation* (1892): "The girls made their hats of rye and wheat straw, and some very pretty bonnets were made of the fibrous substance that grew in the vegetable patch known as the bonnet squash." These inedible squashes are also called "dishcloth gourds" and "loofah." They are widely sold as sponges.

Bonnie Blue flag. The Civil War secession flag of South Carolina, which had a blue field and a single star; also the name of a popular secessionist song. It was at a state convention at Jackson, Mississippi, when that state voted to secede from the Union, that the famous patriotic song of the South was inspired by an immense blue silk banner with a single star that someone carried through the crowd. According to one old story, Arkansas comedian Harry Macarthy witnessed the scene and began writing the song's lyrics, which he finished when the rest of the southern states seceded.

boob tube. *See* COUCH POTATO.

book club. Americas first book club was the Book-of-the-Month Club, founded in April 1926 by Harry Scherman with Robert Haas as president. Its distinguished panel of judges consisted of Dorothy Canfield, Heywood Broun, Henry Seidel Canby, William Allen White, and Christopher Morley, and they chose as the first book-of-the-month Sylvia Townsend Warner's *Lolly Willowes, or the Loving Huntsman* (Viking) to be distributed to 4,750 members. Within 20 years the club had revolutionized the publishing industry and 25 similar clubs were distributing 75 million books, over one-sixth of all American book sales. Customarily, members receive a free book or books upon joining a book club and a free book with every two or three books purchased. Book club editions are often, but not always, printed on cheaper paper. While the clubs have been criticized for inculcating a mediocrity of taste, they have offered many excellent books to their members and there is no doubt that they bring books to areas without bookstores. Ancestors of the book clubs were the circulating libraries of the 19th century, which supplied popular novels to readers for a small subscription price. These libraries often forced publishers to conform to their puritanical standards and made good writing all the more difficult. George Gissing's *New Grub Street* (1891) treats the subject in detail.

boondoggles. One dictionary defines boondoggles as: "Useless, wasteful tasks, 'make-work' projects that are often performed by recipients of a government dole." The word was employed in 1929 by Scoutmaster Robert Link of Rochester, New York, who applied it to the braided leather lanyards made and worn around the neck as a decoration by Boy Scouts. Under the New Deal during the Great Depression, the term was transferred to the relief work for the unemployed that some people, not out of work themselves, thought was as useless as making lanyards, and soon *boondoggling* meant to do any work of no practical value merely to keep or look busy. Before Scoutmaster Link applied *boondoggle* to lanyards it had been a word for a belt, knife sheath, or other product of simple manual skill, and in Scottish dialect it means a marble that you get as a gift, without winning it. The yarn about *boondoggle* being suggested by Daniel Boone idly whittling sticks to throw to his dog does convey the sense of the word, but is just another spurious tale.

booster. Sinclair Lewis's Babbitt was a booster who wore a Booster Club button in his lapel. But Lewis didn't invent the term in his novel. This term for an enthusiastic, often puerile supporter or promoter of a person, team, cause, etc., was born in the American Southwest in about 1890, quickly spreading throughout the country, and has its roots in the verb to boost.

boot camp. U.S. sailors serving during the Spanish-American War wore leggings called *boots,* which came to mean "a navy (or marine) recruit." These recruits trained in what were called boot camps.

Boot Hill. Now a joking name for any cemetery, the term was first applied to any small cemetery where men who died in gunfights, with their boots on, were buried. The first such is said to have been in Deadwood, South Dakota; the Mount Moriah cemetery there is now a big tourist attraction.

boots and saddles! Most Americans are familiar with the old western song "Give Me My Boots and My Saddle," but this familiar cavalry call has nothing to do with boots and saddles, as one might suspect. It derives from the old French cavalry command *Boute selle!* ("Put saddle!"), which the British corrupted to *boot and saddle* and which American cavalrymen further corrupted to *boots and saddles!*

booze. Mr. E. G. or E. S. Booze of either Philadelphia or Kentucky, circa 1840, was a distiller who sold his *booze* under his own name, the bottles often made in the shape of log cabins. But *booze* probably has its roots in the Middle English verb *bousen,* "to drink deeply," which comes from an earlier German word. However, the English use *booze* only for beer and ale and there is no doubt that the labels on our Mr. Booze's bottles influenced the American use of the word for hard liquor and strengthened its general use. Today booze most often signifies cheap, even rotgut whiskey.

border tale. A Western story. "I am sorry to have to lie so outrageously in this yarn. My hero has killed more Indians on one war trail than I have killed in all my life. But I understand this is what expected of border tales. If you think the revolver and Bowie knife are used too freely, you may cut out a fatal shot or stab wherever you think wise." (William F. [Buffalo Bill] Cody in a letter to his editor, 1875).

born-again Christian. This term for a Christian who has found a renewed commitment to Christ has long been known to evangelists, but came into prominence when U.S. presidential candidate Jimmy Carter described himself as a "born-again Christian." The phrase's source is John 3:3 and 3:7: "Jesus answered and said . . . Except a man be born again, he cannot see the kingdom of God . . . Marvel not that I said unto thee, ye must be born again."

Boston. A historical term once used by Indians of the Northwest for any white American, as opposed to the foreign English, French, and so forth. These Bostons were also called Bostonians by the Indians and were so named because so many settlers came from New England or had connections with that great hub of commerce.

Boston accent. Often used outside New England as a synonym for *New England accent,* perhaps because the accent is so strong in the city, although the accent is not the same in all parts of New England. In

Boston one commonly hears such pronunciations as *gull* for *girl, shop* for *sharp, back* for *bark, hot* for *heart,* and *bee-ad* for *bad.*

Boston baked beans. Famous since at least the mid-19th century as the best of baked beans, made with navy beans flavored with molasses and slowly cooked with pork. Baked beans have been the traditional Saturday night supper in New England since early times, though recipes for them vary greatly. Leftover beans were traditionally Sunday breakfast fare.

Boston Brahmin. A Brahmin is a worshipper of the Hindu god Brahma, the creator of the universe. The Brahmin's status as a member of the highest caste in Hinduism inspired the Americanism *Boston Brahmin* for an aristocratic, upper class, conservative Bostonian; the term was first recorded in January 1861 by Oliver Wendell Holmes in his novel *Elsie Venner* as "the Brahmin caste of New England." Holmes found the Boston Brahmins a "harmless, inoffensive, untitled aristocracy . . . which has grown to be a caste by the repetition of the same influences generation after generation" so that it has acquired a distinct character and organization. In November 1947 the *Atlantic Monthly* noted: "The Brahmins do not think of themselves as Brahmins: the word is antique as the wooden cod hanging in the State House." Antique or not the term is still widely used, usually in a humorous way. *Brahmin caste* is a synonym.

Boston Braves. A National League baseball team that was named after the New York City Tammany Hall political machine. Tammany politicians had invested in the club in 1912 and since members of the political club were called "braves," in honor of the Indian chief for whom Tammany was named, the name was applied to players on the baseball team. The Braves moved from Boston to Milwaukee in 1953 and later moved on to Atlanta. *See* DODGERS.

Boston Pops. Members of the Boston Symphony orchestra, founded in 1881 and one of America's oldest symphony orchestras, make up the Boston Pops, which plays more *popular* light music rather than classical music. They usually perform at summer concerts.

Boston strong boy. A nickname of John L. Sullivan, late- 19th-century bareknuckle (no gloves) boxing heavyweight champion. He was also called *The Boston Hercules, Bostons Pet, Bostons Pride and Joy, The Boston Miracle, Young Boston Giant, Bostons Goliath,* and *Bostons Philanthropic Prize-fighter,* among many more nicknames.

Boston Tea Party. The first act of violence in the disputes leading to the Revolutionary War, occurring on December 16, 1773 when members of the Sons of Liberty, incensed by the tax on tea, boarded British ships and dumped 342 chests of tea into Boston Harbor.

boughten goods. Once common as a participal adjective in the U.S., *boughten* is rarely heard any more, though it is listed in the *O.E.D.* as poetic dialect and an Americanism. *Boughten goods* is sometimes used today as a pseudo-rustic term meaning "manufactured or store bought things that are valued above familiar, homemade ones."

bought the farm. As late as the Vietnam War, soldiers killed in action were said to have *bought the farm*. The expression was inspired by the draftees's dream to go home—in many cases to a peaceful farm, or perhaps to buy a farm—in any case, to settle down somewhere far away from the army and war. "Well, he finally did buy the farm," a friend could say on hearing of the death of such a man, and the expression was used so often that *bought the farm* became an ironic synonym for death. The phrase dates to World War II or earlier. Here's another guess at its origin: When a farmer takes a bank mortgage there is a life insurance claim that is built into the payment, so that when the farmer dies the farm becomes the property of his estate; hence, he has finally bought the farm.

bouncer; checker-out. The American *bouncer,* for "a person who acts as a guard in a disco, nightclub, brothel, or bar, someone who bounces out unruly people," dates back to Civil War days. *Checker-out* is the British term for the same, but it seems to have been coined later, in about 1880.

bourbon. *Bourbon whiskey* takes its name from Bourbon County, Kentucky, named for France's Bourbon kings, and home of the first still that produced it. The word *Bourbon* for a political reactionary also derives from France's Bourbon kings, a dynasty that reigned for over 200 years beginning in 1589, and of whom it was said that they "forgot nothing and learned nothing." *The Dictionary of Americanisms* gives its first use for a political diehard as 1876.

Bourbon Street. Another storied American street, this one named for the French Bourbon kings (see BOURBON above). In *Love and Money*

(1954), Erskine Caldwell called the noted New Orleans street "that Southern gentleman's skid row."

Bowditch. A name for the navigation handbook *American Practical Navigator,* prepared by American navigator, astronomer, and mathematician Nathaniel Bowditch (1773–1838) in 1802 and published in a series of editions ever since. Nathaniel Bowditch left school in Salem, Massachussetts, at age 10 and went to sea, where he studied navigation, correcting some 8,000 errors in the leading guide of his time. So respected was Bowditch and his work on navigation that ships of all nations flew their flags at half-mast when he died.

bowery; bowery boys. *Bowery* derives from the Dutch word for "farm," *bowerij,* and this was originally its meaning in early New York. But the word came to be applied to an area in downtown Manhattan that was originally the site of a farm and became the city's most famous skid row, *the Bowery,* long noted in song and story for its saloons and cheap hotels. It is also the name of a street, stretching from Chatham Square to Cooper Square, that was once an Indian path. Huntz Hall, Leo Gorcey, and the other *Bowery Boys* of movie fame take their names from a number of real gangs dating back as far as the 1700s. Other gangs of the day, to name only a few, include the Dead Rabbits, the Roach Guards, the Shirt Tails, and the Plug Uglies. Hell-Cat Maggie, a female member of the violent Dead Rabbits, "filed her front teeth to points and wore artificial brass fingernails," according to Luc Sante's *Low Life* (1991).

to bowl. In some U.S. prisons no talking is allowed after lights out. Prisoners have been known to circumvent this rule by flushing the toilets in their cells until they are dry and can be used as "telephones." When they talk into the empty bowl their voices can be heard clearly in the next cell. *To bowl* has thus come to mean to call another prisoner at night.

bowl game; bowl. The first football bowl game ever recorded was the 1916 Pasadena Bowl (which was a year later renamed the Rose Bowl). *Bowl*, however, had been a synonym for a football stadium since 1914, when the Yale University stadium was first called the Yale Bowl.

boy meets girl. A phrase meaning any conventional love story. Also *girl meets boy*. Cleaning out William Faulkner's desk after he left the Warner Brothers writing factory in the 1930s, coworkers found the fruits of his labor: an empty whiskey bottle and a piece of paper on which he had written, more than 500 times, *boy meets girl.*

the boys. *The boys,* for "political hangers-on," has a long history in America, dating back to at least 1832.

boysenberry. Americans have always been pie makers without peer, thanks to sugar resources close by, an abundance of native fruit, and a willingness to experiment. The blackberry, long regarded as a nuisance and called a bramble or brambleberry in England, is a case in point. Many varieties of blackberries have been developed here, long before anyone paid attention to the family *Rubus* in Europe. Among them is the boysenberry, a prolific, trailing variety that is a cross between the BLACKBERRY, RASPBERRY, and LOGANBERRY, another eponymous berry. The boysenberry, a dark wine-red fruit that tastes something like a raspberry, was developed by California botanist Rudolf Boysen in the early 1900s. Single plants commonly produce two quarts of the large 3/4-inch round, 11/2-inch-long fruit.

bozzonga. I haven't found this word meaning "ass" or "behind" in any dictionary, slang or otherwise, but it was definitely used by tennis star Billie Jean King in September 1973. "I hate sitting around on my bozzonga," she told a television interviewer at the time, referring to her need to play. Maybe Billie Jean invented the word.

bracero. Any Mexican laborer in the U.S. Formerly meaning a Mexican migrant picker legally admitted to the U.S., the word derives from the Spanish *bracero,* "a person with strong arms."

Brahma. A famous western cattle breed first imported from India, its place of origin, by South Carolinian Dr. James Bolton Davis in 1849. *See* BOSTON BRAHMIN.

Brahmin. *See* BOSTON BRAHMIN.

brain chill. A recent American expression describing the shooting head pain suffered by those who eat ice cream too fast. Also called brain freeze.

brain trust. James M. Kieran of the *New York Times* called the group of experts surrounding presidential candidate Franklin Delano Roosevelt the brains trust in his 1932 dispatches, the term having previously been used in sarcastic reference to the first American general staff in 1901, not at all in the same sense. Headline writers quickly chopped off the cumbersome s, and by the time Roosevelt became president his larger group of experts was called the brain trust. Brain trust now is applied to trusted business as well as government advisers.

brainwashing. *Brainwashing* was coined during the Korean War, when a number of American prisoners of war violated military codes after being captured, imprisoned, interrogated, and tortured by the North Koreans and Chinese. The vivid term is not an Americanism, however, being a direct translation of the Mandarin Chinese *hsi,* "to wash," and *nao,* "brain."

brass tacks. There are no brass tacks, only brass-headed ones, used because they rust less easily. The American expression, which has been traced back only to 1903, though it may have been common before then, has several possible origins. Brassheaded tacks were used in upholstering chairs, especially at the foundations of the chairs, and in taking a chair apart to reupholster it from the bottom up, craftsmen might have said they were getting down to business, to the root of the matter, getting down to the brass tacks. There is no solid evidence for this theory, however, just as there is none for the country-store hypothesis. Merchants in country stores, it's said, hammered brass-headed tacks at intervals into their fabric department counters to indicate lengths of a yard, a half-yard and a quarter-yard. After a customer selected the cloth she wanted, the merchant would say, "All right, now we'll get down to brass tacks—I'll measure it up for you." This certainly was a practice in country stores and a common one at about the time the expression is first recorded.

brave as a badger. Ernest Hemingway called his friend foreign correspondent Herbert Matthews *brave as a badger* in the early 1930s. The badger is indeed a brave mammalian creature, furiously protecting its burrow. It gets its name from the French word *baucenc,* which refers to the animal's badgelike markings on its head. *See* badger for more about the creature, which gives its name to Michigan, the Badger State.

breadline. In *The Dictionary of Americanisms, breadline* is said to have been first recorded in 1900, but no specific account of its origin offered. However, in his fascinating book *Here at the New Yorker,* Brendan Gill attributes the expression to the Fleischmann family from whose yeast fortune rose the *New Yorker* magazine. The family ran the Vienna Model Bakery in New York City during the late 1870s: "In order to call attention to the freshness of Fleischmann's bread and also, it appears, because of an innate generosity, Lewis [Fleischmann] made a practice of giving away at 11 every evening whatever amount of bread had not been sold during the day. The poor lined up to receive it at the bakery door; hence our word 'breadline.'" The term had its widest use during the Great Depression 50 years later.

brides of the multitude. A colorful euphemism for prostitutes used in the early West, though the expression may not have been coined there.

brig. *Brig,* for "a prison on a ship," is an Americanism first recorded in 1852. One theory has it that pirates called "brigands" sailed on "brigandines" or "brigantines," small, two-masted sailing vessels, the name of which was soon shortened to *brig.* Since the brigands were criminals and were often in jail, the name of the type of ship they sailed supposedly became associated with jail cells.

broad. *Broad* has meant both a promiscuous woman and any young woman since the 1920s, though it is generally used today, when it is used, to mean a young woman—not necessarily a promiscuous one, but not someone toward whom much respect is shown. The Americanism may derive from *bawd,* but was more likely suggested by broad breasts and buttocks.

Broadway; B'way. By the mid-19th century most New York playhouses were located on Broadway or nearby, but the name *Broadway* wasn't used to attract customers until 1800, when *The Black Crook,* a strange hybrid of ballet and melodrama, was produced. This extravaganza ran over a year on Broadway and toured for more than 20 years, advertising itself as "the original Broadway production." After that the name *Broadway* was commonly used both in describing a successful touring company and in attracting visitors to New York as well. *The Black Crook* also did much to further burlesque, employing a long line of chorus girls in flesh-colored tights, which proved sensational at the time. Broadway is, of course, the best-known street in New York City, though rivaled in fame by Wall Street, Park Avenue, and Fifth Avenue. According to the *Dictionary of Americanisms,* the first recorded use of the name *Broadway* for the street was 1673; before then it had been called High Street. Originally an Indian trail, it now runs 17 miles through Manhattan and four miles through the Bronx. It has been called the longest street in the world, but doesn't come close, the record being held by Toronto's 1,178.3-mile-long Yonge Street. Columnist Walter Winchell may have coined the popular spelling *B'way. See* GREAT WHITE WAY.

broderick. His tactics wouldn't be officially approved today, but Johnny (The Boffer) Broderick is still remembered as a tough New York City cop who relied on his fists as much as his police revolver. Known as the world's toughest cop, Detective Broderick worked "the Broadway beat," dealing out punishment with his fists on the spot so often that *to broderick* became a synonym for "to clobber." Broderick once flattened the hoodlum Jack (Legs) Diamond, and he knocked out and captured Francis (Two-Gun) Crowley before Crowley could find the courage to shoot. Another time he battered two men molesting a woman, threw them through a plate-glass window and then arrested them for malicious destruction of property. In fact, Bellevue Hospital used him as an exhibit to show how much punishment the human hand could take. Broderick, an image of sartorial splendor, was used as a bodyguard by many celebrities, including Franklin Roosevelt and Jack Dempsey. Dempsey confessed that the detective was the only man he wouldn't care to fight outside the ring. This graduate of New York's gashouse district was immortalized by Damon Runyon as Johnny Bran- nigan and played by Edward G. Robinson in *Bullets or Ballots*. By the time he retired in 1947, after 25 years on the force, Broderick had won eight medals for heroism. Broadway gamblers once gave 9-5 odds that he would be killed on any given day, but he died in his bed in 1966, 72 years old.

broker than the Ten Commandments. A humorous expression from the 1930s, during the Great Depression. Wrote Henry Roth in *From Bondage* (1996), a novel set in that period: "Listen Bud, I'm flat broke. I'm broker'n the Ten Commandments."

bronco. A name (from the Spanish for rough and wild) given to small, half-wild American horses descended from steeds that escaped from early Spanish settlements. Any wild, unbroken horse is also called a bronco or bronc.

bronco-buster. A cowboy who breaks wild horses to the saddle; also called a *bronc-buster, bronco-peeler, bronc-rider, bronc- twister, bronc-fighter, bronc-snapper, bronc-scratcher,* and *bronc-stomper.*

the Bronx. The Bronx, one of New York City's five boroughs, takes its name from Jonas Bronck, a Dane who first settled the area for the Dutch West India Company in 1641. Points of interest in the celebrated borough are the Bronx Zoo and Botanic Gardens, the Edgar Allan Poe cottage, and Yankee Stadium, "the house that Ruth built." The Bronx River runs from Westchester County through the Bronx and into the East River. The *Bronx cocktail* was named in honor of the borough, or invented there in about 1919. Long associated with baseball, the razz, or raspberry, called the Bronx cheer wasn't born at Yankee Stadium, home of baseball's New York Yankees. It may derive from the Spanish word *branca,* "a rude shout," or have originated at the National Theater in the Bronx. We know for certain only that the term was first recorded in 1929.

Bronx Bombers. This nickname for the New York Yankees, who make their home in THE BRONX, first appeared in the *New York Post* in 1936. Baseball historian Paul Dickson says the name became popular when heavyweight champion Joe Louis was known as the Brown Bomber. *See* JOE LOUIS.

Bronx cheer. Long associated with baseball, the razz, or raspberry, called the *Bronx cheer,* wasn't born in Yankee Stadium in the Bronx, the home of baseball's New York Yankees, as many baseball fans believe. It may derive from the Spanish word *branca,* "a rude shout," and possibly originated at the old National Theatre in the Bronx. We only know for certain that the term was first recorded in 1929 and that many players have received Bronx cheers in Yankee Stadium.

Brooklyn. A borough of New York City almost as well known as Manhattan. Officially it is designated King's County, but no one calls it that. In 1645 the area was named Breuckelen after an ancient village in the Netherlands. Over the years this changed to Brockland, Brocklin, Brookline, and finally Brooklyn.

a Brooklyn; Woolworth; mother-in-law. Surely Brooklyn is the only borough that lends its name to a bowling term. The New York City borough gives us the word *Brooklyn* meaning a hit made on the side of the headpin opposite to the arm bowling the ball. Another eponymous bowling term is the *Woolworth*, a split of the pins leaving the "five and ten" pins still standing. The bowling term *mother-in-law* refers to the left rear pin in the pin formation.

Brooklyn Bridge. Called the "Eighth Wonder of the World" upon its opening, this bridge joining Brooklyn and Manhattan spans 1,595.5 feet between its towers and was at one time the longest bridge to use steel for greater stability. John Augustus Roebling (1806–69), the inventor of wire cable, designed the bridge but died in a ferry accident during the early stages of construction. His son Washington Roebling (1837–1926) took charge after his father's death. In 1872, Roebling became paralyzed, suffering from the bends, a common affliction among the men working the massive bottomless caissons used to sink the bridge towers onto the solid bedrock beneath the East River. From then until the end of construction, Roebling's wife acted as his intermediary while he looked on through a telescope from the window of his Columbia Heights apartment. Twelve people were trampled to death in the crowd that rushed to cross the bridge when it first opened on May 24, 1883. Almost from that year on, *buying the Brooklyn Bridge* has become a phrase symbolizing gullibility—though it's doubtful that any con man ever really sold it to anyone.

Brooklynese. Betty Boop, Popeye the Sailor Man, and Bugs Bunny all speak Brooklynese. *Brooklynese* is a synonym for the worst of New York speech, coined about 1945. It is an extreme form of New York talk that had its golden age 60 or so years ago and has been heard less ever since. Someone long ago defined *Brooklynese* as what you have a bad case of if you recite the sentence "There were thirty purple birds sitting on a curb, burping and chirping and eating dirty worms, brother," as "Dere were toity poiple boids sittin onna coib, boipin and choipin an eatin doity woims, brudda."

Brooklyn side. When a bowler hits into the wrong pocket of pins (the one opposite his bowling hand, for example, the 1–3 pocket if he's right-handed) the hit is called a *Brooklyn side* or a *Brooklyn,* as in "You've been hitting the Brooklyn side all night."

brother, can you spare a dime? A popular song published in 1932 had these words as its title and they quickly became the common plea of panhandlers throughout America during the Great Depression. American songwriter E. Y. (Yip) Harburg (1898–1981) wrote the 1932 song, which was an American pop hit throughout the Great Depression. Among many other songs, Harburg also wrote the lyrics to "It's Only a Paper Moon" (1932), "Over the Rainbow" (1939); and "Follow the Yellow Brick Road," the last two for the movie *The Wizard of Oz* (1939).

the Brown Bomber. *See* JOE LOUIS.

Bubba. *Bubba,* chiefly among blacks in the American South, is a term of address meaning "brother" and is used by friends as well as relatives. But reference works generally fail to note that the word is also commonly used to mean a white southerner. An essay in the *New York Times* by Molly Ivins put it this way: "In theory, the battle for Southern voters revolves around the stereotypical white Southerner, usually known as 'Bubba' who is partial to country music and conservative politics. But as Presidential politics move into the states of the Confederacy, the biggest question about Bubba may not be how he will vote but how to find him." *Bubba* is also a nickname in the press for former president William Jefferson Clinton, "the man from Hope (Arkansas)."

buck; pass the buck. The American slang word for a dollar may have its origins in animal skins that were classified as "bucks" and "does." The bucks, larger and more valuable than does (some 500,000 of them were traded every year in 18th-century America), could have become a part of early American business terminology (ca. 1800) and later become slang for a dollar. But *buck*'s origin could just as well be in poker. A marker called a *buck* (perhaps after a buck horn knife made from a deer's anthers) was placed next to a poker player in the game's heyday, during the late 19th century, to remind him that it was his turn to deal next. When silver dollars were used as the markers, they could have taken the name *buck* for their own. Although markers called *bucks* may or may not have given us the slang term for a dollar, they are almost certainly responsible for the expression *to pass the buck,* "to evade responsibility"— just as poker players passed on the responsibility for the deal when they passed the buck. Buck is also a derogatory term for an Indian man that dates back to the early 19th century. *Buck* *warrior* and *buck aborigine* were synonymous, though they are rarely, if ever, used anymore.

buckaroo. *Buckaroo,* for "a cowboy," is a corruption of the Spanish *vaquero,* meaning the same. The first recorded quotation using the word, in a letter from Texas, shows the mispronunciation of *vaquero* by Americans: "These rancheros are surrounded by peons and *bakharas* or herdsmen." The mispronunciation "bakhara" was further corrupted to "buckhara," "buckayro," and finally *buckaroo. Buckaroo* has probably lasted because it is a good descriptive word, suggesting a cowboy on a bucking horse. It inspired well over 50 other American slang words ending in "-aroo" or "-eroo." *Stinkaroo,* a bad play or movie, still has wide currency, as does *the old switcheroo,* the act of substituting one thing for another. Others not so familiar anymore are *antsaroo,* ants in his pants; *jugaroo,* a jail; and *ziparoo,* energy.

bucket letter. During the largely ineffective administration of President John Quincy Adams, a series of anonymous letters were sent to the president by David Holt of Georgia, writing under the pseudonym Edward Bucket. These letters, widely published, became familiar to many Americans, and for a number of years a *bucket letter* became the name for any anonymous letter. Such a letter was also called a "bucket."

bucket shop. Before it became the term for "an illegal brokerage house that cheats its customers," *bucket shop* was the designation for "an unsavory bar where patrons could buy beer by the buckets." However, in 1882, the Chicago Board of Trade prohibited grain transactions of less than 5,000 bushels. Illegitimate brokerage houses began trading in smaller lots and whenever larger, legitimate houses dealt illegally in smaller lots they sent down for a "bucketful" to the bucket shops.

buckeye. American pioneers in what is now Ohio so named this horse chestnut tree because its dark-brown nut resembles the eye of a buck deer "when the shell first cracks and exposes it to sight." A useful tree whose soft wood, cut into long shavings, even made ladies' hats and whose very roots were made into a soap, the buckeye *(Aesculus glabra)* eventually gave its name to all the natives of the BUCKEYE STATE. The nuts, or buckeye beans, of the tree were carried as good-luck charms and thought to ward off piles, rheumatism, and chills, among other maladies.

buckeye State. A nickname for Ohio, after the buckeye tree (see BUCKEYE). Like Virginia, Ohio has also been called the Mother of Presidents (Presidents Grant, Hayes, Garfield, Benjamin Harrison, McKinley, Taft, and Harding all hailed from Ohio). In the early 1800s Ohio was called the Yankee State because so many of its settlers were from New England.

buck-nekked. Completely naked. "'They got drunk and crashed the door in on him and found him buck-nekked, dancing the highland fling. A man fifty years old, seven foot tall, with a head like a peanut." (William Faulkner, *Sanctuary*, 1931) Other similar terms are *buck ass-naked, buck born-naked*, and *stark buck-naked*.

buck nun. An old cowboy term for a single, celibate man or recluse who lives by himself without a woman, often in winter camps.

the buck stops here. President Harry S. Truman (1884–1972) probably coined this saying indicating that the Oval Office and the president bear the final responsibility for any policy or action. Since then it has been used widely and is frequently a sign on the boss's desk, as it was on Truman's. *Pass the buck*, above, probably suggested Truman's invention.

buff; in the buff. So many buffalo hides were taken in the 19th century that buff coats made of them became very fashionable, the undyed yellowish coats giving us the word *buff;* the verb *buff* "to polish," entered the language from the strips of buffalo hide that were used to bring metals like bronze to a high polish. Even the word *buff* for an avid devotee of some activity or subject owes its life to *buffalo.* Buffalo robes were the winter gear of firemen in the middle of the 19th century. The amateur firefighters who rushed to blazes emulated the professionals by wearing buffcoats made of buffalo skins and were called buffs as a result. The expression *in the buff,* "in the nude," derives from the soft yellow buff skins made from buffalo hides, which looked something like bare human skin tanned by the sun. Buff is also one of the most unusual acronym nicknames. According to Frederick Forsyth in *The Fist of God* (1993): "The B-52 Stratofortress [bomber] is not called the Buff because it is painted a tan or dun-brown color. The word is not even a derivation of the first two syllables of its number—*Bee-Fifty-two.* It just stands for Big Ugly Fat Fucker." Buffs dropped 40 percent of the entire bomb tonnage during the Gulf War. Each plane can carry 51 750-pound bombs.

buffalo. Most people believe that *buffalo* is a misnomer, a name applied with zoological inexactitude to the American bison. Cortes described the creature as "a rare Mexican bull, with crooked shoulders, a hump on its back like a camel and with hair like a lion," but later explorers thought it was the Asian or African water buffalo and called it after the Spanish *bufalo,* already used in Europe as the name for those animals. Actually the water buffalo and the American buffalo both belong to the bison family, so the real mistake of early explorers was in calling the native American animal simply *buffalo* and not qualifying it with a name such as *prairie buffalo.*

Buffalo Bill. Colonel William Frederick Cody (1846–1917), the peerless horseman and sharpshooter who became the original Buffalo Bill, earned his nickname as a market hunter for buffalo (bison) hides and as a contractor supplying buffalo meat to workers building the Union Pacific Railroad in 1867. To his glory then, and shame now, he killed 4,280 buffalo in one year, mostly for their hides and tongues. It is hard to separate truth from fiction in Cody's life, his fame owing much to the dime novels that made him a celebrity in the late 19th century. Buffalo Bill was a herder, a Pony Express rider, a scout and cavalryman for the U.S. Army in the Civil War, and an Indian fighter who is said to have killed the Cheyenne chief Yellow-hand single-handedly. He was a member of the Nebraska state legislature. His Wild West Show, which he organized in 1883, toured the United States and Europe, bringing him great personal fame, yet financial problems caused this legendary American hero to die in poverty and relative obscurity. Today his name conjures up visions of "sportsmen" picking off buffalo from the platforms of moving trains, abundant buffalo meat rotting on the plains, and the destruction of the great herds. Thanks to early conservationists, some 20,000 American bison survive today, protected on government ranges.

buffalo chips. Dried buffalo dung. Louis L'Amour describes their gathering and use by wagon team women in his novel *Comstock Lode* (1981): "There was a space of wagon-tongue lashed there and a sheet of canvas . . . 'What's that for?' 'Buffalo chips,' a bystander said. 'The women folks walk behind the wagon and pick up buffalo chips and toss them onto that canvas. They're the only fuel you are likely to find.'" American resourcefulness at its most fundamental.

the buffalo gnat. "The most detestable thing in creation," one American pioneer traveling West called this vicious pest. "Before you are conscious of its presence, it has bitten your face, ears and neck in 10,000 places. My face at one time had the appearance of one with smallpox, my eyes were swollen up so much that I could hardly see, and my ears as thick as my hand."

buffalo nickel. The old buffalo nickel, 1.2 billion of which were minted in the United States for 25 years starting in 1913, is among the handsomest of American coins, especially the realistic profile of the Indian chief on the coin's front and the bison on the reverse. In February 2005, the U.S. Mint released a new buffalo nickel with several differences. The Indian on the original coin was actually a composite of *three* Native American chiefs—Iron Tail, Big Tree, and Two Moons— who posed for sculptor James Earle Fraser in 1911. The bison's name was Black Diamond.

buffalo soldier. An American Indian name for African-American soldiers stationed in the West. One explanation of the name is given by F. M. A. Roe in *Army Letters* (1872): "The officers say the negroes make good soldiers and fight like fiends . . . The Indians call them 'buffalo soldiers,' because their wooly heads are so much like the matted cushion that is between the horns of the buffalo." *The Encyclopedia of African-American Heritage* (2000) states "The name is said to have originated with the Plains Indians, who likened the soldier's bravery to that of the buffalo, and because the soldiers' curly black hair was reminiscent of a buffalo mane."

Bull Durham. Long the most popular brand of tobacco rolled into cigarettes or smoked in pipes by cowboys. Recently the title of a movie.

bull in a china shop. Back in 1936 bandleader Fred Waring lost a bet to actor Paul Douglas and had to lead a bull through Plummer's China Shop in New York City. Waring agreed to make good any damage the bull might do, but Ferdinand walked up and down the aisles with aristocratic grace, whereas his leader knocked over a table of china. Obviously bulls aren't as clumsy and reckless in delicate situations as the old saying holds, but the expression has been common in English since before 1834, when Frederick Marryat used it in his novel *Jacob Faithful.*

bull pen. Early in this century the imposing Bull Durham Tobacco signs behind outfield fences in American baseball parks pictured a big brightly colored bull, proclaiming that any batter whose home run hit the bull would get $50 and two bags of Bull Durham. Pitchers usually warmed up near these Bull Durham signs, which may be why warm-up areas for relief pitchers are called *bull pens* today, although the word could have derived from the word *bull pen* that had meant a stockade for prisoners since 1809. Or perhaps the two meanings reinforced each other.

bullshit. Utter nonsense, a flagrant, outrageous lie. This American expletive is first recorded in 1914 but is almost certainly a century or more older. Common euphemisms for it include bull, bushwa, and BS. Flinging, slinging, and throwing the bull is done by a bullshit artist— and much less commonly, a Spanish athlete. "I enclose a prize sample of bullshit," James Joyce wrote in a 1914 letter to Ezra Pound.

bummers. A Southern nickname for Union general William Tecumseh Sherman's soldiers as they made their way plundering and burning across Georgia in Sherman's fabled March to the Sea during the Civil War. They were also called "scabs," "huns," "scavengers," "hateful," "despised," "fiends," "redhanded devils" and "human fungi." But *Bummer* became the only word more anathema to Southerners than that hated word *Yankee.* After looting a town named Barnwell, the Bummers set it on fire and jokingly renamed it Burnwell.

bunk. The Missouri Compromise was being hotly debated the morning of February 25, 1820 when long-winded Congressman Felix Walker of Buncombe County, North Carolina rose on the floor of the House of Representatives and insisted that he be heard before a vote was taken. "Old Oil Jug," as his fellow congressmen called him after his well-lubricated vocal cords, did not address himself to the monumental question of the extension of slavery; his interminable oration actually had little to do with anything and important members began interrupting him with cries of "Question, Question!" On being asked what purpose his speech served, Walker calmy remarked, "You're not hurting my feelings, gentlemen. I am not speaking for your ears. I am only talking for Buncombe." Old Oil Jug apparently had written his speech some time before and believed he would ingratiate himself with the voters back home if he delivered it in the midst of a great debate, but the strategy didn't work, judging by the fact that he lost the next election. Yet his reply, "I am talking for Buncombe," was widely published in newspapers covering the debate and became a synonym for talking nonsense. Eventually, *Buncombe* became *bunkum* and it finally took the shortened form of *bunk* (in the 1850s), meaning not only "bombastic political talk," but "any empty, inflated speech obviously meant to fool people."

Burbank; Burbank plum; Burbank potato. There has been muted controversy over whether the plant breeder Luther Burbank (1849–1926) was a "plant wizard" or something of a failure. Burbank was born in Lancaster, Massachusetts, and there developed the Burbank potato, his most important achievement, while just a boy experimenting with seeds in his mother's garden. At 26 he moved to Santa Rosa, California, using the $150 he made from the sale of his potato to pay for the journey. It was in Santa Rosa, his "chosen spot of the earth," that he bred almost all the varieties of fruit, vegetables, and ornamentals for which he became famous. These included at least 66 new fruits, 12 new bush fruits, seven tree nuts, and nine vegetables, of which a number, notably the Burbank plum, bear his name. He once grew half a million strawberry plants to obtain one prize plant. However, according to Dr. W. L. Howard (University of California Agricultural Experiment Station Bulletin, 1945), only a few of the several hundred varieties developed by Burbank have stood the test of time. The patient Burbank was not the first American plant breeder—Thomas Jefferson, George Washington Carver, and Charles Hovey, originator of the Hovey strawberry, came long before him. Burbank was strongly influenced by Darwin's *The Variation of Animals and Plants Under Domestication*. His credo can be summed up in his statement "I shall be contented if, because of me, there shall be better fruits and fairer flowers." Burbank did have a sense of humor, unlike some of his critics. The renowned horticulturist was working in his experimental garden one day when approached by an obnoxious neighbor:

> "Well, what on earth are you working on now?" the man asked.
> "I'm trying to cross an eggplant and milkweed,"
> Burbank replied.

"What in heaven do you expect to get from that?" asked the neighbor. "Custard pie," said Burbank calmly.

The city of Burbank, California was named for the famous plant breeder.

burbs; suburb. For better or worse, *burbs* has been American slang for *suburbs* for the last decade or so. I record it here mainly because I haven't seen it in any dictionary. *Suburbs* wasn't used much in America until about 1940, though the word dates back to 14th-century England, where it meant residential areas outside a town or city, deriving from the Latin *suburbium,* formed from *sub,* "near," and *urbs,* "city."

burgoo. The rich southern American stew called *burgoo* probably takes its name from a similar stew that American seamen used to make, which, in turn, may derive its name from the Arabic *burghul,* "bruised grain." The word, however, is first recorded out West as *burgou,* in 1837, and may be a corruption of "barbecue." Someone has noted about *burgoo:* "No two people tell the same story about its origin and no two people will give you the same recipe."

buried; buried in booze. *Buried,* and sometimes *buried in booze,* was popular slang for "dead drunk" in the 1920s during Prohibition, when the ingredients in BOOZE could kill more quickly.

burlesque. The American burlesque in which stripteasers performed owes something to traditional burlesque, which is comedy employing satire or caricature (the word *burlesque* in fact deriving from the Italian *burla,* ridicule). But burlesque derived more directly from the minstrel show and variety theater. American burlesque, rarely produced today, featured often raunchy dialect and slapstick comedians, song and dance acts, and scantily dressed chorus girls as well as bump- and-grind strippers. It operated in circuits distinct from vaudeville after the turn of the 20th century, mainly in the Columbia and Empire Circuits, and grew more daring until police raids inspired by laws proposed by New York mayor La Guardia led to the closing of the famed Minsky burlesque houses and others during the Great Depression. The best-known and most artistic stripper of the golden era was Gypsy Rose Lee (born Rose Louise Hovick), who began her show business career as a child song-and-dance act and wrote mystery novels after her burlesque days ended. Fanny Brice, Bobby Clark, Phil Silvers, and Abbott and Costello were among the many great talents who worked in burlesque.

burrito. A tortilla wrapped around meat, beans, cheese, or other fillings. *Burrito* is Spanish for "little burro." The word was originally confined to the U.S. Southwest but is used nationwide now with the spreading popularity of Mexican food.

by the snakes of Babylon! An old exclamation rarely, if ever, heard anymore. Other old-fashioned U.S. exclamations include: By chowder! By crackie! By dad! By fire! By gary! By ginger! By gory! By gull! By gum! By the holy smut! By the livin' laws! By scissors! By smutt! and By zounds!

C

caballero. Deriving from the Spanish meaning "a man on horseback," *caballero* came to signify "a gentleman" as well. It also meant, in the words of a Texas cowboy early in the 19th century, "a hardened but gay cowboy who can jump on his horse any minute and tell the world to go to hell."

cabinet. A term heard in Massachusetts and Rhode Island for what is commonly called a milkshake in other places; it was possibly so named because the drugstore that first concocted it in Fall River, Massachusetts, kept the ice cream in a cabinet attached to the soda fountain. But perhaps the name has something to do with the earlier *cabinet pudding,* which is also a sweet dessert.

cablegram; telegram. First used in 1868, the word *cablegram* initially met with some resistance, scholars condemning it as a hybrid derived from Latin ("cable") and Greek ("gram"). Use the all-Greek *calogram* instead of the New York City-born monster, they suggested, but few agreed and the coinage proved durable. Something of the same happened with the earlier coinage *telegram,* which we know was invented by a friend of a *man* who wrote a letter to the *Albany Evening Journal* on April 6, 1852, asking that it be adopted in place of the clumsy "telegraphic dispatch" used at the time. Grammarians pointed out that *telegram* was not properly formed from its Greek elements and suggested "telegraphemie" instead, but the "barbaric new Yankee word" won out in the test of time. Such improperly formed words are of course common in English and there is a liberal supply of hybrids like *cablegram,* including such common words as because, dentist, grateful, starvation, talkative, and parliament.

cackleberry. A humorous American designation for eggs, dating back a century or so. It is said to have originated in early logging camps.

Cadillac. Cadillac, which is of course a trade name, has long been to expensive automobiles what *ford* has been to lowpriced cars. Ironically, the Detroit Automobile Company, formed by Henry Ford in 1899, was the forerunner of the Cadillac Company, Cadillac later being absorbed by General Motors. The Cadillac, in the United States and elsewhere, has become a symbol of success to some, vulgar pretension to others, and is a synonym for an expensive car to all. It bears the name of Antoine de la Mothe Cadillac (1658–1730), a minor nobleman and French colonial governor who, in 1701, founded Detroit as an important post for French control of the fur trade. Cadillac also established a trading post in what is now Cadillac, Michigan, on Lake Cadillac. Unlike the car bearing his name, the Frenchman seems to have been popular with no one. Neither Indians nor settlers could get along with him at Fort Pontchartrain (present-day Detroit), and his later governorship of the vast Louisiana Territory (1711–16) met with similar hostility. Cadillac, recalled to France, died in his native Gascony.

café society. Said to be coined one night in 1919 by newspaper society columnist Cholly Knickerbocker (Maury Paul) when he saw a number of prominent socialites dining out at the Ritz-Carlton in midtown Manhattan. Up to that time, supposedly, most of this breed dined at home. Paramount Pictures later paid Lucius Beebe, another city newspaper columnist, $50,000 for using the term *café society* as the title of a movie starring Madeleine Carroll—thinking he had invented the expression.

But it is fairly certain that Champagne Cholly (as Paul was also known) deserves the honor. He is also said to have invented glamour girl, an old standby, but is mostly responsible for such thankfully extinct cutesy coinages as sweetie sweets (nice people) and doughy dowagers (rich people).

cafeteria. A relatively young Americanism, *cafeteria* was probably introduced in 1893 at the Chicago World's Fair. It derives, however, from the Spanish *cafetería,* meaning the same.

calabash. Since the mid-19th century a *calabash* has meant an empty-headed person, someone with nobody home upstairs, in U.S. slang. *Calabash* in this sense derives from the gourd of the same name, which comes from the Arabic *qar 'ah yabisah,* "empty gourd." Sherlock Holmes's famous pipe, readers may recall, was made from a hollowed-out calabash gourd.

Calendar Islands. The Calendar Islands in Maine's Casco Bay are among the most appropriately named of island groups—there are exactly 365 of them.

California. Lexicographers aren't positive about the origin of *California,* but the state may be named after a woman named Calafia in an old Spanish romance, Calafia ruling over an island called California. On the other hand, other etymologists insist that *California* is a Catalan word meaning "hot oven"—a story that's not good for the tourist trade.

California blanket. A humorous term for layers of newspapers used as blankets. The Americanism dates back to the early 1900s, when it was apparently invented by hoboes in California.

California breakfast. A derogatory expression that, according to a January 1962 *Western Folklore* article, means "a cigarette and an orange."

California collar. A joking term given to the hangman's noose when vigilante justice ruled in early California.

California fever. The desire to go to California, the term first recorded not when gold was discovered but after explorer J. C. Frémont journeyed there in 1844.

California Joe. An American frontiersman whose real name was Moses Milner. A sharpshooter during the Civil War, he was appointed chief of scouts by Generals Custer and Sheridan. It is said that his new rank lasted only two hours, after he got so drunk that he had to be demoted. He died in a private fight in 1876, when only 46.

California prayer book. A joking term for playing cards, popular in gold-rush days.

California widow. The common ancestor of American golf widows, football widows, baseball widows, fishing widows, and computer widows, to name but a few species. *California widow* dates back to the 1850 gold rush in California, when women throughout the U.S. lost their husbands for a year or forever while the men tried their luck or pursued their fantasies in the gold fields. One such widow advertised in a San Francisco newspaper: "Husband Wanted—Whereas my husband has lately left my bed and board without provocation on my part, I hereby advertise for a suitable person to *fill the vacancy.*" It should be noted that the term *American widow* preceded all those noted above; it was used in England to describe a woman whose husband had left home to seek a fortune in America.

call his bluff. This widely used phrase certainly originated in American poker games of the early 19th century, bluffing being an integral part of poker, and *to call* meaning to match a bet. Some etymologists trace *bluff* itself back to the Low German *bluffen,* "to frighten by menacing conduct," which became the Dutch *buffen,* "to make a trick at cards," but *bluff* is first recorded in an 1838 account of an American poker game.

Cambridge flag. A popular name for the first flag of the American Continental Army at the start of the Revolutionary War. Its official name was the Grand Union flag (because it had been patterned on the British Grand Union flag with its red and white stripes and crosses), but it was popularly called the Cambridge flag because it was first flown near Boston and Cambridge, Massachusetts.

Camp David. The U.S. presidential retreat was named by President Dwight D. Eisenhower after his grandson, David Eisenhower.

Previously the retreat in the beautiful verdant Catoctin Mountains of Maryland was named Shangri-La by President Franklin Roosevelt after the refuge in James Hilton's 1933 novel *Lost Horizon.*

the canary that couldn't fly. The nickname gangsters gave to Kid Twist Reles, who informed on Murder, Inc., in the 1930s and was consequently pushed to his death from the window of a Coney Island hotel while he was being guarded by lawmen.

canfield. Lonely people playing solitaire can at least have the company of Richard C. Canfield (1855–1941), for this American gambler invented the world's most popular game of solitaire one summer toward the end of the 19th century during breaks from the gaming tables at the fashionable resort of Saratoga Springs, New York. Canfield based his new game, named *canfield* after himself, on the solitaire game called klondike, which gold miners in Alaska had invented a few decades before.

cannel coal. Found in Kentucky and Indiana, *cannel coal* is "a brightly burning coal rich in hydrogen that burns well in open fireplaces" and is becoming popular again as fireplaces become more common. Because it gives off a lot of light compared with other coals, it was first called "candle coal," the name eventually corrupted to *cannel.*

canoe; paddle your own canoe. Abraham Lincoln's frequent use of the phrase *paddle your own canoe* did much to make it popular, but Captain Frederick Marryat, that unflattering critic of American manners, seems to have been the first to have used the expression in its figurative sense, "be independent," in his novel The *Settlers in Canada* (1844). *Canoe* probably derives from the Arawak word *canoa,* for "a small boat carved from a tree trunk," which Columbus recorded in his diary and introduced into Spanish.

can of worms. Any source of complex problems or troubles, usually unpredictable. The Americanism is first recorded in 1927 and is chiefly heard in the form of *don't open that can of worms. Can* here refers to an unopened can of food with worms or maggots inside.

Can't anyone here play this game? Casey Stengel, legendary manager of the New York Mets (and the New York Yankees previously), uttered this plaintive cry when one of his players committed two errors to lose an extra-inning game during the 1962 season. The hapless Mets finished last that year, 62 ½ games out of first place, losing more games than any other 20th-century team. Writer Jimmy Breslin called the Mets "a team . . . for losers, just like nearly everybody else in life." Since Stengel said them, the words have been widely used outside of baseball as a humorous admonition to anyone who can't do a job right. Incidentally, Stengel's real name was Charles Dillon Stengel. His nickname *Casey* came from *K.C.,* because he hailed from Kansas City.

canyon. Used mostly in the U.S. for a very deep valley or gorge with steep sides, sometimes with water flowing at the bottom; the word derives from the Spanish *canon* (a large tube or funnel).

Cape Cod turkey. New Englanders have called baked codfish Cape Cod turkey for many years, at least since the mid-19th century, just as melted cheese has been called *welsh rabbit* the world over.

the Capital of the World; the Second City of the World. Former New York City mayor Rudolf Giuliani has in recent years used this sobriquet for New York. But he didn't invent it. The name was given to the city in 1939 when the World's Fair was held there and became popular again when the United Nations made New York its home. In 1898, when a reorganization of the city took in Brooklyn and other parts, New York City became known as the Second City of the World, London being the First City. In recent times Chicago has commonly been called the Second City among American cities.

capitol. A building in which a state legislature meets, or, when capitalized, the building where the U.S. Congress meets. The name comes from ancient Rome's Capitoline hill, on the summit of which was erected the great temple of the city's guardian, Jupiter Optimas Maximus. In A.D. 340 the Capitol was saved from the Gauls when the sacred geese kept there awakened its defenders, who repulsed a night attack. The U.S. Capitol building has 365 steps, one for each day of the year. In 1835 Richard Laurence, a deranged house painter, tried to assassinate President Andrew Jackson in the Capitol rotunda, unsuccessfully when both of his pistols failed to fire.

Capone. The 1920s criminal's name became synonymous both for an American mobster and for the cheap cigars he liked to smoke.

Carolina rice. Some sources say that the first rice successfully grown in South Carolina was introduced into Charleston in 1694 by a Dutch brig out of Madagascar, while others hold that Yankee shipmaster Captain John Thurber presented a packet of Madagascar rice to one of the early settlers on pulling into Charleston harbor late in the 1680s. According to the latter story, the settler planted the rice rather than dining on it, and after it sprouted, he gave seed to his friends, who in turn raised rice on their fertile land. Charleston and the Carolina low country soon became the "Rice Coast," rice fortunes building Charleston and marking the beginning of a plantocracy considered by many to be the New World aristocracy. The Madagascar rice raised there was being called Carolina rice or golden rice by 1787.

carry the ball. The person in charge *carries the ball* and has been doing so since the 1920s, when the football term began to be used figuratively by Americans.

carry you; run a car. In the American South *carry you* means "drive you to the store in a car," and one is taught "how to run a car," *not* how to drive a car.

Carson City. The capital of Nevada is so named after Kit Carson (1809–68), John C. Frémont's expedition guide and a Union Civil War general. The Los Angeles suburb called Carson City is also named for him and so is a California lake.

Carvel. In 1934 Thomas Andreas Carvelas, a Yonkers, New York, resident, invented a machine for making soft, frozen custard ice cream, which he sold from a truck, competing with such rivals as the Good Humor man. Carvelas later legally changed his name to Tom Carvel and sold franchises that made the Carvel name a household word for soft ice cream by the 1960s.

Casablanca. When Warner Bros. warned the Marx Brothers not to use the name "Casablanca" in their film *A Night in Casablanca* because (the studio claimed) this would infringe upon the title of Warner's movie *Casablanca,* Groucho Marx wrote the company the following letter now in the Groucho collection of the Library of Congress. Jack Warner, who regarded actors as "bums" and writers as "schmucks with Underwoods," was not amused. "Apparently there is more than one way of conquering a city and holding it as your own," Groucho wrote. "For example, up to the time that we contemplated making a picture, I had no idea that the city of Casablanca belonged to Warner Bros. However, it was only a few days after our announcement appeared that we received a long ominous document warning us not to use the name 'Casablanca.' It seems in 1471, Ferdinand Balboa Warner, the great-great-grandfather of Harry and Jack, while looking for a short-cut to the city of Burbank, had stumbled on the shores of Africa and, raising his alpenstock, which he later turned in for a hundred shares of the common, he named it Casablanca. I just can't understand your attitude. Even if they plan on releasing the picture, I am sure that the average movie fan could learn to distinguish between Ingrid Bergman and Harpo. I don't know whether I could, but I certainly would like to try. You claim you own Casablanca and that no one else can use that name without your permission. What about Warner Brothers—do you own that too? You probably have the right to use the name Warner, but what about Brothers? Professionally, we were brothers long before you were. Even before us, there had been other brothers—the Smith Brothers, the Brothers Karamazov, Dan Brothers, an outfielder with Detroit and 'Brother, can you spare a dime?' This was originally 'Brothers, can you spare a dime,' but this was spreading a dime pretty thin. The younger Warner Brother calls himself Jack. Does he claim that, too? It's not an original name—it was used long before he was born. Offhand, I can think of two Jacks—there was Jack of 'Jack and the Beanstalk' and Jack the Ripper, who cut quite a figure in his day . . ." And so the letter went on a la Groucho. Needless to say, *A Night in Casablanca* remained *A Night in Casablanca.*

case. Criminals case or survey a place in order to get useful information to enable them to rob it. This underworld expression dates back to early 20th-century America and has been adopted by the British and Australians.

cash on the barrelhead. Though there is no proof of it, the origins of this expression most likely lie in the makeshift saloons on the American frontier over a century ago, which were often no more than a room in a log cabin with a barrel serving as both booze container and counter. No credit was extended, and any customer who wanted a smack of tarantula juice, or any rotgut likely to make him brave enough not to want to pay, was required to put down cash on the barrelhead, or counter.

cash register. The term *cash register* was devised by the machine's inventor—Dayton, Ohio restaurant owner James J. Ritty—who called it the "Cash Register and Indicator" in his patent filed March 26, 1879. Ritty invented the machine to help prevent his cashiers from stealing and, in fact, called it the Incorruptible Cashier. Unfortunately, he sold out his company after two years, discouraged by slow sales, never really cashing in on what would prove to be a billion-dollar invention.

catch colt. A Western euphemism for an illegitimate child, called an *old-field colt* and a *woods colt* in other areas. Originally the term meant a colt that wasn't the result of its owner intentionally breeding its parents.

cat on a hot tin roof. Best known today as the title of Tennessee Williams's famous play, the expression has been in wide use in America since the turn of the 19th century. *Like a cat on a hot tin roof* derives from a similar British phrase, *like a cat on hot bricks,* which was first recorded about 1880 and also means someone ill at ease, uncomfortable, not at home in a place or situation.

the cat's meow. There is a large litter of terms equating the cat with excellence, all of them Americanisms first recorded in the early 1920s. These are *the cat's meow, the cat's nuts, the cat's whiskers, the cat's pajamas,* and *the cat's kittens.* What is especially excellent about a cat's meow or any of the other collection of cat terms remains a mystery.

cattle call. Alfred Hitchcock infamously called actors "cattle," and the term is still used in Hollywood. So is *cattle call,* first recorded in 1952, an open casting call or audition of many actors for one part or more parts. A cattle call for models is called a "go-see." The use of *cattle* as a derogatory term for people dates back to at least 1673, when it is first recorded in this sense. The theatrical use of the term may have originated with actors who thought they were treated like cattle.

cattle singer. An interesting Americanism explained by Edna Ferber in *Cimarron* (1930):

> . . . Shanghai Wiley, up from Texas, was the most famous cattle singer in the whole Southwest. . . . Possessed of a remarkably high sweet tenor voice . . . he had been known to quiet a whole herd of restless cattle on the verge of a mad stampede. It was an art he had learned when a cowboy on the range. Many cowboys had it, but none possessed the magic soothing quality of Shanghai's voice. It was reputed to have in it the sorcery of the superhuman. It was told of him that in a milling herd, their nostrils distended, their flanks heaving, he had been seen to leap from the back of one maddened steer to another, traveling that moving mass that was like a shifting sea, singing to them in his magic tenor, stopping them just as they were about to plunge into the Rio Grande.

caucus. In American politics party leaders hold caucuses, off-the-record meetings, to select leaders and form policy. These leaders are in one sense counselors or advisers, and it is probably the Algonquin Indian word *caucauasu,* meaning "counselor or adviser," that gives us the Americanism *caucus,* first recorded in 1773.

caught between the hammer and the anvil. To be surrounded by powerful enemy forces. The allusion is to the blacksmith's hammer and anvil, but the expression was first heard by most Americans from the lips of General Tommy R. Franks, regional commander of American forces in the war against terrorism (2001), who referred to Al-Queda forces trapped on the battlefield in Afghanistan.

cellar. *Cellar,* for "the lowest position in league rank for a baseball team" is first recorded in a *New York Times* headline of July 9, 1922:

"Red Sox Are Up Again. Leave Cellar to Athletics by Taking Final of Series, 4 to 1." Thus the Philadelphia Athletics were the first baseball team to be in the cellar. Cellar, for "an underground room or basement," dates back to the 14th century and derives from the Latin *cella,* "cell."

cent. *Cent* is an Americanism introduced during the Revolution by Gouverneur Morris to replace the British word "penny." Though both words are still used today, *cent,* deriving from the Latin *centum* for "one-hundredth," (of a dollar) is more common than PENNY.

Centennial State. Colorado has had the nickname Centennial State since it was admitted into the Union in 1876. It has also been called the Switzerland of America (New Hampshire, New Jersey, West Virginia and Maine also claim this title) the Silver State (Nevada claims this one, too) and the Treasure State (Montana is its competitor here).

Central Park. Work began on the great Manhattan park in 1857 based on designs by Frederick Law Olmsted and Calvert Vaux. The park was partially inspired by public grounds in great European cities and was meant to improve New York's reputation and provide a recreational area for its citizens. The orginal grounds covered 700 acres running from 59th Street to 106th Street between Fifth Avenue and Eighth Avenue. Olmsted and Vaux's design called for a combination of pastoral settings and recreational facilities and included features such as the Sheep Meadow and carriage drives. The park opened in 1859 and in 1863 its northern edge moved to 110th Street, increasing the grounds to 843 acres. In the 1930s progressive reformers and Parks Commissioner Robert Moses built numerous playgrounds at the park's edges, constructed ballfields, renovated the zoo, and increased recreational activities. Since its opening, the park has been an important part of New York life, particularly in summertime. Among the park's best-known features are the Children's Zoo, the Delacorte Theater, the Carousel, the Great Lawn, the Metropolitan Museum of Art, and Tavern on the Green restaurant.

chain lightning. Lightning bolts that appear to move very quickly in wavy and zigzag lines. The term is an Americanism coined in about 1825.

cheapskate; a good skate. Revolutionary War soldiers liked to sing the Scottish song "Maggie Lauder," the chorus of which chided a *blatherskate,* a gabby person full of nonsense or hot air. The song is a very old one, dating back to the 17th century, and the word blatherskate is older still, formed from *bladder,* an obsolete English word for an inflated pretentious man, a windbag, and a contemptuous use of the word *skate,* referring to the common food fish. Why the skate was chosen for the humorous word isn't clear, perhaps because it was believed to inflate itself like a blowfish, or possibly just because it was common. In any case, "Maggie Lauder" made *blatherskate* popular in America and later, in the 19th century, when Americans invented their native word *cheapskate,* for a tightwad, they borrowed the *skate* from it. This is a more roundabout explanation than the theory that the *skate* in *cheapskate* comes from a British slang word for chap, but it seems more logical, as *skate* in the sense of *chap* never had much currency in the U.S., except in the term *good skate,* meaning a good person.

checkered cabs. New York City taxis with checkered line along the sides and around the roof. Thousands of them worker city streets in days past, but the last one was retired in 2000.

chenangoe. Upstate New York farms in Chenango County supplied many of the longshoremen who worked the New York waterfront in the late 19th century. So many, in fact, that *chenangoe* became a term for any longshoreman who loads cargo from railroad barges to ships. Before this the chenangoe had been a popular variety of potato.

Cherokee. The name of this Indian tribe is a mystery, their name perhaps stolen from them like their land. "The word *Cherokee* itself has no meaning in the Indian language," writes Michael Frome in *Strangers in High Places* (1966). "It may have had its origin in the time of the [Fernando] de Soto expedition (1540) with the word Achelaque, modified in stages to spell Cherokee, until not even their name remained to them." *See trail of tears.*

Chevrolet. Swiss engineer Louis Chevrolet worked for U.S. car manufacturer William Durant as a racing driver. When Durant opened his new automobile company, he named it the Chevrolet Motor Company after Chevrolet because, he explained, his driver's name "had a musical sound and the romance of foreign origin."

chewing gum. The world's first modern chewing gum was Adams' New York Gum No.1—Snapping and Stretching. (Previously there were gums made of spruce sap, paraffin, and other substances.) Adams' was concocted by Thomas Adams Sr. on his Jersey City kitchen stove around 1869 and later manufactured in New York City. Adams' was the first commercial gum to be made with chicle and this milky liquid from the sapodilla tree was, according to one story, supplied to the inventor by General Antonio Lopez de Santa Anna, Mexican conqueror of the Alamo, who was exiled in Staten Island at the time. Adams first tried to make a cheap rubber substitute from the chicle, as Santa Anna had urged him to do; he failed but then came up with the great gum idea. Later his company merged with eight others into the American Chicle Company. The first successful *bubblegum* was invented by Fleer's employee Walter Diemer in 1928.

Chicago. The Windy City unfortunately derives its name from an Indian word that means "place of the bad smell," "place of skunk smells," or "skunktown." There is only a slight chance that the Indian word means "wild onion place," as has been suggested.

the Chicago way. Eliot Ness, played by Kevin Costner, is told the meaning of this expression in the movie *The Untouchables* (2000) by a tough Chicago cop named Malone, played by Sean Connery: "If you open the can on these worms you must be prepared to go all the way, because they're not gonna give up the fight until one of you is dead," he says. "You wanna know how you do it? They pull a knife, you pull a gun. He sends one of yours to the hospital, you send one of his to the morgue. That's the Chicago way, and that's how you get Capone. Now do you want to do that? Are you ready to do that?"

Chicano. An American of Mexican descent. One explanation claims this word is a contraction of the Spanish for "I am not a boy." Another suggests it comes from the ending of the word *Mexicano,* which the Aztecs pronounced "Meshicano," this eventually shortened to *shicano* and then *chicano.*

chickaree. A name in many parts of the U.S. for the red squirrel, the appellation deriving from the cry the red squirrel makes.

chicken feed. Chickens were fed grain too poor for any other use by American pioneers, and these pieces of poor-quality grain had to be small so the chickens could swallow them. This obviously suggested the contemptuous term *chicken feed* for small change (pennies, nickels, and dimes) to riverboat gamblers fleecing small-town suckers. The first in-print mention of the expression is in *Colonel [Davy] Crockett's Exploits* (1836): "I stood looking on, seeing him pick up chicken feed from the green horns." By extension, *chicken feed* has come to mean any small or insignificant amount of money, and even (rarely today) misleading information deliberately supplied or leaked by a government to spies employed by another government.

chicken guts. A humorous term for the gold trim on the cuffs of Confederate uniforms during the Civil War. Also a name used by children for the symbol "&," the ampersand.

chicken ranch. Unlike most sexual euphemisms, this synonym for "a brothel" takes its name from a real place. The original Chicken Ranch was a bordello in Gilbert, Texas, early in this century, so named because poor farmer clients often paid for their visits with chickens. It is celebrated in the play *The Best Little Whorehouse in Texas*.

chicken scratch; crow tracks. These are Americanisms for illegible handwriting. *Chicken scratch* is first recorded in 1956 but is probably much older, while *crow tracks* dates back to at least 1875. Variations are *hen tracks* and *turkey tracks*.

Chinaman's chance. The Chinese immigrants who built so many miles of American railroads often tried to make their fortune by working old claims and streams abandoned by white prospectors during the California gold rush of 1849. They had an extremely poor chance of finding any gold in such abandoned claims, and thus *a Chinaman's chance* came to mean "no chance at all." The poor lot of Chinese in a segregated society probably reinforced the phrase, for the Chinese had as poor a chance on the railroads and other places as they did in the gold fields.

chintzy. *Chintzy* is American slang for "cheap," or "poorly made," or even "stingy," dating back to about the 1940s. But it comes from the plural of the Hindu word *chint,* for "a glazed cotton fabric with flowery designs" first made in India. The British mistook the plural of the word, *chints,* for the singular, applying it to the cloth and eventually spelling it *chintz*. Regarded as a cheap material in America, *chintz* finally gave us the word *chintzy*.

chip on one's shoulder. In 1830 the *Long Island Telegraph* in Hempstead, New York reported that "When two churlish boys were determined to fight, a *chip* would be placed on the shoulder of one, and the other demanded to knock it off at his peril." From this New York State boyhood custom, first recorded above, comes the expression *to have a chip on one's shoulder,* "to be sullen or angry, looking for a fight." The phrase itself isn't recorded until 1934, but is probably much older.

Choctaw. *Choctaw,* a fancy step in ice-skating, and southern slang for unintelligible speech, is from the Choctaw Indian tribe of southern Mississippi. The Choctaws, named from the Spanish *chato* ("flattened") for their practice of flattening the heads of male infants, fought against the British during the American Revolution and aided the United States in later years against the Creeks. They ceded their lands to the government in 1832, the majority moving to reservations in what is now Oklahoma.

cholmondely. Spelled *cholmondely* and pronounced *chumley* this is an old South Carolinian way to say *chimney.*

chopped liver. Said of something or someone trivial. First recorded in a famous line of American comedian Jimmy Durante: "Now that ain't chopped liver!" Often heard today in the half-humorous complaint "What am I, chopped liver?"

chop suey. Chop suey isn't native to China; in fact, most accounts of its origin say that the dish was invented in America. The widely accepted theory, advanced by Herbert Asbury in his *Gangs of New York* (1928), makes the tasty melange the brainchild of a San Francisco dishwasher, though the Chinese dishwasher is sometimes promoted to a "cook in a California gold mining camp." I've traced the term's invention, however, to 1896, when it was concocted in New York by Chinese ambassador Li Hung-chang's chef, who tried to devise a dish appealing to both American and Chinese tastes. Since the ambassador had three chefs, it's hard to say which one invented chop suey. The name has nothing to do with the English word "chop," deriving instead from the Cantonese dialect *shap sui,* which means "pieces of mixed bits," *sui* being the Chinese for "bits." The chef who invented it took leftover pieces of pork and chicken and cooked them together with bean sprouts, green peppers, mushrooms, and seasonings in a gravy, serving it with rice and soy sauce.

chow. *Ch'ao,* the Mandarin Chinese for "to fry or cook," probably gives us the word *chow,* an Americanism first recorded in the 1850s in California, where there were many Chinese laborers and cooks working on the railroads.

chowder. *Chowder* derives from the French *chaudière,* stew pot, the word brought to the New World by Breton fishermen who settled the Maritime Provinces of Canada. The soup called a clam chowder is made with milk, vegetables, and clams in Maine and Massachusetts, this being the famous New England clam chowder. But in Rhode Island and as far away as New York, it often is made with water, vegetables, tomatoes, and clams, this called Manhattan clam chowder. The two schools are not at all tolerant of each other. One Maine legislator, in fact, introduced a bill making it *illegal* to add tomatoes to chowder within the state of Maine, the penalty being that the offender dig up a barrel of clams at high tide.

Chrysler Building. A skyscraper on Lexington Avenue in Manhattan that was briefly the tallest building in the world. The story is told in *The New York City Guide* (1939): "William Van Alen, architect of the Chrysler Building, and his former partner, H. Crain Severance, became rivals when each was commissioned to design the world's tallest building. When the Chrysler tower seemed likely to terminate at 925 feet, the builders of the Bank of Manhattan Company structure (or Manhattan Company Building) at 40 Wall Street (designed by Severance and Yasuo Matsui) decided to halt their operations at

927 feet. Meanwhile, steelworkers were secretly assembling the rust-less steel section of the Chrysler spire, which, when lifted through the dome and bolted into place, brought the building to its triumphant height of 1,048 feet. Subsequently the Empire State Building stole the laurels."

chuck; chuck wagon. Food or provisions in general; a meal. The term is an Americanism first used in about 1840 and probably derives from the cut of meat (beef) called chuck. The first chuck wagon was made from a surplus Civil War army wagon in 1867 by rancher Charles Goodnight. By the 1880s the term was common for a wagon carrying provisions and equipment for cooking, the Studebaker Company by then manufacturing them for $75 to $100.

Churchill Downs. *Downs* are open, rolling, upland country. These are located in Louisville, Kentucky, and are named not after British great Winston Churchill but for the original property owners, the brothers John and Henry Churchill. Churchill Downs has been synonymous with the Kentucky Derby, established there in 1875 as an annual race for three-year-olds. The Kentucky Derby itself was named after the English Derby (pronounced Darby) at Epson Downs, first held in 1780 when established by the 12th earl of Derby. The first Kentucky Derby, the oldest American horse race, awarded the winner a purse of $1,000, plus the entry fees of all the horses.

Cincinnati. Cincinnati, Ohio, takes its name from the Society of the *Cincinnati,* honoring the Roman statesman Cincinnatus, which former Revolutionary officers in the area founded in 1783.

Cincinnatus. In the early days of the republic George Washington was called the Cincinnatus of America, after the hero of that name who in about 458 B.C. came out of retirement on his farm to lead the Roman army to victory. Returning to the plow, Cincinnatus again served as dictator many years later to successfully avert a civil war. Like Lucius Quinctius Cincinnatus, Washington was a simple, dignified man. *See* CINCINNATI.

CINCUS; FIB. No doubt the most embarrassing acronym in naval history was CINCUS (pronounced "sink us"), which stood for the *C*ommander *in c*hief of the *U*nited *S*tates Navy before World War II, but was dropped from use following Pearl Harbor. Another amusing nautical acronym is FIB, standing for the *F*isherman's *I*nformation *B*ureau of Chicago.

circus; charity circus. The expression *charity circus* for a circus that donates part of its proceeds to charity dates back to famous American circus owner and clown Dan Rice, who helped popularize his circus by donating part of the proceeds in the 1850s and gave performances for the Union cause during the Civil War. Circuses in America go back to at least 1785, however, and circuses were popular in Roman times, the word *circus* itself deriving from the Latin *circus* for ring. A *three ring circus* is thus, strictly speaking, "a three ring ring."

city. Manhattan, one of the five boroughs of New York City, is *the city* to anyone living in any of the other four boroughs, and that person would usually say "I'm going to the city" if he or she was going to Manhattan, although "I'm going to Manhattan" might also be used.

Out in the suburbs of Long Island, Connecticut, and New Jersey, however, one might say "I'm going to the city" and mean he or she is going to the boroughs of Brooklyn, Queens, Staten Island, or the Bronx as well.

City of Corruption. An old name for San Francisco, California, in the late 19th century, when vigilantes patrolled the city streets night and day.

City of the Saints. Salt Lake City, Utah, home of the Mormon Church, or Church of Jesus Christ of Latter-day Saints.

City Where the West Begins. A nickname for Fort Worth, Texas.

Civil War. The northern name for what some southerners called the War, the Revolution, the War of Independence, the Second War of Independence, the Second War of Secession, the Confederate War, the Glorious Cause, the War Between the States, the Unpleasantness, the Second American Revolution, the War for Constitutional Liberty, the War for Nationality, the War for Separation, the War for Southern Freedom, the War for Southern Independence, the War for Southern Nationality, the War for Southern Rights, the War for States' Rights, the War of the North and South, the War of the Sixties, the War to Suppress Yankee Arrogance, the Yankee Invasion, the Late Unpleasantness, and Mr. Lincoln's War. All of these terms, including *Civil War,* were first recorded in 1861. *See* ABE LINCOLN WAR.

claim jumper. One who illegally takes possession of another's land claim. Wrote Philip Johnston in *Lost and Living Cities of the California Gold Rush* (1948): "Occasionally, a claim jumper was hauled into court; but the practice of locating another man's ground became distinctly hazardous, it did not occur with the frequency that many writers of Western fiction would have us believe."

clam chowder. By New England definition clam chowder is a dish made with clams, vegetables and *milk*—never with a tomato base. Manhattan clam chowder, however, is *always* made with tomatoes. This great American gastronomic controversy became national news in February 1939 when Assemblyman James Seeder introduced a bill into the Maine legislature making the use of tomatoes in clam chowder illegal. The punishment his unenacted bill specified: Make any offender harvest two bushels of clams at high tide.

clam up. *Clam up* is an Americanism for "to become silent, refuse to disclose information," dating back to 1916 and referring to the difficulty of opening the "lips" of the clam. *Clam,* for "mouth," has been common in America since the early 19th century. *Close as a clam,* describing a stingy person, is an older expression that probably originated in England.

clay pigeon. George Ligowsky of Cincinnati, Ohio, was in spirit an early conservationist who deplored the practice of using live birds in target shooting. One afternoon while watching boys skipping flat stones over the surface of a pond, he got the idea of making a clay target that could be released and shot at in place of pigeons or other birds. Ligowsky patented his invention in 1881, calling them flying targets, but because they usually took the place of pigeons, they quickly came to be called clay pigeons. Since then, for obvious reasons, *clay pigeons* has also become widespread American slang for an easy target, someone who is easily duped, a sucker.

clean up. In the early 19th century, American farmers used the expression *to clean up* as a synonym for gathering the harvest, stripping all the grain from a field. However, this doesn't appear to be the source when the expression means "to make an exceptional financial success," a "big haul." In this sense *clean up* came into the language after the gold strikes toward the end of the 19th century. It apparently derives from the mining term *clean-up,* which describes the process of separating gold from the gravel and rock that collected in the sluices or at the stamping mill.

Cleveland Indians. There has been controversy recently over whether sports teams should be given Indian names, which has been a practice for over a century. One of the oldest was the name *Cleveland Indians,* the winning entry in a 1915 newspaper contest to rename the team. (It was formerly known as the Naps, in honor of star second baseman Napoleon Lajoie, who had just retired.) The team's new name honored Louis Sockalexis, a Penonscot Indian from Old Town, Maine, who had played college ball at Holy Cross and Notre Dame before signing with Cleveland in 1897 to become the first American Indian to play in the majors. After an excellent rookie year in which he batted .338 and was known for his power hitting and strong throwing arm, Sockalexis apparently succumbed to the pressures of his situation, which included loud war whoops from the fans when he came to bat. He began drinking heavily, and his playing deteriorated until he was dropped from the club in 1899 Although he played only 94 games, he remains the only person after whom an existing major league baseball team was named. Football's Kansas City Chiefs were named after the mayor of Kansas City, who was instrumental in bringing the franchise from Dallas to Missouri and was popularly nicknamed "the Chief." Other teams bearing "Indian" related designations include football's Washington Redskins and basketball's Golden State Warriors. Baseball's Atlanta Braves took the name of their predecessor, the Boston Braves, who were named not for any American Indians but for the emblem (an Indian brave) of New York City's Tammany Hall political machine—members of which had invested in the team.

clipped ears. Though the term isn't recorded in *A Dictionary of Americanisms,* Australians who migrated to the California gold fields in 1849 were often called *clipped ears,* because a certain number of them had been criminals who had suffered the punishment of ear clipping in Australia.

cockamamie. *Cockamamie* means something worthless or trifling, even absurd or strange; a *cockamamie* excuse or story is an implausible, ridiculous one. The word may be a corruption of *decalcomania* ("a cheap picture or design on specially prepared paper that is transferred to china, wood, etc."), a word youngsters on New York's Lower East Side early in the century found tiring to pronounce and impossible to spell.

code talkers. (1) A group of Navajo Indians selected by the U.S. Army to send combat messages in their own language, which the Japanese in the World War II Pacific theater could not decipher. (2) A smaller group of Comanche U.S. soldiers that performed the same duty against the Germans for the Allies in Europe.

Coke; cola. Coke, or Coca-Cola (both registered trademarks), was invented by Atlanta, Georgia, druggist Dr. John S. Pemberton in 1886, and is so named because its original ingredients were derived from coca leaves and cola nuts. *Coke* is also slang for *cocaine* and for this reason the Coca-Cola Company long avoided use of this name—especially because, up until 1909, Coca-Cola did contain minute amounts of cocaine. While the Supreme Court declared *Coca-Cola* and *Coke* exclusive trademarks, *cola* was ruled a generic word that anyone could use. Coca-Cola's slogans "The pause that refreshes" and "Coke is it" are also well known. In 1985 a Mr. Frederick Koch (pronounced "Coke") of Guilford, Vermont, got tired of people pronouncing his last name "Kotch" and changed it to Coke-Is-It. Coca-Cola objected to the use of its trademark, but finally reached a settlement with Mr. Coke-Is-It, letting him keep his new name. For the record, the actual coiner of the name Coca-Cola was Pemberton's bookkeeper, Frank M. Robinson, who invented it in 1893. In those early days Coca-Cola was advertised as the "Esteemed Brain Tonic and Intellectual Beverage."

cold fish. An emotionally cold, impassive person, either a man or a woman. The expression, first recorded in the early 1920s in the U.S., can also mean a sexually cold or frigid person.

cold war. *Cold war,* for a situation where two nations aren't actually at war but are doing everything they can to damage each other short of war, is first recorded in 1947, when Walter Lippmann's *The Cold War,* a study of American-Soviet relations, was published. More specifically, others advise that *cold war* was named "in a 1947 speech by Bernard Baruch, written by Herbert Bayard Swope." But George Orwell wrote in 1945 of "A State which was . . . in a permanent state of 'cold war' with its neighbors."

colt. When Samuel Colt (1814–62) ran away to sea from his home in Hartford, Connecticut at 16, he spent his lonely nights on deck whittling a wooden model of the Colt revolver that was to make him famous. Young Colt had several metal models made of his gun upon arriving home and patented his invention. He built his armory into the largest in the world, his use of interchangeable parts and the production line making him one of the richest men in America. As for the Colt, the first pistol that could be effectively employed by a man on horseback, it played a more important part in the conquest of the West than any other weapon, the famed "six-shooter" becoming so popular that its name became a generic term for revolver. *Colt* for a young horse comes from the Old English *colt* meaning the same.

come up and see me sometime. The still much-imitated words of actress Mae West to her leading man Cary Grant in the 1933 film *She Done Him Wrong.* Her actual words, however, were, "Why don't you come up some time and see me?" Another memorable Mae West line is her "Beulah, peel me a grape!" to her maid in the movie *I'm No Angel* (1933).

comeuppance. Whether this expression is an Americanism or not is the subject of some dispute; it is first recorded in America in 1859 and in England some 20 years later, if that proves anything. *Comeuppance* means "just desserts" or "merited punishment," and has several dialect versions in different areas, including *comings* and *come-uppings,* the British once using *come-uppings* for a flogging. Possibly the expression *come up,* "to present oneself for judgment before a tribunal," fathered the phrase.

commercial. An American term for a radio or TV ad. The term was first recorded on a 1923 *Eveready Flashlight Hour* radio show. According to one ad executive, ad agencies today air 3000 commercials a year. The highest price ever paid for a commercial was the $1.3 million paid for a 30-second spot by Pepsi Cola during Super Bowl XXXI in 1997.

common. When in 1948 Henry Wallace campaigned with the slogan that this was "the century of the common man," many southerners had trouble understanding at first, for *common* is often a term of contempt in the South, far more than in the rest of the United States. It can also be a complimentary term for an unassuming, friendly person, as in "He's a real common man."

commonwealth. Officially, Massachusetts is not a U.S. state, but a commonwealth, as are Virginia, Maryland, Pennsylvania, and Kentucky. Technically, Rhode Island is not exactly a state, either; its official title is the State of Rhode Island and Providence Plantations.

commute. The verb *to commute* developed as a back formation from the noun *commutation* at about the time of the Civil War—Americans were commuting to work on the train even at that early date. *Commute* later became the word for a railroad ticket, a shortening of "commutation ticket." *Commute* has its roots in the Latin *commutare,* to change, thus someone commuting is changing from one place to another.

comparison shopper. Comparison shoppers had their heyday from the 1920s to the 1960s. They originated, however, in the early 20th century price wars of department stores and were at first simply a clerk whom a buyer would send across the street to get an idea of his competitor's prices. Then comparison departments were formed, the average New York department store employing four or five professional shoppers, "the eyes and ears of the store," to study the stock, prices, and customers of rival stores and report back to their employers. This was essential to stores like Macy's with its long-standing policy of selling all merchandise at 6 percent below the prices of other stores. Macy's comparison shoppers were so wily that they sometimes wore disguises.

compass cactus. Western settlers in the U.S. gave this name to the barrel cactus *(Echinocactus)* because it almost always leans southwest, and they could tell directions by it.

compassionate conservatism. A philosophy stressing using conservative concepts to improve society. It was coined by Michael Gerson, White House speechwriter for President George W. Bush during his two administrations.

competitive golf. The great American golfer Robert Tyre "Bobby" Jones (1902–71) defined competitive golf as a game played on a five-inch course, in the space between the ears.

complected. The journals of the Lewis and Clark expedition in 1806 contain the first recorded use of the word *complected* for being of a particular facial complexion. The word is used throughout the U.S., as in "She is dark complected and he is rather light complected."

con; con game; con man. Just after the Civil War, one of the most common frauds in America was the sale of fake gold mine stock in the West. Sometimes gold would be salted in played-out "mines" to fool "marks," but the swindlers who worked the scheme usually settled for a small score from a great number of investors and never bothered about tricking up a real mine. Investors were often reluctant to advance funds without examining the property, however, and the swindlers asked their victims to make a small investment in advance "just as a gesture of confidence," deposits that they quickly absconded with. The trick was soon dubbed the *confidence game,* and, in time, its fast-moving practitioners became known as *con men.* Reinforcing the word is the idea that victims of a con game are bamboozled into confidence that they're going to make a killing. To con, in this sense, has nothing to do with the older English verb *to con,* to study or commit to memory, which derives from the Middle English *cunnen,* "to try." *Con games* were practiced, of course, long before this word for them was coined. On the American continent, for example, Mayan swindlers painstakingly drilled small holes in cocoa beans, emptied out their precious powder and refilled them with dirt before selling them to Europeans.

Confederate states. The U.S. Confederate states, which seceded from the Union, were Alabama, Arkansas, Florida, Georgia, Louisiana, Mississippi, North Carolina, South Carolina, Tennessee, Texas, and Virginia.

conk. A once popular hairstyle worn by African-Americans that straightens and waves curly hair. It probably takes its name from the slang *conk* for head and/or from the commercial preparation Congolene used to so fashion hair. The term is used widely throughout the United States, but its point of origin is unknown. It is also called a process.

Connecticut. "The Nutmeg State," the fifth to enter the Union, in 1788, takes its name from the Mohegan Indian *quinnitukqut,* "at the long tidal river," in reference to the state's location on what is now the Connecticut River.

conniption fit. The English dialect word *canapshus,* meaning "ill-tempered, captious," is the ancestor of the Americanism *conniption,* for "a fit of rage or anger." A person can go into conniptions, have a conniption fit, or go into a fit of conniptions—all mean the same. The expression is first recorded in 1833: "Ant Keziah fell down in a conniption fit."

cookin' with gas. Efficient gas ranges were common in the United States before World War I, models including the 1912 Lindemann with four burners, a broiler, and an oven for $57. But starting in the

1930s, the U.S. gas industry began a public relations campaign trying to convince consumers to use gas rather than increasingly popular electric ranges. This resulted in the widely used saying *now you're cookin' with gas,* "now you've got the right idea, are on the right track," etc. The same is true of the synonym *to cook on the front burner* ("Brother, you're cookin' on the front burner").

a coon's age. Meaning "a very long time," *a coon's age* is an Americanism recorded in 1843 and probably related to the old English expression "in a crow's age," meaning the same. The American term is an improvement, if only because the raccoon usually lives longer—up to 13 years in the wild—than the crow.

cooper. Dr. Kenneth Cooper, an American physician, wrote a book on aerobic exercise, including jogging, that was a worldwide bestseller in the 1960s. No word honors him in the U.S. for the many lives he saved, but in Brazil the word *cooper* means to go jogging.

coot stew. A few generations ago people actually enjoyed this dish. Wrote one feisty Yankee world traveler in the late 19th century: "Frederick's pressed duck at the Tour d'Argent isn't bad, but it can't hold a candle to coot stew." There is a real recipe for coot stew, but the anonymous old Maine recipe for it is more famous: "Place the bird in a kettle of water with a red building brick free of mortar and blemishes. Parboil that coot and brick together for three hours. Pour off the water, fill the kettle, and again parboil three hours. Once more throw off the water, refill the kettle, and this time let the coot and brick simmer together overnight. In the morning throw away the coot and eat the brick."

corker. Someone or something very good, remarkable, as in: "He's a real corker." The term is American, possibly with Irish roots, and is first recorded in 1891.

corner the market. This term arose in U.S. financial circles toward the middle of the 19th century. Used generally today, it originally meant only to buy "one kind of stock or commodity, thereby driving potential buyers and sellers into a corner because they have no option but to yield to the price demands of those controlling the stock."

corn pone. *Corn pone* is a famous southern American cornmeal cake or bread, defined by *Bartlett* in 1859 as "a superior type of corn bread, made with milk and eggs and cooked in a pan." It is often called "corn bread." *Cornpone* has also come to be a derogatory term for someone or something rural and unsophisticated: "That's a cornpone story." The word *pone* comes from the Powhatan Indian word *apan,* something baked.

corny. *Corny,* for something old-fashioned, unsophisticated, and unsubtle, what is often called "tacky" in today's slang, has its origin in America's Corn Belt. Comedians playing to unsophisticated "corn-fed" audiences in the Midwest gave them the corn-fed humor they wanted, so much so that corn came to be known as "what farmers feed pigs and comedians feed farmers." Soon *corn-fed humor* became simply *corny jokes,* the phrase possibly helped along by the Italian word *carne* "cheap meat," being applied to the "cheap jokes" the comedians told. *Corny* eventually was used to describe anything old-fashioned, full of clichés, or mawkishly sentimental.

cotton-pickin'. Despicable, wretched, damned; now sometimes used in a humorous sense. The term has its roots in the inferior status of poor farmers and field hands in the southern United States and dates back to the 19th century. The word is often heard in the expression "Get your cotton-pickin' hands off me!"

Cotton State. A nickname for Alabama, which is also called the Lizard State, and the Yellow Hammer State (after the beautiful yellow-hammer woodpecker, or after the yellowish homedyed uniforms of Alabama Confederate soldiers).

cottonwood blossom. In the Old West, an outlaw hanged from the limb of any tree was called a cottonwood blossom after the common cottonwood tree *(Populus balsamifera)*, which was often used as a gallows tree. This use of the cottonwood led to the saying *have the cottonwood on him,* meaning to have the advantage over someone. Among the most unusual American desserts of pioneer days was cottonwood ice cream, a sweet, pulpy white mass scraped in the spring from the inner bark of the cottonwood.

couch potato. A phrase from a pun. *Couch potato* means a lazy, inactive person who does little else in leisiure time save lie on the couch watching TV. As for the punning derivation of *couch potato,* first came the slang term *boob tube* for television, recorded in 1963. Someone who watched too much of the boob tube was shortly after dubbed a "boob-tuber." *Boob tuber* suggested the potato, a plant tuber, to Tom Iacino of Pasadena, California, in 1976, and he invented the term *couch potato,* which he registered as a trademark eight years later. Soon after his inventive punning, Iacino and some friends formed a club called the Couch Potatoes, which appeared in the 1979 Pasadena Doo Dah

Parade, in which they lay on couches watching TV while their float was pulled through the streets. Little remained but for cartoonist Robert Armstrong to draw the familiar image of a couch potato—a potato sprawled out on a couch watching TV—for his book *Dr. Spudd's Etiquette for the Couch Potato* (1982).

cough up. Four centuries ago *to cough up* meant to disclose. It did not take on its present meaning of "to pay up or hand over" until the end of the 19th century, probably originating in this sense as American criminal slang. One theory is that underworld suspects tried to bribe police officers with money instead of coughing up information about crimes, and that *cough up* then came to mean "pay up."

country mile. Any long distance; a widely used Americanism that apparently originated a century ago in some rural area. Also called a country block. In baseball we often hear the expression "He hit the ball a country mile."

country pay. Trading in early American country stores was often conducted by barter, or country pay, as it was called, with customers exchanging corn, wheat, rye, and flax, or articles of household manufacture like blankets and baskets for goods on the merchant's shelves. Homemade Indian brooms, maple syrup, aphrodisiac ginseng (sold in China), barrel staves, dried fruits, the potash and charcoal left when forests were burned down to clear land, even Indian wampum—all these and a hundred other things were used as country pay.

country stores. Far from being "fancy" or "citified," American country stores traded with customers everywhere in rural areas. For more than 20 years after paper bags were invented in 1850, clerks were still wrapping most packages into "pokes," brown wrapping paper adeptly shaped into cornucopias, folded over, and tied with string. *See* COUNTRY PAY.

cowabunga! *Cowabunga!* has recently come to be used as a general cry of delight, due to its popularization by the Teenage Mutant Ninja Turtles and Bart Simpson of television fame. An earlier TV character, Chief Thunderthud of the *Howdy Doody Show*, used the expression in the 1950s, and it was picked up by surfers in the 60s.

cowboy. A term first applied to members of Tory bands in New York state who rustled cows, but by the mid-19th century, it came to mean a man who herds and tends cattle on a ranch, most of his work done on horseback. Because of Hollywood westerns, *cowboy* has also taken on the meaning of any reckless person, such as a speeding automobile driver. Ironically, in recent times the word has been applied as much to handlers of sheep as to handlers of cattle.

Cowboy President. A nickname given to President Theodore Roosevelt, who was a North Dakota ranchman from 1884-86 and remained interested in cowboy life.

cowboys and Indians. No one knows exactly when children started playing cowboys and Indians in the 19th century (or possibly earlier), but the first recorded use of this name for the game has been traced to 1887.

cowgirl. When it was first recorded in 1884, *cowgirl* meant a female rancher or a rancher's daughter; it later came to mean a cowpuncher as well.

cowpoke; cowpuncher. Cowpokes and cowpunchers were originally cowboys who poked cattle onto railroad cars with long poles. The terms, first recorded in 1880, were soon applied to all cowboys.

Coyote State. A nickname for South Dakota, after the prairie wolf *(Canis latrans)* resident there. South Dakota has also been called the Artesian State, the Sunshine State, the Blizzard State and the Land of Plenty.

crabburger. A hamburger-shaped pattie made of crabmeat and served on a hamburger roll. A favorite in Louisiana.

crabs in a bucket. The words of a resident in a New York City housing project where feuds and crime have caused death and suffering (*New York Times,* August 23, 2004): "It's crabs in a bucket out here. They're all climbing up over each other to get out, but meanwhile they're all pulling each other back down." Crabs are commonly stored in a bushel basket or bucket when caught while crabbing.

crack. Very potent, addictive, chemically purified cocaine that is smoked through a glass pipe. Crack cocaine takes its name from the crackling sound the drug mixture makes when it is crystallized to form "rocks." The term was first recorded in *Time* magazine in 1985 and only a year more passed before *crackheads* was applied to those addicted to the substance.

cracker. A poor white person, especially one from Georgia (the Cracker State), so called, perhaps, from their use of cracked corn. Originally the expression was *corncracker,* someone who cracks corn to make grits or cornmeal. At one time (1766), *cracker* meant "a liar," but when, after the Civil War, many people in the South became too poor to buy cornmeal and had to make their own, *cracker* came to mean a backwoodsman and then a poor white, generally a person living in the southern states of Georgia and Florida. Others say that cracker was originally applied to Florida cowboys and derived from their cracking their whips as they herded cattle. In any case, the term is generally an offensive one and is now regarded as a racial epithet that is a violation under the Florida Hate Crimes Act. Many people, however, are proud to call themselves *Georgia crackers, Florida crackers,* etc., just so long as they're doing the calling.

Cradle of American Liberty. A nickname for Massachusetts, where the Revolutionary War began. However, Boston is called the Cradle of the Revolution as well as the City of Nations. Faneuil Hall in Boston is also called the Cradle of Liberty.

Cradle of the Confederacy. A nickname given to Montgomery, Alabama, where the seceded southern states met on February 4, 1861, to form the Confederate States of America.

crash. *Crash* in the sense of to *crash a party* is an Americanism that derives from *gate-crasher,* an American expression that originated in about 1920. The latter term has its roots in the idea of a person forcing his way through a gate into a sporting event. *Gate-crashing* is not much heard of anymore, but *crashing* and *party-crashing* are commonly used.

crazy as a bedbug. That great Yankee homespun humorist Seba Smith (1792–1868) may have coined *crazy as a bedbug* in the series of letters by "Major Jack Downing" that he published in his newspaper, *The Portland Courier,* in 1832: "Nabby ran about from house to house like a crazy bedbug." *Crazy as a bedbug* means completely crazy. It may be that bedbugs scoot about crazily at times, or that their victims jump out of bed and run around crazily when bitten by them. The word *bedbug,* incidentally, is also an American invention.

crazy like a fox. The fox is, of course, traditionally regarded as sly and crafty. Its reputation for cunning led to the Americanism *crazy like a fox,* which is first recorded in 1908 and is used to describe someone who seems to be a fool but is putting on an act and is really exceedingly clever.

creasing. (1) A painful method of capturing a wild horse by shooting it in the crest of the neck above the cervical vertebrae and stunning it.

The practice is recorded in Texas as early as 1820. (2) Barely wounding someone: "He just creased him."

credit. According to J. P. Morgan, loans are made safe by character rather than collateral. This idea is reflected in the word *credit*, which derives from the Latin *credo*, meaning "I believe," which indicates that the person giving credit "believes" in the person to whom he gives it. The word, in its financial sense, was first recorded in 1542.

Crescent City. A nickname for New Orleans, because, according to Joseph Ingraham in *The South-West* (1835), "it is uilt around the segment of a circle formed by a graceful curve f the Mississippi River."

crooked as a barrel of snakes; crooked as a dog's hind leg; crooked as a barrel of fishhooks. Someone very dishonest or sly is *crooked as a barrel of snakes,* this Americanism dates back to the 19th century. The Americanism *crooked as a dog's hind leg* means the same and was first recorded at about the same time, as does the reference to fishhooks. "He was the mayor but crooked as a barrel of fishhooks."

crud. An Americanism dating back to the early 1920s in army use, *crud* doesn't come directly from the Middle English *crudd,* for "coagulated solids of milk, or curds," even though Shakespeare used the word *crudy* in this sense. It probably derives from the mispronunciation of the word *curdled* as *cruddled,* anything curdled or cruddled being undesirable crud. The word first described semen sticking to the body or clothes after sexual intercourse, and was probably so named for this, but is now used mainly as a synonym for feces, or, even more commonly, for "anything dirty, inferior, worthless, ugly, or disgusting."

curse of the Bambino. A curse against the Boston Red Sox's winning baseball's World Series said to be in effect since Red Sox owner Harry Frazee sold Ruth to the New York Yankees in 1920.

curveball. The word *curveball* has been traced to William Arthur "Candy" Cummings (1848–1924), a Brooklyn Hall of Famer, who is credited with inventing baseball's curveball in 1867. Cummings's curve was inspired by the shells that he skimmed across a Brooklyn beach as a youngster, but he perfected it by experimenting with a baseball that he bought for a nickel.

the customer is always right. American retailer H. Gordon ielfridge (1856–1947) coined this slogan when he opened his uge department store, Selfridge's, in London. Before this, while working for Marshall Field & Co. in Chicago, he coined the expression "———shopping days until Christmas."

cut a wide (big) swath. This Americanism, meaning "to make a big pompous show, to appear important," dates back to the early 19th century or before. "Gracious me! How he was strutting up the sidewalk—didn't he cut a swath!" exclaimed one writer in 1843. The term is a farming one, a *swath* being "the amount of grass or any crop cut down with one sweep of a scythe."

cut one's foot. To *cut one's foot* means to step in cow dung. The euphemism, traced back to the Appalachians, was first recorded in 1899 and still has some currency in rural areas today. A variation is *to cut one's foot on a Chinese razor.*

cut up (or split) the melon. This means to divide the spoils or profits of any kind, each person getting a slice of the tasty melon, or profits. Surprisingly, it is a relatively recent term, dating back only to 1906 or so, when it arose as Wall Street jargon for the distribution of extra, unexpected dividends to stockholders.

cyberspace. American author William Gibson coined this word in a 1982 short story, popularizing it in his novel *Neuromancer* (1984). Based on *cybernetics,* first recorded in 1948, *cyberspace* is the space of virtual reality. Published in 20 languages, his novel earned Gibson the title "Father of Cyberspace." But the derivation goes back to the ancient Greeks, who coined it from their word *cyber*, meaning navigator.

D

D (River). This river, usually called the D, flowing into the Pacific Ocean from Devil's Lake in Lincoln City, Oregon, is the shortest-named body of water anywhere.

Da Brooklyn National Antem. Written years ago by Orter Anonamus when Brooklynites all spoke Brooklynese:

> Da Spring is sprung Da grass is riz
> I wunnah weah da boidies is?
> Da boid is on da wing?—dat's absoid!
> From what I hoid da wing is on da boid.

dago; wop; guinea. *Dago* is an offensive word that may derive from the name of a saint. Mencken traces this disparaging term to 1832, when it was used in Louisiana to describe a Spaniard, not an Italian. But *dago* is a corruption of the very common Spanish name Diego, or alludes to St. Diego, Spain's patron saint, or both. *Diego* was used in Elizabethan times for a "swarthy" Spanish or Portuguese seaman. As recently as the beginning of this century the word also meant the Italian language, as well as a professor or student of Italian. The pejorative term is not heard as often today as its derivative, *dago red,* "any cheap wine" *Dago* may also come from "day come, day go" a term reputedly used by early Italian laborers in expressing their patient philosophy. Far more offensive is *wop,* which arose toward the end of the 19th century. This ugly word comes from a relatively innocuous one, the Neapolitan *guappo,* a term used by immigrant laborers signifying a showy, pretentious person. Similarly, the offensive *guinea* may have originally referred to Italian laborers working for the equivalent of a guinea a day.

daisy cutter. A 15,000-pound U.S. bomb that explodes just above the ground. The euphemistic name was first heard during the war on terrorism in 2001.

Damnation Alley. An alley in Boston so named because it was wide enough for only one oxcart, so that whenever two teamsters met going in opposite directions the air was blue with *damns* and much stronger curses.

damned if you do, damned if you don't. Early American evangelist Lorenzo Dow (d. 1834) coined these words while condemning other preachers who "make the Bible clash and contradict itself, by preaching somewhat like this: 'You can and you can't—You shall and you shan't—You will and you won't— And you will be damned if you do— And you will be damned if you don't.' "

damsel in distress. A damsel is a young unmarried woman of good birth. This dated term thrived in old Hollywood films, in which gallant knights in shining armor invariably rescued damsels in distress. *Damsel* comes from the Latin *domina,* "mistress."

dance hall hostess. Western dance halls like Dodge City's *Variety* were often combined saloons, gambling houses, and brothels. By the 1870s, *dance hall hostess* became a euphemism for prostitutes like the Variety's Squirrel-Tooth Colie, Big Nose Kate, and Hambone Jane.

Daniel Boone. "A good gun, a good horse, and a good wife," in that order, were the ingredients for Daniel Boone's prescription for happiness. The American pioneer's name has long been synonymous with a frontiersman, an intrepid explorer or hunter, and a resourceful backwoodsman. Boone's accomplishments have been exaggerated in popular accounts, but there is no doubt that his explorations opened the way for millions. Born near Reading, Pennsylvania, the great folk hero moved to North Carolina with his Quaker family in his early years. After serving under British General Braddock as a wagoner, he explored Florida, and fought as a lieutenant colonel of militia during the American Revolution, among many other activities. But his major contribution was the blazing of the famous Wilderness Road, which he and a band of 30 men forged in March, 1775, to found Boonesboro on the Kentucky River. Daniel and his wife, Rebecca, figure in more frontier lore than any other pioneers, and he has been commemorated in numerous place names. Boone was 86 when he died in 1820, a legend in his own time.

dark meat; white meat. These were originally American euphemisms for the leg and the breast, respectively, of turkey and other fowl, *leg* and *breast* being embarrassing words in Victorian times. The words are still frequently used, but descriptively now and not euphemistically.

Davis Cup. While still an undergraduate at Harvard in 1900, American statesman and sportsman Dwight Filley Davis (1879–1945) donated a silver cup to be presented as a national trophy to that country winning an international championship contest in lawn tennis. The cup still bears his name.

Davy Crockett. David (Davy) Crockett, as the song goes, was "a son of the wild frontier" from his earliest years. Born in 1786 in Limestone, Tennessee, Davy was hired out to a passing cattle driver by his Irish immigrant father when only 12; he wandered the frontier until he turned 15, before finally returning home. He became a colonel in the Tennessee militia under Andrew Jackson during the Creek War, and after serving as a justice of the peace and state legislator, acted on a humorous suggestion that he run for Congress in 1827. Much to his surprise, he won the election. Crockett served two terms in Congress, and was noted in Washington for his backwoods dress and shrewd native humor, though many of the comments often attributed to him are largely apocryphal. His motto was "Be sure you are right, then go ahead." When defeated for reelection in 1835—mainly because he opposed Jacksonian banking and Indian policies—he moved to Texas, where he joined the Texas war for independence from Mexico. On March 6, 1836, Colonel Crockett was killed with the defenders of the Alamo. The folk hero's famous autobiography, *A Narrative of the Life of David Crockett of the State of Tennessee* (1834), was probably dictated, but is written in his robust style, complete with many examples of the tall tale.

deadbeat. Though *deadbeat* meant an exhausted, almost dead person at the beginning of the 19th century, by about 1863 it had become American slang for "a hobo or sponger riding the rails." The idea of hoboes not paying their way, riding trains free, inspired the present prevailing use of *deadbeat* for "someone who doesn't pay his debts."

dead letter office. A place where undeliverable letters (no return address, etc.) go. The U.S. Postal Service has long had no office of that name, changing it in 1994 to the Mail Recovery Center. But dead letter office will live on in poem and story, especially in Herman Melville's "Bartleby the Scrivener" (1856), which suggests that Bartleby was a clerk in the dead letter office, where its strange atmosphere may have affected his strange attitude toward life. Some critics hold that the neglect of Melville's novels led him to regard his work as "dead letters."

deadline. This expression has its origin in the infamous Confederate prison camp at Andersonville during the Civil War. There the deadline was a line marked 17 feet from the camp fence. Any prisoner who crossed that line was shot dead by the guards. It seems that newspaper reporters and editors were the first to use the word in its present sense of a time when a task must be finished. They applied it to the time when a story had to be completed; if the story wasn't in by that time, it was in effect killed or dead for that edition.

deadman's hand. James Butler "Wild Bill" Hickok, only 39, had come to Deadwood, Dakota Territory, in 1876 to make a stake for the bride he had just taken, but lawless elements, fearing his appointment as town marshall, hired gunman Jack McCall to assassinate him, giving McCall 300 dollars and all the cheap whiskey he needed for courage. Wild Bill was playing cards in the No. 10 saloon (his back to the open door for only the second time in his days of gunfighting) when McCall sneaked in and shot him in the back of the head, the bullet passing through his brain and striking the cardplayer across the table from him in the arm. Hickok's last hand, which he held tight in a death grip, was aces and eights, which has ever since been called the deadman's hand. McCall, freed by a packed miner's court, was later convicted by a federal court, his plea of "double jeopardy" disregarded on the ground that the miner's court had no jurisdiction. He was later hanged for his crime.

dead presidents. Slang for paper money of any denomination, as all the presidents pictured on U.S. currency are dead because U.S. law forbids any living person's likeness on currency. The term was first recorded in New York's Harlem in 1944 and now is used throughout the country.

decibel. "Watson, come here; I want you." These were the un-dramatic words spoken by inventor Alexander Graham Bell to his lab assistant on March 10, 1876, the first complete sentence conveyed over the telephone. Bell was a Scottish immigrant who in 1871 came to the United States, where he lectured to teachers of the deaf on his father's visible speech method and opened his own school of vocal physiology in Boston. In the course of work on his harmonic telegraph, he invented the first practical telephone, an idea he had conceived as early as 1865. Later inventions included the first practical phonograph record, the audiometer, and a telephonic probe for locating bullets in the human body. The Bell Telephone Company was formed in July, 1877. The inventor died in 1922, aged 75. *Bel,* a unit of measuring the loudness of electrical signals, and *decibel,* ⅒ of a *bel,* both honor his name.

Deep Throat. The code name of Mark Felt, former assistant director of the FBI during the Nixon administration, who gave *Washington Post* reporter Robert Woodward information about the 1972 Watergate break-in. *Deep Throat* was borrowed by Woodward and fellow reporter Carl Bernstein from the well-known pornographic film of that name. *Deep Throat* has become a synonym for any secret source, just as *Watergate* (the Watergate office-apartment complex in Washington, D.C., which housed the headquarters of the Democratic National Committee) has for any scandal. *Gemstone,* the secret code name for the Watergate break-in, has been all but forgotten. The pornographic movie *Deep Throat* (1972) made over a halfbillion dollars, but Linda Lovelace, the pseudonym of the woman who starred in it, wasn't paid a cent. Linda Lovelace claimed that her husband at the time forced her to appear in the film, holding a gun at her back, and that the movie depicted her rape. Her story is told in her autobiography, *Out of Bondage,* published a few years before she died in an auto accident in 2002, age 53.

Delaware. Mencken points out that the map of this country is "besprinkled with place names from at least half a hundred languages, living and dead." Of the eight classes he lists as their sources, "surnames" comes first. *Delaware* falls into this category, being the first alphabetically of American states that take their names from the names of individuals. The Diamond State commemorates English soldier Thomas West, Baron De La Warr (1577–1618), who in 1609 was appointed the first governor of Virginia by the Virginia Company. Delaware Bay was named for Lord De La Warr by Sir Samuel Argall, who discovered it when the governor sent him on an expedition to locate supplies for the starving settlers at Jamestown; both Delaware and the Delaware Indians derive their names from this body of water. De La Warr had been appointed governor of Virginia for life, but died on his second trip from England to the colony and was buried at sea.

dem bums. This nickname for the Brooklyn Dodgers, beloved of memory, was given to them by an irate fan seated behind home plate at a home game in Ebbets Field during the Great Depression. Particularly incensed at one error he shouted, "Ya bum, ya, yez bums, yez! " and his words, reported by a baseball writer, stuck as an endearing nickname for the team. It was in 1900 that the team was named the Dodgers, after all Brooklynites, who were called trolley dodgers by Manhattanites, contemptuous of all the trolleys in the borough. *See* DODGERS.

demoralize. *Demoralize* has the distinction of being the only word coined by the great American dictionary maker Noah Webster. Webster invented the word in 1794 when writing of the French Revolution and the bad effects such civil wars had on the morals of the people involved. He did not borrow it from the French word *demoraliser,* as many people thought, but made it by simply placing the common prefix *de* on the English word *moralize.*

Dennis the Menace. A name given to any mischievous but good-hearted overactive, mostly good-intentioned child, after the freckled-faced cartoon character Dennis the Menace drawn by cartoonist Hank Ketcham (1920–2001). Hank Ketcham drew his creation from 1950 to 1994, when he retired and a team of artists took over his strip, which now appears in over 1,000 newspapers in 48 countries and 19 languages. According to Mr. Ketcham, the cartoon character Dennis was named after the cartoonist's four-year-old son. The real-life Dennis wrecked his bedroom while he was supposed to be napping one afternoon, leading his mother to shout, "Your son is a menace!"

department store. The term *department store* isn't recorded until 1887, when a New York establishment advertised itself as H.H. Heyn's Department Store, though the idea of separate departments in stores can be found in print at least 40 years earlier, when an article in *Hunt's Merchandising Magazine* told of "tubes connecting with each department of a store, from the garret to the cellar, so that if a person in a department . . . wishes to communicate with the employer, he can do so without leaving his station."

derby. *Derby* is the American name for a version of the domeshaped felt hat that the English call a bowler. The man it honors also has the English Derby at Epsom Downs and the Kentucky Derby at Churchill Downs named for him. The 12th earl of Derby, Edward Stanley (d. 1834), came from a family that traced its origins to William the Conqueror. He had a great interest in horse racing but little in his wife—a mutual feeling—and so devoted most of his time to the improvement of the breed. Races had long been held at Epsom Downs, but in 1780 the earl started a series of annual contests for three-year-olds, the races named in his honor because he both suggested them and was such a convivial host each season at The Oaks, a house near the course that had belonged to his uncle General "Johnny" Burgoyne. The Derby became so popular that almost a century later, in 1875, the Kentucky Derby adopted part of its name. After the Civil War, American spectators at the "Blue Ribbon of the Turf" noticed that English sportsmen often wore odd-shaped bowler hats. A few were brought back home, where it is said that a Connecticut manufacturer made a stiff felt, narrow-brimmed version that an unknown New York store clerk sold as "hats like the English wear at the Derby." In any event, *derby* became the American term for bowler, the most popular headwear for men up until the 1920s. *See* CHURCHILL DOWNS.

derringer. This is the small but deadly large-bored gun that in real life has been the choice of a large variety of villains, including assassin John Wilkes Booth. The pistol is named for Philadelphia gunsmith Henry Deringer, who invented it in 1835. Posterity cheated Deringer a bit, though, for the stubby gun came to be spelled with a double *r*.

Deseret. A place-name used in the Utah Territory by the Mormons in 1850. The word is a coined one from the *Book of Mormon* and means "honeybee," a symbol of hard work and cooperation. What is now Utah was called the State of Deseret, and Salt Lake City was called Deseret.

destroyer. This relatively light, fast, naval combat ship was first called the *torpedo boat destroyer* after what was then its primary mission. The first U.S. destroyer was the 273-ton USS *Farragut,* named after U.S. admiral David Farragut, a Civil War hero.

Dewey decimal system. The father of American library science, Melvil Dewey (1851–1931), first proposed his famous Dewey decimal system in 1876 while serving as acting librarian at Amherst College. It is now used by some 85 percent of all libraries. The classification scheme, invented when he was in his early twenties, divides the entire field of knowledge into nine main classes (from 000 to 999), a second set of numbers following a decimal point indicating the special subject of a book within its main class. A man of fantastic energy and originality, Dewey later became chief librarian at Columbia College (1883–*88*), where he founded, in 1887, the first American school of library science. As director of the New York State Library (1889–1906), he reorganized the state library, making it one of the most efficient in the nation, and originated the system of traveling libraries. Dewey also helped found the American Library Association, the New York State Association, and the *Library Journal.* He crusaded for simplified spelling and use of the metric system, among many other causes.

Dick Smith. *Dick Smith* or *Dick Smither* refers to a solitary, selfish, cheap man with short arms and deep pockets, who would never order a round for other drinkers at a bar, though he'd always accept a free drink. The eponymous expression, first recorded in 1876 in the *Congressional Record,* may be based on a real Michigan lumberjack of that name. A quiet, unsociable baseball player named Dick Smith is another possibility, as is Richard Penn Smith (1799–1854), a Philadelphia playwright who introduced romantic tragedy in the U.S. and was indebted to the work of several French and English playwrights as models for his own work.

diddledees. An unusual Americanism meaning pine needles. It has been suggested that since diddledees are sometimes used as kindling, they take their name from the diddledee tree or shrub of the Falkland Islands, which is also used for fuel. The term could have been brought to America by whalers a century or so ago. In various regions of the U.S., pine needles are also called needles, spills, pins, twinkles, straws, tags, and shats.

dime novel. American publisher Erastus Flavel Beadle (1821–94) named all such melodramatic, often lurid, romantic or adventure paperbacks in 1860 when he first called books that he published the *Dime Book Series.* The first book issued in his series was *Malaeska, the Indian Wife of the White Hunter.* The "dollar books for a dime," as it was advertised, sold over 300,0 copies its first year.

dingbat; dingus, etc. *Dingbat,* a favorite expression of Archie Bunker's, is American in origin, going back to at least 1861, when it meant "anything that can be thrown with force or dashed violently at another object," according to Farmer's *Americanisms* (1899). The word possibly derives from *bat,* "a piece of wood or metal," and *ding,* "to throw." But *dingbat* came to be used in describing anything of which the proper name is unknown to or forgotten by a speaker, much as we more frequently use such meaningless words as *thingamabob* (an extension of the word *thing* that goes back to the late 17th century), *thingamajig, dingus, doohickey, whatsit,* and other infixes. A father describing how to assemble a complicated piece of equipment, such as a child's toy, might say: "You put this *thingamajig* into this *doohickey* and tighten this *doodad* and this *thingamabob;* then you take this *dingus* over here near this *gismo* and attach it to this *hickeymadoodle* so that it barely touches the *thin-gamadoodle* there near the *whatchamacallit*—then you have to grease it up with this *jeesalamsylborax* or the damn *dingbat* won't work!" *Dingbat* has also served over the years as a slang term for "a gadget, money, buns or biscuits, a woman, and a hobo or bum." But Archie Bunker's contemptuous use of the word for a "nut," an ineffectual, bumbling fool (that is, anyone he doesn't agree with), may come directly from the Australian *dingbats,* meaning "eccentric or mad." *Dingbats* are also the small marks and printers' decorations used in publishing.

dinner on horseback. A famous dinner given by American millionaire C. K. Billings at Louis Sherry's restaurant in 1903. The guests, all men, lounged in the saddle astride horses that had been brought to the ballroom by elevator. The diners ate pheasant from feed bags and drank champagne from large rubber casks. It was said that Billings spent $50,000 for the feast, including the planting of sod on the ballroom floor. A couple of years later, in 1905, millionaire Diamond Jim Brady topped Billings with a dinner he gave for his racehorse Gold Heels; it cost over $100,000, including the $60,000 he spent for diamond jewelry for each guest.

dirt farmer. A farmer who works his own farm rather than employing tenants or hired hands. The U.S. term dates back to about 1920.

dirty look. A reproving glance of disgust or annoyance: "She threw him a dirty look." The Americanism is first recorded in 1928.

Dirty Thirties. The 1930s, when terrible dust storms afflicted the Great Plains of the U.S., causing many deaths and great financial loss.

dirty word. A taboo word, an obscenity. The U.S. term is first recorded in about 1835 and its extended meaning is applied to anything considered unmentionable or reprehensible, as in "His name is a dirty word." What is a dirty word, of course, depends on the mind or heart of the beholder or listener. A famous *list* of dirty words is American comedian George Carlin's radio comedy routine about seven dirty words that are prohibited on the air. The FCC banned Carlin's "Seven Dirty Words" and was upheld by the U.S. Supreme Court, which deemed the words indecent but not obscene. The Indecent Seven are *fuck, shit, cunt, cocksucker, piss, tits,* and *motherfucker.*

Disneyan. Among Walt Disney's 39 awards from the Academy of Motion Picture Sciences, and his more than 800 awards and decorations for his work from other sources, there is one that honors him "for creating a new art form in which good was spread throughout the world." It is on this creation that his fame rests secure. Walter Elias Disney (1901–66) did not invent the animated cartoon but brought it to perfection and created characters that have become a permanent part of American folklore *(see* MICKEY MOUSE*).* His many full-length animated motion pictures *(Snow White and the Seven Dwarfs, Bambi, Fantasia, Dumbo, Pinocchio, Cinderella, Alice in Wonderland, Robin Hood, Peter Pan,* and so on) set a standard for all others. Disney's Mickey Mouse film *Steamboat Willie* was the first animated sound cartoon and he is credited with the invention of the storyboard and other innovative cartoon techniques. On another less creative level, the artist has been invidiously called "the Henry Ford of the entertainment industry" for his Disneyland in California and the Disney World in Florida. Like Henry Ford—and Disney films were his favorites—Disney's was a typical American success story: humble beginnings (although his family traces its origins to England's noble D'Isney clan), hard work, and hardships of every description. Even the success marred by crass commercialism in later years is not unfamiliar. Yet the genius triumphs in the end. Disney's characters remain, in the words of British artist David Low, "the most significant figures in graphic art since Leonardo."

district attorney. A cowboy stew containing cheap or unmentionable ingredients, such as sweetbreads, guts, and kidneys. It is so named because of the cowboy's hatred of legal authorities. Also called county attorney and son-of-a-bitch stew.

District of Maine. Until 1820 the area that i s now the state of Maine was a part of Massachusetts known as the District of Maine.

Dixie; Dixieland. It sounds incredible, but the first *Dixieland* or *Dixie* may have been in New York City. Some etymologists lean to the following derivation of the word given by the *Charlestown Courier* of June 11, 1885: "When slavery existed in New York, one Dixie owned a large tract of land on Manhattan Island, and a large number of slaves. The increase of the slaves and of the abolition sentiment caused an emigration of the slaves to more thorough and secure slave sections, and the Negroes who were thus sent off (many being born there) naturally looked back to their old houses, where they had lived in clover, with feelings of regret, as they could not imagine any place like Dixie's.

Hence it became synonymous with an ideal location combining ease, comfort, and material happiness of every description." Although no slave "lived in clover," the explanation seems somewhat less doubtful than other theories about Dixie—that it derives from the 18th-century Mason Dixon line, or that the word comes from the French-Creole word *dix,* meaning "10," which was prominently printed on the back of 10-dollar notes issued by a New Orleans bank before the Civil War.

Dixie cup. The American Water Supply Company's vending machines sold a drink of water in a disposable paper cup for one cent beginning in 1906, the cup possibly called a *Dixie cup* because it was so reliable—like the old *10*-dollar bills issued in Louisiana prior to the Civil War (*see* DIXIE). In years to come the Dixie cup was frequently applied to ice cream sold in a small cup as opposed to Popsicles, or ice-cream pops, and cones.

do a Brodie. As a result of his famous leap off the Brooklyn Bridge, Steve Brodie's name became a byword—in the form of to *do* (*or pull*) *a Brodie*—for "taking a great chance, even taking a suicidal leap." Brodie made his jump from the Manhattan side of the Brooklyn Bridge on July 23, 1886, to win a $200 barroom bet. Eluding guards on the bridge, the 23-year-old daredevil climbed to the lowest cable and plummeted 135 feet into the water below, where friends were waiting to retrieve him in a rowboat. He was arrested for endangering his life and reprimanded by a judge, but that didn't stop him from making future leaps off other bridges. Some say that Brodie never jumped at all, an unproved theory, and many at the time belittled his claim. It is said that Brodie once angered boxer Jim Corbett's father by predicting that John L. Sullivan would knock his son out. "So you're the fellow who jumped over the Brooklyn Bridge," the elder Corbett said when the two met for the first time. "No, I jumped *off of* it," Brodie corrected him. "Oh," replied Corbett, "I thought you jumped *over* it. Any damn fool can jump off it."

Dodgers. The incomparable Brooklyn Dodgers, who became comparable after their move to Los Angeles, were called the Dodgers because Manhattanites contemptuously referred to all Brooklynites as "trolley dodgers" at the turn of the century, the bustling borough being famed for its numerous trolleys, especially in the central Borough Hall area. Attempts were made to change the name to the Superbas, the Kings, and the Robins, all to no avail. Some baseball team names just seem to catch on while others don't. The Boston Bees, for example, were named by a distinguished committee of baseball writers from a choice of 1,300 names, but people stubbornly called them the Braves, a name they retained after they moved to Milwaukee. The Cincinnati Reds tried to become known as the Redlegs to avoid identification with communism, but their name remains the Reds. *See also* DEM BUMS.

Does Macy's tell Gimbels? Gimbels department store has long gone out of business, but this expression is still commonly heard. The by now proverbial words arose from a friendly, well- publicized, and well-advertised retailing war between the two giant New York department stores. The expression possibly originated as a publicity gag, perhaps as a line in an Eddie Cantor comedy skit when a stooge asked Cantor to reveal some dark secret and the comedian replied, "Does Macy's tell Gimbels?" Actually, Macy's often told Gimbels and vice versa. One time Gimbels ran an ad calling attention to Macy's fabulous annual flower show, heading it: "Does Gimbels tell Macy's? No, Gimbels tells the world!" On another occasion, in 1955, both stores posted signs on their buildings directing shoppers to the other's store. The Gimbels-Macy's rivalry was further publicized in the film *Miracle on 34th Street,* in which Macy's directs customers to Gimbels when it doesn't have a particular item in stock.

doesn't know beans. Boston, home of the "bean eaters," "home of the bean and the cod," may be behind the phrase. Walsh, in his *Handybook of Literary Curiosities* (1892), says that the American expression originated as a sly dig at Boston's pretensions to culture, a hint that Bostonians knew that Boston baked beans were good to eat, that they were made from small white "pea beans"—even if Bostonians knew nothing else. It may also be that the American phrase is a negative rendering of the British saying "he knows how many beans make five"—that is, he is no fool, he's well informed—an expression that probably originated in the days when children learned to count by using beans. But *he doesn't know beans,* "he don't know from nothing," possibly has a much simpler origin that either of these theories. It probably refers to the fact that beans are little things of no great worth, as in the expression "not worth a row (or hill) of beans."

dog eat dog. According to the *Dictionary of Americanisms,* this is a phrase from the American frontier first recorded in 1834. It means ruthless competition with no holds barred; everyone for himself or herself; tit for tat. British poet Thomas Gray in an 1858 letter quoted a saying meaning exactly the opposite: "I cannot promise any special instruction and shall take no fee. 'Dog does not eat dog' is the saying, you know." Whether these two sayings arose independently or have something to do with each other hasn't been firmly established.

dogfight. A term used by cowboys for a fistfight; many cowboys, preferring to fight with weapons, thought dogfights were beneath them, reasoning that if they were intended to fight like dogs they would have been born with longer teeth and claws.

dogie. The American cowboy has been shouting "git along, little dogie" for more than a century, but no one knows where the word *dogie,* for "a motherless calf," comes from. Maybe it derives from "dough-guts," referring to the bloated bellies of such calves, perhaps *dogie* is a clipped form of the Spanish *adobe,* ("mud"), possibly the cows were so small that they were playfully called "doggies" and the pronunciation changed. Since some American cowboys were black there is also the possibility that the Bambara *dogo,* "small, short," is the source, or the Afro-Creole *dogi,* meaning the same. Your guess is as good as any etymologist's.

dog's life; to go to the dogs; die like a dog; dirty dog. Dogs aren't the prized, often pampered pets in other countries that they are in America. In the East they are often considered pariahs, scavengers of the streets, and the Chinese, Koreans, and Japanese, among other Asians, commonly eat them. Englishmen of earlier times used dogs primarily for hunting and kept them outside or in a rude shelter, not generally as house pets. The dogs were fed table scraps there wasn't any further use for, and these they had to fight over. It didn't seem ideal, a dog's life, and Englishmen of the 16th century began to compare anyone who had become impoverished, who was going to utter ruin naturally or morally, to their maltreated canines. *To lead a dog's life* was to be bothered every moment, never to be left in peace; *to go to the dogs* was to become just like the helpless animals; and *to die like a dog* was to come to a miserable, shameful end. There were many other similar phrases that arose before the dogs had their day in England and America, including *throw it to the dogs,* "to throw something away that's worthless"; and of course *a dirty dog,* "a morally reprehensible or filthy person."

doing a land-office business. Before the Civil War, the U.S. government established land offices for the allotment of government-owned land in western territories just opened to settlers. These agencies registered applicants, and the rush of citizens lining up on mornings long before the office opened made the expression *doing a land-office business,* "a tremendous amount of business," part of the language by at least 1853. Adding to the queues were prospectors filing mining claims, which were also handled by land offices. After several decades the phrase was applied figuratively to a great business in something other than land, even, in one case I remember, to a land-office business in fish.

do it while standing on one foot. This Americanism means to do something easily and quickly, to encapsulate or describe it with little effort, as in "She explained her theory to reporters while standing on one foot."

don't change horses in midstream. The phrase, possibly suggested to Abraham Lincoln by an old Dutch farmer he knew, is recorded almost a quarter of a century before Lincoln said it. But Lincoln immortalized the expression when he accepted his nomination for the presidency in 1864. Waving aside any suggestions that the honor was a personal one, he told the Republicans that he was sure they hadn't decided he was "the greatest or the best man in America, but rather, . . . have concluded it is not best to swap horses while crossing the river, and have further concluded that I am not so poor a horse that they might not make a botch of it in trying to swap." Over the years "the river," which was of course the Civil War, was abbreviated to "midstream" and the saying *don't change horses in midstream* came to mean "don't change leaders in a crisis."

don't look back, something might be gaining on you. Sage advice from baseball great Leroy "Satchel" Paige, who would have been one of the greatest pitchers in the major leagues if the color barrier had been broken earlier. Paige's five additional rules were: 1) avoid fried meats which angry up the blood; 2) if your stomach disputes you, lie down and pacify it with cool thoughts; 3) keep your juices flowing by jangling around gently as you move; 4) go very gently on the vices, such as carrying on in society—the social ramble ain't restful; and 5) avoid running at all times.

don't stick your neck out. Chickens, for some reason still known only to chickens, usually stretch out their necks when put on the chopping block, making it all the easier for the butcher to chop their heads off. Probably our expression, a warning to someone not to expose himself to danger or criticism when this can be avoided, which is American slang from the late 19th century, originated from the bloody barnyard image. Lynchings have also been suggested, but lynched men rarely stick their necks out for the noose.

don't take any wooden nickels. First recorded in about 1915, this expression was originally a warning from friends and relatives to rubes leaving the sticks in the great migration from rural areas to the big cities at the turn of the century. It was a humorous adjuration meaning beware of those city slickers, for no real wooden nickels were ever counterfeited—they would have cost more to make than they'd have been worth. Ironically, country boys were the ones who possibly *did* succeed in passing off wooden objects as the real thing. Yankee peddlers as early as 1825 allegedly sold wooden nutmegs, which cost manufacturers a quarter of a cent apiece, mixed in with lots of real nutmegs worth four cents each.

doodlebug. An American word probably dating back to California at the beginning of the 20th century for any divining rod said to be able to locate oil and other minerals. The term is usually applied to the bogus divining rods of con men. The word was also used during World War II to describe the German flying bomb or V-1, and previously was the name of a tiger beetle or its larva.

doofus. Originally American slang of the late 1950s meaning "a fool, a dope, a jerk," or any combination of the three. Some writers claim the word is an alteration of *goofus* for the same, while others say it is of Yiddish or German origin. Australians would call a doofus a "donk."

dooley. Another name for a sweet potato and yam in the American South, possibly named after someone who developed a superior variety—which makes that individual one of the few people to have a vegetable named after him or her. *Dooley* also refers to an outdoor toilet building in parts of the South, apparently named after a contractor who built such public structures for the federal government during the Great Depression.

a doozy. Something special, outstanding, as in "That's a doozy of a coat you've got," or, in the negative, "That's a doozy of a cut you've got." An Americanism first recorded in the early 1900s, it may be an alteration of *daisy*, influenced by the last name of the great Italian actress Eleanora Duse (1859–1924), who was indeed *a doozy* of a thespian.

double in brass. To be versatile, to be able to do more than one thing well, or to hold two jobs in order to make more money. In its earliest recorded use, the American expression meant to play in a circus act and perform in a circus band as well. It was very common for a circus performer in the 1880s to play in the brass band when not performing as a clown, acrobat, or equestrian, and it is still sometimes the practice in small one-ring circuses. So *to double in brass* became circus talk of the day, was adopted by actors to describe an actor playing two parts in the same play, and then passed into general use.

doughboy. This word for a U.S. Army infantryman may have originated from the term *adobe,* which Spaniards in the Southwest called military personnel, though this is only one of several possible explanations for the term.

Dow Jones. Short for the *Dow Jones Industrial Average,* the Dow Jones is the average daily price of selected industrial stocks. It was first published in 1884, five years before its founders, Charles Henry Dow and Edward D. Jones, began to publish the *Wall Street Journal.* In 1909 their company was acquired by Walker Barron, of *Barron's Financial Weekly.*

down the creek, boys. A drinking toast. Used in Ernest Hemingway's short story "Up in Michigan."

down to the wire. For over a century *wire* has been synonymous with the finish line in horse racing, because of the wire stretched across the track that the horses passed under at the end of a race. The *Oxford English Dictionary* records the term from William McPaul's *Ike Glidden* (1902): "The conquering colt swept under the wire for a nose ahead of the trotter." But Mitford Mathew's *A Dictionary of Americanisms* cites an earlier, 1887 U.S. newspaper usage of *wire,* claiming it as an Americanism. *A Dictionary of Americanisms* goes on to date *down to the wire* as an expression first recorded in 1950 in the newspaper account of a baseball game. Widely used as slang now for "to the very last moment or the very end," it is also heard as *to go to the wire.*

do you know where your children are? A catchphrase coined by television broadcaster Tom Gregory and first used in the early 1960s. Gregory was viciously mugged at that time, the violence ending his career.

draftee. First recorded in an 1866 Civil War memoir, *draftee* was surely used before this during the war, probably as soon as the Confederate Conscription Act of 1862 and the Union Draft Law of 1863 were passed. In the North single men 20 to 45 and married men 20 to 35 were drafted, while the South conscripted all men 18 to 35. Most men volunteered, however; only about 2 percent of the Union Army consisting of draftees. During World War II *draftee* and other *ee*-ending words (such as *trainee, enlistee, escapee,* and *amputee)* were widely used. *Draft* in the sense of "conscript" comes from the "to draw or pull" meaning of the verb *to draft.*

drive-in. The first U.S. drive-in movie opened in Camden, New Jersey, on June 6, 1933, admission to this 400-car site costing 25 cents for the double feature. Richard M. Hollingshead, Jr., had used the term *drive-in* a month earlier when he patented the system. Within about 25 years there were more than 4,000 U.S. drive-ins. Very few are left today.

drop a dime. To make a phone call to police detectives informing on someone. *Dime dropper* refers to a *rat,* a *snitch,* a *stool pigeon,* among other choice terms. The term, still in use, dates back to the 1960s, when a phone call cost a dime.

Dr. Pepper. The popular soft drink was so named by Texas druggist Wade Morrison in 1885 after a certain Miss Pepper, a Virginia belle whose father ended their courtship. The "tonic, brain food and exhilarant" (as it was called then) was invented by Charles Aldeston, a clerk in Morrison's store.

the dry salvages. A small but well-known group of rocks, with a beacon, off the coast of Cape Ann, Massachusetts, *Salvages* here rhymes with *assuages,* perhaps because "the dry salvages" is a corruption of *les trios sauvages.* "The Dry Salvages" is the title of a poem by T. S. Eliot.

duck in a noose. A phrase that figured as a sidelight in the sniper killings case that terrified the Washington, D.C., area for three weeks in the fall of 2002. The sniper wanted the chief of police of Montgomery County to repeat this phrase, which he had mentioned in a phone call, and Chief Moose did as he requested at a late-night news conference. What the sniper meant by the phrase was revealed in a Cherokee folk tale, "The Rabbit, the Otter and Duck Hunting." In the tale, according to Celestine Bohlin writing in the *New York Times* (10/24/02), "a boastful rabbit is challenged by an otter to capture a duck. The rabbit manages to slip a noose around the neck of a duck, which then takes off, with the rabbit hanging on for dear life. The duck flies higher and higher, and finally the rabbit loses its grip and falls into an old sycamore tree where it is trapped . . ." Obviously, the sniper regarded himself as the escaping duck who couldn't be caught, and the police as the hapless rabbit that would never catch him.

dude ranch. At first a term for tourist ranches in the West but now used to describe such places everywhere, from the Catskills to the Texas Panhandle.

duh. An exclamation now widely used in the U.S. to make fun of someone after that person has spoken, indicating that he or she has said or done something stupid or obvious. The expression dates back to the early 1940s and may have been introduced or popularized by ventriloquist Edgar Bergen's dummy Mortimer Snerd, a rustic moron who constantly had the word put in his mouth.

dust bowl. Severe dust storms beginning in 1934 destroyed crops and dried the soil in the southern High Plains of the United States, largely because this land in Kansas, Colorado, Oklahoma, New Mexico, and Texas had been poorly farmed for years. The Great Depression, drought, and the dust forced large numbers of people to migrate from the area, which was first called the *dust bowl* in a story written by Associated Press reporter Robert Geiger in April 1935. The dust storms lasted almost a decade and dust from them blew as far as 300 miles out into the Atlantic, where it coated ships. *See also* OKIES, DIRTY THIRTIES.

E

eagle shits on Friday. At least since the years of the Great Depression, U.S. workingmen have used this phrase meaning "payday is Friday," and the term may date back to the Spanish-American War. The eagle, of course, is the one on the U.S. dollar. A euphemism for the expression is *the eagle screams on Friday.*

ear biter. Government jobs weren't always so safe, secure, and uneventful, as this obsolete term shows. In 1845 a special agent of the U.S. Post Office bit off the ear of an opponent in a fight. For some time afterward all post office special agents were facetiously called *ear biters* as a result.

the earth moved. "Did the earth move for you?" These joking words said to one's lover after sex were apparently invented or popularized by Ernest Hemingway in *For Whom The Bell Tolls* (1940) when he has Maria say to Robert Jordan, " 'Did the earth never move for thee before?' 'Never,' he said truly." *For Whom The Bell Tolls* itself comes from a sermon by John Donne: "No man is an *Iland* intire of it selfe; every man is a peece of the *Continent* . . . And therefore never send to know for whom the *bell* tolls; It tolls for *thee.* "

ear to the ground. Rámon Adams wrote in *Western Words* (1944) that old plainsmen often placed a silk neckerchief on the ground and thus could hear the sounds of men and horses miles away. Even if plainsmen and American Indians didn't hear distant hoofteats by putting their ears to the ground, so many writers of Westerns have attributed this skill to them that the practice has become well known. The phrase is first recorded in 1900 in the *Congressional Record,* meaning to use caution, to go slowly and listen frequently. Since then someone with *an ear to the ground* has become someone try ing to determine signs of the future, trying to find out what's coming.

easy as rolling off a log; logrolling. No one seems to know the origin of the first expression, which dates back to Colonial times. One ingenious theory suggests that colonists searching for home sites in the wilderness would leave their toddlers seated on dry logs temporarily while they explored the area and that the round-bottomed children often rolled off the logs, not knowing how to keep their balance. The metaphor could just as likely have derived from colonists rolling logs off toward a building site, across a meadow or down a hill. Logs can be quite heavy, though, and difficult to move, which explains the origins of *logrolling.* When an early settler in the West was building a log cabin, his neighbors helped him roll the heavy logs to the home site, or helped him clear the land of felled trees, with the understanding that he would do the same for them if need be. Eventually the frontier expression *logrolling* came to describe this mutual "backscratching," passing into politics by 1838 as the practice of one lawmaker voting for a bill sponsored by another if his colleague reciprocates and votes for a bill sponsored by him—the political deal, "help me roll this one, I'll help you roll that one past the opposition."

easy as taking candy from a baby. An expression meaning "anything very easy to do," which probably doesn't date back much before the 1930s. Neither does *easy as ABC* or *easy as shooting fish in a barrel,* among other similar sayings, all of which seem to have been inspired by the old Americanism EASY AS ROLLING OFF A LOG.

easy street; to live on easy street. To be well-off financially or to be rich, to live in comfortable circumstances. The earliest known reference to this expression is in 1897. A little later in 1901 it was used by American author George V. Hobart in his novel *It's Up To You,* where he describes a prosperous young man who had it made and could "walk up and down Easy Street." *On easy street* could, however, have some relation to the old English expression an *easy road,* "a road that can be traveled without discomfort or difficulty," an expression that was used figuratively by Shakespeare.

eat crow. During an armistice toward the end of the War of 1812, an American soldier out hunting crossed the Niagara River past British lines. Finding no better game, he shot a crow, but a British officer heard the shot and surprised him. The Britisher tricked the Yankee out of the rifle with which he shot so well. He then turned the gun on the American, demanding that he take a bite out of the crow he had shot as a punishment for violating British territory. The American complied, but when the officer returned his weapon and told him to leave, he covered the Englishman and forced him to eat the rest of the crow. That is the origin of the expression *to eat crow,* "to be forced to do something extremely disagreeable," as related in an 1888 issue of the *Atlanta Constitution.* Although *to eat crow* is possibly a much older expression, the saying first appeared in print in 1877 and the story may well be true—nothing better has been suggested. The concept behind *to eat crow* is that crows are not good eating, but the flesh of young ones was once esteemed and I have it on the authority of the Remington Arms Co. that even old crows aren't so bad if you simply "skin the bird, salt and cut it into pieces, parboil till tender and then fry with butter and onions." I'll eat crow if someone conclusively proves that the rec ipe isn't authentic.

eat dog for another. Various American Indian tribes ate dog meat, and at least one was called *the Dogeaters* by their enemies. When white men sat at Indian councils where dog meat was served, those who didn't relish the comestible could, without offending their host, put a silver dollar on the dish and pass it along, the next man taking the dollar and eating the dog. From this practice arose the American political expression *to eat dog for another.*

eat humble pie. Here is an expression probably born as a pun. The *humble* in this pie has nothing to do etymologically with the word *humble*, "lowly," which is from the Latin *humilis*, "low or slight." Umbles or numbles (from the Latin *lumbulus*, "little loin") were the innards—the heart, liver, and entrails—of deer and were often made into a pie. Sir Walter Scott called this dish "the best," and an old recipe for it (1475) instructed "For to serve a Lord"—but some thought it fit only for servants. When the lord of a manor and his guests dined on venison, the menials ate umble pie made from the innards of the deer. Anyone who ate umble pie was therefore in a position of inferiority—he or she was humbled—and some anonymous punster in the time of William the Conqueror, realizing this, changed *umble pie* to *humble pie,* the pun all the more effective because in several British dialects, especially the Cockney, the *h* is silent and *humble* is pronounced *umble* anyway. So the play upon words gave us the common expression *to eat humble pie,* meaning to suffer humiliation, to apologize, or to abase oneself.

eatin' a green 'simmon. The *'simmon* in this 19th-century Americanism is a persimmon, which takes its name from the Cree *pasiminan* (dried fruit). Although the fruit is delicious when thoroughly ripe, a green unripe persimmon is so sour it could make you whistle, which led to the expression *he looks like he's been eatin' a green 'simmon.* On the other hand, ripe persimmons suggested *walking off with the* *persimmons* (walking off with the prize), which also dates back to the 1850s.

eat the Yank way. To Brits, who have long called Americans Yanks, this phrase means to hold the fork in the right hand, as Americans generally do.

Edgar Allan Poe cottage. Often called "New York's chief literary shrine," this little cottage at Fordham in the Bronx is the place where Poe's wife, Virginia, died of tuberculosis during the terrible winter of 1846–47 when she and Poe were desperately poor and close to starving. Poe wrote "The Raven" and "The Pit and the Pendulum," among other great works. He was paid $10 for "The Raven," immediately recognized as a work of genius when it appeared, and it was a year and a half before he pried loose his money from the *New York Mirror.*

edgy. *Edgy* for nervous or irritable is an Americanism first recorded as late as 1931. However, it derives from the expression *on edge,* which has been common since the beginning of the century. No doubt the latter is patterned on someone on the edge of a precipice, close to falling. The *mulligrubs, jimjams, shakes, fantods,* and *willies* are all earlier synonyms.

Edison; Edison effect. When Thomas Alva Edison died in 1931, aged 84, the *New York Times* devoted four and a half full pages to his obituary, calling him the greatest benefactor of humanity in modern times. His name is a synonym for inventor and his more than 1,300 United States and foreign patents establish him as probably the world's greatest genius in the practical application of scientific principles. Born in Milan, Ohio, reared in Port Huron, Michigan, Edison had been interested in science since childhood—so curious in fact, that he once fed another boy a large dose of Seidlitz powders to see if the gas generated would enable him to fly. He had less than three months of formal schooling, was educated by his schoolteacher mother, and at 12 became a newspaper boy on the Grand Trunk Railway—his hearing became impaired at that time by a cuff on the ear from a railroad conductor. Edison's first successful invention was an improved stock ticker, which he proceeded to manufacture. He then devoted his full time to the "invention business." The Wizard of Menlo Park—where one of his first shops was located—soon had a new laboratory in West Orange, New Jersey, where he could "build anything from a lady's watch to a locomotive." A list of only his most noted inventions is still almost unbelieveable. These included assisting in the invention of the typewriter; invention of the carbon telephone transmitter; the first commercially practical electric light; an entire complex system, complete with many inventions, for the distribution of electricity for light and power, which resulted in the first central electric light power plant in the world in New York City; an electric automobile; the first full-sized electric motor; electric railway signals; station-to- station wireless telegraphy; an efficient alkaline storage battery; the magnetic ore separator; paraffin paper; an improved Portland cement; the Dictaphone; a mimeograph machine; the phonograph; the fluoroscope; and a motion-picture machine called the kinetoscope, from which developed the modern motion picture. Many of his inventions spawned giant modern industries— the electric light, his telephone transmitter, the phonograph, and the motion-picture camera being only four such discoveries. Ironically, the Edison effect, one of the few discoveries named for him, was not exploited by the inventor. It is the principle of the radio vacuum tube that made radio and television possible. The Edison base of light sockets also bears the immortal inventor's name, as does a town in central New Jersey. One of his five children, Charles Edison, served as that state's governor.

editorial. *Editorial* is an Americanism for what the British call a *leader* or *lead article,* that is, an article expressing the views of the editor or publisher of a periodical. The word is first recorded in 1830 and still hasn't caught on in England.

effing. *Effing* or *effen* has been a euphemism for *fucking* in America since at least the early 1960s, though it is first recorded in a *New York Times Magazine* article by Anthony Burgess in 1972: "I have already had several abusive phone calls, telling me to eff-off back to effing Russia, you effing, corksacking limey effer."

egghead. Usually a term of mild contempt or derision applied to intellectuals, *egghead* was first used in its present sense to describe candidate Adlai Stevenson and his advisers during the 1952 presidential campaign. Though the physical description better fit Stevenson's opponent, General Dwight D. Eisenhower, the term echoed the popular misconception that all intellectuals have high brows and heads shaped like eggs, the same kind of heads cartoonists give to "superior beings" from outer space. The continued popularity of the expression seems to suggest, sadly enough, that though these heads be admittedly full of brains, they are alien to the "common person." But *egghead* is often used humorously, even endearingly, and may yet become a word with no stigma attached to it.

eggs benedict. Oscar of the Waldorf once confirmed the story that *eggs benedict* was invented by a man suffering from a hangover. It seems that early one morning in 1894, Samuel Benedict, a prominent New York socialite, tread softly into the old Waldorf-Astoria Hotel after a night of partying—his head hurt that much. But he had what he thought was the perfect cure for his splitting headache—a breakfast of poached eggs served on buttered toast and topped with bacon and hollandaise sauce. Oscar, the maitre d'hotel, thought this combination excellent, but substituted an English muffin for the toast and ham for the bacon, naming the dish in Benedict's honor. Whether the cure worked or not isn't recorded, and another version of the tale claims that the dish was created between Oscar and New Yorker Mrs. Le Grand Benedict.

Egypt of the West. President Lincoln coined this term in an 1862 message to Congress. It was a name for the interior area of the United States between the Alleghenies and the Rocky Mountains.

Eighteen-hundred-and-freeze to death. A humorous name for the year of 1817, when an unusually cold winter in New England was followed by a cold spring, and the weather continued to be so unseasonable that many crops failed. Some sources put the years as 1816–17 and include the summer of 1816 as a very cold one when crops failed.

eight-hour day; five-day week. Henry Ford brought attention to the *eight-hour day* and *five-day week* for workers in 1926 when he instituted them at the Ford Motor Company plant in Detroit. However, a small number of workers had worked such hours before this, and the former term is recorded a quarter-century earlier.

Ellis Island; Castle Garden. Ellis Island was the United States's chief immigration station from 1892 until 1943. Previously Castle Garden, an old Dutch fort that had been converted into a noted opera house and amusement hall, had processed immigrants from 1855 to 1892 in Battery Park at the southern tip of Manhattan. Located in upper New York Bay, Ellis Island originally occupied three acres but was built up with landfill to 27.5 acres to accommodate the millions of people arriving there. During its use as an immigration center from 1892 to 1943, the Ellis Island facilities processed 16 million immigrants, roughly 70 percent of all immigrants to the United States in that period. People arriving there were screened for various undesirable factors such as contagious illnesses or mental deficiency before being granted entry to the United States. When the government began screening prospective immigrants in their native countries, Ellis Island fell into disuse. The government offered it for sale in the 1950s but could not find an adequate buyer, and the island eventually became a national monument under the care of the National Park Service. In 1998, most of Ellis Island officially became part of New Jersey after many years of legal debate over whether it actually belonged to that state or New York. Ellis Island was once called "Oyster Island" because of the abundant oysters in its waters. It was also called the "Isle of Tears," after the many people who were rejected at the center.

e-mail. A relatively new expression that is an American abbreviation of *electronic mail,* coined in the early 1980s. Making fun of the traditional, much slower ordinary postal system is the expression *snail mail.*

embedding. A U.S. policy permitting accredited war correspondents to live and travel with the military, often in combat situations. Embedded reporters have been permitted since the beginning of the second Iraq War (Operation Iraqi Freedom) in 2003.

Emigration Road. A nickname for the Oregon Trail, which brought so many settlers West and was called by a traveler in 1862 "the best and longest natural highway in the world."

Empire State. A nickname for New York State, possibly because George Washington called New York "the seat of Empire" in 1784. The EMPIRE STATE BUILDING, formerly the tallest building on earth, is named for it. New York was also once called "The Gateway to the West."

Empire State Building. It isn't widely known that the Empire State Building was jokingly called the "Empty State Building" because many of its floors were not rented for some 15 years after its completion in 1931. It takes its official name from New York State's sobriquet, the Empire State, which George Washington inspired when in discussing the 13 original states he referred to New York State as "the seat of the Empire." Until 1972 the Empire State Building was the tallest building in the world at 1,250 feet. It was surpassed as New York's tallest building by the TWIN TOWERS of the World Trade Center at 1,350 feet, until those great buildings were destroyed by terrorists in 2001. Today the Empire State Building is the second tallest building in the U.S., bested by Chicago's Sears Tower at 1,454 feet. The tallest building in the world is the Petronas Towers (1,483 feet) in Kuala Lumpur, Malaysia. The Empire State Building was featured unforgettably in the movie classic *King Kong* (1933), and in 1945 a B-25 crashed into its side in an accident similar to the terrorist act that destroyed the Twin Towers, though with much less loss of life.

enjoy every sandwich. According to the *New York Times* (January 30, 2006), this phrase was coined by singer-songwriter Warren Zevon (d. 2003) "and is well on its way to becoming the baby-boom mortality mantra."

entangling alliances. George Washington didn't invent this political expression often attributed to him, even if he was against alliances with other countries that could entangle or ensnare the U.S. The words are Thomas Jefferson's, from his inaugural address in 1801: ". . . honest friendship with all nations—entangling alliances with none. . . ."

E Pluribus Unum. The motto on the obverse side of the Great Seal of the United States may come from an expression found on the title page of the British *Gentlemen's Magazine,* widely circulated in America for several decades after 1731. The title page of the magazine's first volume shows a hand holding a bouquet over the epigraph *E Pluribus Unum.* The Latin words mean, in this case, "From many, one," and are as fitting for a bouquet of flowers as they are for a nation composed of many former colonies. Other possibilities, however, include a line in Virgil's poem "Moretum," which deals with the making of a salad and reads *color est e pluribus unus,* probably the first use of the phrase in any form, and an essay by Richard Steele in *The Spectator* (August 20, 1711), which opens with the Latin phrase *Exempta juvat spiris e pluribus unus* ("Better one thorn plucked than all remain"). The Continental Congress ordered the President of Congress to have a seal in 1776 and *E Pluribus Unum* appeared on the first seal, as well as on many early coins. Congress adopted the motto in 1781 and it still appears on U.S. coins as well as on the Great Seal.

Equality State. Wyoming is called the Equality State because its Territorial Legislature was the first to grant women the vote, in 1863. For the same reason it is called the Suffrage State.

eternal Quiz Kid. A name *Time* magazine bestowed upon U.S. historian Arthur M. Schlesinger Jr. (1917–2007), somewhat sarcastically.

euchre. *Euchre,* to cheat or to swindle, comes from the American card game of euchre, which was very popular in the West in the early 19th century. Gamblers cheated at the game so frequently that its name became synonymous with their chicanery.

Everglades. Since the early 19th century this term, apparently an Americanism, has been applied to the low, marshy region overgrown with tall grass in Florida. It has been suggested that the "ever" in the word is used loosely in the sense of "interminable."

Evergreen State. A nickname for Washington State, after its abundance of evergreen forests. Washington is also called the Chinook State in honor of the Indian tribe once numerous there. *See* CHINOOK.

everything's coming up roses. Any enterprise is going very well, splendidly, profitably. The American expression is first recorded in 1959 as the title of a song in the musical *Gypsy;* the phrase may also have some connection with *come up smelling like a rose,* or *step (fall) in shit and come up smelling like roses.*

everything worthwhile doing is either immoral, illegal, or fattening. A by-now proverbial saying often attributed to New York wit Alexander Woollcott, a member of the Algonquin Round Table.

Evil One; Evil Empire; Evil Man Number One. The first is a term coined by President George W. Bush, or his speechwriter, for the terrorist Osama bin Laden after the destruction of the World Trade Center on September 11, 2001. The younger Bush probably knew that the Iraqis had called his father, President George Bush, "Evil Man Number One." Previous to this, beginning in 1983, President Ronald Reagan called the Soviet Union "The Evil Empire." Long before both Bushes and Reagan, poet John Milton used the *Evil One* as a name for the Devil in *Paradise Lost* (1667). *See* THE GREAT COMMUNICATOR.

expletive deleted. *Expletive deleted* has quickly become a euphemism to use in place of a curse, especially for four-letter words. The phrase originated in the 1970s after Watergate, deriving of course from the transcripts of President Nixon's White House tapes in which many curses are rendered as "expletive deleted."

exurb. American social historian A. C. Spectorsky invented this term in his book *The Exurbanites* (1950). He used it to describe regions beyond the suburbs of a city, semirural areas inhabited mainly by rich people.

the eyes are the windows of the soul At least one source calls this a proverb of the mid-16th century. However, John Green-leaf Whittier (1807–92) used it in his poem "My Psalm" and in recent times Cormac McCarthy quotes it in his novel *No Country for Old Men* (2005): "They say the eyes are the windows of the soul. I don't know what them eyes was the windows to and I guess I'd as soon not know."

F

face. According to one police detective (*New York Times,* 3/15/92) *face* has taken on a new meaning in recent times: "He's a guy who looks like a mobster's supposed to look . . . They [the mob] send him to scare the hell out of someone, like 'Go send a face.'"

face the music. Though not listed by Mathews, this appears to be an Americanism first recorded in 1850. Meaning "to face up to the consequences of one's actions" it may have originally been army slang, alluding to the "Rogue's March" being played when an offender was drummed out of the service.

faction. A combination of parts of *fact* and *fiction,* this originally U.S. genre is based on real events and/or characters. It was first recorded in 1967.

a fade barn. Of all the major American dialects, the southern is the most consistently difficult to translate. Among the most amusing examples is the expression *a fade barn* that the editors of the *Dictionary of American Regional English* tried to track down for a couple of years. The editors knew that the expression existed because field interviews had recorded it in North Carolina without establishing its meaning. When a Raleigh newspaper joined in the search, the answer was quickly apparent. Dozens of correspondents chided the editors for not knowing, in the words of one North

Carolinian, that "a fade barn is what you stow fade [feed] for the livestock."

fail-safe. The fail-safe system, intended to help prevent nuclear war, was developed by the Strategic Air Command of the U.S. Air Force in the 1950s. Under the fail-safe procedure a bomber had to return home without dropping its bombs if specific orders to drop the bombs weren't received. Thus a failure to receive such a radio message would be a failure on the safe side that wouldn't accidentally trigger a nuclear war. The term *fail-safe* is now used to describe any precautionary system.

fall guy. In American professional wrestling during the 1890s, just like today, many of the bouts were fixed, with a loser picked beforehand. This may have resulted in the term *fall guy* being applied to the loser, the wrestler who took a fall, the words later coming to mean any person who takes the blame for the actions of others. But there is no proof of this theory. The earliest quotation using the term *fall guy*, in 1904, links it to the underworld, and even before that in 1893 *fall* is recorded as a criminal arrest or conviction, making the wrestling connection seem unlikely.

fancy footwork. Originally a term from American boxing describing the footwork of a skillful boxer in the ring, fancy footwork has come to mean any clever evasion or maneuver. It probably dates back to the early 1900s, when there were a lot of fast, clever boxers around.

Faneuil Hall. Pronounced FAN-ul or FAN-yul; a historic building in Boston, Massachusetts. An old rhyme instructs how to pronounce this famous landmark:

When you speak of the market
That's known as Faneuil,
Kindly pronounce it
To rhyme with Dan'l.

fanny. This euphemism may be an unknown personification, the diminutive of the feminine name Frances, or it may have a more objectionable history than the word it replaces. For Partridge suggests that the euphemism for "backside" comes from the eponymous heroine of John Cleland's hardly euphemistic novel *Fanny Hill* (1749). The term in this sense is originally an American one, however, probably deriving from the English slang use of Cleland's *Fanny* for "the female pudenda." Or else Americans were reading *Fanny Hill* long before it was legally permissible to do so. Cleland's classic of brothel life, which he wrote to escape debtor's prison, has already been made into a movie, had had vast sales in paperback and, judging by recent examples, may indeed finally prove euphemistic for its genre. Another etymologist feels that *fanny* may come from the obsolete expression *fancy vulva;* still another source traces the word to a pun on *fundament* (which became *fun,* then *fan,* then *fanny*), and *Webster's* derives it from "the fanciful euphemism 'Aunt Fanny' for the buttocks."

farm out. Branch Rickey, then with the St. Louis Cardinals, founded baseball's first farm system in 1918, buying stock in minor league teams on which he cultivated new players for the Cardinals. These clubs became widely known as farm teams and the major league players sent down to them from the parent club for more seasoning (or forever) were said to be farmed out. (The expression had been used for the sale of a major leaguer to the minors 15 years or so before this.) The term is now also used to mean assigning work to another person by financial agreement.

fat cat. *Fat cat* for a rich contributor to political compaign funds was coined by *Baltimore Sun* writer Frank R. Kent in his 1928 book *Political Behavior.* Today it also means any rich, secure person.

fat city. This American slang, first recorded in 1964, means being very well off, sitting pretty, as in "I was nowhere, but I got a break and now I'm in fat city." Sometimes capitalized.

Father Knickerbocker. A synonym for New York City. The prominent Dutch Knickerbocker family settled near Albany, New York, in about 1674. Among its prosperous descendants was the wealthy Herman Knickerbocker (b. 1779), the great-great-grandson and namesake of the family founder, who became known as "the prince of Schaghticoke" for his great manor along the Schaghticoke River. So when Washington Irving burlesqued a pompous guidebook of the day with his *A History of New York from the Beginning of the World to the End of the Dutch Dynasty* (1809), he decided to capitalize on the old familiar name, choosing the pseudonym Diedrich Knickerbocker. Irving could not have concocted a better name in satirizing the stodgy Dutch burghers than this thinly veiled alias for the well-known Dutch "prince," although the first great book of comic literature written by an American was also a satire on Jeffersonian democracy, pedantry, and literary classics. Soon his humorous work became known as *Knickerbocker's History of New York,* but it wasn't until English caricaturist George Cruikshank illustrated a later edition in the 1850s that the Knickerbocker family name was bestowed on the loose-fitting, blousy knee breeches known today as *knickers.* The trouser style is no longer worn by schoolboys but was revived some time ago as a fashion for women. The British still call women's underwear *knickers.* As a result of Irving's work *Father Knickerbocker* became an early synonym for New York City, *Knickerbocker* was adopted by a school of local writers called the *Knickerbocker Group,* and an early New York City literary journal was called The *Knickerbocker Magazine* (1833–65). Much later it became the name of New York's professional basketball team, the New York Knicks.

Father of American Football. While serving as a member of the Intercollegiate Football Rules Committee for 48 years, Walter Chauncey Camp (1859–1925) was responsible for so many rules governing American football that he can truly be said to have laid the foundations for the modern game. The Yale coach was being called the Father of American Football by 1920, five years before his death at one of the committee meetings.

Fatso; Ratso. *Fatso* as the nickname for a fat person is an Americanism dating back to the Great Depression years, which were hardly fat years. The word is first recorded in a Damon Runyon tale and later gained in popularity when it became the name of a button-popping character in the comic strip *Smilin' Jack*. It may have suggested *Ratso* for an unkempt unsavory person, most notably the character Ratso Rizzo in the film *Midnight Cowboy*.

Faulknenian. Resembling the writing style of U.S. author William Faulkner (1897–962), often in reference to Faulkner's long, convoluted, often sparsely punctuated sentences.

F.B.I. Its abbreviation was being used almost as soon as the Federal Bureau of Investigation was named in 1935. The first recorded use of the initials, however, came a year later, in 1936, when it was used in an article describing "Baby Face" Nelson shooting it out with an FBI agent.

Today F.B.I. or FBI is usually used instead of the longer name. The bureau is also called the *Feds*, which was the name the *Confeds* (Confederates) used for federal U.S. troops during the Civil War. *See* G-MAN.

fear. "The only thing we have to fear is fear itself—nameless, unreasoning, unjustified terror . . ." From President Franklin D Roosevelt's first inaugural address, March 14, 1933.

featherbedding. "What do you want, feather beds?" management supposedly snapped when Rock Island Railroad freight crews complained that their caboose bunks were too hard. This has been cited as the origin of the term *featherbedding*, for "unions forcing employers to hire more men than necessary for a job." It is certain, however, only that the expression was first recorded during a labor dispute in 1943.

featherbed lane. Any bad, unpaved, rutted road. According to an old unlikely story, George Washington had housewives pave a road with featherbeds (bedcovers) so that the Redcoats wouldn't hear his troops marching by at night—this giving rise to the term.

feather in his cap. American Indians of various tribes often wore feathers to show their past bravery in wars. This custom led to the Americanism *a feather in his cap*, "an honor or an accomplishment of which a person can be proud."

Feds. *See* F.B.I; G-MAN.

feel one's oats. Someone feeling his oats or full of oats is in high spirits, full of pep, so full of himself that he may even be showing off a bit. The allusion is to lively horses fed on oats and the expression is American, first recorded in 1843 by Canadian Thomas Haliburton, the humorist whose Sam Slick gave us "cry over spilt milk" and other expressions. Men, women, and children can feel their oats, but only young men are said to sow their wild oats.

fellow traveler. Used since the 1930s to describe a sympathizer with a cause, though not one who joins that cause. The term was used disparagingly in the 1950s about people thought sympathetic to the communist cause.

fence-mending. Secretary of the Treasury John Sherman, later to author the Sherman Anti-Trust Act, decided to run for the Senate in 1879, knowing that he would shortly lose his Cabinet post because President Rutherford B. Hayes wouldn't be running for reelection. When he visited his Ohio farm, he told reporters "I have come back to mend my fences" and reporters assumed he meant political fences, not the ones around the farm. Soon after, *fence-mending* came to mean "trying to gather political support at home by making personal contacts," and "patching up disagreements," the last its most common use today.

15 minutes of fame. Thirty-five years ago, in 1968, Andy Warhol proclaimed, "In the future everybody will be famous for fifteen minutes."

The leader of the pop art movement died 15 *years* ago and he is still world famous, as are his words.

fifty-fifty. Fifty-fifty—50 percent for one party, 50 percent for the other—is still a common Americanism for "equally divided." An expression that one would guess is much older, it is first recorded in a 1913 *Saturday Evening Post* article, though it may date back to the late 19th century or earlier.

the 51st state. A name President John F. Kennedy bestowed upon *Meet the Press,* so great has been its influence on American politics. The show first aired in 1947 and has been broadcast every week since then, with a panel of newsmen interviewing guests.

54-40 or fight. James Polk won election to the American presidency in 1844 with this slogan, which referred to the ousting of the British from the whole of the Columbia River country up to latitude 54 degrees 40 minutes N. After his election Polk discarded the slogan and settled the Oregon question without going to war. The sarcastic Whig slogan "Who is James K. Polk?" inspired the myth that Polk was a political nonentity and weak president. In truth, he was one of the hardest-working of all presidents, attained almost all his stated aims, and added more territory to the U.S. than any president except Jefferson.

fight fire with fire. An Americanism, possibly deriving from the use of backfires to help extinguish great prairie and forest fires in the early West. Settlers would set fire to a circle or strip of land in the path of a blaze but at a good distance from it, then extinguish it and leave a barren patch so that the advancing fire would have nothing to feed on and so would burn itself out. Fighting fire with fire could be a dangerous practice, for the backfire might get out of control itself, so the expression came to mean "any desperate measure involving great risk."

filibuster. Deriving from the Dutch *vribuiter,* "freebooter or pirate," *filibuster* was originally used in American English to describe gun-runners in Central America, men who engaged in war with a country with whom their own country was at peace. Over the years the word came to mean "obstruction of legislation in the U.S. Senate by prolonged speechmaking," after a congressman described one such obstruction as "filibustering against the U.S."

fine-haired sons of bitches. A derogatory term for gentlemanly, "civilized" types in the early West. "'I despise all you fine-haired sons of bitches,' he heard someone say."

fingerpointing. In its sense of accusing someone, frequently unfairly, the expression is said to date back to 1941, when *Social Focus* magazine said northern states shouldn't be *fingerpointing* at lynchings in southern states when they had their own race riots.

fink. The original *fink* may have been either a Pinkerton man or a cop named Albert Fink, who worked for railroads in the American South. Mencken prefers the former explanation, tracing the term to the 1892 Homestead steel strike when Pinkerton men were hired as strikebreakers, these brutal "Pinks" becoming *finks* in time, the word synonymous with the earlier "scab" or the British "blackleg." Finks were anathema to the early labor movement, but the word is now used to describe not only "a strikebreaker but any treacherous, contemptible person or a police informer." Mr. Albert Fink could just as well have inspired the term in similar fashion. The German-born Fink, according to a reliable source, long headed a staff of detectives with the Louisville and Nashville Railroad and then switched to the New York Trunk Line Association in about 1875. He was not involved in railroad labor disputes, but his operatives probably policed rates charged on the lines and some of them were likely planted spies who came to be known as *finks*. This gives the word more a management than a labor flavor, but it is possible that *fink* gained currency in this way before being adopted by union men. It is at least as plausible as the transformation of "Pinks" to finks. *Ratfink* is a stronger variant of *fink* that originated in the U.S. within the last 30 years or so.

fire away Flanagan. A historical phrase dating back to the Revolutionary War. It means "to keep it up, go on, continue," according to the *Dictionary of Americanisms* (1951). Whether there was a real Flanagan is unknown, but the expression was first recorded by Philip Freneau in a 1783 poem: "Scarce a broadside was ended 'till another began again—By Jove! It was nothing but Fire away Flanagan!" This poem referenced an attack on the Fraunces Tavern, a restaurant still open today in New York City. It was then known as the Queen's Head Tavern, owned by Samuel Francis, a fierce anti-Royalist who later changed his name.

firebug. *Firebug* derives from those bugs who have enthusiasms often amounting to manias. That this is an old American expression is evidenced by the fact that Oliver Wendell Holmes used it figuratively, writing of "political firebugs" in his book *The Poet at the Breakfast*

Table (1872). That is the first recorded use of the term, which generally means "a pyromaniac, someone mentally unbalanced who lights fires for his pleasure." But people with a mania for anything have been called bugs in America since at least the early 19th century; we have had our slavery bugs, those who wished to see slavery extended into the West, and we still have our money bugs, whose sole interest is money.

fire-eater. An often violent, always uncompromising believer. The expression has its roots in the southern cause before and during the Civil War, the term dating back to the 1840s. Anonymous doggerel of the day described the fire-eaters:

> "Down in a small Palmetto State the curious ones may find
> A ripping, tearing gentleman, of an uncommon kind,
> A staggering, swaggering sort of chap who takes his whisky straight
> And frequently condemns his eyes to that ultimate vengeance which
> a clergyman of high-standing has assured must be a sinner's fate;
> This South Carolina gentleman, one of the present time."

first, one must endure. Ernest Hemingway took this as his lifelong motto, the words a translation of French: *Il faut (d'abord) durer,* meaning one must endure in order to finally win.

the first hundred years are the hardest. Hollywood writer and cynical wit Wilson Mizner and America's greatest word inventor T. A. Dorgan vie for the authorship of this humorous saying about life in general. Dorgan seems the more likely candidate, considering his creation of such American masterpieces, among many others, as *dumbbell, dumbhead, Dumb Dora, nobody home upstairs* (dumb), *applesauce* (for insincere flattery), *drugstore cowboy, lounge lizard, chin music* (pointless talk), *the once-over, the cat's meow, the cat's pajamas, flat tire, you said it, for crying out loud, see what the boys in the backroom will have,* and *the only place you'll find sympathy is in the dictionary.*

First Lady. The first First Lady of (or in) the land was Dolley Madison, according to one old story, but most writers say the honorary title dates from the mid-19th century, long after Dolley served as Thomas Jefferson's and later her husband, James Madison's, official hostess. The first mention of *First Lady* is in British correspondent William Russell's *My Diary North and South* (1863): "The gentleman . . . has some charming little pieces of gossip about the first Lady in the Land [then Mary Todd Lincoln]." Dolley Madison did, however, die in 1849, so there might be some connection between her and the title. The term is also used, usually uncapitalized, for a prominent woman in any profession, as in "She's the first lady of the American theater." An old joke makes *First Lady* a synonym for spare ribs, because Eve was made from Adam's spare rib. Jacqueline Kennedy is the only First Lady who didn't want to be called *First Lady.* She said it sounded like the name of a saddle horse.

the first million is the hardest. The U.S. catchphrase arose in about 1920, when millionaires were far less common, though hardly unheard of.

fit to be tied. Somebody filled with such great anger, outrage, that one has to tie him up to calm him down. Apparently an American idiom.

five-and-ten. A name still occasionally heard for stores like F.W. Woolworth, long after it was possible to buy anything there for a nickel or a dime. Five-and-tens, or five-and-ten-cent stores, flourished from the mid-19th to the mid-20th century in America, with Woolworth's (founded by Frank Woolworth in 1879 as a five-cent store) being the most notable chain. Such stores are even remembered in popular song lyrics, including "I found my million-dollar baby in a five-and-ten-cent store," and "and if that diamond ring don't shine, poppa's gonna take you to the five-and-dime."

fix. *Fix,* for the dishonest prearranging of games, races, or other sports events, is an Americanism first recorded in 1881 to describe tampering with a horse to prevent it from winning a race. It may be a shortened version of an earlier term with the same meaning, *fix up.*

flake. *Flake* has meant "a packet of cocaine" since the 1920s, but it first appeared in its meaning of an odd, eccentric person, often a colorful, likable eccentric, in the 1950s, probably in baseball. It possibly referred originally to "offi>eat San Francisco outfielder Jackie Brandt, from whose mind, it was said, things seemed to flake off and disappear," according to Tim Considine, writing in the *New York Times Magazine* and quoted in Paul Dickson's *The Dickson Baseball Dictionary* (1989). Then again, the *flake* of eccentricity could derive from association with the narcotics sense of the word. Stuart Berg Flexner's *Listening to America* (1982) says *flake* appeared "in professional football in the early 1970s, especially when referring to John Don Looney (who couldn't, after all, be called merely a looney . . .), who attacked tackling dummies in anger and seldom heeded signs . . ." In any case, consistent sports use of the word made it common American slang.

flapper. The word *flapper* didn't originate in the JAZZ AGE. *Flapper* was originally a British expression meaning a young girl, first recorded in 1888. This word may have derived from the flapping of the pigtails such young girls often wore, but, on the other hand, it could come from *flap,* a loose woman, which was used as far back as the early 17th century. Another possibility is the late 18th-century British *flapper* meaning a duck too young to fly. By 1915 Americans may have finally adopted one or another of these British words to describe the wild, flighty, unconventional, pleasure-loving young women of the Roaring Twenties who boldly smoked cigarettes; drank from a flask; wore short dresses, no corsets, and stockings rolled beneath the knees; had bobbed hair; loved to dance with their "sheiks"; and were also called *jazz babies, hot mamas,* and *whoopee mamas.* Or the scandalous American *flapper* could descend from the British *flapper* that was used in the late 19th century to mean a very young, immoral teenager, especially one who had been trained for vice. "They all want flappers," a sedate British actress complained in 1927, "and I can't flap." Another possible origin of the word is the flapping sound of unbuckled galoshes American girls favored as a fashion fad in the 1920s. The *New Dictionary of American Slang* (1986) suggests "the idea of an unfledged bird *flapping* its wings as dancers did when dancing the Charleston." Take your choice.

flattery will get you nowhere. A common U.S. phrase dating back to about 1945 and meaning don't bother flattering me, you haven't got a chance of it working.

flattop. Though the *Langley,* a converted coal ship commissioned in 1922, was America's first aircraft carrier, no one thought of calling any aircraft carrier a *flattop* until World War II, when the United States built 150 carriers.

flea market. These bargain markets have nothing to do with fleas. *Flea market* has been an American expression as far back as Dutch colonial days when there was a very real Vallie (Valley) Market at the valley, or foot, of Maiden Lane in downtown Manhattan. The Vallie Market came to be abbreviated to *Vlie Market* and this was soon being pronounced *Flea Market*. Today there is a flea market *(marché auxpuces)* area in Paris.

Flickertail State. An old nickname for North Dakota, because of its many flickertail squirrels.

float like a butterfly, sting like a bee. Words describing Muhammad Ali's boxing technique. His trainer and friend Bundini Brown coined the phrase when Ali was still Cassius Clay in the 1960s. One of Ali's major opponents in his fights was Joe Frazier, whom he taunted whenever he could, calling him an "ugly old bear," among other choice insults. Today Frazier calls him the Butterfly.

floor-through. An American term, heard in New York City, for an apartment in a small apartment building, such as a brownstone, that takes up an entire floor. "They rented a nice floor-through."

floorwalker. "Dandified ushers," the first department store floorwalkers were called, and in the 1890s that was often exactly what they were. Dressed in either a black frock or a cutaway coat, with gray-striped trousers, a very high collar, and a rose in the buttonhole, the floorwalker was usually a spiffy, or smarmy, exceedingly polite living directory, who pompously patrolled the aisles, the arbiter elegantiarum of conduct and store etiquette. Charlie Chaplin knew the type well and portrayed one in his film *The Floorwalker*. Today floorwalkers are more often called *floor managers,* their main job still the supervision of sales personnel and assistance of customers.

floozie. "Flat-Foot Floogy with the Floy Floy," a popular song in 1945, spelled *floozie* differently, but it meant the same. A floosie, floogy, flugie, or even faloosie is a gaudily dressed, dumb, disrespectable, frequently high-spirited woman, often a prostitute. If the word derives from *Flossie,* a nickname for Florence, no one has proved it, and the word was first recorded in the form of *flugie* at the turn of the century. Hollywood's HAYS CODE banned *floozie,* along with *red-hot mamma* and other words, but the term got a breath of new life with the song mentioned above, which describes a floozie with what it seems is a kind of venereal disease, the floy floy. This American slang, as a British writer observes, is "picturesque" and should be retained for its "blousy flowery atmosphere" suggesting "good spirits, gaudy flowered dresses, and bad but delightful perfume."

flopper. In American slang for over a century, a *flopper* can be a swindler; a beggar displaying or feigning a disability; or a person who switches political parties for his own benefit. *Flopper* is also another name for a flounder, a fish known for its flopping from one side to the other when caught and landed on the deck of a boat. Unrecorded anywhere I've looked, this last term was mentioned in the 1940s film *Man on the Ledge.*

Florida. "The Sunshine State" was the Florida Territory before being admitted to the Union as the 27th state in 1845. *Florida* means "land of flowers" in Spanish, Ponce de Leon naming it in 1513 with "flowery Easter" in mind.

Florida room. A term used in Florida and other states for I living room with large windows to catch the sun; also called a sun room.

flourish. An old euphemism for the sex act used by Virginii tobacco planter, author, and colonial official William Byrd, who kept a secret diary in shorthand as an avocation, never intending for it to be published. He had no inhibitions about married love, judging by his entry for July 30, 1710: "In the afternoon my wife and I had a little quarrel which I reconciled with a flourish. Then she read a sermon in Dr. Tillitson to me. It is to be observed that the flourish was performed on the billiard table."

flying machine. The Wright brothers, Orville and Wilbur, liked to call their epochal invention a *flying machine,* never an *airplane, aeroplane, aerial ship,* or *aerial machine.* The term *flying machine* is recorded as far back as 1730. The name of the Wright's plane, which on December 17, 1903, near Kitty Hawk, North Carolina, made the first powered flight in a heavier- than-air craft, was the *Wright Flyer,* an appellation they chose in honor of something so down-to-earth as a bicycle brand these bicycle shop owners (and high school dropouts) made and sold back in their Dayton, Ohio, store. A place with a *hawk* in it would be a wonderful location for the world's first airplane flight, but the Wright flight actually took place not in Kitty Hawk, as is usually said, but on Kill Devil Hill, a place close by.

flying saucer. U.S. pilot Kenneth Arnold is said to have been the first earthling to sight a flying saucer, in June 1947, near Mount Ranier in Washington State. Arnold has also been credited with naming the dish-shaped object many believed to have come from outer space. But unidentified flying objects have been reported since at least 1878 in America, when a Texas *Daily News* story told of a flying object "about the size of a large saucer" that some pedestrian had spotted directly over and far above his head. In any case, there have been thousands of sightings since Arnold's, but no landing so far as we know.

The Flying Tomato. A nickname of red-headed Shaun White, the world's best-known snowboarder. His shoulder-length red locks flow behind him as he flies downhill. White began his career when only seven. He often did stunt work for child stars.

fly off the handle. Axes in American pioneer days were frequently handmade, frontiersmen whittling their own handles and attaching axe-heads shipped from back East. Because they were often crudely fitted to the helve, these axe-heads often flew off the handle while woodsmen were chopping down trees or preparing firewood, sometimes injuring the axeman or people nearby. The sudden flying of the head off the axe, and the trouble this caused, naturally suggested a sudden wild outburst of anger, the loss of self-control, or the losing of one's head that the expression *to fly off the handle* describes. The expression is first recorded in John Neal's novel *Brother Jonathan; or the New Englanders* (1825) as *off the handle,* but isn't known in its full form until 1844, when it was used in still another of Thomas Haliburton's "Sam Slick" tales. *See* FEEL ONE'S OATS.

fly-up-the-creek. We don't hear this expression today, but it is recorded as early as 1845 as the nickname for a resident of Florida. Floridians were so called because *fly-up-the-creek* is a popular name of the small green heron common in the state. Walt Whitman used the expression in this sense and it later meant "a giddy capricious person."

Fog City. A local name for San Francisco, named proudly by natives.

Foggy Bottom. This derogatory name for the U.S. State Department in Washington, D.C., is said to have been coined by Washington *Post* columnist Edward Folliard in the early 1940s. Previously *Foggy Bottom* was a marshy area of the Potomac River where the State Department is now located. This (and the foggy GOBBLEDYGOOK of official State Department papers) accounts for the persistence of the disparaging name.

fog's so thick you kin hardly spit. A Maine saying recorded in John Wallace, *Village Down East* (1943).

fohn. The famous dry spring wind, varying from warm to hot, that blows along and down the valleys on the northern side of the Alps, melting snow in its path. Its name derives from the Latin *Favonius* for the West Wind.

follow the tongue. A phrase common among Americans following the rutted Oregon Trail west in the 1840s and 1850s at about three miles an hour. "At night," writes David Dary in *The Oregon Trail* (2005), "the tongue of the lead wagon was pointed toward the North Star, so that the wagon train could orient itself the next morning."

fool's gold. A term coined in the American West around 1875 for iron or copper pyrites, which are sometimes mistaken for gold; used figuratively to mean anything that deceives a person. "'That's fool's gold. See how green those flakes look in the light? Real gold don't do that'" wrote Anke Kristke in *Women of the West* (1990).

the fool's tax. No reference consulted lists this term, but the *New York Times* cites it in an editorial (8/29/01): "Lotteries have collectively taken the name 'the fool's tax' because the odds of winning are so small . . . [Powerball, for example, offers odds of one in 80 million] . . . In New York State, as many as one in every eleven players is a compulsive gambler feeding an addiction."

for crying out loud. An Americanism first recorded in 1924, but probably dating back earlier, *for crying out loud* is what is called a "minced oath," a euphemism that may have originated when someone started to say "For Christ's sake!" but got only as far as the first syllable of the second word, realized the curse was inappropriate in the circumstances, and changed the offensive word to "crying." It's hard to believe that this common expression was consciously invented by someone. But it has been traced to American cartoonist and prolific word coiner Thomas Aloysius (TAD) Dorgan (1877–1929).

Ford. John Dillinger, the first "public enemy number one," once wrote Henry Ford extolling the performance of his car as a getaway vehicle. That curious incident shows just how widespread was the Ford's really incalculable influence on society, both good and bad. Henry Ford's motor cars, though not the first invented, put America and the world on wheels, his assembly-line and mass-production methods marking the beginning of modern industry, and his "Five Dollar Day" heralding a new era for labor. Ford (1863–1947), born on a farm near Detroit, Michigan, founded the Ford Motor Company in 1903. First came his two-cylinder Model A and then in 1909 the immortal Model T, the Tin Lizzie, the flivver, America's monument to love, available in any color so long as it was black. Fifteen million of these cars were built over almost 20 years—a record that lasted until the Volkswagen broke it in 1972—and any cheap, dependable car became known as a ford. The word is usually capitalized now, but Ford still remains a symbol of American mechanical ingenuity. Though he was often controversial and foolish in his public life, no one has ever doubted the inventor's genius. He is honored today by both the motor company bearing his name and the philanthropic Ford Foundation.

FORD TO CITY: DROP DEAD. In a speech on October 29, 1975, President Gerald R. Ford denied ever refusing New York City federal financial assistance. Possibly he merely implied such a rejection. In any event, the headline FORD TO CITY . . . that the *New York Daily News* printed on its front page became a lasting literary piece no matter how short.

Forefather's Day. A New England holiday, celebrated mostly in Massachusetts on December 21, that commemorates the Pilgrims' landing at Plymouth in 1620. Traditionally, samp porridge is served on this day, which is not a legal holiday. The annual holiday was first celebrated at Plymouth, Massachusetts, in 1769.

foreigner. A word used in New England meaning someone not born in a town or area, even if he or she has lived there for many years.

forget it! As an expression of annoyance or anger meaning "never mind," *forget* it! has been popular since before 1912, when the Americanism, in the form of *aw, forget it,* was discussed in a scholarly work on slang. The term enjoyed a resurgence of popularity in the hippie 1960s.

forgotten man. Franklin Roosevelt popularized this phrase when running for president in 1932, applying it to all those suffering during the Great Depression whom government had done little to help. The term was invented, however, by Yale professor William G. Sumner, who in 1883 applied it to the American workingman, the decent, average American citizen.

fortune cookies. The cookie with a fortune inside was invented in 1918 by David Jung, a contemporary Chinese immigrant who had established Los Angeles's Hong Kong Noodle Company. Jung got the idea after noting how bored customers got while waiting for their orders in Chinese restaurants. He employed a Presbyterian minister (the first fortune cookie author!) to write condensations of biblical messages and later hired Marie Raine, the wife of one of his salesmen, who became the Shakespeare of fortune cookies, writing thousands of classic fortunes such as "Your feet shall walk upon a plush carpet of contentment." The Hong Kong Noodle Company is still in business, as are hundreds of other fortune cookie "publishers." Notable ones include Misfortune Cookies of Los Angeles: "Look forward to love and marriage, but not with the same person" Today fortune cookies are of course served at the end of a meal.

40 acres and a mule. A promise, with no basis in fact, made by dishonest politicians to newly freed slaves after the Civil War. Each freed slave, they said, would receive 40 acres of land and a mule to work it with. "When we were children we used to ridicule the slogan 'forty acres and a mule' as a stupid deception used by the Yankees to get the black men to vote for the Republicans," wrote Katherine Lumpking in *The Making of a Southerner* (1947).

40 miles of bad road. The old expression from the American West describes any very ugly or unattractive person or place, as in "She looks like 40 miles of bad road and he looks 10 miles longer."

49er. A person who went to California in 1849 during the gold rush, or someone in favor of the use of the 49th parallel of latitude as a compromise boundary line in the Oregon boundary dispute with Great Britain.

40 rod lightning. Whiskey in the early West could literally kill a man and was thus given colorful names, none more vivid than *40 rod lightning*—which likened it to a rifle or shot that could kill a man at 40 yards.

Forty Thieves. A common name in the mid-19th century for the Common Council of aldermen that governed New York City. Their name was suggested by a dangerous gang of the time with the same name. The infamous Boss Tweed came from the ranks of the Forty Thieves council.

foul ball. A ball hit outside of the fair playing area in baseball has been called a foul ball since the 1860s. By the 1920s the term was being used generally for any useless, inadequate or contemptible person, and specifically for an inferior boxer, a palooka. The great American word inventor and cartoonist T. A. Dorgan is said to be the first person to use the expression in this extended sense. More recently *foul ball* has been used to mean an outsider.

The Four Freedoms. On January 6, 1941, U.S. President Franklin Delano Roosevelt declared as the goals of the nation's policy: freedom of speech, freedom of worship, freedom from want, and freedom from fear. These became widely known as the Four Freedoms.

the Four Hundred. Society columnist Ward McAllister coined this term in 1889, when he claimed only 400 people formed New York City's high society. The old story says "400" was chosen because Mrs. Astor's ballroom held only that number, but the truth is that she often invited twice that many people to parties held there.

four-letter man. *Four-letter man* for "an excellent athlete" originated in college sports and originally meant someone who earned a letter in football, baseball, basketball, and track. Since its first use in early 20th-century America it has also come to be slang for a stupid person, from the four letters of *dumb,* and a contemptible person, from the four letters of *shit.* Amos Alonso Stagg, longtime football coach at the University of Chicago, was the first to award monograms of the first letter of a school's name to athletes and these monograms were being called letters by 1961 Stagg himself was called "the grand old man of football."

fourscore and seven. The words *fourscore and seven* are from American president Abraham Lincoln's classic Gettysburg Address, delivered on November 19, 1863, dedicating the National Cemetery at Gettysburg, Pennsylvania, where a great and bloody battle of the Civil War had been fought. The two-minute or so speech famously began: "Fourscore and seven years ago our fathers brought forth upon this continent a new nation, conceived in liberty and dedicated to the proposition that men are created equal." It ended: "We here highly resolve that these dead shall not have died in vain—that this nation, under God, shall have a new birth of freedom—and that government of the people, by the people, for the people, shall not perish from the earth." It is one of the most famous and most quoted speeches, or prose poems, in history and used the words *under God* long before the Pledge of Allegiance to the flag (June 1954).

fox-trot. One story has it that actor Harry Fox's original trotting type of dance was a show-stopper in a 1913 Broadway hit musical. The show's producers realized the dance had promotional value and hired the noted social dancing teacher Oscar Duryea to modify it and introduce it as the *Fox Trot* to the public. This he did and the fox-trot has been America's most popular slow dance ever since. The story does jibe with the fact that the term is first recorded as *Fox* (with a capital *F*) *trot* in an RCA Victor Catalog in 1915.

fragging. *Fragging* came into the language during the Vietnam War. Meaning the intentional wounding or killing of an officer by his own troops, it takes its name from the fragmentation grenades sometimes used to accomplish this.

Frankie Bailey's. Only movie star Betty Grable's "million-dollar legs" can compare with the gams of American performer Frankie Bailey, who was the toast of the town in the Gay Nineties. Miss Bailey's shapely stems were so celebrated that *Frankie Bailey's* became the term for any sexy, pleasing pair of legs.

a Frankie Yale. All but obsolete today, *a* Frankie Yale means something cheap and useless, after the rotgut liquor and badly made cigars mobster Frankie Yale (1895–1927) forced his speakeasy clients to buy in the 1920s. Yale was killed in New York's first machine-gun assassination.

Frankly my dear, I don't give a damn. *I don't give a damn* is first recorded in America in the 1890s. Its most famous use was in *Gone with the Wind* (1939), when Rhett Butler tells Scarlett O'Hara this iconic line.

Fredonia. In 1827 a group of adventurers tried to set up a Texan republic called Fredonia; the name Fredonia had been invented in about 1800 by Dr. Samuel Latham Mitchell as a term for the United States, "a land where things are freely done," and was borrowed by the unsuccessful adventurers. Fredonia, incidentally, was the name of Groucho Marx's homeland in the film *Duck Soup*.

free soil, free speech, free labor, free men. This was the slogan of the American Free-soil Party during the election of 1848. The slogan referred to the party's opposition to the extension of slavery into any of the territories newly acquired from Mexico. With former President Martin Van Buren as its candidate, the Free-soilers polled nearly 300,000 votes and were a decisive factor in the victory of the Whigs over the Democrats. In 1854 the Free-soil Party was absorbed into the new Republican Party.

freeze-out poker. No limit freeze-out poker was invented and named by legendary Walter Clyde "Puggy" Pearson (1929–2006), a Las Vegas gambler who introduced the tournament of freeze-out, now called the World Series of Poker, in which all players start with the same amount of chips and play until one player wins everything. The colorful Pearson, a member of the Poker Hall of Fame, wrote and often performed an autobiographical song called "The Roving Gambler."

French fried potatoes. Many youngsters think McDonald's invented them, but they were conceived in Belgium toward the middle of the 19th century. From there the Belgian fries spread in popularity to France, and the method of deep frying them soon imported to America, where they are still known under the misnomer *French fries*.

French toast. In America *French toast* refers to sliced bread soaked in a mixture of eggs and milk before frying the dish golden brown. In England the popular breakfast dish is simply sliced bread fried in bacon fat or butter. The French themselves make it the same way Americans do, calling it *pain perdu* ("lost bread") since the bread is "lost" in the other ingriedents.

Frisbee. *Frisbee* is the trademarked name for a plastic, concave disk used in catching games between two or more players, who spin the disk off into the air with a flick of the wrist. The disk and name are said to have been inspired by a similar game played by Yale students, who tossed about disposable metal pie tins that came from pies made by the Frisbie Pie Company of Bridgeport, Connecticut. The modern plastic Frisbee, however, is said to have been invented by William Morrison, who sold it to the Wham-O Manufacturing Company in 1955 and whose name is on the patent. Then Ed Headrick (1924–2002), head of research at Wham-O, further improved the product, changing its name from the *Pluto Platter* to *Frisbee,* a name that Wham-O says does not derive from the pie company name, despite the similarity, coming instead from a once-popular comic strip called "Mr. Frisbie." It is estimated that about 4 million people play Frisbee; no one knows how many dogs play. Just before his death Mr. Headrick told a reporter that "Frisbyterians," loyal Frisbee enthusiasts, don't go to purgatory when they die: "We just land up on the roof and lay there."

from away. Used to describe anyone residing in Maine who doesn't hail from the state. The expression is also heard on the North Fork of Long Island, New York, and can mean a summer visitor as well.

from soup to nuts. An American expression for "everything," apparently coined in the late 1920s and obviously based on the menu of a sumptuous meal or banquet at which everything from a first course of soup to a last course of nuts is served. *In the soup* is an Americanism meaning "in trouble."

from the sublime to the ridiculous. This very common expression most often means from one extreme to the other, or from the noble to the ignoble. Sometimes it is heard, erroneously, as *from the ridiculous to the sublime*. The phrase has been traced to English and American patriot Tom Paine, who wrote in *The Age of Reason* (1794–95): "The sublime and the ridiculous are often so nearly related that it is difficult to class them separately, and one step above the ridiculous makes the sublime again." Paine spent 11 months in prison in between the writing of the first two parts of his great book.

from the word go. From the start, the beginning, the very first. This lasting expression is first recorded in the autobiography *The Life and Adventures of Colonel David Crockett of West Tennessee* (1833): "I was plaguy well pleased with her from the word go."

frozen Yankee Doodle. A famous saying from brilliant American conversationalist Thomas Gold Appleton about the Boston Art Museum, torn down in 1908. Appleton said that if architecture was frozen music, this building was "frozen Yankee Doodle."

fuhgeddaboutit. The New York pronunciation of the expression *forget about it* has thanks to the movies (see *Mickey Blue Eyes)* and television (see *The Sopranos)* become well known all over the world. It is usually the equivalent of "don't mention it, it's no trouble at all," "no problem," etc., in response to a "thank you." But it can also mean "no way!" "I won't even consider it," etc.

Fulbright scholarship. A Fulbright is a scholarship grant provided under the U.S. Congress Fulbright Act (1946), which was introduced by Senator James William Fulbright (1905–1995) and has been awarded to a large number of now prominent Americans.

Fuller Brush man. Alfred C. Fuller, founder of the Fuller Brush Company, liked to quote the boosterism "'American' terminates in 'I can' and 'Dough' begins with 'Do,'" which he may have invented. Fuller, who built his door-to-door business into a $130 million enterprise, died in 1973, aged 88. At one point his ubiquitous Fuller Brush men and Fullerettes (female salesmen) called on 85 of every 100 American homes, even made home deliveries by dog sled in Alaska. These modern-day peddlers weren't welcome everywhere—some communities still have laws against any door-to-door salesmen calling without a specific invitation—but for the most part they were American favorites. Disney's big bad wolf in the *Three Little Pigs* film disguised himself as a Fuller Brush man, Red Skelton played the lead in the movie *The Fuller Brush Man,* and Lucille Ball starred in *The Fuller Brush Girl.* Fuller Brush men were the subject of about as many off-color jokes as the traveling salesman and the farmer's daughter.

Fun City. A well-known nickname for New York City said to have originated in 1966 with Mayor John V. Lindsay (1921–2001) on his first day in office when a reporter asked if he was happy he'd been elected. "I still think it's a fun city" Lindsay replied. Author Dick Schapp first capitalized the name in his *Herald Tribune* column "What's New in Fun City."

funnies. Another name for the funny papers, comic books, comics, comic strips, etc. The comics is recorded in about 1920, but may be older. Mayor Fiorello LaGuardia used to read the Sunday funnies to youngsters listening to him on the radio. See you in the funny papers used to be a humorous farewell; it even made it to the pages of Faulkner's classic *The Sound and the Fury* (1928–29).

fur-lined purgatory. A phrase coined by American poet Richard P. Blackmur (1904–65) to describe working as an editor for Henry Luce at *Time-Life* publications.

fuss and feathers. Nonsense over nothing at all. The expression dates back to the 19th century, a time when *Old Fuss and Feathers* was the nickname of U.S. general Winfield Scott, a very vain man, all 300 pounds of him. Scott, a genuine American hero and a general from the War of 1812 through the Civil War, was said to love himself, food, and wine—in that order. Dressed to the nines in his splendid self-designed gold-braided uniform and plumed hat, he was "almost a parade by himself" as he waddled down the street. As a contemporary put it: "What a wonderful mixture of gasconade, ostentation, fuss, feathers, bluster and genuine soldierly talent and courage is this same Winfield Scott." *See* GREAT SCOTT!

fuzz. Most etymologists have given up as a lost cause the derivation of *fuzz* for the police or a police officer, but here are a few suggestions for the Americanism's origin. *Fuzz,* which apparently was born in the early 1920s, may contemptuously refer to "fuzzy" lint or hair on the uniforms of police officers. It may also have originally been black slang for the hairy body of a white person, although no such usage has been documented. The *New Dictionary of American Slang* (1986) says it was first black slang for "man with the fuzzy balls," meaning a white man. *Fuzz* has to be marked "Origin Unknown."

G

gabfest. *Gabfest* is an Americanism, which like all *fest* words *(e.g.,* talk-fest, funfest) half derives from the annual family fest (from the German *Fest,* "festival") held by the German-American Turner family beginning in the mid-19th century. The *Turner fest* was the model for *gabfest,* first recorded in 1897, but *gab* had been used in England for "to talk fluently, very well, or too much." *Gab* may be an old Norse word, or may be onomatopoeic like *gabble,* and has been used since at least 1670. *Gift of gab* ("He's got a gift of gab"), the ability to talk well or convincingly, dates back to 1681 in England, while *gabby,* too, is British, first recorded in 1719.

gag rules. Gag rules restrict or prevent discussion on a particular subject by a legislative body. The term is an Americanism first recorded in 1810, though gag tactics were used as early as 1798 in Congress to try to restrict freedom of the press.

Gallup Poll. The Gallup Poll is the best known, though not the first, public-opinion poll. It was originated by Dr. George Horace Gallup (b. 1901), a professor of journalism at Northwestern University. Gallup developed his technique about 1933, basing it on carefully phrased questions and scientifically selected samples. He became prominent nationally by predicting the outcome of the 1936 American presidential election, when many other pollsters failed. His poll, operating both at home and abroad, has proved remarkably accurate but is far from infallible. In the 1948 national elections, for example, Gallup chose the late Governor Thomas E. Dewey over incumbent President Truman.

gamble away the sun before sunrise. This saying about gold and riches might be considered the first American proverb, though it isn't recorded in *Bartlett's* or any other book of quotations. The expression surely is old enough, dating back to 1533, when Pizarro conquered Cuzco, the capital of the Inca Empire, and stripped the Peruvian metropolis of gold and silver. One cavalryman got as his share of the booty a splendid golden image of the sun "which raised on a plate of burnished gold spread over the walls in a recess of the great temple" and which was so beautifully crafted that he did not have it melted down into coins, as was the usual practice. But the horseman came to symbolize the vice of gambling. That same night, before the sun had set on another day, he lost the fabulous golden image of the sun at cards or dice, and his comrades coined the saying *Juega el Sol antes que amanezca:* "He gambles (or plays) away the sun before sunrise," which crossed the ocean from America on Pizarro's gold-laden galleons and became proverbial in Spain.

gandy dancer. There are several theories about this term for a railroad construction worker, which is immortalized in the song "The Gandy Dancer's Ball." One says *gandy dancer* is an American hobo term for fellow tramps who helped build the transcontinental railroad. Another claims the expression comes from the gander-like movements of these men as they worked, while a third and most probable theory opts for Chicago's Gandy Manufacturing Co., which made prominently marked track-laying tools used by the workers.

gangbuster. H. L. Mencken said, "Gang-buster was launched in 1935 to describe Thomas E. Dewey (a prominent New York district attorney who prosecuted organized crime and later became governor and an unsuccessful Republican candidate for president). The radio program *Gangbusters,* introduced in 1936, popularized the term, and it has since been applied to any law enforcement officer engaged in breaking up gangs. *To do gangbusters* is to be very successful, as in "The show did gangbusters," or "The book sold like gangbusters," while *come on like gangbusters* means to approach something very aggressively and energetically, like the opening of a *Gangbuster* radio program with its machine guns, sirens, etc.

Garden State. A nickname for New Jersey, which has had an abundance of nicknames, including the Jersey Blue State, New Spain, the Clam State, and even, strangely, the Switzerland of America (which mountainous New Hampshire has also been called). In the late 19th century New Jersey was known as the Mosquito State, though its mosquitos are no match for Alaska's.

Garrison finish. Holding Montana back from the pack until they came into the homestretch, "Snapper" Garrison suddenly stood high in the stirrups, bending low over the horse's mane in his famous "Yankee seat" and whipped the mount toward the finish line, moving up with a rush and winning the 1882 Suburban Handicap by a nose. This race made jockey Edward H. Garrison an American turf hero. Garrison, who died in 1931, aged 70, used his new technique many times over his long career, winning many of his races in the last furlong, and the Garrison finish became so well-known that it was applied to any close horse race, finally becoming synonymous with all last-minute efforts—in sports, politics, or any other field.

Gate City. A nickname now or in the past for several cities, including Atlanta and Louisville, because they are each situated at the entrance to a region. Atlanta is also called the Gate City of the South.

Gatling gun. The Gatling gun won fame as the best of the 11 mostly eponymous Civil War machine guns (including the Ripley; the Ager "Coffee Mill"; the Claxon; the Gorgas; and the Williams, which, when used by the Confederates on May 3, 1862, became the first machine gun to be fired in warfare). Designed by Doctor Richard Jordan Gatling (1818–1903), a North Carolina physician and inventor, the Gatling was perfected by 1862 but adopted by Union forces too late to be used in more than a few battles. Mounted on wheels, it had a cluster of 5 to 10 barrels that revolved around a central shaft. The gunner, by turning a hand crank, controlled the rate of fire, up to 350 rounds per minute. Despite the weapon's late introduction, the Gatling's effective range of 2,000 yards had a strong psychological effect on the Confederacy; adopted by many nations after the Civil War, it remained in use until about 1900. Although the weapon is of only historical importance today, as the precursor of the modern machine gun, another word deriving from it has wide currency. *Gat,* a slang term for a small gun, apparently arose as a humorous exaggeration. By 1880, however, fictional characters were talking of having gatlins under their coats and it wasn't long before *gatlin,* or *gatling,* was shortened to *gat.*

gee! An American euphemism for "Jesus!" *gee!* dates back to only 1895. Its antecedents are *jewillikin* (1851); *gee whillikins!* (1857); *gee whiz!* (1895); *gee whitaker!* (1895); and *holy gee!* Since then we have had *jeez!* (1900); *jeepers!* (1920s); and *jeepers creepers!* (1934).

Gentlemen prefer blondes. *Gentlemen Prefer Blondes* (1925) was the title of the Anita Loos (1893–1981) novel, but the words in the text were, "Gentlemen always seem to remember blondes." Her famous book, made into a play and movie, had such diverse admirers as James Joyce, George Santayana, Mussolini, and Churchill, and was written as a spoof of her good friend Mencken's taste for "dumb blondes." Loos herself was a brunette and wrote a sequel to her book, *But Gentlemen*

Marry Brunettes (1926), among over a hundred books and screenplays, including her script for D. W. Griffith's masterpiece *Intolerance*. She considered Hollywood a "mink-lined rut," and, as for men, "always believed in the old adage, 'Leave them while you're looking good.'"

Geronimo! Chiricahua Apache leader Geronimo is said to have made a daring leap on horseback to escape U.S. cavalry pursuers at Medicine Bluffs, Oklahoma. As he leaped to freedom down a steep cliff and into a river below he supposedly cried out his name in defiance of the troopers. There is no mention of this incident in the great warrior and prophet's autobiography, which he dictated to a white writer before his death under military confinement at Fort Sill, Oklahoma, in 1909. But by that time Geronimo was an old man, well over 70, and had converted to the Dutch Reformed Church; little remained of the brave leader who in protecting his people's land against white settlers had terrorized the American Southwest and northern Mexico with cunning, brutal raids and whose actions became western legend. The cry *Geronimo!* is part of that legend and was adopted as the battle cry of American paratroopers leaping from their planes in World War II. The 82nd Airborne at Fort Bragg, North Carolina first used it, taking it either from the oral legend about Geronimo or from the popular movie featuring the Indian warrior, showing near the paratrooper training center at the time.

gerrymander. Above editor Benjamin Russell's desk in the offices of the *Centinel,* a Massachusetts Federalist newspaper, hung the serpentine-shaped map of a new Essex County senatorial district that began at Salisbury and included Amesbury, Haverhill, Methuen, Andover, Middleton, Danvers, Lynnfield, Salem, Marblehead, Lynn, and Chelsea. This political monster was part of a general reshaping of voting districts that the Democratic-Republican-controlled state legislature had enacted with the approval of incumbent Governor

Elbridge Gerry. The arbitrary redistricting would have happily enabled the Jeffersonians to concentrate Federalist power in a few districts and remain in the majority after the then yearly gubernatorial elections of 1812, and was of course opposed by the Federalists. So when the celebrated painter Gilbert Stuart visited the *Centinel* offices one day before the elections, editor Russell indignantly pointed to the monstrous map on the wall, inspiring Stuart to take a crayon and add head, wings, and claws to the already lizard-shaped district. "That will do for a salamander," the artist said when he had finished. "A *Gerry*-mander, you mean," Russell replied, and a name for the political creature was born, *gerrymander* coming into use as a verb within a year.

get a horse! A phrase from the early age of the automobile in the U.S. when motor cars were often mired in ditches or chugged slowly down the street, and people, especially children, would shout "get a horse!" to the motorists manning them. The phrase is not obsolete as some writers have it. I have heard it directed at runners or joggers several times in the last few years—mostly by children.

get lost. U.S. servicemen brought this native expression with them overseas during World War II. It means "get out of here, get off my back, don't bother me."

get more bang for the buck. These words, frequently heard today, have nothing to do with sex and ladies of the night, as has been suggested, although *bang* is slang for copulate. The expression means to get more value for your money and was apparently coined by President Dwight Eisenhower's defense secretary, Charles E. Wilson, in applauding a policy aiming for "more basic [national] security at less cost." Wilson's words were more exactly, "a bigger bang for the buck," and *bang* here means "firepower," not sex. More details can be found in William Safire's *The New Language of Politicians* (1968).

get one's dander up. Many of the early Yankee humorists—Seba Smith, Charles Davis, Thomas Haliburton—used this Americanism for "to get angry," and it is found in the *Life of Davy Crockett.* It is one of those expressions with a handful of plausible explanations. The most amusing is that the *dander* in the phrase is an English dialect form of *dandruff* that was used in the Victorian era; someone with his dander up, according to this theory, would be wrathfully tearing up his hair by the fistful, dandruff flying in the process. Another likely source is the West Indian *dander,* for a ferment used in the preparation of molasses, which would suggest a rising ferment of anger. The Dutch *donder,* "thunder," has also been nominated, for it is used in the Dutch phrase *op donderon,* "to burst into a sudden rage." And then there is the far-fetched theory that *dander* is a telescoped form of "damned anger." And if these aren't enough, we have the possibilities that *dander* comes from an English dialect word for "anger"; from the Scots *danders,* for "hot embers"; and from the Romany *dander,* "to bite."

get one's ducks in a row. American bowling alleys were the first to introduce duck pins, short slender bowling pins unlike the rotund pins that the English used. Pin boys who set up these pins (before the advent of automatic bowling machines) had the job of getting their ducks in a row. Soon the expression *I've got my ducks in a row* was being used by anyone who had completed any arrangements.

getty. Pronounced JET-ee. An old term for a streetcorner organ grinder, usually one with a monkey trained to collect coins thrown by the audience. Sometimes the getty's monkey would climb up the apartment windows to get the coins. Today the term is mainly remembered in an old song "The Sidewalks of New York": "And the getty plays the organ on the sidewalks of New York."

Gettysburg Address. *See* FOURSCORE AND SEVEN.

gimme a dope. *Gimme a dope* still means "give me a Coca-Cola" in the southern U.S., especially among teenagers. This isn't recent slang, but dates back to the late 19th century, when the fabled soft drink was touted as a tonic and contained a minute amount of cocaine.

give 'em hell. Harry Truman and his supporters didn't originate this Americanism during the Presidential election of 1948. The expression has been traced back to the early 19th century and has military origins. In 1851 it was recorded in *Harper's Magazine:* "At daybreak old Rily shouted, 'Forward and give them h-ll!'" Four years earlier, during the Battle of Buena Vista in the Mexican War, General Zachary Taylor had exhorted his men to "Give 'em hell!" after the enemy launched a fierce attack.

give me liberty or give me death. The full quotation from Patrick Henry in the 1775 Virginia provincial convention was supposedly, "Is life so dear, or peace so sweet, as to be purchased at the price of chains and slavery? Forbid it, Almighty God! I know not what course others may take, but as for me, give me liberty or give me death." The last seven words constitute the first quotation millions of American schoolchildren have learned over the past two centuries, but there is no record that Patrick Henry ever spoke them, and they may have been invented by Henry's biographer William Wirt 41 years later. The whole matter is discussed in Bill Bryson's *Made In America* (1994), which makes reference to learned papers on the subject.

give my regards to Broadway. This catchphrase comes from George M. Cohan's song "Give My Regards to Broadway," which was first performed in Cohan's play *Little Johnny Jones.*

give someone the gate. *Giving someone the gate,* "firing him, showing him the door," has been American slang since at least 1921, when it first appeared in print. There is some precedent for it, however, in the old English phrase *to give or grant the gate to,* that is, to let someone pass through the castle gate and out to the road, which the *O.E.D.* traces back to 1440. The American term is of course negative, but ironic use of the earlier *give the gate to* could have inspired it.

glare ice. A term used mostly in the northeastern U.S. for a sheet of smooth, very slippery ice, which is also called "a glare of ice." It is probably called "glare" because of its intense shining.

glittering generalities. American attorney Rufus Choate (1799–1859) coined this term for cliches, empty words, and platitudes in a letter to a friend about the Declaration of Independence: "the glittering and sounding generalities of natural rights which make up the Declaration of Independence." Less well-known, but truer, is Ralph

Waldo Emerson's remark when he heard of Choate's coinage: "Glittering generalities! They are blazing ubiquities!"

G-man. In about 1932 the name *G-man* originated in the underworld for special agents of the Department of Justice, Division of Investigation, who had been organized since 1908. Criminals meant government men when they coined *G-men,* which the newspapers and the movies quickly adopted. *Feds, Dee Jays* and *Whiskers* (for Uncle Sam's Agents) were other names G-men were called by, the last two designations obsolete today.

G.O.A.T. An acronym for "Greatest of All Time," a company owned by former heavyweight champion Muhammad Ali. Ali recently sold 80 percent of the marketing rights to his name for $50 million.

goatee. The style of chin whiskers cut in the form of a tuft like that of a he-goat apparently became popular in mid-19th-century America, when the word *goatee* is first recorded. *Goatee* simply means "little goat" and the Americanism is first recorded in 1842 as *goaty. Billygoat beard* or *billygoat whiskers* means the same and is first recorded in the mid-1880s.

goat meat. An American euphemism for venison, deer hunted and killed out of the legal hunting season. There are several synonyms, including *goat mutton.*

gob. The U.S. Navy banned the use of *gob* for a sailor in the early 1920s, claiming it was undignified. Like most such com-stockery, the ban on *gob* failed, but the navy might have been right about its lack of dignity, considering the word's possible origins. *Gob*, first recorded in 1909, probably comes either from *gobble*, an allusion to the way many sailors reputedly ate, or from the word *gob*, for "spit," in reference to English coast guardsmen who were called *gobbies* in the past because they were in the habit of expectorating so much. Little better is the suggestion that the word is from the Irish *gob*, "mouth," as in the expression *shut your gob*. Sailors might then have been compared to "big mouths" or something similar.

gobbledygook. *Gobbledygook* means obscure, verbose, bureaucratic language characterized by circumlocution and jargon, and usually refers to the meaningless officialese turned out by government agencies. The late Representative Maury Maverick coined the word in 1944 when he was chairman of the Smaller War Plant Committee in Congress. Maverick had just attended a meeting of the committee, at which phrases such as "cause an investigation to be made with a view to ascertaining" were rife. He wrote a memo condemning such officialese and labeled it *gobbledygook*, later explaining that he was thinking of the gobbling of turkeys while they strutted pompously. BAFFLEGAB, JARGANTUAN, PUDDER, and PENTAGONESE are all synonyms. George Orwell's "translation" of Lord Nelson's immortal phrase "England expects every man to do his duty" is a good example of gobbledygook: "England anticipates that, as regards the current emergency, personnel will face up to the issues, and exercise appropriately the functions allocated to their respective occupational groups."

"God Bless America." American composer Irving Berlin, who emigrated with his parents from Russia to the U.S. when five years old, wrote the unofficial American national anthem while serving in the army during World War I at Camp Upton in Yaphank, a Long Island, New York, farm town. Berlin wrote the song for the benefit musical revue *Yip, Yip, Yaphank,* which was performed entirely by soldiers, but he felt the lyrics were too solemn for the show and filed it away. In 1938, when singer Kate Smith requested a song for her popular radio program, he suggested "God Bless America," and it became an American classic before World War II to the present-day war on terrorism. Berlin, who died in 1989 at 101, donated all the song's millions in royalties to the Boy Scouts. The seldom sung first verse of the song goes: "While the storm clouds gather, far across the sea/Let us swear allegiance to a land that's free/Let us all be grateful for a land so fair/As we raise our voices in solemn prayer." *See* AMERICA THE BEAUTIFUL, AMERICA; STARS AND STRIPES, STAR-SPANGLED BANNER; YANKEE DOODLE DANDY.

God should be allowed to just watch the game. The great entertainer Yogi Berra is supposed to have made this remark from behind the plate after watching Chicago White Sox batter Minnie Minoso appeal for divine intervention by drawing a cross in the dust on home plate. The story has become sports legend, but syndicated columnist William Safire recently contacted the former Yankee catcher and Yogi denied he ever said it. Yogiisms Yogi hasn't denied include "I've been playing 18 years and you can observe a lot by watching" (on his managerial abilities); "He can run anytime he wants—I'm giving him the red light" (on giving a player permission to steal a base); and the much-quoted "It ain't over till it's over."

go fly a kite. Get out of here, go away, stop bothering me, go to hell, get lost. Still heard, though not so often as it once was. The expression may be older but is first recorded in a 1928 number of the *Saturday Evening Post.*

go for broke. Make your greatest effort. Now widely used in all the United States, it is a Hawaiian expression that began its English life as the World War II slogan of the 42nd Regimental Combat Team.

go for the long ball. This contemporary American slang means to take a big risk for a big gain. It does not come from baseball but from football, referring to long desperate passes made in the last minutes of a game.

going fishing. A baseball term, dating back at least to the 1930s, for a batter who swings at bad pitches out of the strike zone that he should take as balls, usually pitches high and outside. *Fishing trip* is a synonym.

going . . . going . . . gone. Any New York Yankee fan of the 1950s will remember this phrase, which became the trademark of Yankee radio announcer Mel Allen (1913–96) in describing a home run or a hit in the process of becoming a home run. Just as well known were the native Alabamian's words *How 'bout that?*, a comment about how pleasing or depressing or dramatic something was.

going like 60. In 1860 a terrible drought in the Missouri and Arkansas valleys devastated that part of the country, lasting more than a year. Some tracers of lost word origins believe that the memory of the drought was so vivid that people began linking the year 1860 with extremes of any kind. But the drought could only have reinforced and possibly accelerated the meaning of the popular expression *going like 60,* for it was used by James Russell Lowell in his *Biglow Papers* in 1848 ("Though like sixty all along I fumed an' fussed") and was recorded in an early 1860 slang dictionary as "[to go] at a good rate, briskly."

Perhaps 60 is used simply to express a large number, as an abbreviation of "like 60 miles an hour," or something similar. "Forty" was used in this way at least since Shakespeare's *Coriolanus* (1607), and in *Uncle Tom's Cabin* (1852) a character says: "I has principles and I stick to them like forty."

goldbrick. Con men working Western mining properties toward the end of the 19th century sometimes sold gullible investors lead or iron bricks coated with gold paint, representing them as the real thing. One Patrick Burke of St. Louis is recorded as having paid $3,700 for such a "gold" brick in 1887. This all-too-common confidence scheme gave the name *goldbrick* to any swindle or fakery. Later, soldiers picked up the expression and used the phrase *to goldbrick* in its present meaning of avoiding work or shirking duty. The phrase is first recorded in 1914 in this sense, applied to army lieutenants appointed from civilian life.

gold digger. Long before gold digger meant a mercenary woman, a use first recorded in 1915, it signified a miner in California gold fields such as Jackass Gulf, Puke Ravine, Greenhorn Canyon, and Rattlesnake Bar. In fact, the term *gold digger,* for a miner, is recorded in 1830 during America's first gold rush, which took place in northern Georgia. It was gold diggers of the most mercenary kind that a humorous Western song referred to in one of its verses:

> "The miners came in '49
> The whores in '51
> And when they got together
> They produced the native son."

golden parachute. A contract guaranteeing a company executive very generous benefits, including severance pay, if one loses a job because the company is sold or merged. The American term is first recorded in 1981 but is actually an offshoot of the earlier British golden handshake, which dates back to 1960 and means essentially the same, except that the golden parachute is contractual.

Golden State. A nickname for California since Gold Rush days a century and a half ago. It has also been called El Dorado and the Bear State, after its grizzly bears.

Goldwynism. "Include me out," "In two words: impossible," and "We have passed a lot of water since then" (for "a lot of water has passed under the bridge") are but three legendary Goldwynisms. An American film pioneer, Samuel Goldwyn has long been considered a modern "Mr. Malaprop," unrivaled for his fractured English. Goldwyn, born in Warsaw, Poland, on August 27, 1882, founded Goldwyn Pictures Corporation, which became part of Metro-Goldwyn-Mayer in 1924, and later turned independent producer. He died in 1974. No doubt many of the thousands of Goldwynisms attributed to him—word manglings, mixed metaphors, malapropisms, grammatical blunders, and the like—were invented by press agents, writers, friends, and enemies. But genuine or not, they became part of the legend surrounding the man.

gone today, here tomorrow. This twist on the old saw "here today, gone tomorrow" is attributed to the publisher Alfred Knopf (1892–1984). He was talking about book returns from bookstores.

good for you! An American expression of approval or congratulations since at least 1861. It is equivalent to *well done!* or *well said!* Sometimes the variation *good on you!* is used.

Good Gray Poet. We Americans haven't bestowed affectionate sobriquets on many of our poets, but Walt Whitman (1819–92), surely our greatest poet, is an exception. Whitman was given the name Good Gray Poet by William Douglas O'Connor, who used the words as the title of his 1866 book, which was written in defense of his friend Whitman when the poet was fired from his clerkship in the Indian Bureau of the Department of the Interior on the grounds that his poetry collection *Leaves of Grass* was immoral. Much later, Whitman wrote the preface for his friend's *Three Tales,* which was published posthumously in 1892 and included a story called "The Carpenter," a Christ-like portrait of the poet. In his old age, with his full flowing gray beard, Whitman seemed more the Good Gray Poet than ever.

goodnighting. Students of the old West may be aware that bulls on long cattle drives often suffered from chaffing of the testicles, which frequently swelled so large that the animal sickened and died. The remedy was to cut off the testicle bag, push the testicles up into the body and sew the cut—a process that enabled the bulls to travel well and did not impair their breeding. This remedy was called goodnighting, after cattleman Charles Goodnight, who invented it, and is surely among the most unusual of words named after people.

good ole boy. Though it is used nationally now, a *good ole boy* is still generally a white southern male exemplifying the masculine ideals of the region; any amiable southerner, provided he likes guns, hunting, fishing, drinking, football, and women, in roughly that order; or a loyal southerner, rich or poor, devoted to all things southern. The term had popular use in the mid-1960s. Said the late Billy Carter, President Jimmy Carter's brother, of the good ole boy: "A good ole boy . . . is somebody that rides around in a pickup truck . . . and drinks beer and throws 'em out the window." *(Redneck Power: The Wit and Wisdom of Billy Carter,* 1977.) Perhaps older than *good ole boy* is the little-heard *good ole rebel,* which derives from a song entitled "Good Old Rebel" written by Innes Randolph in the 1870s: "I am a good old rebel—/ Yes, that's just what I am—/ And for this land of freedom/ I do not give a damn. I'm glad I fit agin 'em/ And I only wish we'd won;/ And I don't ax no pardon/ For anything I've done." Hemingway uses *good ole boy* in *A Farewell to Arms* (1929): "You're a good old boy," the author says to his friend Captain Rinaldi.

good-time Charlie; good-time girl. *Good-time Charlie* refers to an affable, sociable, convivial man, the term perhaps coined by that great American word inventor T. A. Dorgan *(see* HOT DOG), who first used it in 1927, probably before anyone else. Not long after this, in 1928, the term *good-time girl* is first recorded. It usually describes a convivial young woman who is looking to have a good time, to play, anything for a laugh, much the same as a good-time Charlie.

goof off; goofy. Goofing off, "wasting time," originated in the U.S. armed forces during World War II. It implies shirking like a silly or goofy person, a *goof,* which word derives from the English dialect word *goff,* "a simpleton," first recorded in 1570.

goon. Alice the Goon, a big stupid creature who appeared in E. C. Segar's comic strip "Popeye, the Thimble Theatre" in the late 1930s, gave her name to both stupid people called goons and the big stupid thugs called goons. Segar (1894–1938) may have fashioned the name from the 1895 slang term *goony,* for "a simpleton," but he could also have blended *g*orilla and bab*oon* or even *g*oof and bab*oon.*

go out on a limb. To go out on a limb is to take a chance, to make a chancy prediction, as in "I'll go out on a limb and say he'll win in a landslide." The expression is an Americanism dating back to the later 19th century; the word *limb* is of course a tree limb.

go over big. To become a big success, a great hit. Apparently the expression is from the world of entertainment. Its first mention in print suggests this: "A comedy that 'goes over big' and is very funny is often referred to as a 'wow.'" (*American Speech* 10/21/27).

G.O.P.; G.O.P stands for *G*rand *O*ld *P*arty, the official nickname of the U.S. Republican Party. First used in 1887, when it also meant "get out and push" (your own horse or car).

go peddle your papers. Far more common today than 50 years ago, this American expression has a variety of meanings depending on the situation it is used in, including go away, get lost, be a good guy and leave, go away before you get hurt, mind your own business, leave us alone, etc.

Gopher State. The most popular nickname for Minnesota, though it prefers the North Star State and the motto *L'Étoilei du Nord* is on its state shield. It has also been called the Bread and Butter State, the Bread Basket of the Nation, the Wheat State, the Cream and Pitcher of the Nation, and the Playground of the Nation.

Gordon Bennett! James Gordon Bennett (1841–1918), the son of the founder of the *New York Herald*, was an eccentric who ran the paper well but had little or no regard for money. Once he gave a train guard a $14,000 tip. Another time he threw a batch of money into a roaring fireplace to watch it burn but became angry and flung the bills back into the flames when a young man tried to salvage them. When he found someone seated at his favorite table in a Monte Carlo restaurant, he bought the place for $40,000, evicted the diners, sat down to eat—and when he left gave the restaurant back to its original owners as a tip. Bennett had a thing for restaurants. As he strolled through them to his reserved table, he liked to yank tablecloths off all the tables in his way. He'd then hand the head-waiter a large wad of cash to distribute to the disturbed and stained diners. He did this so often that the expression *Gordon Bennett!* became (and remains, in England) a cry of anyone soiled by a clumsy waiter.

go someone one better. A common American expression today, *to go someone one better* means to exceed the performance of someone else. It began life as a poker term (which it still is) in the early 19th century, meaning to raise the bet one more chip over someone who has bet before you.

Gotham. Washington Irving first called New York Gotham in his *Salmagundi Papers* (1807), because its residents reminded him of the legendary inhabitants of the English town of Gotham. An old tale has it that these villagers had discouraged King John from building a castle in their town, and taxing them for it, by feigning madness—trying to drown fish, sweep the moon's reflection off the waters, etc. This legend led to more stories about the villagers, collected in a book called *Merrie Tales of the Mad Men of Gotham*, and Irving, reading of these alternately wise and foolish people, thought that they resembled New Yorkers.

go west, young man, go west. In America *go west* came to stand for new life and hope instead of death with the expansion of the frontier. There is some controversy about who said *go west, young man* first, however. Horace Greeley used the expression in an editorial in his *New York Tribune:* "Go west, young man, and grow with the country." Later, as the phrase grew in popularity, Greeley said that his inspiration was John Babsone Lane Soule, who wrote "Go West, young man" in an 1851 article in the *Terre Haute Express.* Greeley even reprinted Soule's article from the Indiana newspaper to give credit where it was due, but several writers insisted that Greeley had given them identical advice before Soule had written the piece. William S. Verity said that the great editor had coined the expression a full year before Soule.

go while the going's good. Bogart says this to Hepburn in their film *The African Queen* (1951) while trying to persuade her to leave Africa where World War I German troops are brutally expelling all others. Those infamous leeches that were all over Bogart in their escape were only rubber and were stuck to Bogey with waterproof glue. Each "leech" contained a small "blood sac" that broke when peeled off.

grace under pressure. This phrase is often attributed to American president John F. Kennedy, but it was really author Ernest Hemingway's coinage and credo. JFK borrowed the expression from Hemingway.

graft. This American term for dishonest earnings, usually of politicians, isn't recorded until 1859. Its origins are unclear, but the word may derive from the British slang *graft,* for "any kind of work, especially illicit work," which, in turn, may come from the British *graer,* "to dig," influenced, Partridge says, by the gardening *graft.* The gardening *graft* derives, ultimately, from the Greek word *grapheion,* "a bone or wood pencil-like instrument used for writing on wax tablets." Someone in early times possibly thought that a *grapheion* resembled a twig for grafting.

Graham crackers, etc. Young Presbyterian minister Sylvester Graham (1794–851) became so ardent a temperance advocate that he not only traveled far and wide to lecture on the demon rum, but invented a vegetable diet that he was sure would cure those suffering from the evils of drink. Graham soon extended his mission to include changing America's sinful eating habits. Meats and fats, he said, led to sexual excesses and mustard and catsup could cause insanity, but Graham mainly urged the substitution of homemade unsifted whole wheat flour for white flour. Modern science has affirmed his belief that refining flour robs it of vitamins and minerals, and most of his regimen, including vegetables and fruits in the diet, fresh air while sleeping, moderate eating, and abundant exercise, is now widely accepted. His memorials are the *Graham flour, Graham bread,* and *Graham crackers* that his followers ate and dedicated to him.

grand. *Grand* for a thousand dollars is American slang that dates back to at least 1900, and is probably so named because it is "a grand sum of money." *Grand* was abbreviated to a *G* or a *G-note* within 20 years or so. An older term for a thousand dollars is a *thou,* first recorded in 1869 and still used; a newer term meaning the same is *a big one,* which seems to have been coined about 50 years ago, about the time that *large* for a thousand dollars is first recorded.

grandbaby. A common term for a grandchild that dates back to at least 1916; heard recently (1991) from a southern woman in the Empire State Building in New York City, of all places: "I got three grandbabies down home." *Grand boy* is a male grandbaby.

Grand Ole Opry. The Grand Ole Opry is "the oldest continuously live" U.S. radio program. Debuting on Nashville, Tennessee's, WSM radio on November 28, 1925, it quickly became the most famous of all such country and western formats. Today, the Grand Ole Opry is an entertainment complex, drawing hundred of thousands of people to see live shows.

The Granite State. A nickname for New Hampshire. The state's granite industry, storytellers say, was established as a result of locals drilling for salt. In 1827 citizens drilled hole after hole searching for the precious condiment, only to give it up as a bad job upon striking layer after layer of granite. Soon after, they decided to mine the granite.

the grapevine. Some 15 years after Samuel Morse transmitted his famous "what hath God wrought" message, a long telegraph line was strung from Virginia City to Placerville, California, so crudely strung, it's said, that people jokingly compared the line with a sagging grapevine. I can find no record of this, but, in any case, grapevines were associated with telegraph lines somewhere along the line, for by the time of the Civil War a report *by grapevine telegraph* was common slang for a rumor. The idea behind the expression is probably not rumors sent over real telegraph lines, but the telegraphic speed with which rumormongers can transmit canards with their own rude mouth-to-mouth telegraph system.

grass roots. "A little classic of the poetic imagination," the *New York Times* once called this phrase, but whose "poetic imagination" we don't know. In 1935, when the Republican Party was seeking a broader base of support among the voters, John Hamilton of Topeka, Kansas used the words in describing the "new" G.O.P. No one has traced the phrase back further in print, but one respected etymologist has testified that he heard the expression back in rural Ohio in about 1885. A term dear to politicians, it simply means to get down to basic facts or underlying principles, its appeal becoming more nostalgic as more concrete replaces grass. *Grass roots* itself, for "basics, fundamentals," has been traced to 1932 when used, appropriately enough, to describe the candidacy of Oklahoma Governor William H. ("Alfalfa Bill") Murray for the Democratic presidential nomination. It, too, probably stems from the prairie farms of the West.

Great American Desert. The idea of a Great American Desert in the West discouraged many people from settling in the region, which they thought was uninhabitable. The term *Great American Desert* was used in newspapers and geographies as early as 1834. Before this, the area, which is part of the Great Plains, was called the Great Desert, this term recorded 50 years earlier.

The Great American Novel. This term sprang up toward the end of the 19th century. Frank Norris wrote: "The Great American Novel is not extinct like the Dodo, but mythical like the Hippogriff . . . the thing to be looked for is not the Great American Novelist, but the Great Novelist who shall also be American." Observed Jack London a little later: "I'd rather win a water-fight in a swimming pool, or remain astride a horse that is trying to get out from under me, than write the great American novel."

great balls of fire! This very popular exclamation was inspired by the legendary rock-and-roll singer Jerry Lee Lewis's song "Great Balls of Fire!" and the movie suggested by the song. Jerry Lee Lewis (b. 1935) is a U.S. country-western and rock-and-roll singer. *The great balls of fire* exclamation dates, however, to the 19th century.

Great Communicator. A name in praise of Ronald Wilson Reagan (b. 1911), celebrated for his skills in dealing with people. The former movies and television star served as U.S. president from 1981–89. Reagan died in 2004, age 93, the longest lived U.S. president. He did like the title *The Great Communicator*, yet in his speeches he delivered many memorable lines, including his description of the then Soviet Union as the evil empire. Shortly after being shot by assassin John W. Hinckley Jr. in 1981, he told his wife, in spite of great pain, "Honey, I forgot to duck" (really a Jack Dempsey quip on losing the heavyweight championship), and quipped to surgeons about to operate on him: "Please tell me you're Republicans [his own party]." In Germany Reagan urged Soviet leader Mikhail Gorbachev to destroy the Berlin Wall between

East and West: "Mr. Gorbachev, tear down this wall!" Later, after the Berlin Wall came tumbling down, a 6,000-pound section of it was sent to Reagan for his presidential library, where it can be seen today.

Great Depression. The greatest economic depression began with the U.S. stock market collapse in 1929, which dropped the Dow Jones average to its all-time low of 41.22 in 1932. In 1929 the Dow stood at 381.7, while today it is close to 13,000.

the Greatest. A nickname of Muhammad Ali, world heavyweight boxing champion in 1964. "I am the greatest!" Ali usee to say, "I am the prettiest," etc., etc. But the champ always acknowledged it was the flamboyant wrestler Gorgeous George who coined the words.

greatest show on earth. See THERE'S A SUCKER BORN EVERY MINUTE.

the Great Lakes. Lakes Erie, Huron, Michigan, Ontario, and Superior are between the United States and Canada. These connected lakes, containing the world's largest freshwater area, are joined with the Atlantic Ocean by the St. Lawrence Seaway.

Great Scott! Old Fuss-and-Feathers, General Winfield Scott, a brigadier general at only 28, was well known for his arrogant swagger, and his opponents may have jeeringly dubbed him "Great Scott" with this in mind. On the other hand, the hero of the Mexican War and the Whig candidate for president in 1852 wasn't the only Scottophile in the country—his many supporters may have named him "Great Scott" in admiration of his great dignity. At any rate, the exclamation *Great Scott!* hasn't been traced back before Old Fuss-and-Feathers' day and he could certainly have been responsible for the expression in one way or another. That the term is just a euphemism for "Great God!," a play on the German *Gott,* is a simpler but not necessarily truer explanation.

the great unwashed. In 1901 the *Congressional Record* noted that "the Democratic Party has long been known as the 'great unwashed.'" By then the epithet was at least 50 years old. *The great unwashed* is still heard today occasionally in reference to what the speaker believes are "the lower classes," but is not applied to the Democrats. In the late 18th century the British had called the rabble of the French Revolution the great unwashed.

Great White Hope. *See* JACK JOHNSON.

The Great White Way. This nickname for the Manhattan theatrical or entertainment district, a reference to all the lights there, was coined by Albert Bigelow Paine, best known today as Mark Twain's first biographer, and used as the title of his novel *The Great White Way* (1901), which is about the Antarctic, not Broadway.

Green Berets. Another name for the U.S. Special Forces, which are the core of the American Special Operations Community. These elite troops are named for the dashing green berets they wear as part of their uniform and are thought to number over 10,000. They are trained mainly at the U.S. Army John Kennedy Special Warfare Center and School at Fort Bragg, North Carolina ("The Schoolhouse"), especially in guerrilla fighting. The first Green Berets were advisers to the South Vietnamese army in the early 1960s. *Green Beanies* is a derogatory or humorous term for the Green Berets.

greenmail. Patterned on *blackmail*, which it strictly is, *greenmail* was coined on Wall Street in 1983, *green* suggested by the color of U.S. currency. When one company buys enough shares in another to threaten a takeover, the "greenmail" company is forced to buy the shares back at a higher price to avoid that possibility.

Green Mountain State. A nickname for Vermont first recorded in 1838 but suggested by *Green Mountain Boy*, a Vermont inhabitant, which goes back to 1772 when a militia of Green Mountain Boys was organized to protect the state's boundary lines.

Green Revolution. U.S. agronomist Norman E. Borlaug (b. 1914) is widely regarded as the father of the Green Revolution, a 1960s expression meaning increased and diversified crop yields in countries that could barely feed their own.

green rot. Descriptive American slang from Civil War times that is a synonym for gangrene, as is mortification. Green rot is so-called because the skin is first pale but becomes red or bronze and finally is green in color. It was common on the battlefields.

Greenwich Village. A lower Manhattan district of New York famous as a literary and artistic community since the early 20th century—earlier than that if one considers that Thomas Paine wrote *The Crisis* there and that Edgar Allan Poe lived in the Village for a time. It's called the Village because it was a separate village through the colonial period and into the early 19th century.

grin and bear it A phrase meaning to put up with things. Once very popular thanks to a U.S. cartoon with the same title. A grin is a broad smile, the word dating back to before 1000.

Grinch. A nasty, miserly, Scrooge-like person. Taken from the name of the character in the popular children's book *How the Grinch Stole Christmas* by Dr. Seuss (Theodor Seuss Geisel, 1904–94).

gringo. Many scholars trace this disparaging term for an American to the Spanish *gringo*, "gibberish," which is a corruption of the Spanish word *Griego*, "a Greek." *Gringo*, by this theory, would be related to the old saying "It's all Greek to me," indicating that the Yankees were strange and unfamiliar in their ways to the Mexicans who so named them. But we haven't exhausted all the conjectures by any means. Another etymologist boldly claims "green coat" as the base for *gringo*, and a second theory says that the first two words of the Robert Burns lyric "Green grow the rashes O," a song sung by American soldiers in the Mexican War, is the origin of the contemptuous word—somehow one can't imagine battle-hardened veterans riding along singing: "Green grow the rashes O/ The happiest hours that ere I spent/ Were spent among the lasses O!" If the "gibberish" theory is to be challenged, the most likely contender is Major Samuel Ringgold, a brilliant strategist dreaded by the Mexicans during the Mexican War until he was killed at the Battle of Palo Alto in 1846. Ringgold's name, pronounced with a trilled r and without the last two letters as it normally would be by a Mexican, might yet prove the correct source for the word.

grizzly bear. This fearsome bear has also been called the *silvertop*, because the ends of its hair are silver gray; the *mulebear*, because early prospectors thought it found their mules especially tasty; and *Moccasin Joe*, because its footprints somewhat resemble those of a man wearing moccasins. Indians in California called the bears *Josmites*, "the killers," a word still preserved in the name of the Yosemite Valley and Yosemite National Park. The great beasts were given the name *grizzly*, however, because of their grayish color, not from the word *grisly* meaning horrible or terrible.

groundhog; woodchuck. American settlers named the marmot, or woodchuck *(Arctomys monax)*, the groundhog, perhaps because this member of the squirrel family seems hoggish in the way he burrows through the ground. Or, possibly, *groundhog* is a translation of the Dutch *aardvark* made by Dutch settlers in America, even though the South African aardvark, or earth hog, is a larger burrowing animal than the groundhog. The groundhog isn't a hog then, but his other American name, woodchuck, is no more accurate, for he doesn't chuck wood, either, a fact even the old tongue twister implies: "How much wood would a woodchuck chuck if a woodchuck could chuck wood?" "Woodchuck" has no connection with wood at all, simply deriving from the Cree Indian word *wuchuk* or *otchock* for another animal, the fisher, or pekan, which early settlers corrupted finally to "woodchuck" and applied through mistaken identity to the groundhog.

ground zero. Nuclear bombs are detonated before hitting the ground, and *ground zero* (or hypocenter) refers to the area directly below their explosion. The term dates back to the early 1940s and the first A-BOMB tests, but now also applies to the area around any huge explosion, fire, etc., such as the World Trade Center destruction on September 11, 2001. *Ground zero,* loosely used, means the "most elementary or beginning level," as in "Let's start at ground zero."

Grrrrreeeat! American actor Thurl Ravenscroft, who died at the age of 91 in 2005, liked to say that he was the only man in the world who had made a career with one word. That word was Grrrrreeeat! and he coined it as the roar of Tony the Tiger, the amiable cartoon character used in ads for Kellogg's Frosted Flakes breakfast cereal. Not only did he create the roar, he acted as Tony's voice for over 50 years, roaring Grrrrreeeat! thousands of times. Additional voices he created included, among many others, those of characters from the Disney movies *The Jungle Book, Mary Poppins,* and *Lady and the Tramp. See* WHAT'S UP, DOC?

grunt. *Grunt,* as in "He grunts and groans," is an onomatopoeic word that imitates the sound of grunting. The use of *grunt* for an American infantryman, who does a lot of grunting and groaning, probably dates back no further than the late 1950s and did not become common for "dogfaces" until the Vietnam War. One story has Marine Corps pilots coining the term.

G-string. Stripteasers, who sometimes call this a "gadget," aren't responsible for the word. *G-string* is an Americanism first used to describe an Indian's loincloth or breechclout in the 19th century. It could be that some fiddler in the West compared the heaviest of violin strings, the G string, to the length of sinew or gut that Indians tied around their waists to hold up their breechclouts. But even the heaviest of violin strings wouldn't really do the job. Perhaps the *g* is just a euphemistic shortening of "groin," an indecent word at the time. The burlesque G-string is of course far smaller than the Indian variety and must have seemed even skimpier a century ago, considering the Brunhildian builds of yesterday's ecdysiasts. One burlesque company of the day proudly advertised "two tons of women" and had only 20 strippers.

G.T.T. A historical term common in the 19th century standing for "Gone to Texas," apparently derived from *G. T.T.* signs that emigrants hung on the doors of their homes and businesses when they went west. Soon these initials came to be entered by lawmen in their record books when a wanted man couldn't be located. Finally, they became a designation for any disreputable man.

Gullah. The American dialect called Gullah, with some 5,000 African terms in it, takes its name either from *Ngola* ("Angola") or from the West African Gola tribe. It is spoken on the Sea Islands and along the South Carolina-Georgia coast.

gully-washer. An Americanism meaning a heavy rain. One old story has it that in the Ashland *Virginia Herald-Progress* someone advertised: "Wanted: One good rain. No 10-minute gully-washers need apply."

gunkhole; gunk. A gunkhole is a deep mudhole. One theory has it that the word *gunk* here is old Scottish meaning "to hoax or fool" and that *gunkhole* is used to mean a mudhole because "some fool once thought he could walk in mud and it let him down." But one guess is as good as another for the origins of these early Americanisms. *Gunk* refers to any thick or sticky substance ("He cleaned the gunk off it"). Originally the word was the trademark of a degreasing solvent, patented by a U.S. company in 1932.

guyascutus. Early Americans invented this humorous historical term, which describes a cow with short legs on one side so that it could better walk around the steep Vermont hills. The pronunciation is generally "guy-as-cut-as."

gyro ball. In baseball, a new name for a screwball, made famous by pitcher Dizzy Dean.

H

hair in the butter. A very delicate or sensitive situation. This Americanism dating from the early 20th century refers to the difficulty of removing a single hair from a piece of butter. Wrote Molly Ivins in *Molly Ivins Can't Say That, Can She?* (1991): "The Great Iranian Arms Caper is not only hair in the butter, I'd say someone's thrown a skunk in the churchhouse as well."

hair-raising. This Americanism came into the language too late, about 1910, for it to be associated with Indians or Indian hunters taking scalps. There is no evidence that horrible accounts of Indians or whites "lifting or raising hair" inspired the synonym for "frightening." Most likely the term is a streamlining of the old expression *to make one's hair stand on end.*

half-back. A new term, rarely recorded, for northern Americans, usually retired, who relocate in Florida, find it too hot in the summer but don't want to return to northern winters and so go halfway back, to settle in North Carolina.

half-breed. An offensive term for the offspring of an American Indian and a white person; first recorded in 1760, though later much used in the West. It is now used as offensive slang for the offspring of parents of different racial origin.

hamburger. Most authorities say that the hamburger first appeared in the U.S. in 1884 under the name of *Hamburg steak,* after the place of its origin, Hamburg, Germany. But the town of Hamburg, New York persistently claims that America's favorite quick food was invented there in the summer of 1885 and named for the burger's birthplace. According to this tale, its inventors were Charles and Frank Menches from Ohio, vendors who ran out of pork at their concession at the Erie County Fair. Since the first recorded use of *hamburger* seems to have been in 1902, according to the *O.E.D.,* Hamburg, New York could be the source. *White Castles, McDonalds* and *Wimpey-burgers* (for the Popeye comic-strip character who ate prodigious amounts of them) are synonyms for hamburgers.

hand over fist. Seamen reached the rigging on old sailing ships by climbing hand over hand up a thick rope—a skill sailors prided themselves on—and when sails were hoisted, the same hand over hand technique prevailed, just as it did when ropes or even fish were hauled in. American seamen in the 19th century changed this expression to the more descriptive *hand over fist,* which shows one fist clenching a rope and a loose hand passing over it to make another fist on the rope, etc. The rapid ascent on the ropes and the act of hauling in nets soon suggested someone rising rapidly in the business world and hauling in money, which is what we still mean when we say someone is making money *hand over fist.*

hands-in-the-pocket weather. A colorful Pennsylvania Dutch idiom meaning very cold weather.

Handsome Frank. The nickname of Franklin Pierce (1804–69), the 14th president, who was a friend of Nathaniel Hawthorne and appointed him to the consulship at Liverpool, England. As vain as he was handsome, the genial Pierce was rumored to be an alcoholic in his late years. His friend, the dignified Millard Fillmore, America's 13th president, rivaled Pierce in looks, as did 29th president Warren Harding, who carried on several affairs during his blessedly short term in office and had the looks of a matinee idol. Other good-looking presidents include James Garfield, Chester Arthur, Ronald Reagan, and Gerald Ford (who once worked as a male model). JFK was (or could be) charming rather than handsome. The most foppish of presidents was Martin Van Buren, who was called Petticoat et, among about a dozen insulting nicknames. *See* OK; PRESIDENTIAL NICKNAMES.

hanging around. This expression meaning to idle or loiter about is possibly the ancestor of *hangout,* a place for hanging around, and today's popular phrase *hanging out,* idling about. *The Dictionary of American Slang* gives its origin as the late 19th century, but it is definitely older than this, since Oliver Wendell Holmes uses it as an Americanism in his novel *Elsie Venner* (1861), putting it in quotes.

hang in there. This common Americanism, meaning "to refuse to give up" and "to stick with it," originally hails from the world of boxing, where managers exhorted exhausted fighters to finish a round or a bout, even to hang on to the ropes. In recent years the expression has come to be used as common parting words to someone in trouble, or in fact to anyone, since everyone in this life is usually up against the ropes in one way or another. Similarly, a frequent answer from anyone asked how he or she is: "I'm hanging in there."

hang it up. American slang since about the 1920s for "to quit work or retire," *hang it up* is a shortened term for the baseball expression *to* *hang up one's spikes* ("One more season and I'll hang up my spikes") meaning the same. A less frequent variation among men is *hang up one's jockstrap,* a phrase of more recent vintage.

hang out your shingle. To become a doctor or lawyer, among other professions. The Americanism comes from pioneer days, when doctors did use shingles for their signs.

Hangtown fry. Placerville, California, used to be nicknamed Hangtown because a good number of men were hanged there—or so the story goes. *Hangtown fry* refers to an omelet made of eggs, fried oysters, bacon, and onions that was invented during the gold rush in Placerville, or Hangtown.

hang up one's spikes; hang up the gloves. Strictly speaking, the phrase *hang up one's spikes* means "to retire" from professional baseball, football, or any sport in which spiked shoes are worn, as in "Slugger Mark McGwire has decided to hang up his spikes." However, the expression is used lightly for to retire from anything. The term was first recorded in 1942, the same year boxing's *hang up the gloves* made its initial appearance.

hapa haoli. In Hawaii this term means a person who is half white. *Hapa* here is the English word half assimilated phonologically into Hawaiian, with *l* dropped, *f* replaced by *p*, and the first vowel added. *Haoli* (pronounced HOW-lee) means white.

happening. Artist Allan Kaprow, who called himself an "unartist," coined the term *happening* in the late 1950s, its first printed appearance in The Nation of November 1959. A happening is an improvised performance or spectacle, often involving group or audience participation. Kaprow (1927–2006) was strongly influenced by Jackson Pollack and John Cage, among others.

happy landin' with Landon. The Republicans coined this campaign slogan for Alfred M. Landon in 1936, when he ran against Franklin D. Roosevelt for president. It was more like a crash landing than a "happy landin'," Landon suffering one of the most devastating defeats in American political history.

a hard day's work makes a soft bed. An old New England proverb rarely heard anymore.

Harper's Ferry, West Virginia. This beautiful little town in easternmost West Virginia on the bluffs at the confluence of the Potomac and Shenandoah Rivers is famous in American history because the old fanatic abolitionist John Brown was captured and hanged there just before the Civil War. The town takes its name from one Robert Harper, who established a ferry at the site in 1747.

Harry S. Truman. The S in the American president's name has been the subject of stories for over half a century now. According to an April 12, 1945 Associated Press dispatch, "[It] is just an initial—it has no name significance. It represents a compromise by his parents. One of his grandfathers had the first name of Solomon; the other Shippe. Not wanting to play favorites, the President's parents decided on the S."

Harvard beets. Harvard beets, often called pickled beets, are made from sliced beets cooked in sugar, cornstarch, vinegar, and water. There is no record that the dish was invented at Harvard University, but it is said that the unknown chef noticed the resemblance in the color of the deep red beets to the crimson jersies of the then vaunted Harvard football team. Harvard, the first institution of higher learning in North America, bears the name of John Harvard (1607–38), an English minister who lived for a time in Charlestown, Massachusetts, and later willed the fledgling university half his estate and his library of over 400 books. Cambridge, Massachusetts, where Harvard is located, was named for England's Cambridge University.

hasta la vista, baby. This phrase has become a well-known U.S. cliche since Arnold Schwarzenegger uttered it in his film *Terminator 2* (1980). It means "goodbye," *adios* in Spanish, Schwarzenegger uttering it as he dispatched a victim. Other less hackneyed Spanish terms for goodbye include *hasta luego* and *hasta mañana* (see you tomorrow).

hate someone's guts; have his guts for garters. The former phrase is first recorded in a 1901 letter to Teddy Roosevelt from William Allen White, famous independent publisher and editor of the (Kansas) *Emporia Gazette*. White, however, used the euphemism *intestines* in his letter: "I hate his intestines. It seems to me that there is no man in American politics that I have such an utter loathing and contempt for." The latter *guts* phrase sounds as if it might be from Texas, but I cannot find it recorded anywhere. I've heard it two or three times, as in "He'd better be on time or I'll have his guts for garters!"

Hatfield-McCoy feud. *See* RAZORBACK.

haul ass. To leave with haste, depart quickly. "Let's haul ass out of here." The term originated in the South but has some national use today.

have a bear by the tail. This is another of those colorful expressions (see A BEAR FOR WORK) that arose in America during the first half of the 19th century. *To have a bear by the tail* is to be in a bad situation— you're in trouble whether you hold on or let go!

have a brick in one's hat. To be drunk. According to Mainer Timothy W. Robinson *(American Speech,* 1948): "At the time [matches] were made so that one using them had to have a brick to scratch them on, and the saying was that he carried a brick in his hat, so when anyone had been to the store [for liquor] and walked a little crooked, the boys would say 'he had a brick in his hat.' " This may or may not be the origin of the expression, but it is an old one—Longfellow used it in his poem *Kavanaugh* (1849).

have a burr in (under) his saddle. An old Western expression still said of someone who is extremely irritated or agitated, even impatient.

have at one's fingertips. To have thorough familiarity or knowledge of a subject. The phrase isn't recorded until 1870 in America, but it is obviously an elaboration of the much earlier *to have at one's fingers' ends,* which is recorded in England in 1553 as a familiar saying.

have fishhooks in one's pocket. To be very cheap. First recorded in 1913, the Americanism may have originated much earlier with Long Island, New York, sea captain Samuel Mulford. Mulford lined his pockets with fishhooks to foil pickpockets when he visited London before the American Revolution. His ploy worked.

have one's number on it. The widely accepted belief in the American military that the bullet, grenade, shell, or bomb that kills one is marked by fate with one's number. *Number* could refer to one's serial number; American soldiers all wore identity tags or DOG TAGS at the time the expression was first recorded during World War I.

have other fish to fry. To be busy, usually with something important, so that one can't do anything else at the moment. The old American phrase is still heard today, often with variations, as in this example from the television series *The West Wing* (7/25/01): "I've got a bigger fish to fry."

have the edge. A player to the left of the dealer in 19th-century American poker games often had the right to continue in the game or drop out. This was called *to have the age,* and the poker term began to be used outside the game, as when Mark Twain in a 1907 magazine article wrote, "How could I talk when he was talking? He 'held the age' as the poker-clergy say." Soon the *age* in the expression became *edge,* due to the similarity in pronunciation and the aptness of *edge* in the phrase, and *to have the edge* came to mean to have any advantage.

have the inside track. This phrase means "to have an advantageous position in any competitive situation." The expression is from American track and field and dates back to the mid-19th century. The inside track or lane on a race course is the shortest and the runner positioned in it has the least distance to run (which is why many races have staggered starts).

have the luck of Hiram Smith. Few, if any, soldiers have been as unlucky as Hiram Smith, who fought in the Aroostook War of 1836–39, a war between New Brunswick and Maine over land near the Aroostook River on the U.S.-Canadian border. When New Brunswick sent loggers into the area, Maine authorities recruited a force to eject them. There were several clashes between 1838 and 1839 before an agreement was reached by General Winfield Scott's troops, the conflict known as the "Bloodless War." However, one person was killed in the war—luckless Hiram Smith, the only person to die in the entire war, whose luck was at least as bad as any soldier before or since.

Hawkeye State. A nickname for Iowa dating back to at least 1839, when *Hawkeye* described an Iowan. Candidates for the original Hawkeye after whom Iowans were named include a great Indian chief; newspaper editor James Gardiner Edwards, known as "Old Hawkeye"; and Natty Bumppo, hero of James Fenimore Cooper's *The Last of the Mohicans* (1826), whose nickname was Hawkeye.

Hays Code. Long the moral code of the American film industry, the *Hays Code* commemorates Will Harrison Hays (1879–1954). "Czar" of the movies, Hays served as first president of the Motion Picture Producers and Distributors of America from 1922 to 1945. A former chairman of the Republican National Committee and postmaster general under Harding, he helped formulate the so-called *Hays Code* in 1934 and zealously administered it from what was dubbed the Hays Office.

haywire. A fairly recent autobiography entitled *Haywire* shows that this Americanism still has a long life ahead of it, even though its rural origins are remote from most Americans now. Someone or something gone haywire is confused, out of order, deranged, crazy. The expression is first recorded toward the beginning of the century and was suggested by the baling wire, or haywire, that farmers and ranchers used to tie bales of hay. When a bale of hay was opened with a hatchet to feed livestock this thin sharpened wire would spring out and whirl about a farmer, the sharp ends frequently cutting him or snagging in his clothing. Old haywire lying around—and there was of course much of it—also wound about the legs of horses and other livestock, hopelessly tangling them up. Finally, farmers used old haywire to make temporary repairs on everything from machinery to fences and houses—temporary repairs that were often never made permanent and gave their places a disorderly look. All of these associations, from the crazy leaping of the wire to the tangling up of livestock and the disorder created by haywire, contributed to the coining of the colorful expression, which probably dates back to the 19th century, though first recorded in 1910.

headline. Newspaper headlines are an American invention that came into frequent use during the Civil War, but the earliest known example blared forth from the front page of the Tory *New York Gazette* and the *Weekly Mercury* on October 20, 1777. Fortunately for the United States the headline was all wrong:

> Glorious News from the Southward. Washington Knocked up—The Bloodiest Battle in America—6,000 of his Men Gone—100 Wagons to Carry the Wounded—General Howe is at present in Germantown—Washington 30 Miles Back in a Shattered Condition—Their Stoutest Frigate Taken and One Deserted—They are Tired—And Talk of Finishing the Campaigne.

hear a different drummer. The expression is from Henry David Thoreau's *Walden* (1850): "If a man does not keep pace with his companions, perhaps it is because he hears a different drummer. Let him step to the music which he hears, however measured or far away." A variation is *march to a different drummer.*

heavy hitter. A batter who consistently hits the ball hard, a power hitter, has been called a heavy hitter in baseball since at least the first recording of the term in 1887. By extension the term has come to apply to anyone powerful in any profession or undertaking, giving us *political heavy hitters, literary heavy hitters,* etc.

he can run, but he can't hide. American fighter Joe Louis (1914–1981) said this before his bout with challenger Billy Conn in 1946 for the heavyweight title. Conn had a reputation for fancy footwork, but Louis caught up with him and knocked him out.

heebie jeebies. Cartoonist Billie DeBeck (1890–1942), who invented "hotsy totsy," "hot mama," and other slang expressions, is credited by Mencken with this coinage, for "a feeling of nervousness, fright, or worry"—the willies or jitters. What he based the rhyming compound on, outside of a sheer joy of sound, is hard to say. One guess is that it is a "reduplicated perversion" of "creepy" or "the creeps." More likely DeBeck took the expression from the name of a dance called the Heebie-Jeebies popular in the 1920s, a dance that inspired a popular song titled "Heebie Jeebies" (1926). The dance, of American Indian ancestry, is said "to represent the incantations made by Red Indian witch doctors before a sacrifice."

He has a leak that will send him to hell. A nineteenth-century American expression, nautical in origin, describing someone or something with a fatal flaw.

Heimlich maneuver. U.S. physician Henry J. Heimlich (b. 1920) will be long remembered for this emergency rescue procedure used on someone choking on a foreign object. Dr. Heimlich invented the procedure in 1970, and it has since saved thousands of lives.

Heisman Trophy. The Heisman Memorial Trophy has been called the ultima Thule for undergraduate football players, being awarded annually since 1935 to the best of their breed in the country. It is named for John W. Heisman, former Georgia Tech coach. Called "Shut the Gates of Mercy" Heisman, the coach was a great mentor, though not noted for being a gentleman on the playing field. On one occasion he allowed his team to rack up an incredible 222 points against an opponent. Notable Heisman Trophy winners include Tom Harmon of Michigan (1940), Paul Hornung of Notre Dame (1956), and O. J. Simpson of

Southern California (1968). Jay Berwanger of the University of Chicago won the initial award in 1935.

he kept us out of war. The political slogan *he kept us out of war* has been used in two American presidential campaigns. The Democrats used it in 1916 to help return Woodrow Wilson to the White House, only to have Wilson ask Congress to declare war on Germany a year later, "to make the world safe for democracy." In 1956 the Republicans used it to sell Dwight D. Eisenhower as a peacemaker in Korea, though it took a backseat to the very popular "I like Ike."

Hell and Texas. Civil War general Phil Sheridan said that if he owned both Hell and Texas, he'd "rent out Texas and live in Hell."

hell on wheels. Union Pacific Railroad construction gangs in the 1860s lived in boxcars that were pulled along as the line progressed. Traveling and living with these hard-drinking, often violent men were gamblers, prostitutes, and other unsavory characters. The wild congregation assembled in the boxcars suggested the population of hell to settlers, and the transient town was called *hell-on-wheels,* a colorful term soon applied to any violent, vicious person or lawless place.

hell's kitchen. As that part of hell where the fires are hottest, hell's kitchen would be unpleasant indeed, which is why it came to mean any very unpleasant, disreputable place. The expression is first recorded in Davy Crockett's *An Account of Col. Crockett's Tour to the North and Down East* (1834). By 1879 it was being used as a name for an infamous district on New York City's West Side, which Mitford Mathews tells us was "once regarded as the home of thieves and gunmen." The Stovepipe was part of it, and nearby were the tenements of Poverty Gap.

hero. The *New York Times* (October 15, 2003) says that "in 1936, Clementine Paddleford, the legendary food writer on the *New York Herald Tribune,* unwittingly named the sandwich, saying, 'You'd have to be a hero to finish one.' The same source quotes Howard Robboy, a sociologist who is an authority on the subject, as saying the hero (then called the Italian sandwich) "was first made in New York in the late 19th century on the premises of Petrucci's Wines and Brandies at 488 Ninth Avenue near 37th St. The site is now Manganaro Foods. . . ."

hero sandwich; poor boy. New York City's Italian hero sandwiches, the term first recorded in the 1920s, are named for their heroic size, not for Charles Lindbergh or any specific hero of the Roaring Twenties. Hero sandwiches are surely among the most numerous-named things in English. Synonyms include such terms as *hoagies* (in Philadelphia), *submarines* or *subs* (in Pittsburgh and elsewhere), *torpedos* (Los Angeles), *wedgies* (Rhode Island), *wedges* (New York State), *bombers* (New York State), *Garibaldis* (Wisconsin), *Cuban sandwiches* (Miami), *Italian sandwiches* (Maine), *Italians* (Midwest), *grinders* (New England), *spuckies* (pronounced "spookies"; Boston), *rockets* (New York State), *zeps* or *zeppelins* (several states), and *poor boys* (New Orleans), though this last one is made with French instead of Italian bread and can feature oysters. *Blimpie* is a trade name for a similar sandwich, and *Dagwood* refers to any huge sandwich—after "Blondie" comic strip character Dagwood Bumstead's midnight snack creations. That's 20 in all—and there must be more!

he sold his saddle. A phrase from the American West meaning a cowboy has retired from the cowboy life.

Hetty Green. One of America's most outrageous misers was the notorious Henrietta ("Hetty") Green, who had a balance of over $31 million in the bank yet was so cheap that her son had to have his leg amputated because he received no medical treatment while she shopped around for a free medical clinic. Hetty, who left an estate of $94 million, was famous for not spending a cent if she didn't have to.

hickory. *Pawcohiccora* was the name American Indians near Jamestown, Virginia gave to the milky liquor they obtained from nuts from a tree that abounded in the area. Colonists called the milky liquor and nuts *hiccora,* or *hickory,* abandoning the first part of the Indian word, and eventually applied the word *hickory* to the useful tree the nuts came from, which supplied them with a stony, tough wood good for many purposes.

highfalutin. Pretentious, pompous. The Americanism, dating back at least to 1839, may be a variation on *high-flown.* Ernest Weekley, in *An Etymological Dictionary of Modern English* (1921), wants to know if "this type of oratory is due to Red Indian influence" on Americans, though he does admit "we [British] can do a little in the same line . . . ." As an example of highfalutin American language he cites one of Dickens's portrayals of American stereotypes in *Martin Chuzzlewit* (1843–44): "He is a true born child of this free hemisphere! Verdant as the mountains of our country; bright and flowing as our mineral licks; unspoiled by withering conventionalities as air our broad and boundless perearers! Rough he may be. So air our buffalers. But he is a child of natur' and child of freedom; and his boastful answer to the despot and the tyrant is that his bright home is in the settin' sun."

high five. *High-fiving* is a celebratory gesture where two participants raise their hands over their heads and slap each other's hands. The high five is often seen after a good play in sports, and indeed, University of Louisville basketball players Wiley Brown, Daryl Cleveland, and Derek Smith claimed to have invented it in 1979 during preseason practice as an odd, attention-getting gesture of triumph. However, hand slapping is also a way of greeting, especially among African-Americans. *The New Dictionary of American Slang* (1986) says the high five is "Chiefly used by and adopted from athletes, who themselves adopted the style from black colleagues."

high hat. Jack Conway, a former baseball player and vaudevillian who became editor of the show business newspaper *Variety,* coined the expression *high hat,* for "a snob," in 1924. It suggests an affected rich or nouveau riche man in a high silk hat and tails strolling about town with his nose almost as high as his hat, and it gave birth to the expression *to high hat,* to snub or act patronizingly. The prolific Conway—Walter Winchell called him "my tutor of slanguage"—died in 1928. *Belly laugh, pushover, to click* (succeed), *baloney* (bunk), S.A. (sex appeal), *payoff,* and *palooka* are among his other memorable coinages.

High Hopes. A popular song composed by Sammy Cahn that became the Democratic campaign song in 1960 when John Kennedy ran for president.

hijack. Back in Prohibition days, the story goes, criminals who robbed trucks of their loads of whiskey commanded their drivers to "Stick 'em up high, Jack!" or "Up high, Jack!" From their command they were called *highjackers,* then *hijackers,* and the word *hijack* became part of the language. Another explanation is that the crooks pretended to be friends of the drivers, calling out "Hi, Jack!"

hillbilly. Despite TV sitcoms like *The Beverly Hillbillies,* the word *hillbilly* is a derogatory name for hill people or highlanders, a designation, insulting at best, that has in the past provoked fights to the death. *Hillbilly* is first recorded in 1900 and usually implies laziness, ignorance, and stupidity. Highlanders don't mind being called "hillbillies" by other mountain folk, but they do object to flatlanders or "furriners" using the term.

his name is mud. Dr. Samuel Alexander Mudd (1833–83), a Maryland physician and Confederate sympathizer, set the broken left leg of Lincoln's assassin, John Wilkes Booth, who escaped from Ford's Theater by leaping to the stage from President Lincoln's box, breaking his leg when he landed. Dr. Mudd had nothing to do with the assassination or any escape plot, but in the hysteria of the moment he was sentenced to life imprisonment, though President Andrew Johnson pardoned him in 1869. Mudd's name (robbed of a d) has ever since been associated by many with the phrase *his name is mud,* and most undeservedly so. In the first place, this is a British phrase, not an Americanism. Second, according to Eric Partridge's highly respected *Dictionary of Slang and Unconventional English* (1961 ed.), *his name is mud* is first recorded in 1823 England, 10 years before Mudd was born, and is probably a few years older. The 1823 quotation Partridge gives is: " 'And his name is mud!' ejaculated upon the conclusion of a silly oration. . . ." Partridge's definition of the phrase is the same as most American definitions: "one has been badly defeated, one is in utter disgrace." Rather than being inspired by poor Dr. Mudd, the expression was almost certainly suggested by the universal dislike or even loathing of plain old mud, which has never been exactly popular with humankind.

hit below the belt. An English boxing rule early in the 18th century, to hit below the belt became a general Americanism by 1928, meaning to take unfair advantage.

hitch your wagon to a star. Set your goals high, aim high. These oft-quoted words were written by American philosopher Ralph Waldo Emerson in his essay "Civilization" in *Society and Solitude* (1810).

hit the hay. To go to sleep, as in "We all hit the hay early after that first day of climbing." Obviously, all the hay around suggests a rural origin and the phrase is first recorded in 1880s America. It may even derive from *hit the sack*, the sack in the phrase meaning a sack containing bedding like straw since the 17th century.

hit the road, Jack, and don't come back. Get out of here an don't bother us. A U.S. black expression since about 1950, but has become a song lyric as well.

Hit the sack. *See* HIT THE HAY

hit the wall. Though it is ignored in all dictionaries, so far as I know, this expression was born in the mid-1970s, when marathon running became popular in the United States. The *wall* is a point in a 26-mile 385-yard marathon run (usually at the 18- to-20 mile mark) when a runner seems to lose everything physically, hits up against a wall, so to speak, and can go no farther—at least not at his or her customary pace. It can be a terrible feeling, especially if one hasn't trained properly for the marathon, but most runners pull themselves over the wall and go on to finish. Figuratively, the phrase is now used to describe any situation in life that stops a person's progress and seems to make it impossible to go on.

Hoboken. For no good reason this New Jersey city across the river from New York (and Frank Sinatra's birthplace) has been the butt of jokes for over a century, just the mention of its name getting a laugh. Hackensack and Secaucus (once noted for its pig farms) have had much the same trouble.

Hog and Hominy State. A old nickname for Tennessee.

hog wild. To become wildly excited or irrational due to excitement, anger, or even happiness. The Americanism probably originated in the mid 19th century, though it isn't recorded until about 50 years later. It obviously refers to the way hogs become wildly excited when aroused and is just as obviously another phrase from the farm, still hanging in there long after most Americans began buying their bacon wrapped in cellophane.

Ho, ho, ho! The booming voice of the Jolly Green Giant in the famous TV commercial for Green Giant foods beginning in the 1950s. The advertising jingle was sung by Elmer Dresslar (1925–2005).

hold one's feet to the fire. This Americanism dates back to the 19th century and means to force someone to do something. It may have originated somewhere on the frontier, although the form of torture is surely much older.

hold the fort. Union General William Tecumseh Sherman is said to have invented this expression in 1864, when he wired the words to General Corse. Since the Civil War the words have not been used literally and have come to mean to take charge of any post or position, giving the job, temporary as it may be, your best efforts. It is sometimes heard as *hold down the fort.* General Sherman also suggested the phrase *40 acres and a mule* when, in a field order of 1865, he authorized that "Every family shall have a plot of not more than forty acres of tillable ground." Southern blacks took this to mean that all shareholders' plantations would at the end of the war be divided up into 40-acre plots that would be distributed to their slaves along with a mule to work them. The mule in the phrase was probably suggested by the old expression *three acres and a cow,* a common promise of British politicians.

hold your horses. Harness racing at American country fairs about a century and a half ago probably inspired the expression *hold your horses.* The amateur drivers, frequently young and inexperienced, often started their charges before a race had begun, leading the starter and the spectators to shout "Hold your horses!" By the 1840s the expression was being used to urge human patience in general.

Holland Tunnel. The tunnel connecting Manhattan and Jersey City has nothing to do with Holland or the Dutch. It is named for the great chief engineer who designed it, Clifford M. Holland. The tunnel opened in 1927.

Hollywood. There is no proof for the tale that the film capital of the world, laid out in 1887, was first called Holywood by its pious founders, this corrupted to Hollywood as the town corrupted. Hollywood may have been named for the native California holly or toyon *(Heteromeles arbutifolia)*, a large shrub that isn't a true holly but whose scarlet berries, borne from Christmas to Easter, suggest the holly and are much used for Christmas ornaments. Most probably, however, Tinseltown takes its name from the name of a ranch in the area owned by Mr. and Mrs. Harry Henderson, or from a hamlet named Hollywood in 1887 by the Wilcox family, who farmed in the area. It is hard to find anyone with many kind words for Hollywood. "It's hard to tell where Hollywood ends and the DTs begin," said W. C. Fields. "Hollywood's a trip through a sewer in a glass-bottomed boat," said Wilson Mizner. "Hollywood impresses me as being ten million dollars worth of intricate and highly ingenious machinery functioning elaborately to put skin on baloney," observed drama critic George Jean Nathan. Said comedian Fred Allen: "All the sincerity in Hollywood can be put into a gnat's navel and you'd still have room for three caraway seeds and an agent's heart."

Hollywoodese. A term referring to the hyped-up speech of movie people. "Hollywood talks and thinks in superlatives," Leo Rosten wrote

60 years ago in *The Movie Colony*. "Movie people do not 'like' things; they are 'mad' about them. They do not dislike things; they 'loathe' or 'detest' them. . . . The revealing story is told of two movie producers meeting on the street; 'How's your picture doing?' asked the first. 'Excellent.' 'Only excellent? That's too bad!' "

The Hollywood Golden Rule. "Who ever has the gold makes the rules."

holy cow! A trademark phrase associated with former Yankee baseball star Phil Rizzuto, who often used it in his baseball commentaries during a ballgame. "Scooter" Rizzuto, who died at age 89 on August 15, 2007, always claimed that his high school baseball coach encouraged him to use *Holy Cow!* instead of any real profanity. Yankee manager Casey Stengel called one of the shortstop's brilliant plays "the greatest play I ever saw." On the other hand, Rizzuto himself for some reason called any elder who made an error a "huckleberry."

home court advantage. An expression from basketball that has become part of the American lexicon, *home court advantage* means the psychological advantage one has in familiar surroundings, where one knows the terrain better and has a sympathetic audience.

home run. The term *home run* in baseball was first recorded in 1856 and, as Stuart Berg Flexner pointed out in *Listening to America,* it "couldn't have appeared much sooner because it wasn't until the late 1840s and early 50s that *home* was used in games to mean the place one tried to reach in order to win or score . . ." A home run was also called a *home* at the time, but *homer* isn't recorded until 1891. It should be noted that *home run* was a cricket term before it was used in baseball. Because it is the ultimate hit in baseball, a *home run* has come to mean a great accomplishment in any field.

Homestead State. An old nickname for Oklahoma because so much of the state was settled by homesteaders under the Congressional Homestead Act of 1862.

homophobia. An aversion to gay or homosexual people and behavior based on this aversion. Writing in the *New York Times* letters column (January 30, 2005), George Weinberg claimed he invented the word: "As a clinical psychologist, I was struck in the early 1960s by the atrocities committed against gay men and women by psychologists as well as by others. I became a devoted activist for gay rights, which to me are nothing more or less than human rights. I was the first to identify the adverse reaction to gays as phobic, and I coined the word 'homophobia.'"

Honest Abe. The most common nickname for Abraham Lincoln, inspired by the "every schoolboy knows" stories of his honesty. *The Rail Splitter* is another well-known Lincoln nickname, from his splitting fence rails as a young man in Illinois. Least known is his derogatory nickname *Spot Lincoln,* because as a congressman he had questioned President Polk's story that Mexico started the Mexican War on U.S. soil, Lincoln demanding that the spot where this had happened be identified. In the South Lincoln was often called *Old Abe* and his enemies also called him the *Ape* (based on Abe and his aspect), as well as the *Baboon.* Blacks often called Lincoln *Uncle Abe* and his White House staff affectionately called him the *Tycoon,* the first use in America of this

Japanese term for a military leader. Lincoln, of course, is also known as the *Liberator,* the *Emancipator* and the *Great Emancipator,* for his freeing of 4 million slaves. His wife was known as the *She-Wolf* and, rarely, *Mrs. President;* many of her contemporaries thought her bad-tempered and meddling.

hoodlum. A youthful ruffian and a gangster. The word *hoodlum* may derive from the Bavarian *hodalump* meaning the same. But there is no concrete proof of this and there are several other theories, these also unproved. All we really know is that *hoodlum,* first recorded in San Francisco in 1871, is now standard English. One source (Weekley) even calls the word "a perverted backspelling of Muldoon."

Hooverize, etc. Before becoming the 31st president of the United States Herbert Clark Hoover (1874–1964) had a distinguished career as an engineer and administrator, popularizing scientific management among businessmen and inspiring the building on the Colorado River of Boulder (now Hoover) Dam, for example. Hoover first came to national attention as the head of various European relief agencies and as U.S. Food Administrator during World War I. In the latter capacity he met the food crisis by ending farm hoarding of crops, curbing speculation, and urging Americans to live by "the gospel of the clean plate" and to institute "wheatless and meatless" days. It was only a few days after these suggestions that the term *to Hooverize* began to appear in newspapers around the country, and housewives soon adopted the phrase when discussing ways to stretch food. Later, when Hoover was president during the Great Depression, more than a few derogatory terms bearing his name were invented. Shoes with hobs in them were Hoover shoes, and Hoover blankets were newspapers bums slept under. The Hoover cart was a southern mule-drawn wagon made from the rear axle and chassis of a discarded automobile, and a Hooverville was a collection of shacks housing the unemployed at the edges of cities throughout the country. Later Hoover Commissions under both Truman and Eisenhower studied the reorganization of the executive branch of government and suggested many improvements that were adopted. The Hoover vacuum cleaner—*hoover* long a synonym for vacuum cleaner—is named for the man who founded the Hoover company in the 1920s.

hop on the bandwagon. Barnum and earlier showmen perfected the American bandwagon—a brass band perched atop a brightly decked dray pulled by a team of horses—but politicians quickly adopted it for national and local election campaigns. It wasn't, however, until the handsome silver-throated champion of silver, William Jennings Bryan, ran for president for a second time in 1901 that the expression to *hop on the bandwagon*, "to rush to join a popular movement," entered the language. The phrase remembers local politicians and ward heelers hopping up on Bryan's bandwagons as they banged and rolled through town, to show the support for their candidate and help create enthusiasm for him.

hornswoggle. Hornswoggle, "to bamboozle or cheat," is one of the few extravagant American phrases of the early 19th century surviving today. It is described as "a fanciful formation" by Mathews and first attested in 1829 in Kentucky, but no one knows who coined it. It may be related to the English dialect word *connyfogle*, "to deceive in order to win a woman's sexual favors," which is rooted in the English slang *cunny* for vagina.

horse sense. *Horse sense* for good plain common sense comes from the American West, about 1850, inspired by the cowboys' trusty intelligent little cow ponies, trained even to do a good deal of cattle-herding work without directions from their riders (as noted in *The Nation*, August 18, 1870).

Hosackia. Few people know that New York City's Rockefeller Center was once the site of the famous Elgin Gardens, one of the first botanic gardens in America. The Elgin Gardens were established by Dr. David Hosack (1769–1835) who subsequently deeded them to Columbia University, long the landlord of Radio City. Hosack, a professor at Columbia, is remembered as the physician who attended Alexander Hamilton after his fatal duel with Aaron Burr. He served on the first faculty of Columbia's College of Physicians and Surgeons, and helped found Bellevue Hospital as well as founding and serving as first president of the now defunct Rutgers Medical College. Hosack wrote a number of medical and botanical books, including a biography of Casper Wistar *(see* WISTERIA*)*. *Hosackia,* a genus of over 50 species of perennial herbs of the pea family, is named for him. Its most cultivated species is *H. gracilis,* "witch's teeth," a rock-garden plant about 12 inches high with pretty rose-pink flowers borne in small umbels.

hot dog. According to concessionaire Harry Stevens, who first served grilled franks on a split roll in about 1900, the franks were dubbed hot dogs by that prolific word inventor sports cartoonist T. A. Dorgan after he sampled them. "TAD" possibly had in mind the fact that many people believed frankfurters were made from dog meat at the time, and no doubt heard Stevens' vendors crying out "Get your red hots!" on cold days. Dorgan even drew the hot dog as a dachshund on a roll, leading the indignant Coney Island Chamber of Commerce to ban the use of the term *hot dog* by concessionaires there (they could be called only *Coney Islands, red hots* and *frankfurters). Hot dog!* became an ejaculation of approval by 1906, one that is still heard occasionally; *hot diggity dog!* was invented during the Roaring Twenties. Dorgan at least popularized the term *hot dog,* which may have been around since the late 1880s. In fact, *hot dog* for a frankfurter is recorded in the college newspaper *The Yale Record* in 1895 in a humorous poem about someone who "bites the dog" when it's placed inside a bun.

hotfoot. U.S. author Damon Runyon was the first to record and define the practical joke called a *hotfoot,* in a 1937 story. Wrote Runyon: "The way you give a hotfoot is to sneak up behind some guy, stick a paper match in his shoe between the sole and the upper . . . and then light the match." This is usually done while the practical joker's confederate distracts the victim. The word is not related to *hotfoot* meaning "rapidly, with speed," as in "Let's hotfoot it out of here."

hot potato. *Hot potato* can mean a "delicate situation," something to be handled with great care. It is said to derive from the phrase *drop someone* (or *something*) *like a hot potato* and was first recorded in 1950. Over 70 years older, however, is *hot potato* for an energetic person or for a sexy woman, the last sometimes called a *hot patootie,* which was apparently an American invention during World War I.

hotter than a two-dollar pistol. An old Americanism meaning very hot, an allusion to cheap 19th-century pistols that got hot when fired.

house that Ruth built. A familiar name for Yankee Stadium in the Bronx, New York, the house that Ruth built was constructed in 1923 to hold the huge crowds that came out in large part to see baseball immortal George Herman ("Babe") Ruth. Previous to this the Yankees played in the nearby Polo Grounds, which remained the home of the National League New York Giants until it was torn down years later. (Yankee Stadium was completely reconstructed in 1976 and eventually replaced in 2008 with the "new" Yankee Stadium constructed nearby.)

Howard Beach wait. People speaking on the phone in New York City's Howard Beach have developed what is known as the Howard Beach wait to let a plane go over the house. The wait is for the jets landing at and taking off from John F. Kennedy International Airport, their flight paths often directly over Howard Beach. The same could be said of all the communities bordering JFK. Some seven miles to the east in Nassau County, the village of Cedarhurst is noted for Cedarhurst Alley, a flight path directly over the residential community.

How do you like them apples? An American expression that means "what do you think of that?" *How do you like them apples?* was first recorded in 1941 and is still heard; *"How do you like them grapes?* came on the scene 15 years earlier and may be obsolete today.

howdy. Generally regarded as an expression born in the American West, *howdy,* a contraction of "how do you do?," began life as a southern expression and was taken West by Confederate Civil War veterans. It is first recorded in 1840.

how the other half lives. This expression for "how people belonging to another class live" usually refers to the rich today, but it originally referred to the poor. The words derive from the title of social reformer

Jacob Riis's book *How the Other Half Lives* (1890), describing the lives of New York City poor people.

hubba-hubba. "A delirious delight in language making," Mencken calls the coining of *hubba-hubba*. The expression was ubiquitous during World War II, made famous by a leering Bob Hope, the linguistic equivalent of a wolf whistle that was uttered lasciviously when an attractive woman walked past a group of men. Sexual but highly complimentary, it was often *hubba hubba hubba*, the third awesome *hubba* thrown in for added emphasis if body language warranted it. Anyway, we're told that the term originated with "flyboys," U.S. airmen who got it from Chinese airmen being trained at a Florida air base early in World War II. Supposedly it is a corruption of the familiar Chinese greeting *how-pu-how*. A second theory, wholly unpalatable, traces the expression to *Hubba*, "a cry given to warn fishermen of the approach of pilchards."

huckleberry. The first American settlers noticed the wild huckleberry, comparing it with the English bilberry, and first calling it a *hurtleberry* or *hirtleberry*, from which its present name derives. Huckleberries were so little, plentiful, and common a fruit that a *huckleberry* became early 19th-century slang for a small amount or a person of no consequence, both of these expressions probably inspiring Mark Twain to name his hero Huckleberry Finn. The berry was also used in the colloquial phrase *as thick as huckleberries,* very thick, and *to get the huckleberry,* to be laughed at or ridiculed, a predecessor of sorts of the raspberry (razz), or Bronx Cheer. *To be a huckleberry to someone's persimmon* meant, in 19th-century frontier vernacular, to be nothing in comparison with someone else. Huckleberries, which are not a true berry but a drupe fruit, belong to the *Gaylussacia genus,* which was so named in honor of French chemist Joseph-Louis Gay-Lussac (1778–1850).

huddle. The football huddle may have been invented and named by Herb McCracken (1900–95) when coach of the Lafayette College football team in 1924. According to Coach McCracken's *New York Times* obituary (3/25/95): "Aware that Penn State had memorized its offensive signals, he ordered his players not to start each down at the line of scrimmage. Instead, he told them to gather behind the line to learn the next play in secret, and the *huddle* was invented." But some sources credit Amos Alonzo Stagg with earlier inventing the huddle while coaching at the University of Chicago. Still others credit coach Bob Zuppke of the University of Illinois in the early 1920s, and Zuppke certainly did make the huddle a standard part of the game. There are other claimants, too, and there is not sufficient evidence to crown any one of them.

hula hoop. Another of the great toy fads of the 20th century (see FRIS-BEE), the hula hoop was invented about 1956 by an Australian toymaker, who based the plastic hoop on a wooden exercise hoop of gymnastic classes. Marketed by the U.S. Wham-O toy company, as the Frisbee was, the hula hoop sold up to 40 million in 1958, mostly to teenagers who gyrated them on their hips in and out of school until the fad ended.

hula-hula. The Hawaiian name for this pantomime story-dance is simply *hula*, the dance noted for its highly styled hand imagery, which uses many of the over 700,000 "distinctive movements of the hands, arms, fingers and face by which information can be transferred without speech." During World War II, Japanese soldiers posing as Filipinos often tried to penetrate Allied lines in the Philippines. Suspects were given *hula-hula* to pronounce and the Japanese infiltrators who, unlike the Filipinos, had trouble with their l's, invariably pronounced it "hura-hura," sealing their fate.

hully-gully. The *New York Times* once described the "dignified" hully-gully disco dance as "like Wyatt Earp drawing his guns, Dean Martin downing drinks . . ." Deriving from the twist in the 1960s, the dance may be so called because some of its gestures are similar to gestures used in the southern children's guessing game hull-gull.

hummingbird. These beautiful little American birds, some of which weigh less than a penny, take their name from the humming sound their wings make when they hover over a flower. The "flying jewels" were so admired in early times that American Indians often dried and pressed them for use as earrings.

hunky-dory. No one is certain about it, but a product called Hunki-dori, a breath freshener introduced in 1868, may have given us the American expression *everything is hunky-dory,* or O.K. We do know for sure that *hunky-dory* is first recorded the same year that Hunkidori was introduced. The old tale that the word comes from the name of a pleasure street in Yokohama much frequented by American sailors seems to be spurious. According to Carl Whittke in *Tambo and Bones* (1930): " 'Josiphus Orange Blossom,' a popular song . . . in reference to Civil War days, contained the phrases 'red hot hunky dory contraband.' The Christy's [a minstrel group] made the song so popular that the American people adopted 'hunky-dory' as part of their vocabulary." Still another theory has the expression deriving in 1866 from *hunk,* a New York dialect word for "home base," which in turn derives from Dutch *honk,* "good."

hush puppy. These cakes of deep-fried cornmeal batter, very popular in the South, have been traced back only to the time of World War I; at least the name isn't recorded before then. The most common explanation for the odd name is that hunters tossed bits of the cakes to their dogs, telling them to *"hush, puppy."* A perhaps more authentic version notes that the cakes were first made in Florida, where people often fried fish outdoors in large pans, attracting dogs who would whine and bark. To quiet the dogs, the cook would fry up some cornmeal cakes and throw them to the dogs, shouting, "Hush, puppies!" *Hush puppie*s for soft shoes or slippers seem to have been so named by the first company to manufacture them, in the 1960s.

hyphenated Americans. Starting as contemptuous slang in the late 19th century, *hyphenated American* meant any naturalized citizen who regarded himself as both American and of the country from which he came (Irish-American, German-American, etc.). Today, the term is not generally contemptuous and refers to one's ancestry and to racial and religious groups as well.

I

I am the greatest. Pugilist Muhammad Ali said this, but he didn't believe it. The world heavyweight champ admitted that he borrowed the phrase from wrestler Gorgeous George and used it for publicity purposes.

I cannot tell a lie (Pa). The folktale of George Washington cutting down the cherry tree and admitting it to his father ("I cannot tell a lie, Pa") is one of the most persistent in American history. It is first recorded in the Reverend Mason L. Weems's *Life of Washington* (1800), told to him by an old lady who had spent much time with the family. No one has ever *disproved* this story, though there is some evidence that it was current as a country tale before Parson Weems printed it. Weems's book went through over 40 editions, and millions of Americans were raised on the story, including Abraham Lincoln, who borrowed a copy of the book, and when it was damaged by a sudden rain had to work three days to pay its owner for it. All we can say with certainty is that like most folklore the tale was exaggerated over the years: a tree stripped of bark becoming the chopped-down tree, "I can't tell a lie, Pa," becoming "Father, I cannot tell a lie."

"I could have been a contender." The well-known words of former boxer Terry Malloy (played by Marlon Brando) in the 1954 Oscar winner *On the Waterfront.* Malloy, disappointed with his life, a small-time hood by now, made the confession to his brother. Other *On the Waterfront* Oscar winners include Budd Schulberg, best original story and screenplay; Elia Kazan, best director; and Brando, best actor.

Idaho. *Idaho* may be the only state name that is a complete fraud—at any rate, its name may mean nothing at all. Many sources derive the word *Idaho* from a Shoshonean Indian word meaning "gem of the mountain," but the Idaho State Historical Society claims that there never was any such Indian word and that *Idaho* and its translation was the phony creation of a mining lobbyist who suggested it to Congress as the name for the territory we now know as Colorado. Congress rejected the name, but it caught on among gold prospectors along the Columbia River, and when it was proposed in 1863 as the name for what we know today as Idaho, Congress approved it and the Idaho Territory was born. The origin of the word may be Shoshonean, however, though it does not mean "gem of the mountain" or "Behold! The sun is coming down the mountain," as another writer suggested. Idaho residents, in fact, ought to forget about the real Shoshone word that *Idaho* may have derived from, for that word would be *Idahi*, a Kiowa curse for the Comanches that translates roughly as "eaters of feces," "performers of unnatural acts," "sources of foul odors," etc.

Idaho baked potato. Very few potatoes are named and known for their place of origin. First known as the Early Rose potato, a variety discovered by the great horticulturist Luther Burbank in his New England garden in 1872, this famed versatile tuber went through some 40 years of breeding before it became known as the Idaho. Strangely enough, this well-known name was made famous by a New York department store "taster." William Titon, better known as Titon the Taster, worked 60 years for Macy's and was the store's final authority on all groceries, wines, and liquors. Among other accomplishments, Titon discovered the Idaho potato in 1926 while buying apples for Macy's and promoted it until the spud's name became synonymous with baked potato, for which Idaho's governor wrote a letter of thanks to the store.

I'd rather not go there. I'd rather not talk about that or say anything about it. A U.S. phrase dating back 20 years or less.

I'd sooner sleep in the pasture and pick corn out of horsedroppings. I'd rather do almost anything else than what you propose. This little-known humorous Americanism dates back to the early 19th century.

If I can't dance, it's not my revolution. The expression originated with American anarchist Emma Goldman (1869–1940) in the early 1900s, after her lover and fellow anarchist, Alexander Berkman, berated her one night for dancing wildly in a radical hangout.

if the glove doesn't fit, you must acquit. A little ditty often attributed to Johnny Cochran (1938–2005), one of the lawyers defending O. J. Simpson in his 1994 murder trial. A bloody glove had been found at the Simpson house and the prosecutor asked Simpson to see if it fit him. "If the glove doesn't fit, you must acquit," Cochran told the jury as Simpson tried unsuccessfully to pull it on. Though another member of the "Dream Team," Gerald Uelman, apparently suggested the rhyme, Cochran later wrote: "It's the line that eventually will be cited by *Barlett's Familiar Quotations,* the line endlessly quoted to me by people, the line by which I'll be remembered, and I suspect it will probably be my epitaph."

If you ain't the lead horse, the scenery never changes. A humorous American expression I've only found in Thomas McGuane's *Keep the Change* (1989): "My old man used to say, 'If you ain't the lead horse, the scenery never changes.' Now it looks like I might lose the place. I need to get out front with that lead horse."

if you can make it in New York, you can make it anywhere. Probably coined by a New Yorker, this phrase dates back at least 30 years, possibly more. It was popularized in the song "New York, New York," written by Fred Ebb and John Kander and recorded by Liza Minnelli in 1977 and by Frank Sinatra in 1980.

If you can't lick 'em, join 'em. This Americanism probably dates back to the late 19th or early 20th century. Cynical and pragmatic, it comes from the political precincts, as one would expect.

If you can't stand the heat, get out of the kitchen. The aphorism is usually attributed to President HARRY S TRUMAN but there is some evidence that he got it from his military adviser General Harry Vaughn, who got it from who knows where. It has also been suggested, with no proof, that what the salty Truman really liked to say was "If you can't stand the stink get out of the shithouse."

if you don't do, you're gonna get done. I first heard this phrase about swindling in the 1934 Loretta Young and Cary Grant movie *Born to Be Bad,* but the idea behind it is much older. For example, the so-called Chicago Golden Rule (Do de other feller before he do you) dates back to about 1902.

If you don't like the weather, just wait a minute. A saying referring to the mercurial nature of New England weather attributed to Mark Twain, who despite his many years in the region, never got used to the weather.

If you need anything, just whistle. When Humphrey Bogart died and was cremated in 1957, his wife, Lauren Bacall, placed a small gold whistle in the urn with his ashes. Inscribed on the whistle is a variation on the famous line she delivered to Bogey in their first film together, *To Have and Have Not*: "If you need anything, just whistle." Her exact words had been, "If you need me, just whistle," but no one remembers it that way.

if you peel that onion a little farther. An American expression, its exact origin unknown, meaning "as you examine something a little closer" it begins to take on a new appearance or meaning, as in. "On its surface the tax bill seems to help the poor, but if you peel that onion a little farther, you begin to find that's not the case at all." An onion, of course, has many layers.

I gotta million of 'em. Often said by a comedian, or any joke- teller, after telling a gag. The words are associated with American comedian Jimmy Durante (1893–1980) and thus may date back to the early 1900s, when the beloved "Schnozzola" appeared in vaudeville. Durante ended all his radio shows with the still mysterious, raspy words, "Good night, Mrs. Calabash, wherever you are."

I have found it. The motto of Sacramento, the capital of California; its nickname is the Golden State. The golden poppy, Sacramento's flower, is another gold-related saying adopted after gold was discovered ("I have found it") in 1848 at Sutter's Mill, near Sacramento.

I'll be there with bells on. Early-18th-century Conestoga wagons usually arrived at their destination with bronze bells ringing, giving rise to this Americanism. These same Conestogas are responsible for traffic moving on the right side of the road in the U.S. rather than on the left as in Britain. According to one authority, the Conestogas were "best guided from the left and so afforded a clear view ahead only when driven from the right side of the road. Drivers of other vehicles found it not only wise not to argue but convenient to follow in the ruts made by the heavy wagons and habit soon became law."

Illinois. This central "Prairie State" is named for the Illinois Indians, as the French called the confederation of six Indian tribes in the area. Frenchmen were the first Europeans to enter Illinois territory, in 1673. They changed the Indian name *Hileni* or *Ileni,* meaning "man," to *Illin*, adding their *ois* plural. Since the Indian plural is *uk, Illinois* might be *Illinuk* today if they hadn't done so. The Illinois group is almost extinct today, numbering between 200 and 300, compared to an estimated 8,000 in the 17th century.

Illinois baboon. A derogatory name given to Abraham Lincoln by his detractors, sometimes shortened to the baboon and sometimes changed to Illinois gorilla and Gorilla.

Illinois gorilla. A derogatory nickname for Abraham Lincoln during the Civil War. "He was long detained in Washington, having interviews with Abe, the Gorilla; Seward, the Raven; and Feathers Scott." (*Richmond Dispatch*, November 13, 1861). Lincoln was also called the Illinois gorilla. His own secretary of war, Edwin Stanton, called him the original gorilla. *See also* ILLINOIS BABOON.

I ♥ New York. Mary Wells Lawrence of the Wells Lawrence Green advertising agency coined the ubiquitous tourism slogan for New York City. Ms. Lawrence, the first woman to own a major ad agency, also invented the famous Alka Seltza "Plop Plop" jingle, among many other ads.

I'm a curly-tailed wolf with a pink ass and this is my night to howl. A humorous oath heard among drinkers of potent moonshines and recorded by students of American Mountain dialect.

I'm as mad as hell and I'm not gonna take this anymore. A celebrated speech by actor Peter Finch in the movie *Network* (1976). He won the Oscar for best actor in the film and became the only actor to win an Oscar posthumously since he died of a heart attack shortly after the film.

I'm from Missouri. During the Civil War, an officer of the Northern army fell upon a body of Confederate troops commanded by a Missourian. The Northerner demanded a surrender, saying he had so many thousand men in his unit. The Confederate commander, game to the core, said he didn't believe the Northerner's boast of numerical superiority and appended the now famous expression, "I'm from Missouri; you'll have to show me." Dr. Walter B. Stevens recorded this proud derivation of the phrase in *A Colonial History of Missouri* (1921), but other authorities support the following derogatory origin: Miners from the lead district of southwest Missouri had been imported to work the mines in Leadville, Colorado, sometime after the Civil War. They were unfamiliar with the mining procedures in Leadville and fellow workers regarded them as slow to learn, their pit bosses constantly using the expression, "He's from Missouri; you'll have to show him." Residents of the "Show Me" state obviously favor the former theory, in which "I'm from Mizorra" is a badge of distinction, signifying native skepticism and shrewdness.

in a New York minute. A very short time, instantly. "He did it in a New York minute." A popular expression that was first recorded in print in 1967, though William Safire, in *Coming to Terms* (1980), quotes an informant who says his father, who died in 1929, age 69, often used the expression.

in a pig's ear. A euphemism for the American slang phrase in a pig's ass, which means *never*, as in "In a pig's ass I'll work on Saturday." In a pig's eye is also used.

in a pig's eye. A fiery emphatic denial meaning "never," "not a chance," "like hell," as in "In a pig's eye you could beat me." Variations on the well-known Americanism include in a pig's ass and in a pig's ear.

Indian giver. Tradition holds that American Indians took back their gifts when they didn't get equally valuable ones in return. Some Indians were no doubt *Indian givers*; others, however, got insulted if they received *more* than they gave. Instances of Indians *Indian-giving* are hard to come by, and even the *Handbook of American Indians* (1901), published by the Smithsonian Institution, defines the practice as an "alleged custom." Perhaps the expression is explained by the fact that *Indian* was once widely used as a synonym for bogus or false. Many of the nearly 500 terms prefixed with *Indian* unfairly impugn the Indian's honesty or intelligence—even *honest Injun* was originally meant sarcastically, and *Indian summer* means a false summer.

Indians don't count. An offensive boast of gunmen in the early Southwest, who supposedly kept a count of all but Indians and Mexicans that they killed. Also heard was *Mexicans don't count*.

I never missed one in my heart. Veteran major-league baseball umpire Bill Klem, who retired in 1941, said this to assure his admirers and detractors that he had never made a call, right or wrong, that he didn't believe was right. The expression is now used by people in and out of sports as a profession of sincerity.

in God we trust. Mind Your Business was the first motto used on a U.S. coin. *In God We Trust*, the motto now found on all American coins large enough to hold it, was authorized by two Congressional acts of 1865. It was used on the eagle (the $10 gold piece), the double eagle (the $20 gold piece), the half eagle (the $5 gold piece), the silver dollar, the half dollar, and the quarter—and still appears on those latter three coins. This motto inspired the humorous slogan *In God We Trusted, In Kansas We Busted* that settlers in Kansas, bankrupt by the severe droughts from 1887 to 1891, painted on their old covered wagons when they returned East.

in hock. In the game of faro, much played in 19th-century America, the last card in the box was called the *hocketty card* (from a word of unknown origin), this card later said *to be in hock*, as was any player who bet on the last card. This was a bad bet, most often a losing one, so that *to be in hock* soon meant "to owe money." Pawnshops were a convenient place to get money to pay debts, so they became known as *hock shops*, and *to be in hock* soon meant to have some or all one's valuable possessions in a hock shop or, generally, to be in very bad financial shape.

In Hoover we trusted, now we are busted. Herbert Hoover won the U.S. Presidency in 1928 with his party's slogans *a chicken in every pot* and *rum, Romanism, and rebellion,* the latter a reference to his opponent Al Smith's Catholicism. He lost the presidency in 1932, in the midst of the Great Depression, Franklin D. Roosevelt's supporters calling for "New Deal" and chanting in *Hoover we trusted, now we are busted.*

in like Flynn. Chicago's "Boss" Flynn's machine never lost an election and was always "in office," inspiring the expression *in like Flynn*, meaning "to have it made." The popularity of movie actor Errol Flynn and his amorous activities helped popularize the phrase in the early 1940s.

in Macy's window. A synonym for the ultimate in public exposure: "If we do that we might as well be in Macy's window." Traditional window displays date back to the early 1880s when the use of plate glass on a wide scale made display windows a standard feature of department stores. Macy's display windows in New York were long the most prominent among them, especially those in their flagship store on West 34th Street, "The World's Largest Store" with over 2.2 million square feet of floor space. In fact, Macy's old 14th Street store in Manhattan was famous for its Christmas displays as far back as the mid-1800s, featuring a collection of toys revolving on a belt.

in over your head. Another phrase whose origin may be the swimming pool, like go in off the deep end (qv). This American expression means "to be in a situation one can't control," as someone who didn't know how to swim would be if he or she jumped in at the deep end of the pool.

interrobang. This is the very newest of punctuation marks, devised by an American typecasting company in the 1970s. A combination question mark and exclamation point, it is used after an expression that could be both a question and exclamation, such as "Where's the fire?!" Resembling an exclamation point superimposed on a question mark, it takes its name from the *interro* in *interrogation* and the printers' slang *bang* for an exclamation point.

interview. Media interviews can be traced back to 1859, at about the time of John Brown's raid on Harper's Ferry. At this time abolitionist Gerrit Smith gave an interview to a *New York Herald* reporter who remained anonymous. Other sources, however, claim that journalist Anne Royall invented the form in an 1825 story about President John Quincy Adams.

intestinal fortitude. The head coach of Ohio State University's football team, Dr. John W. Wilce, is said to have invented this word for "guts" in 1915 as "a protest against the lurid language of the gridiron and locker room," *guts* then being considered "improper for drawing-room conversation." They don't make coaches like Dr. Wilce anymore, nor locker rooms so mild.

In Texas the cattle come first, then the men, then the horses, and last the women. An old Texas saying quoted by Edna Ferber in *Giant* (1952).

in the doghouse. The expression *in the doghouse*, "out of favor or undergoing punishment," isn't of ancient origin but is an Americanism first recorded toward the end of the 19th century. Possibly the term originated during the African slave trade, when sailors locked the hatches at night, to prevent slaves from escaping, and slept on deck in tiny sleeping cubicles called "doghouses." There is no evidence, however, to support this theory, or any other for that matter.

in the ketchup. Meaning the same as *in the red* (qv), the U.S. slang dates from the mid-20th century.

in the red. An American term that since the early 1900s has meant "to do business at a loss for a certain period." The term derives from the practice of accountants using red ink to enter debits in a firm's books. *In the black* means operating at a profit.

in two shakes of a lamb's tail. A lamb can shake its tail twice quite rapidly, apparently more quickly than many animals can shake their tails once, which explains this Americanism, meaning "in hardly any time at all." The expression dates back to the early 1800s and no one knows who coined it. Possibly it is a humorous extension of the older British phrase *in two shakes*, meaning the same, and probably alluding to the quick shaking of a dice box.

I only regret that I have but one life to give for my country. Supposedly the last words that American spy Nathan Hale said on the gallows before he was hanged by the British. According to the recently discovered diary of British officer Captain Frederick Mackenzie, what he really said was, "It is the duty of every good officer to obey any orders given him by his commander- in-chief." Hale was executed on September 22, 1776. British author Joseph Addison's play *Cato* (1713) has the words "What pity it is that we can die but once to serve our country."

Iowa. Nicknamed the *Hawkeye State* (after a resident sharpeyed Indian chief), our 29th state, which entered the Union in 1846, is so called from the name of the Sioux *Ioways* or *Aiouez*, meaning "sleepy ones." The tribe, however, didn't consider themselves lazy, calling themselves the *Pahoja*, "gray snow." A rival tribe had named them "the sleepy ones."

iron dog. What is an iron dog? To Alaskans it's a snowmobile. Why? Because it gets people around like the sturdy dogs that once pulled them through the snow.

Iroquois. These Indians often ended their speeches with "Hi-roquoue!"—meaning "I have spoken with strong emotion!" To the ears of French explorers in North America this sounded like *Iroquois*, the name they gave to the Indian tribe.

I say it's spinach and I say the hell with it. E. B. White wrote the caption that became this catchphrase, for a 1928 Carl Rose cartoon in the *New Yorker* showing a spoiled little girl who rejects her mother's offer of broccoli with these words—which have come to mean, "When I'm indulging my prejudices I don't want to be confused with facts." The phrase's abbreviated form, *spinach*, however, means the same as boloney, malarkey, bull, etc.

itchy trigger finger. To have an itchy trigger finger is to be quick on the trigger, to be quick to act, itching to go, impetuous or even alert. The American expression was first recorded in 1903 as *to have trigger itch*. Within 30 years or so it took its present form.

It's a great life if you don't weaken. Often said derisively or ironically after something has gone wrong. Probably an Americanism, the phrase dates back to World War I and is commonly heard today.

It's a naive domestic burgundy without any breeding but I think you'll be amused by its presumptions. This originated as the caption under a James Thurber drawing of a pretentious oenologist offering a glass to a friend. It is an expression that has been used jokingly by many a host pretending to be a "wine expert" while dispensing a $3.99 special.

It's a new ball game. Since about 1940 Americans have been using this catchphrase to mean "What's past is past, we start over from here." Though it could have come from several sports, the saying almost certainly has its origins in baseball and sounds like something a baseball announcer may have spontaneously invented. The expression is often "It's a whole new ball game."

It's chess, not checkers. It's complicated, with no easy answer to a question, chess being a much more difficult game than checkers. This relatively recent phrase is an Americanism that has been used by government officials answering the questions of reporters at press conferences.

It's how you played the game. Sportswriter Grantland Rice, who coined the term the *Four Horsemen* to describe Notre Dame's famous backfield in an account of a Notre Dame-Army game ("Outlined against a blue-gray October sky, the Four Horsemen rode again . . .") is also responsible for *it's how you played the game.* The much-loved writer, who died in 1954 at the age of 73, first used the expression in a poem he published in one of his "The Sportlight" columns:

> When the One Great Scorer comes
> To mark against your name,
> He writes—not that you won or lost—
> But how you played the game.

Itsy Bitsy Teenie Weenie Yellow Polka Dot Bikini. A 1960 hit song written by Paul Vance and his songwriting partner Lee Pockriss. The song was about a girl with a new kind of bathing suit, one so different and skimpy that she was afraid to come out of her locker wearing it. The bashful girl was based on Mr. Vance's wife Rose, who was thinking of buying a bikini and nervous about it.

I vant to be alone. Aside from some GOLDWYNISMS, this may be the single most famous quotation to come out of Hollywood, partly because it is a sentiment uncharacteristic of most film stars. Too bad that Greta Garbo didn't say it. The legendary actress has made it clear for history that what she really said was: "I want to be *let* alone."

Ivy League. The colleges referred to as the *Ivy League* are Harvard, Yale, Princeton, Dartmouth, Cornell, Brown, Columbia, and the University of Pennsylvania. They are all "old-line institutions," with thick-vined, aged ivy covering their walls, and the designation at first applied specifically to their football teams. Sportswriter Caswell Adams coined the term in the mid-thirties. At the time Fordham University's football team was among the best in the East. A fellow journalist compared Columbia and Princeton to Fordham, and Adams replied, "Oh they're just Ivy League," recalling later that he said this "with complete humorous disparagement in mind."

I Want You! The words on the most famous recruiting poster of World War I, which showed Uncle Sam looking out and pointing at the viewer. It was by American artist and writer James Montgomery Flagg (1877–1960).

J

jack. *Jack,* for money in general, is an Americanism first recorded in 1859, but the expression is probably older, possibly deriving from the expression *to make one's jack,* "to succeed in one's endeavors," first attested in 1778. This expression, in turn, may come from the British slang *jack,* for "a farthing and a counter used at gaming tables," which dates back to about 1700. Also, a home run in baseball. The term was originally a verb, first recorded in 1979, meaning to hit a ball hard, jack it, especially for a long home run. But though it is unrecorded in any dictionary, jack also has come to mean a home run itself. Speaking of Giant's star Barry Bonds, an opposing player said: "Two years ago he hit 73 jacks. Last year he won a batting title. I don't know what else the guy can do." (*New York Times,* September 9, 2003).

Jack Johnson. John Arthur (Jack) Johnson, his memory recently revived by the play The *Great White Hope,* loudly proclaimed that he reigned as the first black world heavyweight champion in 1908 when he KO'd Englishman Tommy Burns—though his title claim was disputed and not settled until he demolished Jim Jeffries, the original great white hope, in 1910. Johnson held the title until 1915, when giant Jess Willard knocked him out in 26 rounds in Havana, Cuba. The American fighter had often been called the "Big Smoke" in the United States, "smoke" being common slang at the time for Negro. For this reason, and because he was so powerful a man, the German 5.9 howitzer, its shell, and its shell burst were named after Johnson. A formidable weapon, whose shells emitted thick black smoke upon exploding, the Jack Johnson saw action against the Allies during World War I, when Johnson's name was prominent in the news for his fights and love affairs. Johnson, in fact, had fled to Europe in 1913 after being convicted of violating the Mann Act, unjustly or not. The great boxer died in 1946, aged 68.

Jackson, Mississippi. One of the four U.S. state capitals named after presidents. The others are Lincoln, Nebraska, for Abraham Lincoln; Madison, Wisconsin, for James Madison; and Jefferson City, Missouri, for Thomas Jefferson.

Jacuzzi. A trademark name for a whirlpool bath of swirling comforting water that was invented by Candito Jacuzzi (1903–86) and which he first called the "Roman bath." The American inventor made the bath to help his son, who suffered from rheumatoid arthritis.

jag on. To be drunk, as in "He had a jag on." *Jag* here is a 19th-century Americanism for a heavy load of something, such as a wagon full of wood or hay. Figuratively then, someone who has a jag on, carrying a heavy load, more than he or she can handle, is loaded.

jalopy. Here's one whose origins etymologists don't even venture a guess upon. It means, of course, a beaten-up old car or (rarely) airplane (usually called a *crate*). Should you want to investigate, the word seems to have surfaced first in Chicago in about 1924 and was sometimes spelled *jaloppi*. Possibly it derived from the slang of a foreign language. *Rattletrap* and *heap* are synonyms of about the same age.

jambalaya. A New Orleans Creole dish made of rice cooked with ham, sausage, chicken, and shell sh; or a combination of all, along with herbs, and vegetables, especially tomatoes, onions, and peppers. Hence, any diverse collection of things: "the show was a jambalaya of stunts."

java. *Java,* for "coffee," originated as slang among American tramps in the late 19th century. It is obviously an allusion to the coffee-producing island.

jaw-dropping. An expression of disbelief or disappointment; a startling or shocking revelation. The phrase, apparently an Americanism, has becoming more popular recently, especially in political circles.

Jayhawker State. A nickname for Kansas. Kansas has also been called the Battleground of Freedom (in Civil War times), the Garden State (a title it shares with New Jersey), the Garden of the West (Illinois also claims this one), the Grasshopper State (after grasshopper invasions there), the Cyclone State, the Sunflower State (after the state flower), the Squatter State, the Central State, the Dust Bowl State (*see* DUST BOWL) and, best of all, the Navel of the Nation.

jazz. Enough men to form a good jazz group are credited with lending their names to the word. One popular choice is a dancing slave on a plantation near New Orleans, in about 1825—Jasper reputedly was often stirred into a fast step by cries of "Come on, Jazz!" Another is Mr. *Razz*, a band conductor in New Orleans in 1904. Charles, or *Chaz*, Washington, "an eminent ragtime drummer of Vicksburg,

Mississippi circa 1895," is a third candidate. A variation on the first and last choices seems to be Charles Alexander, who, according to an early source, "down in Vicksburg around 1910, became world famous through the song asking everyone to 'come on and hear Alexander's Ragtime Band.' Alexander's first name was Charles, always abbreviated Chas. and pronounced Chazz; at the hot moments they called, 'Come on, Jazz!', whence the *jazz* music." Few scholars accept any of these etymologies, but no better theory has been offered. Attempts to trace the word *jazz* to an African word meaning hurry have failed, and it is doubtful that it derives from either the *chasse* dance step; the Arab *Jazib*, "one who allures"; the African *jaiza*, "the sound of distant drums"; or the Hindu *jazba*, "ardent desire." To complicate matters further, *jazz* was first a verb for sexual intercourse, as it still is today in slang.

Jazz Age. A coinage of F. Scott Fitzgerald for the era of the 1920s in America, a time dominated by youth and jazz music and marked by frenetic hedonism as well as great achievement. Also known as the Roaring Twenties and the Boom, this extravagant era, often treating life as a great party, was depicted in the caricatures of John Held and described in Fitzgerald's classic fiction: *Tales of the Jazz Age* (1922), the first use of the phrase *Jazz Age*; his masterpiece, *The Great Gatsby* (1925); *Flappers and Philosophers* (1920); and his first novel, *This Side of Paradise* (1920). Of the Jazz Age Fitzgerald wrote: "It was an age of miracles, it was an age of art, it was an age of excess, and it was an age of satire."

J. C. Penney. Yes, the "C" in the name of the J. C. Penney department stores does stand for "cash," which was the middle name of the store's founder—James Cash Penney.

jeep. Eugene the Jeep, a character in Elzie Crisler (E.C.) Segar's widely syndicated comic-strip "Popeye," had supernatural powers and could do just about anything. Introduced in 1936, the mythical little animal was well known by World War II when Willis-Overland began manufacturing their versatile, open, 1 1/4-ton, four-wheel-drive vehicles for the armed forces. No one knows for certain, but the vehicle was probably named a *jeep* by U.S. servicemen from the sound of the army term GP (general purpose), this reinforced by the popularity of Eugene the Jeep and the "jeep" noise that he constantly made. In any event, jeep was "in the air at the time," as Mencken says, used as the name for many contrivances, and the official army name for the vehicle—"half-ton-four-by-four command-reconnaissance car"—was definitely in need of improvement. A *peep* was the term invented to distinguish the new half-ton truck from the jeep, but it never really caught on. Wrote famed World War I correspondent Ernie Pyle: "The jeep does everything. . . . It is faithful as a dog, strong as a mule, agile as a goat."

Jefferson City, Missouri. Named after Thomas Jefferson, this is one of the four U.S. state capitals named after presidents. The others are Lincoln, Nebraska, for Abraham Lincoln; Madison, Wisconsin, for James Madison; and Jackson, Mississippi, for Andrew Jackson.

jell; It didn't jell. *Jell* is an Americanism meaning "to congeal or jelly" and may have been invented by Louisa May Alcott in her book *Little Women* (1869), where it is first recorded. The expression *it didn't jell*, "it didn't work, it failed," is first recorded in 1949.

Jell-O. The trademark name of this dessert, made of gelatin, sugar, and fruit flavoring, was coined by Mary Wait, the wife of its inventor, cough medicine maker Pearl B. Wait of LeRoy, New York, in 1897. By

1929, Jell-O and Postum cereal were the nucleus of the huge General Foods Corporation.

Jersey barrier. Cones placed around the scene of an accident, of which there are far too many on the New Jersey highways, to make the site less dangerous.

Jesse James. Jesse Woodson James became a kind of American Robin Hood in his own brief lifetime. A member of the Confederate Quantrill gang in his youth, he and his brother Frank later led the most notorious band of robbers in the country's history. The gang's daring bank and train robberies caused many deaths, but James was regarded as a hero by a public that hated foreclosing banks and greedy railroads. In 1882, changing his name to Thomas Howard, Jesse went into hiding at St. Joseph, Missouri. There, six months later, Robert Ford, "the dirty little coward that shot Mr. Howard," killed him for a reward. Jesse James was only 35 when he died. He is still a folk hero, commemorated in a popular ballad, folktales, movies, novels, and at least one play. Besides being slang for a criminal, a *Jesse James* is a truckman's name for a police magistrate and has been applied by baseball players to umpires.

Jim Crow. Blackface minstrel Thomas D. Rice, "the father of American minstrelsy," introduced the song "Jim Crow" in 1828, claiming to have patterned it on the song and dance of an old field hand named Jim Crow he had observed in Kentucky. Rice's routine, part of a skit called "The Rifle," became so familiar here and on tour in England that a few years later a British antislavery book was titled *The History of Jim Crow*. It is from this book and similar uses of *Jim Crow* to signify a black that the discriminatory laws and practices take their name, though the first Jim Crow laws weren't enacted until 1875 in Tennessee.

jim-kay. An historical term meaning to stu with food to a dangerous point. According to one story, a family kept a pet pig that they named James K. Polk, a er the U.S. president, and fed James (or Jim) K. so much that he burst apart. Thus the president's name became the basis for this odd addition to America's political lexicon.

jocko. Apparently a new name for kill. In a recent trial, a New York gangland lawyer complained that he didn't know the meaning of *jocko*, which the prosecutor said meant to kill (*New York Times*, June 25, 2005). The judge said it really didn't matter, considering the murder and racketeering charges the lawyer's client had already been convicted of: "One could infer that 'jocko' does not mean let's go out and picnic in Central Park." Jocko also means a nincompoop, saphead, a dolt, a natural born fool, etc.

joe. *Joe* may have become slang for coffee, as in a *cuppa joe*, because of the great consumption of it by G.I. Joes during World War II, according to Mark Pendergast in his fascinating book *Uncommon Grounds: The History of Coffee and How It Transformed Our World* (1999). This seems unlikely, as the term is first recorded in 1930 as tramp and underworld slang. Another interesting theory is that the word derives from Stephen Foster's song "Old Black Joe" (1850), a perennial favorite like so many of his songs ("Oh! Susannah," "Swanee," "My Old Kentucky Home," "Camptown Races," "Jeanie with the Light Brown Hair," among others). But no matter how appealing, there is no firm evidence for any of these theories.

Joe Louis. Joe Louis, perhaps the greatest of all heavyweight fighters, came to be nicknamed the *Brown Bomber* for his blockbusting right and the color of his skin. Joe Louis Barrow, born on May 13, 1914, in Lafayette, Alabama, was the son of a sharecropper who died when Joe was four. The family moved to Detroit where Joe helped support them when he was only 16 by taking odd jobs that included work as a sparring partner in a local gym. This led to a boxing career that finally saw him take the heavyweight title from Jim Braddock in 1937. He defended his title more often than any other champion in ring history, and only Jack Dempsey outpolled him in the Associated Press survey of 1950 in which sportswriters picked the best boxers of the century. Louis lost three times in a career interrupted by service in World War II, once (before he became champion) to Max Schmeling, whom he knocked out in a rematch, and then to Rocky Marciano and Ezzard Charles, after he had retired as undefeated heavyweight champion but was attempting a comeback. His ring record included 64 KOs, eight decisions, and one win by default. A *Joe Louis* is synonymous for the utmost in a fighter, a heavyweight without peer.

John Hancock. If John Hancock had done nothing else, he would be remembered for his big, bold, belligerent signature, the first on the Declaration of Independence, writ "so big no Britisher would have to use his spectacles to read it." "King John" Hancock (1737–93), also known as the King of Smugglers, was a Revolutionary patriot who led local merchants in protesting the Stamp Act, heading as he did the largest mercantile firm in Boston. Immensely popular in his own lifetime, he became a major general of militia, a member and president of the Continental Congress, and, except for one term, was elected annually as governor of Massachusetts from 1780 until his death. His name, as everyone knows, is commonly used to mean a signature or as a synonym for *name* itself. *See* JOHN HENRY.

John Henry. Like *John Hancock* above, this is a synonym for a signature or name, but we don't know how the term arose. There is probably no connection here with the black folk hero John Henry, who outdrove a steam drill with his hammer. *John Henry* originated in the American West as cowboy slang and that's all anyone has been able to establish about it.

johnnycake. "New England corn pone" someone has dubbed this flat corn bread once cooked on a board over an open fire. Most scholars agree that no cook named Johnny had a hand in inventing the bread. *Johnnycake* is usually traced to *Shawnee cakes* made by the Shawnee Indians, who by Colonial times were long familiar with corn and its many uses in cooking. Not everyone agrees, though, and one popular theory holds that *johnnycake* is a corruption of *journey-cake*, which is what early travelers called the long-lasting corn breads that they carried in their saddlebags. However, *johnnycake* is recorded before *journeycake* in the form of *jonikin*, "thin, waferlike sheets, toasted on a board . . . eaten at breakfast with butter"; *jonikin* is still used for griddle cakes on the eastern shore of Maryland. The word apparently progressed from *Shawnee cake* to *jonnikin* and *johnnycake*, and then to *journeycake*. Probably when people no longer needed to carry the cakes on journeys, johnnycake became popular again.

Johnny-come-lately. Back in the early 1800s, British sailors called any new or inexperienced hand Johnny Newcomer. American sailors apparently adopted the expression, changing it to Johnny Comelately. The first recorded mention of the term—in an 1839 novel set on the high seas—uses it in this form in referring to a young recruit. The expression soon came to describe newcomers in all walks of life, changing a little more to the familiar *Johnny-come-lately*.

John Wayne. The term *John Wayne* (the movie name of Marion Morrison, 1909–79) can mean a "heroic person" or a "reckless, daring showy person," due to Wayne's star movie roles and his off-camera political views. No one knows how long any of these will last, but *John Wayne* has become the word for about 10 other things, including a John Wayne bar, an Army-field-ration candy bar; a John Wayne cookie or cracker, also Army field rations; a John Wayne hat, a bush hat; and John Wayne High School, after those who quit school to join the army. To John Wayne is to attack someone forcefully with little or no consideration.

John Wesley Hardin. A fabled gunfighter. After John Wesley Hardin (1853-95), killer of some 40 men, the first when he was only 12. Hardin, famous for his *quick cross draw* (crossing his arms to opposite sides and pulling his guns from his vest pockets) died when he was shot in the back of the head while playing cards.

Jonathan apple. The Jonathan apple, named after Jonathan Hasbrouck, an American judge who died in 1846, is fifth in order of commercial importance in America. It is a late fall-ripening apple, bright red and often yellow-striped, its round fruit mildly acid and the trees bearing it very prolific. The Jonathan, grown mainly in the Northwest, is but one of numerous apple varieties commending their growers or other notables. The Gravenstein, Grimes Golden, Macoun, and Stayman are only a few others that come to mind.

josh. The best guess is that the Americanism *josh*, for "to kid" or "fool around," is a merging of *joke* and *bosh*. The pseudonym of an American writer may have something to do with the word, though. Henry Wheeler Shaw (1818–85) wrote his deliberately misspelled crackerbox philosophy under the pen name Josh Billings. Employing dialect, ridiculous spellings, deformed grammar, monstrous logic, puns, malapropisms, and anticlimax, he became one of the most popular literary comedians of his time. The expression *to josh* was used about 18 years before Josh Billings began writing in 1863, but his salty aphorisms probably strengthened its meaning and gave the term wider currency.

joy o' the mountain. This colorful name is given to trailing arbutus in the mountains of the American South. Trailing arbutus (of the *Epigaea* genus) is probably the most fragrant of all wildflowers. The evergreen plant is difficult to cultivate in home gardens, but thrives in the wild.

the juice ain't worth the squeeze. The juice here is orange juice, not liquor, and the saying means it's not worth doing, the effort isn't worth the result. Reported by a Maryland correspondent.

juice loans. Loans made at very high interest. A specialty of the Outfit, a Chicago branch of the Mafia. They are called "street taxes" by loan sharks, who have to pay it to mobsters.

Jumbo. P. T. Barnum purchased the fabled elephant Jumbo from the London Zoological Society in 1881 for "The Barnum and Bailey

Greatest Show on Earth." Jumbo, captured by a hunting party in 1869, was one of the largest elephants ever seen in West Africa; the natives called the six-and-a-half-ton beast by the Swahili word *jumbo*, meaning "chief." He became a great favorite in the London Zoo, giving rides to thousands of children, and his sale to the American showman caused quite an uproar. Within six weeks the incomparable P.T. had reaped $336,000 from the $30,000 investment, and he made Jumbo's name a synonym for "huge" throughout America and the world.

Juneteenth. June 19, in honor of the emancipation date of blacks in Texas, where the holiday is celebrated annually by many African-Americans.

junket. "The term *junket* in America is generally applied to a trip taken by an American official at the expense of the government he serves so nobly and unselfishly," noted a *Detroit Free Press* writer in 1886. The Americanism had been used similarly by Washington Irving in 1809. Our *junket* comes from the British *junket*, for "a banquet," which may derive from the old Norman word *jonquette*, meaning a reed basket in which fish and other things were carried, or "in which sweet cream cheese was brought into town for sale." *Jonquette*, in turn, comes from the Latin *juncus*, "a reed."

just a heartbeat away from the presidency. Presidential candidate Adlai Stevenson coined this phrase in a campaign speech on October 23, 1952. He was referring to Republican vice presidential nominee Richard Nixon, "the young man who asks you to set him one heartbeat from the presidency of the United States."

just like Jell-o on springs. Famously said by Jack Lemmon o Marilyn Monroe walking away in the film *Some Like It Hot* (1959), and since used to describe other sexy women. *Jelly*, not JELL-O, had earlier described this love-potion motion in the popular song lyric "I wish I could shimmy like my sister Kate, / She shakes like jelly on a plate . . ."

just what the doctor ordered. Anything that is most suitable, perfectly relevant. Often heard in the United States since at least the 1940s.

just when I thought I was out, they pull me back in. A lament of the Godfather in the book and movie of the same name when he tries unsuccessfully to break his ties with the mob. the phrase has been heard more commonly recently, in a humorous way.

K

kale. *Kale* is 20th-century American slang for money, as well as a vegetable. The word derives from the Middle English *cale*, a variant of *cole,* for "cabbage." American settlers called this primitive member of the cabbage family *colewarts.*

Kal-el. Superman is an alias or nom de querre in the fight against evil. The comic book hero's real name is Kal-el, bestowed upon him by his parents when he was born on the planet Krypton before it exploded.

Kansas. The Sunflower State, admitted to the Union in 1861 as our 34th state, takes its name from the name of a Sioux tribe meaning "people of the south wind." It had previously been called the Kansas Territory.

katydid. John Bartram, America's first great botanist, first recorded *katydid* (or a word similar to it) in 1751 as the name of the large, green arboreal insect of the locust family known scientifically as *Microcentrum rhombifolium.* The word is of imitative origin, the chattering noise the insect makes sounding like "Katy did! Katy did!"

keeping up with the Joneses. According to his own account, cartoonist Arthur R. ("Pop") Momand lived in a community where many people tried to keep up with the Joneses. Momand and his wife resided in Cedarhurst, New York, one of Long Island's Five Towns, where the average income is still among America's highest. Living "far beyond our means in our endeavor to keep up with the well-to-do class," the Momands were wise enough to quit the scene and move to Manhattan, where they rented a cheap apartment and "Pop" Momand used his Cedarhurst experience to create his once immensely popular *Keeping Up with the Joneses* comic strip, launched in 1913. Momand first thought of calling the strip "Keeping Up with the Smiths," but "finally decided on *Keeping Up with the Joneses* as being more euphonious." His creation ran in American newspapers for over 28 years and appeared in book, movie, and musical-comedy form, giving the expression *keeping up with the Joneses* the wide currency that made it a part of everyday language.

keep on truckin'. Keep going, keep moving, don't quit. Etymologist Joseph T. Shipley wrote that the expression "comes from the great marathon dance contests that were a part of our 1930s scene, when all the partners clung to one another, half-asleep, but on and on moving around the dance hall through the night, like the great trucks that go endlessly across our continent through the dark hours, as they 'keep on truckin' for the prize." This scene was brilliantly depicted in the movie *They Shoot Horses, Don't They?* (1969).

keep the ball rolling. The election of 1840, which pitted President Martin Van Buren running for reelection against "Tippecanoe and Tyler, too"—General William Henry Harrison, legendary hero who fought against the Indians at Tippecanoe, and Virginian John Tyler—brought with it the first modern political campaign. Some historians believe that the election gave us the expression *keep the ball rolling* as well as the word *O.K.* One popular advertising stunt that helped Harrison win was "to keep the ball rolling" for the "log cabin and hard cider candidate." Ten-foot "victory-balls," made of tin and leather and imprinted with the candidate's name, were rolled from city to city for as far as 300 miles. These victory balls did popularize the expression *keep* *the ball rolling,* keep interest from flagging, but the saying undoubtedly dates back to the late 18th century. Of British origin, it alludes either to the game of bandy, a form of hockey where the puck is a small ball, or the game of rugby. In either sport there is no interest in the game if the ball is not rolling. The first form of the expression was *keep the ball up. See* BANDY; O.K.

keep your eye on the ball. Many sports could have spawned the American expression meaning "be closely attentive." Baseball, tennis, golf, and basketball are all candidates, but the saying seems to have derived from the exhortations of college football coaches to their charges at the turn of the century. *To be on the ball,* to be vitally alert or in the know, is apparently an offshoot of this phrase, even though in baseball it has been said of a pitcher who has a wide variety of effective pitches.

keep your fingers crossed. Making the sign of the cross has long been thought to be effective in averting evil, but the use of crossed fingers as a symbol of the cross is American in origin, probably originating as a superstition among blacks in the 17th century. The practice was also thought to bring good luck and resulted in the expression to *keep your fingers crossed,* as well as the belief among schoolchildren and others that a lie told with the fingers (or toes, or legs, etc.) crossed "doesn't count."

keep your shirt on. The stiff, starched shirts worn by American men back in the mid-19th century when this expression originated weren't made for a man to fight in. Therefore, men often removed their shirts when enraged and ready to fight, a practice that is reflected in the older British expression *to get one's shirt out,* "to lose one's temper." *Keep your shirt on* was a natural admonition from someone who didn't want to fight and realized that an argument could be settled if both parties kept calm and collected. *Keep your hair on* and *keep your back hair up* are earlier related expressions for "don't get excited."

Kentucky. The Blue Grass State was admitted to the Union in 1792 as our 15th state, formerly having been Kentucky County, Virginia. It takes its name from the Iroquois *Kentake,* "mead-owland." Historically Kentucky was called "the dark and bloody ground" because it was an Indian no-man's-land used by several tribes as a burial and hunting ground.

Kentucky bite. Heavyweight champion Mike Tyson was hardly the first American to bite off part of an opponent's ear in a fight in or out of the ring. Such tactics were all too common in years past, especially, it seems, in our old Kentucky homes. Melville noted the technique in *White-Jacket* (1844) and Hemingway described it graphically in several of his stories. More recently, Vincent, the new godfather in *Godfather III* bit of part of his rival's ear.

Kentucky bluegrass. A grass (*Poa pratensis*) that grows particularly well in Kentucky but is widely used as a lawn grass throughout the United States.

Kentucky burgoo. A celebrated stew made of chicken or small game, and corn, tomatoes, and onions; traditionally served on Derby Day. *See* KENTUCKY DERBY.

Kentucky colonel. Someone upon whom the honorary title of Colonel is bestowed in Kentucky, though no one takes the title very seriously.

Kentucky Derby. A horse race for three-year-olds held annually since 1875 on the first Saturday in May at Churchill Downs in Louisville, Kentucky; it was named after the English Derby at Epsom Downs, first held in 1780. *See* DERBY.

Kentucky rifle. Famous in American history as the rifle of the pioneers, the long, extremely accurate Kentucky rifle is recorded by this name as early as 1838. The flint-lock muzzleloader should, however, be called the Pennsylvania rifle, for it was first made in that state by Swiss gunsmiths in the 1730s and perfected there. "The British bayonet was no match for the Kentucky rifle," wrote one early chronicler.

Kentucky right turn. According to William Safire's "On Language" column in the *New York Times* (January 27, 1991), this is a humorous term meaning "the maneuver performed when a driver, about to turn right, first swings to the left."

Keystone State. A nickname for Pennsylvania since at least 1803, when it was first recorded. Pennsylvania also has been called the Quaker State, the Steel State, and the Oil State. Keystone was chosen because Pennsylvania was the keystone of the arch that the original 13 colonies loosely formed.

Key West. This southernmost area of Florida and the U.S. takes its English name from Spanish Cayo-Hueso, a small rocky islet to the west.

kick it up a notch. Make something, especially a recipe, a little more intense, better, more flavorful, hotter, etc. The expression is used frequently by Emeril Lagasse, host of the *Emeril Live* television cooking show when he prepares a recipe. It may have its origins in cooking, possibly deriving from a cook turning up the heat a notch on an oven's thermostat.

Kilroy was here. No catchphrase has ever rivaled Kilroy since it appeared on walls and every other available surface during World War II. It was first presumed that Kilroy was fictional; one graffiti expert even insisted that *Kilroy* represented an Oedipal fantasy, combining "kill" with "roi" (the French word for "king"). But word sleuths found that James J. Kilroy, a politician and an inspector in a Quincy, Massachusetts shipyard, coined the slogan. Kilroy chalked the words on ships and crates of equipment to indicate that he had inspected them. From Quincy the phrase traveled on ships and crates all over the world, copied by GIs wherever it went, and Kilroy, who died in Boston in 1962 at the age of 60, became the most widely "published" man since Shakespeare. James Kilroy wrote this about the coinage in the *New York Times Magazine* (Jan. 12, 1947): "On December 5, 1941, I started to work for Bethlehem Steel Company, Fore River Ship Yard, Quincy, Mass., as a rate setter (inspector) . . . I was getting sick of being accused of not looking the jobs over and one day, as I came through the manhole of a tank I had just surveyed, I angrily marked with yellow crayon on the tank top, where the tester could see it, 'KILROY WAS HERE.' "

Kinderhook. Old Kinderhook, the nickname of President Martin Van Buren, is the basis for the universal expression o.k. Old Kinderhook's birthplace, Kinderhook, New York, in turn, takes its name from children. When Henry Hudson anchored the *Half Moon* near this hook of land, he was greeted by Indian children, *Kinder* in German and Dutch. *See also* o.k.

King Cotton. A term once much used to personify the economic supremacy of cotton in the South. Wrote R. H. Stoddard in his poem "King Cotton" (1861): "Ye slaves of curs forgotten/Hats off to great King Cotton!"

Kirby pickle. The Kirby pickle familiar to gardeners is a name applied generally to all pickling cucumbers and definitely is named in honor of a man. It bears the name of the developer of a once-popular pickling cucumber called the *Kirby*—Norvel E. Kirby of Philadelphia's I. N. Simon & Son seed company, now out of business. Simon introduced the Kirby in 1920 and it remained popular until the mid-1930s, when more disease-resistant types replaced it. Its name remained, however, as a designation for all pickling cucumbers.

kissing cousin. *Kissing cousins* is a southern Americanism that dates back before the Civil War. The term first implied a distant blood relationship, but today more often means a very close friend who is considered family. It still is used in its original sense of a relative far removed enough to permit marriage, "an eighth cousin" in the North.

kiss-me-quick. In New England and the southeastern part of the U.S. a kiss-me or a kiss-me-quick was a ridge or depression in a roadway, one that caused a carriage to jolt and possibly throw a girl into her young man's arms. The usage is recorded as late as 1945 in the Southeast and may still be used there to a limited extent.

Klingon. Etymologists have missed including this word in any straight or slang dictionary I've seen. The word has been used to describe a brutal, barbaric, warlike person for some 30 years now, ever since the term was invented for the TV series *Star Trek*. Therein the Klingons are debased warlike beings from the planet Klingon, who look no better than they act.

klutz. Widely used in the U.S. since about 1918, *klutz* was originally a Yiddish term, deriving from the German *Klotz* for "a log or block of wood." It describes a clumsy, graceless person; a bungler, a fool. *Klutz,* however, can also refer to an intelligent person who is badly coordinated. *To klutz* means "to botch up or bungle."

knock (throw) for a loop. To hit someone or something very hard, to defeat, to astonish or upset. This Americanism has been traced back to the early 1920s. Loop may have originally referred to the loop maneuver made by an airplane, but that is only a guess. The expression has several colorful variations, including *knock for a row of ashcans, knock for a row of milk cans, knock for a row of Chinese pagodas,* and, best of all, *knock for a row of tall red totem poles.*

knock the spots off. The origins of this Americanism for "to defeat decisively" are not clear, but some word sleuths believe it is from the world of boxing, reasoning that the expression is first recorded in a sports story and—admittedly reaching on this one—speculating that the spots in question were freckles figuratively knocked off the face of a badly beaten fighter. However, the expression could have its roots in the sharpshooting of 19th-century American marksmen, who could shoot the pips (or spots) out of a playing card nailed to a tree a considerable distance away.

know-how. An Americanism coined about 1830 that means "knowledge of how to do something, expertise." It was first recorded in an 1859 issue of *Spirit of the Times* featuring a story in which one character tells another to charge "fifty cents for the killing" (of livestock) "and fifty cents for the know-how."

know one's cans. Cowboys on the range in the 19th century were usually starved for reading matter and o en read the labels on the cook's tin cans, learning them by heart. A tenderfoot could always be distinguished because he didn't know his cans. The expression isn't recorded in the *Dictionary of Americanisms* but is given in Ray Allen Billington's *America's Frontier Culture* (1977). Wrote Edna Ferber in *Cimmaron* (1930): "The back and the side doors of the dwelling . . . littered with the empty tin cans that mark any new American settlement, and especially one whose drought is relieved by the thirst-quenching coolness of tinned tomatoes and peaches. Perhaps the canned tomato, as much as anything else, made possible the settling of the vast West and Southwest."

Kris Kringle. After nearly a century and a half this synonym for Santa Claus is still heard, even though the words have nothing at all to do with Santa. The term originated in America in about 1830 and was spelled *Krisskring'l* before taking its present form. *Krisskring'l* stemmed from a misunderstanding of the word *Christ-kindlein* used by German immigrants, its meaning not "Santa Claus" but "the Child in the Manger," or "the little Christ child."

Ku Klux Klan. A secret organization that arose in the South after the Civil War to preserve white supremacy. From 1865 to 1877 the name was often applied to all secret political organizations with the same purpose. The term derives from the Greek *kyklos*, circle, plus *klan*, a variant spelling of *clan*. Since 1915 the Klan's official name has been the Knights of the Ku Klux Klan and the organization has directed its words and actions against Jews, Catholics, and the foreign-born as well as African-Americans. An old story holds that the name of the organization is based on the sound of rifle-bolt being operated.

L

Ladies and gentlemen. *Ladies and gentlemen,* as a form of address to a mixed audience, used to be the reverse: It was traditional to say "gentlemen and ladies." The change, putting ladies first, came in early America and first took place in the North, not in the chivalrous South.

ladies of the line. We have all heard of the self-explanatory *ladies of the night,* for prostitutes, but why *ladies of the line?* The expression comes to us from the American West, where prostitutes did business in tents and jerry-built shacks stretched out in lines at the outskirts of towns, mining camps, or railroad yards.

ladies of the night. This American euphemism for prostitutes was popular in the 1870s and is still used today. Interesting collective nouns for such ladies include: *a horde of hookers, a jam of tarts, a wiggle of whores, a flourish of strumpets, an essay of Trollope's, an anthology of pros.*

lagniappe. *Lagniappe,* a "bonus gift" often given by merchants to customers, derives from the American Indian *yapa,* "a present to a customer," which came into Spanish first as *la napa,* "the gift." Pronounced *lanyap,* the word has also been used in Louisiana to mean small-scale bribery.

Lake Superior. Lake Superior is aptly named, for it is the world's largest freshwater lake, with a surface area of 31,800 square miles.

Lake Webster. The body of water with the longest name is located near Webster, Massachusetts, and is called Lake Webster by almost everyone. However, its official, Indian-derived name is composed of 43 letters and 14 syllables, translating into English as "You fish on your side; we fish on our side; nobody fish in the middle." Should anyone want to try pronouncing it, the lake is called Chargoggagoggmanchaugagoggchaubunagungamaug.

La La Land. A humorous name for Los Angeles (L.A.), California, since the early 1980s. In lower case *to be living in la la land* means to be far removed from reality.

lame duck. Before the adoption of the 20th Amendment to the Constitution in 1930, any president or congressman who was defeated for election in November elections still held office until the following March 4. These elected officials were called lame ducks because they were mostly ineffectual, although they could help pass legislation embarrassing to an incoming administration. The "Lame Duck Amendment" eliminated them, but lame-duck appointments to diplomatic posts, etc., can still be made by a defeated, outgoing president. No one is sure where the term *lame duck* comes from. It originated about 125 years ago and may have been suggested by the British *lame duck*, "a person who has lost all his money, who has been financially crippled on the stock exchange." On the other hand it could be native born, a qualification of the American phrase *a dead duck*, an outgoing congressman being not quite dead yet, merely "lamed" until March 4 of the following year.

Land of Blood. A nickname for Kentucky since the early 19th century, when it was famous or infamous for its many Indian wars.

land-office business. Prior to the Civil War, the U.S. government established "land offices" for the allotment of government-owned land in western territories just opened to settlers. These offices registered applicants, and the rush of citizens lining up mornings long before the office opened made the expression *doing a land-office business*, "a tremendous amount of business," part of the language by at least 1853. Adding to the queues were prospectors filing mining claims, which were also handled by land offices. After several decades the phrase was applied figuratively to a great business in something other than land, even, in one case I remember, to a land-office business in fish.

large as life. We owe this popular phrase to one of Thomas C. Haliburton's Sam Slick tales, *The Clockmaker* (1837), in which Sam Slick of Slicksville says of another character: "He marched up and down afore the street door like a peacock, as large as life and twice as natural." Sam's words became a popular catch-phrase in America and still survive in both the original and abbreviated versions.

last of the Mohicans. The Mohicans live—contrary to James Fenimore Cooper's famous story, we have not seen the last of them. Cooper adopted the name of the Algonquian-speaking tribe for the second of his "Leatherstocking Tales," and the title *The Last of the Mohicans* became an expression still used to indicate the last of any group with a certain identity. But the Mohicans—at least mixed-blood remnants of the tribe—still survive near Norwich, Connecticut and in Stock-bridge, Indiana. The Mohicans, or Mahicans, were a powerful group in the past, occupying both banks of the upper Hudson in New York, while another branch, the Mohigans, lived in eastern Connecticut. While settlement and war with the Mohawks pushed them out of these areas—Dutch guns supplied to their enemies hastening their dispersal—and they almost entirely lost their identity. Probably some 800 survive today. The tribe owns a profitable gambling casino on its Connecticut reservation.

latchkey children. Children whose parents both work and who have to let themselves into their homes after school with a key. The term is older than one would think, dating back at least to World War II in America. At that time many mothers worked in defense industries and many fathers served in the armed forces.

law and order. This slogan was employed long before present times in America, notably by Rhode Island's Law and Order Party, which opposed Dorr's rebellion in 1844. It has now been usurped by the series produced by Dick Wolf on NBC.

lay it on with a trowel. An Americanism first recorded in about 1839, at about the same time *lay it on thick* was recorded. Both phrases mean the same, that is to slavishly flatter, exaggerate. A trowel, of course, is a tool used for depositing and working with mortar and plaster.

lazybird. The cowbird *(Molothrus ater)* is called the lazybird in America because the female of the species lays her eggs in the nests of other birds instead of building her own. The term is probably an old one, though first recorded in 1917.

lazy Susan. The British call our *lazy Susan* a dumbwaiter, which the revolving servitor was called in America until relatively recently. It is said that the first use of the term dates back to about 75 years ago when the device was named after some servant it replaced, Susan being a common name for servants at the time. But the earliest quotation that has been found for *lazy Susan* is in 1934, and it could be the creation of some unheralded advertising copywriter. Therefore, *lazy* may not mean a lazy servant at all, referring instead to a hostess too lazy to pass the snacks around, or to the ease with which guests can rotate the device on the spindle and bring the sections containing different foods directly in front of them.

leave in the soup. To leave someone in the lurch or in trouble. The expression is an Americanism first recorded in 1889 in connection with some South Dakota con man who skipped town with a lot of money, leaving many investors in trouble.

Leblang. New York ticket agent Joseph Leblang sold reduced-price tickets to Broadway shows in the 1920s. He was so noted for this that his name became an eponymous word meaning to sell same, or meaning the tickets themselves (Leblangs).

left-handed monkey wrench. There is no such tool, but green workers on a job are sometimes told to find one as a joke. The same applies to a "left-handed screwdriver" or "hammer." The terms are Americanisms, probably dating back to the early 20th century but possibly much older.

left holding the bag. To be left responsible for something, to be the fall guy or scapegoat after the others involved in a crooked scheme have protected themselves from prosecution or absconded. The term is an old Americanism dating back to 1760 or earlier, and Thomas Jefferson used it. The British use the phrases *left holding the can* and *left holding the baby*. *Left holding the bag* is recorded in Royall Tyler's *The Contrast* (1787), the first stage comedy written by an American. In the play Jonathan, the trusty Yankee retainer of the serious-minded American Revolutionary War officer Colonel Manley, is a servant full of homespun shrewdness. After referring to Shay's Rebellion, a 1786 revolt of Massachusetts farmers against high land taxes, Jonathan says: "General Shay has sneaked off and given us the bag to hold."

legalese. When Charles A. Beardsley, then president of the American Bar Association, kidded his fellow lawyers with the famous words "Beware of and eschew pompous prolixity," he was campaigning against what philosopher Jeremy Bentham called "literary garbage," legal talk that has nothing to do with communication. "Legalese" consists principally of long-windedness, stilted phrases such as "Know all men by these presents," redundancies including "separate and apart" or "aid and abet," such quaintisms as "herewith and heretofore," and foreign-language phrases that could easily be translated into plain English: e.g., *caveat emptor* ("let the buyer beware") or *amicus curiae* ("friend of the court"). Despite the efforts of Beardsley and many others, the situation has not improved much over the last millennium. Some, like Sir Thomas More, have believed that it never will. More, a lawyer himself, explained that lawyers are "people whose profession is to disguise matters."

lei. The well-known Hawaiian flower wreath. The garland of flowers is traditionally worn around the neck.

lemonade. *lemonade* is an Americanism for a drink made of lemon juice, water, and sugar, always served cold, usually with ice. To the British, Australians, and New Zealanders, however, *lemonade* means "clear soda pop," often with a lemon flavor, such as the trademarked Sprite or 7-Up.

let her rip. Letting things go at full speed was called *let-her-rip-itiveness* in mid-19th-century America. The Americanism derives from another American expression, *let her rip,* which apparently first referred to railroad locomotives. Americans were always obsessed with speed. Wrote one early train traveler out West: "Git up more steam—this ain't a funeral! Let her rip!"

Let's slip out of these clothes and into a dry martini. A bynow almost proverbial quip by author and wit Robert Benchley. Benchley was known to drink; in fact, he was known to drink more and to be able to hold more than anyone in his circle. "What do you drink so much for?" F. Scott Fitzgerald, of all people, once lectured him. "Don't you know alcohol is slow poison?" "So who's in a hurry?" Benchley replied. Another time he observed, "Drinking makes such fools of people, and people are such fools to begin with, that it's compounding a felony."

letter carrier. An old term for a postman still commonly used in northern California; occasionally heard in metropolitan New York and other areas as well.

Levi's. The word *Levi's* has become more popular in the eastern United States recently as a synonym for jeans, denims, or *dungarees*—probably due to the bright-colored styles that Levi Strauss and Company are manufacturing today. The trademarked name has been around since the gold rush days, though, when a pioneer San Francisco overall manufacturer began making them. Levi Strauss reinforced his heavy blue denims with copper rivets at strain points such as the corners of pockets, this innovation making his product especially valuable to miners, who often loaded their pockets with ore samples. Within a few years the pants were widely known throughout the West, where the name Levi's has always been more common than any other for tight-fitting, heavy blue denims.

Liberty Tree (Elm); Liberty Hall; Liberty Stump. A tree that grew in Boston from which effigies of unpopular people were hanged during the protests over the Stamp Act in 1765. The ground under the tree became known as Liberty Hall. In 1775 the British cut the venerable elm down, and for a time it be came known as the Liberty Stump. Soon after Liberty Trees were being planted all over the country, some say in almost every American town. Most of them died from the disease that struck elms early in the 20th century.

lickety split. Bartlett's *Dictionary of Americanisms* (1859) defines *lickety split* as "very fast, headlong; synonymous with the equally elegant phrase 'full chisel.'" Today *lickety split* is only heard infrequently and it is folksy rather than "elegant." The *lick* in the phrase is probably associated with speed because of the rapidity with which the tongue moves in the mouth, and *split* is perhaps associated with "split second." The Puritans used the phrase, but it wasn't very popular until the mid-19th century. *Lickety cut, lickety switch, lickety click, lickety liver,* and *lickety brindle* were variations on the expression.

lightning pilot. A pilot on the Mississippi River in the 19th century who was lightning quick, who got all the speed possible from his ship, was called a lightning pilot. The term was used by Mark Twain and many other contemporary writers.

like a house on fire. Although log cabins weren't the homes of the earliest American settlers—Swedes settling in Delaware introduced them in 1638—they became a common sight on the western frontier in the 18th and 19th centuries. As practical as they were, these rude wooden structures were tinderboxes once they caught fire. So fast did they burn to the ground that pioneers began to compare the speed of a fast horse to a log cabin burning to the ground, saying he could go *like a house on fire.* By 1809 Washington Irving, under the pseudonym Diedrich Knickerbocker, had given the expression wide currency in his *History of New York from the Beginning of the World to the End of the Dutch Dynasty,* the first great book of comic literature by an American. The phrase soon came to mean "very quickly or energetically."

like Grand Central Station. Very crowded, packed, hectic. In use since the early 1900s, the phrase refers to New York's Grand Central

Terminal, where trains arrive and depart for many destinations, and the busy Grand Central subway stop in the terminal.

like in Macy's window. A synonym for the ultimate in public exposure: "We'll be like in Macy's window." Traditional window displays date back to the early 1880s when the use of plate glass on a wide scale made display windows a standard feature of department stores. Macy's display windows in New York were long the most prominent among them, especially those in their flagship store on 34th Street, "the World's Largest Store" with over 2.2 million square feet of floor space. In fact, Macy's old 14th Street store in Manhattan was famous for its Christmas displays as far back as the mid-1800s, featuring a collection of toys revolving on a belt.

like it or lump it. Be happy with it or just put up with it against your will, resign yourself to it. *Lump it* could come from the word lump, which once meant to gulp down a bitter medicine. The expression dates back to 1791, according to the *Dictionary of Americanisms.*

like pigs in clover. To be completely content, very happy. The first mention of the Americanism was a brief poem in the Boston Gazette (Jan. 7, 1813): "Canadians! Then in droves come over, / And live henceforth like pigs in clover." In Britain pigs in clover describes wealthy people behaving badly, but I've never heard or seen the words used that way in the U.S.

like trying to find flea shit in a pile of pepper. The phrase is used by a U.S. senator in the movie *J.F.K.* (1991), but I'm sure it's older. It means "almost impossible to find," harder by far than finding a needle in a haystack.

like trying to nail Jell-o to a tree. Theodore Roosevelt seems to have invented the idea behind this metaphor, if not the exact words, in a July 2, 1915, letter to William Roscoe Thayer, in which he described the difficulty of negotiating with Colombia regarding the Panama Canal. His exact words were: "You could no more make an agreement with them than you could nail currant jelly to a wall—and the failure to nail currant jelly to a wall is not due to the nail; it is due to the currant jelly."

Lincoln, Nebraska. Named after Abraham Lincoln, this is one of the four U.S. state capitals named after presidents. The others are Madison, Wisconsin, for James Madison; Jefferson City, Missouri, for Thomas Jefferson; and Jackson, Mississippi, for Andrew Jackson.

Lincoln shingles. Hardbread, also dubbed sheet-iron crackers, was called Lincoln shingles by U.S. troops on the frontier. The term is first recorded in Captain Eugene F. Ware's *The Indian War of 1874,* but must date back to Civil War times, given the use of Abraham Lincoln's name. A synonym was *teeth dullers.*

the li-on is busy. This immortal intonation was first used at the Metropolitan Telephone and Telegraph Co.'s old Nassau exchange in New York City, by a Brooklyn-born operator around 1882. Dialing,

Touch-Tone phones, cell phones, and the decline and fall of Brooklynese have made the words rare, possibly obsolete.

litterbug. Litterbug, meaning someone who habitually litters, is an anonymous coinage, probably based on firebug, dating back to the end of World War II. It owes its popularity to the Lakes and Hills Garden Club of Mount Dora, Florida, which used the slogan "Don't be a litterbug!" in a 1950 roadside cleanup campaign.

loaded for bear. Ready for anything, well prepared, heavily armed. "Loaded for b-ar," as the expression was often pronounced, probably goes back to American pioneers hunting in the forests where they had to carry guns loaded with ammunition powerful enough to kill a bear, the most dangerous beast they might encounter. The phrase was first recorded, however, in 1875. Today it can also mean "very drunk."

loafer. Loafer, for "a lazy do-nothing, an idler, or lounger," is apparently an Americanism, first recorded in 1830, deriving from the German *Landlaufer,* "vagabond." Other possible ancestors are the English dialect word *louper,* "vagabond," the expression *to loup the tether,* "to wander," and the Dutch *loof,* "weary." The verb *to loaf* is apparently a back-formation from the noun. *Loafer* has been the name for a slip-on shoe without laces in the U.S. since the 1940s.

lobster shift. Lobster shift, for the newspaper shift commencing at four in the morning, is said to have originated at the defunct *New York Journal-American* early in this century. The newspaper's plant was near the East Side docks and workers on this shift came to work at about the same time lobstermen were putting out to sea in their boats.

lock, stock, and barrel. The firing mechanism, or lock (by which the charge is exploded); the stock (to which the lock and barrel are attached); and the barrel (the tube through which bullets are discharged) are the three components of a firearm that make up the whole gun. Thus the expression *lock, stock, and barrel* means the whole works, the whole of anything. The saying is an Americanism first recorded in Thomas Haliburton's Sam Slick stories (1843), but likely goes back to the muskets of the American Revolution. However, the expression might also be rooted in the *lock* on a country store's door, the *stock,* or goods, inside, and even the *barrel* on which business was often transacted.

log cabin. The first log cabins in America were built by Swedish settlers in Delaware in about 1638. English settlers, who had never seen such structures in England, soon followed the Swedes' example and named the little log houses log cabins.

lollygagging. The *Dictionary of Americanisms* quotes an indignant citizen in the year of our Lord 1868 on "the lascivious lolly-gagging lumps of licenteousness who disgrace the common decencies of life by their love-sick fawnings at our public dances." This is the first recorded use of *lollygagging,* which means "to fool around, dawdle, waste time" and can mean "lovemaking," though this last is no waste of time and my dear old grandmother never used the word in such a way to me.

lone star flag. This name was usually applied to the flag of the Texas Republic but referred to the flags of several southern states in Civil War times, including the flags of Virginia, South Carolina, and Louisiana.

Lone Star State. A nickname for Texas, after the single star on its state flag. Texas has also been called the Beef State, the Jumbo State, the Banner State, and the Blizzard State.

the longest night; the longest day. *The longest night* is another term for the Holocaust (qv). *The longest day* was June 6, 1944, D-day, when the Allies landed in France. It is said that German Field Marshal Erwin Rommel (the Desert Fox) was the first to use the phrase, when he told an aide a few months before the Normandy landing that "the first 24 hours of the invasion" would be decisive, sealing Germany's fate: "For the Allies, as well as Germany, it will be the longest day." Years later, the words would become the title of a famous book and movie.

long green. The first U.S. greenback dollars were printed in 1863 and this term came into use soon after. *Long green* means "a lot of money," suggesting green bills laid in a long line, end to end.

long row to hoe. Rows in American home gardens today, usually a dozen feet or so in length, can't compare to the long rows of corn, beans, and other crops on early American farms. These rows, which often stretched out of sight, had to be weeded by hand at the time and approaching one with hoe in hand was dispiriting, to say the least. The expression a *long row to hoe* was probably well established for any time-consuming, tedious task many years before Davy Crockett first recorded it in 1835. It is still heard in a day when mechanized equipment has replaced hoes on farms, perhaps because, according to a recent poll, some 100 million Americans consider themselves vegetable gardeners.

looks like she swallowed a watermelon seed. A humorous way American mountain folk describe a pregnant woman. The expression dates back to the early 19th Century.

looney tunes. Looney Tunes was originally the name of a Warner Brothers cartoon series that first appeared in 1930, taking its name of course from *looney,* which comes from lunatic. In recent times, *looney tunes* has been used by law enforcement authorities to mean a crazed subject and has had increased general usage in the same sense. President Reagan referred to terrorists and their supporters as looney tunes. It was street slang long before this, however.

Loop. Well known as Chicago's business, shopping, and theatrical center, the Loop was named after the elevated railroad, built in 1897, whose tracks "loop" the district.

Los Angeles. *Los Angeles* is a shortening of the California city's original name: *El Pueblo de Nuestra Senora la Reina de los Angeles de Porcinuncula* ("The town of Our Lady Queen of the Angels of Porcinuncula"). It is more often called *L.A.* Call it "L.A." and it loses 54 letters.

loud and clear. In U.S. aviation radio transmission *loud and clear* means the air weather is perfect for flying. The phrase may date from the early 1920s.

Louisville; Louisville Slugger. Louisville, the largest city in Kentucky, was named for France's Louis XVI in 1780 in recognition of the assistance he had given America during the Revolutionary War. Home of Fort Knox, the Kentucky Derby, the mint julep, many bourbon distilleries, and the only inland United States Coast Guard station, Louisville also houses the famous Hillerich & Bradley's baseball bat factory, where the renowned Louisville Slugger has been made since 1884. The bat is of course named after the city named after a king. Louisville Sluggers are made from prime white ash, one mature tree is needed to make 60 bats, and more than 6 million are turned out each year. Some 2 percent of the annual production goes to professional ballplayers, these fashioned from specifications noted in a 50,000-card file covering the bat preferences of ballplayers past and present.

love child; love brat. *Love child,* for "a child born out of wedlock," isn't a euphemism from Victorian times, as is often said. The kind words date back at least to 1805, when recorded by a writer referring to *love child's* use in another locality. Before this Pope used the similar *babe of love* in the *Dunciad* (1728): "Two babes of love close clinging to her waist." *Love brat,* a nastier variant, is recorded earlier than either expression, sometime in the 17th century.

love tap; love pat. People were probably calling gentle taps indicating love *love taps* long before Mark Twain used the expression in *A*

Connecticut Yankee in King Arthur's Court (1889). But Twain's is the first recorded use of the expression, which may have been suggested by the earlier *love pat*, recorded in 1876.

lower the boom. *Lower the boom* can mean to hit someone hard, as in "Clancy lowered the boom," or to ask someone for a loan. The idea behind the American expression, which probably dates back to the late 19th century, is that of a cargo-loading boom hitting someone.

L7. One rarely hears or sees this late-fifties Hollywood slang for "a square" anymore, perhaps because while it is clever visually, it has no ear appeal. *L7* means square, "not with it" according to bandleader Artie Shaw, because "if you form an L and a 7 with your finger, that's what you get."

luau. The word for a Hawaiian feast often made for tourists.

Lucy Stoner. Use of the "Ms." form of address for a woman today recalls the all-but-forgotten *Lucy Stoners* active earlier in this century. A woman who refused to change her maiden name upon marriage was often called a Lucy Stoner. The term recalls American feminist Lucy Stone (1818–93), who deserves far greater recognition than she has received. On graduation from Oberlin, the only college accepting women at the time, Lucy Stone was 29, and she plunged headlong into the woman suffrage and antislavery causes. Her important work included helping to form the National Woman's Association, of which she was president for three years, and the founding of the *Women's Journal*, the association's official publication for nearly 50 years. An eloquent speaker for women's rights, Lucy Stone became well-known throughout the U.S. In 1855 she married Dr. Henry Brown Blackwell, an antislavery worker, but as a matter of principle she refused to take his name, and she and her husband issued a joint protest against the inequalities in the marriage law. Lucy Stone would never answer to any but her maiden name all her married life, and the Lucy Stone League later emulated her, defending the right of all married women to do so.

Lyme disease. Lyme disease is named after the Connecticut town where it was first recognized in the 1970s. The minuscule tick *Ixodes dammini* harbors the spirochetes of the disabling disease. The ticks are carried to humans by deer and whitefooted mice that leave them on grass and foliage.

lynch. Our word for extralegal hanging definitely comes from the name of a man, but just who was the real Judge Lynch? At least a dozen men have been suggested as candidates for the dubious distinction. Scholarly opinion leans toward Virginia's Captain William Lynch (1742–1820), who was brought to light by Edgar Allan Poe in an editorial on "lynching" that he wrote in 1836 when he edited the *Southern Literary Messenger*. Poe claimed that the "lynch law" originated in 1780 when Captain Lynch and his followers organized to rid Pittsylvania County of a band of ruffians threatening the neighborhood. Poe even affixed a compact drawn up by Lynch and his men to the editorial. William Lynch's identity was further verified by Richard Venables, an old resident of the county, in the May 1859 issue of *Harper's Magazine*. But without evidence of any actual hanging there was still room for doubt. Finally, additional proof was found in the diary of the famous surveyor Andrew Elli-cott, who visited Captain Lynch in 1811 and gained his friendship. William Lynch related how his lynch-men, as they were called, were sworn to secrecy and loyalty to the band. On receiving information accusing someone of a crime, the accused was seized and questioned before a court of sorts. If he did not confess immediately, he was horsewhipped until he did, and sometimes hanged whether he confessed or not.

M

macguffin. Alfred Hitchcock defined the word *macguffin* while talking about his film *Notorious* (1946): "So the question arose, in designing the story for the film, what were the Germans up to down in Rio, what were they doing there? And I thought of the idea that they were collecting samples of uranium 235 from which the future atom bomb would be made. So the producer said, 'Oh, that's a bit far-fetched— what atom bombs?' I said, 'Well, both sides are looking for it . . . [but] if you don't like uranium 235, let's make it industrial diamonds. But it makes no difference, it's what we call the "macguffin" ' . . . The *macguffin* is the thing the spies are after, but the audience *doesn't care*. It could be the plans of a fort, the secret plans of an airplane engine."

Mackinaw blanket; Mackinaw coat. John S. Farmer, in *Americanisms Old and New* (1889) first gave the origins of this term common in America since about 1830: "A superior kind of blanket which derived its distinctive name from the island of Mackinaw, formerly one of the chief posts at which Indian tribes received their grants from the government. A provision of one of the Indian treaties was that part of the payment made to the redskins should be in these superior blankets, and from that fact the name *Mackinaw Blankets* or *Mackinaws* simply was derived." A *Mackinaw coat* is a coat made from a Mackinaw blanket, or from any blanket.

mad as a rained-on rooster. A phrase recently introduced by television commentator Dan Rather.

mad as a wet hen. Hens don't become very upset from getting wet, so this old expression isn't a particularly apt one. An Americanism that dates back to the early 19th century, it was apparently based on the false assumption that a hen, being exclusively a land animal, unlike, say, the duck, would go beserk if caught in the rain or doused with water. Better was the old expression *wet hen* for "a prostitute."

Madison, Wisconsin. Named after James Madison, this is one of the four U.S. state capitals named after presidents. The others are Lincoln, Nebraska, for Abraham Lincoln; Jefferson City, Missouri, for Thomas Jefferson; and Jackson, Mississippi, for Andrew Jackson.

Mae West. This inflatable life jacket was introduced at the beginning of World War II and named for one of the world's most famous sex symbols because it "bulged in the right places." Mae West (1893–1980) starred on Broadway until two of her plays, *Sex* and *Pleasure Man* were closed by the police in 1928. Migrating to Hollywood, she won fame as "Diamond Lil," the "Screen's Bad Girl," and the "Siren of the Screen." Her name, *Webster's* advises, is also given to a twin-turreted tank, a malfunctioning parachute with a two-lobed appearance, and a bulging sail. When told that her name was included in *Webster's*, she said: "I've been in *Who's Who* and I know what's what, but this is the first time I've made the dictionary." Among her many famous sayings are "Peel me a grape, Beulah [her maid]," and "Come up and see me sometime." It is said that Mae West acquired the nickname "Baby Vamp" when she was only five and played a vamp at a church social; she repeated the performance in a stage play the same year, perfecting her famous walk at that time. "I do all my best work in bed," she once replied when a reporter asked her how she went about writing her memoirs. She claimed to be sexually active well into her 80s and once claimed *(not* in her 80s) to have made love with one of her paramours for 15 consecutive hours. Several inventors have claimed they invented the Mae West life jacket, but most authorities choose U.S. inventor Alvin Markus (1885–1943), holder of many patents. See the *New York Times* (May 16, 2005) for an interesting account of the invention.

Magnolia State. A nickname for Mississippi, which was first called the Mudcat State after the large catfish (mudcats) in its waters. It has also been called the Eagle State (probably from the eagle on its state emblem), the Border-Eagle State, the Ground-hog State, the Mud-Waddler State, and the Bayou State.

a mailbox for the dead. While recording the plight of home-less vagrants on the outskirts of Reno, Nevada, American poet Langston Hughes (1902–67) took a long walk and came to a small mountain cemetery. On the cemetery gate there seemed to be a mailbox, though there was no house in sight. Upon reaching the gate he realized that what he saw was only an old board that had warped into the shape of a mailbox. The idea of a "mailbox for the dead," however, caught his fancy, and that night he began a story that would fit the title. During his writing he kept calling his father, whom he had not seen for more than 13 years. The next day Hughes received a telegram informing him that his father had died the night before, at the same time the poet had been writing "A Mailbox for the Dead."

Maine. Maximillian Schele De Vere in *Americanisms* (1871) says that the name *Maine* may have been chosen for the Pine Tree State "in compliment to the Queen of England, who had inherited a province of the same name in France." According to George R. Stewart in *Names on the Land* (1945):

In a New England charter of 1620 the lawyers wrote:

"The country of the Maine Land," words which suggest a general description rather than a name. Two years later, however, a charter was granted to two old sea-dogs of the Royal Navy, Sir Ferdinando Georges and Captain John Mason, and in it the word had certainly ceased to be a description. Dated on August 10, 1622, the charter declared that "all that part of the mainland" the grantees "intend to name the Province of Maine." Some have thought that this name arose because of the greater number of islands off that northern coast, which made men have more reason to speak of "the main." Others have tried to connect it with the Province, or County, of Maine in France. But again, *main* as equaling *chief* or *important* would have been of good omen, if a little boastful. Moreover, about 1611 Captain Mason had served in the Orkneys, and must have known the name as used there.

Mainiacs. A humorous title given to residents of Maine, who are more properly called *Mainers.*

Main Street. *Main Street* is the typically American designation for the principal thoroughfare in a town, while the British synonym is High Street (the *high* denoting importance, not elevation). In early Colonial days, along the East Coast, there were High Streets, some surviving today, but *high* came to suggest elevation in America as the pioneers moved inland toward the mountains. The most famous *Main Street* is found in Sinclair Lewis's novel of the same name, published in 1920. Even New York City has it Main Streets; in fact, Manhattan is the only one of New York City's five boroughs that doesn't have a Main Street. Over the years Main Roads, Main Drags, and Main Stems have also been added.

major league. The baseball terms *major league* and *minor league* date back to 1882, when the National League was called the major league and the American Association (not today's American League) was called the minor league. Later these two leagues merged and the unified teams became known as the major leagues, any league below them being called a minor league. Today, of course, the major leagues are composed of the American and National Leagues, each with two divisions. Because the major leagues are the highest level of professional baseball, the term *major league* has generally come to mean the best of anything. *Big league*, a synonym, also comes from baseball, where it was used as early as 1899.

make fur fly. The cruel "sport" of trapping raccoons and setting dogs on them to see how long the coons could last may have suggested this expression to American pioneers. Certainly the air was filled with fur during such fights. By at least 1825 the saying meant "to attack violently." In the autobiographical *A Narrative of the Life of David Crockett, of the State of Tennessee* (1834) we read: "I knew very well that I was in the devil of a hobble, for my father had been taking a few horns, and was in a good condition to make the fur fly."

make good. To succeed, prosper, or fulfill a promise, as in "He made good on his word." This Americanism was born as a poker term, which is explained in the manual *Poker: How to Play It* (1882): "When all who wish to play has gone in, the person putting the ante . . . can play like the others by 'making good'—that is, putting up in addition to the ante as much more as will make him equal in stake to the rest." By the turn of the 19th century the poker term was being used figuratively.

make him an offer he can't refuse. Used jokingly today, but popularized by the film version of Mario Puzo's *The Godfather* (1972), in which the GODFATHER, played by Marlon Brando, uses it as a veiled threat. One of his confidants tells him that a certain Hollywood producer will never give his godson an important part in a movie he is making. "I'm gonna make him an offer he can't refuse," is the godfather's exact answer, implying the potential of violence to the producer. That violence turns out to be decapitating the producer's prize racehorse and placing the horse's head in the bed where he is sleeping. The phrase is used several times in the *Godfather* movies.

make the feathers fly. To badly beat an opponent in a fight. This Americanism is first recorded in John Neal's romantic novel *Brother Jonathan* (1825): "If my New York master only had hold o' him; he'd make the feathers fly."

make things hum. Since at least the early 18th century, humming, suggesting the blending of many human voices or the activity of busy bees, has been used to express a condition of busy activity. Two hundred years later the expression *to make things hum* was invented in America. Possibly the hum of machines in New England textile factories was the inspiration for the phrase, in reference to the fabled Yankee mechanics who made things hum again when the machines broke down.

make whoopee. *Whoopee* has been an American exclamation of joy or approval since about 1860. However, it was apparently newspaper columnist Walter Winchell who coined the expression *making whoopee,* for "wild merrymaking," the expression then made very familiar by the popular song "Making Whoopee" (1930).

mañana. The Spanish word for tomorrow or sometime in the future. The *land* or *kingdom of mañana* was once a common American term used to mean a place where time was often disregarded, a land of postponement, and often applied to Mexico.

man for breakfast. Lawlessness often went unpunished in the American West and people reading their morning newspapers had their *man for breakfast,* or murder, every day. The expression persisted from the late 19th century well into the 20th century.

man hands. Hands that are large or unfeminine. The term is used to describe a beautiful woman whose overly masculine hands are her only flaw: "She's gorgeous except for those man hands of hers." Coined on the television series *Seinfeld.*

Manhattan; Manhattanization. Since 1898 *Manhattan* has been the name of New York's central borough, and has always been a synonym for New York City itself. From the Manhattan Indians, indirectly, we also have the *Manhattan cocktail,* made with whiskey, sweet vermouth, and bitters, first mixed about 1890; *Manhattan clam chowder,* made with tomatoes, unlike the traditional New England milk clam chowder; and *Manhattan Project,* the code name for the project that developed the first atomic bomb. *Manhattanization* is a word that seems to have originated only recently. In the 1971 fall elections, San Francisco residents were urged to vote for an amendment halting the construction of tall buildings to avoid the Manhattanization of San Francisco.

Manhattan clam chowder. *See* CHOWDER

Manhattan Project. The code name for the group of scientists and administrators who developed the atomic bomb for the United States during World War II.

Manhattan schist. The thick, tough bedrock that makes it possible to build the skyscrapers of Manhattan. Exposures of it can be seen in Central Park.

manifest destiny. The 19th-century belief or doctrine that it was the divine destiny of the United States to expand its territory over the whole of North America. An 1845 editorial by John L. O'Sullivan supporting the U.S. annexation of Texas was the first to use the term: "[It is] our manifest destiny to overspread the continent allotted by Providence for the free development of our yearly multiplying millions."

Mann Act. Widely known as The White Slave Act, the Mann Act was a 1910 U.S. law named for its author, Congressman James-Robert Mann (1856–1922), which forbid under heavy penalties the transportation of women from one state to another for immoral purposes.

man of the Revolution. The patriot called the man of the Revolution in American history isn't George Washington, as one might suspect. Samuel Adams has the honor "because of the leading part he played in bringing about the War of Independence."

man on the horse. We know that this expression meaning "the person in authority or in charge" is an Americanism, but it is first recorded in England. In 1887 a British newspaper writer noted: "The man on the horse . . . to use the picturesque American phrase, is not now Lord Salisbury." No doubt the expression dates back at least 20 years earlier, perhaps to Civil War days.

man without a country. Contrary to what many people have believed since grade school, Edward Everett Hale's famous story "The Man Without a Country" is fictional. Only the name of the main character is real. In the story Lt. Philip Nolan cries out, "Damn the United States! I wish I may never hear of the United States again!" and is of course sentenced to sail the seas all his life on a Navy ship without ever hearing his country's name again. Nothing like this ever happened to the real Philip Nolan, an adventurer whose career Hale used as background. Hale later regretted using the man's name and wrote a book called *Philip Nolan's Friends* (1876), "to repair my fault, and to recall to memory a brave man," as he put it.

many small potatoes and few in a hill. New Englanders, especially Mainers, use this expression for something or somebody of small consequence. It dates back about a century.

maple syrup; maple sugar. "There can't be a remedy better for fortifying the stomach" than maple sugar, a pioneer wrote in 1705. Maple sugar, boiled from maple syrup and the only sugar the first settlers had, has a long history that dates from the time American pioneers learned how to make it from the Indians. The same, of course, applies to maple syrup, another maple-tree product Americans are still familiar with, but there were also maple-derived products like maple water, maple vinegar, maple molasses, maple wax, maple beer, and even maple wine.

Marenisco, Michigan. Another unusual place name, *Marenisco,* Michigan, was coined from the first syllables of the *four* names of its first woman settler: *Mary Relief Niles Scott.*

mark twain. *Mark twain!* means "mark two fathoms (12 feet) deep" and was called out when riverboat leadsmen sounded the river with weighted line. It is well known that former river-boat pilot Samuel Langhorne Clemens took his pen name Mark Twain from the leadsman's call *mark twain!*

Martha's Vineyard. Possibly discovered by Leif Eriksson in the 11th century, Martha's Vineyard, an island about five miles off Massachusetts's southeast coast, was once an important center for whaling and fishing. The Indians called the island Noe-pe, "Amid the Waters," while the Norsemen named it Staumey, "Isle of Currents." It was christened

Martin's Vineyard by English navigator Bartholomew Gosnold in 1602, apparently for no reason in particular. After a century it took the name *Martha's Vineyard*, probably because its name was confused with that of a little neighboring island to the southeast called Martha's Vineyard that had also been named by Gosnold. That little island is now called No Man's Land, after an Indian named Tequenoman.

Marx Brothers. The stage names of the famous family comedy team originated during its early vaudeville days. Groucho was named for the money pouch called a "grouch" that he carried for the act; Chico for the chicks he always chased; Gummo after the rubber boots he wore; Harpo for the harp he played; and Zeppo, it is said, after a trained monkey that once appeared on the same bill as the Marx Brothers.

Maryland. A popular but incorrect belief has it that *Maryland* was named for the Virgin Mary because it was originally settled by Catholics. The Old Line State actually bears the name of Henrietta Maria (1609–69), wife of England's King Charles I and daughter of France's Henry IV. When Maryland was settled under Lord Calvert in 1632 as a haven for persecuted Catholics, Henrietta Maria was a natural selection for its name, and in the original Latin charter the area is called *Terra Mariae*. It seems that Maryland was to be named for King Charles at first, but he already had the Carolinas named after him and suggested "Mariana," as a name honoring his queen. This was rejected by Lord Baltimore because it was the name of a Jesuit who had written against the monarchy and *Terra Mariae* was adopted instead. Maryland, one of the 13 original colonies, bears the name "Old Line State" because of the bravery of her soldiers—men of the line—during the Revolutionary War.

Mason-Dixon line. Although Dixie wasn't named for the Mason-Dixon line, the latter term has come to be used as a figure of speech for an imaginary dividing line between North and South. The Mason-Dixon line has an interesting history. Originally the 244-mile boundary set between Pennsylvania and Maryland in 1763–67 by English surveyors Charles Mason and Jeremiah Dixon, it was extended six years later to include the southern boundary of Pennsylvania and Virginia. The line had been established by English courts to settle a territorial dispute between the Penns of Pennsylvania and the Calverts of Maryland, but the use of *Mason-Dixon line* in Congressional debates during the Missouri Compromise (1819–20) gave the expression wide currency as a dividing line between free and slave states. After the Civil War the term was retained as the boundary between North and South, especially as a demarcation line of customs and philosophy. Its existence probably did influence the popularity of the word DIXIE.

mason jar. With the renewed interest in vegetable gardening and fresh, healthy foods that are raised for taste and not ease of shipping, the mason jar, used for home canning, is coming into prominence again. The wide-mouthed glass jars with either glass or metal screw tops were named for their inventor, New Yorker John Mason, who patented them in 1857.

massa. This American term for "master," long used by slaves, could derive from the English "master," or from the West African *masam,* "chief," or it could be a blend of both. No one knows for sure.

Massachusetts. "Place of the big hill" is the English translation of the Algonquian *Massachusetts.* The Bay State was admitted to the Union in 1788 as our sixth state and had been called the Massachusetts Bay Colony before then. It is now officially called the Commonwealth of Massachusetts.

the Massachusetts game. A version of baseball, similar in some respects to the present game, whose rules were codified in about 1858 and is one of the forebears of real baseball.

Massholes; foreigner. A century ago many more rivalries and much more name-calling existed between states. The name-calling, at least, hasn't ended. Novelist Richard Russo, for example, notes in his fine *Empire Falls* (2001) that summer visitors to Maine from Massachusetts are locally called "Massholes," a memorable derogatory regionalism I can find in no other source. It sounds like a coinage typical of Mainers, who also call people from out of state "foreigners" and might call someone a "grasshole" for working too hard on his lawn.

Master of the Universe. American author Tom Wolfe invented this term in its sense of an extraordinary Wall Street trader, a preeminent moneymaker, in his novel *Bonfire of the Vanities* (1987). Master of the Universe was apparently suggested by a toy doll of the same name.

maverick. Texas lawyer Samuel Augustus Maverick (1803–70) reluctantly became a rancher in 1845 when he acquired a herd of cattle in payment for a debt. Maverick, a hero who was imprisoned twice in the war for independence from Mexico, eventually moved his cattle to the Conquistar Ranch on the Matagorda Peninsula, 50 miles from San Antonio. But he was too involved in other activities to prove much of a rancher. When in 1855 he sold out to A. Toutant de Beauregard, their contract included all the unbranded cattle on the ranch. Since careless hired hands had failed to brand any of Maverick's calves, Beauregard's cowboys claimed every unbranded animal they came upon as a *Maverick*. So, apparently, did some of Maverick's neighbors. Though Sam Maverick never owned another cow, his name soon meant any unbranded stock, and later any person who holds himself apart from the herd, a nonconformist. All of the standard sources give Texan Sam Maverick as the eponym behind this word. But John Gould, in *Maine Lingo* (1975), credits a Sam Maverick who "was already settled on an island in the harbor when the Puritans came in 1630 to establish Boston." Therefore, he "became the only Bostonian permitted to vote without church affiliation" and was considered a "oddball," a "stray," his fame spreading through New England. Gould claims the "use of *maverick* for an unmarked log in a Maine river preceded the meaning of an unbranded calf on the western plain by many years." A good story that may be true, but no specific, dated sources or quotations are given, although Gould says his Maverick "is mentioned often in early Boston records." Could this be a rare, perhaps unprecedented case of two eponyms independently becoming the same word?

McCarthyism. McCarthyism was coined by author Max Lerner and introduced for the first time in his newspaper column on April 5, 1950. The word notes the witch-hunting practices and disregard of civil liberties that his critics accused Senator Joseph McCarthy (1905–57) of using and inspiring during the "Red" scare in the early 1950s. The Wisconsin senator, a great patriot to his supporters, first charged the Democratic administration with allowing communist infiltration of the State Department. After taking on other government departments, he finally met his match when he attacked the army for alleged security lapses. The army, in turn, accused him of seeking special privileges, and while McCarthy was acquitted by the Senate of this charge, he was censured by a vote of 67–22 for his insolent behavior toward Senate committees. Earlier, the McCarthy hearings were televised and his countenance and repeated "Point of order, Mr. Chairman, point of order" became familiar throughout America. His low tactics ruined the lives of many innocent people.

McDonald's. In recent times the trademark name of the American fast-food restaurant has become almost as well-known as *o.k.* and the trademark *coke,* mainly because McDonald's has franchises through-out the world. Often McDonald's is a synonym for a hamburger. The Japanese have borrowed the name from English and altered it slightly to *Makudonarudo.* The original McDonald's (which no longer exists) was on E Street in San Bernardino, California. The original McDonald brothers sold all but three of their stores to Ray Kroc. These three, now owned by the "Pep Boys" (Manny, Moe, and Jack), are the world's only legal non-Kroc McDonald's.

McGurk's Suicide Hall. A New York City Bowery saloon of the 1890s. So named because so many people committed suicide in it: six in 1899 alone. Other colorfully named dives of the so-called genteel Gay Nineties included the Rat Pit, the Hell Hole, the Inferno, the Dump, and the Flea Bag. All were staffed with fearsome bouncers like Eat-'Em-Up Jack McManus of McGurk's.

the McKinley grip. A handshake perfected by William McKinley when he ran for president (and won) in 1897. McKinley would shake with his right hand and hold the elbow with his left. He was said to be able to shake a hand every two seconds, the record for any president.

McMansion; McJob. *McMansion* is a derogatory term first heard in 2000 for a large, very expensive house with no originality of design, one that looks like all the other "mansions" in the area. *Mc* is an allusion to the MCDONALD's fast-food restaurant chain, which has also given us the term *McJob,* coined in the 1980s for any low-paying, unstimulating job.

Medal of Honor. The United States' highest military decoration, awarded to a serviceman who distinguishes himself beyond the call of duty, this blue-ribboned gold star was established by Congress in 1862 as an award for Union heroes in the Civil War.

median strip. The most common term in America for the grassy strip or area separating opposite sides of a highway. Among other terms used to describe this strip are a *meridian* (in the Midwest), a *medial strip* (Pennsylvania), *neutral ground* (Louisiana), a *mall* (upstate New York), and a *divider* (New York City area).

Megan's Law. In 1994 seven-year-old Megan Kanka was murdered by a previously convicted child molester who lived near her New Jersey home. Public outrage led to a state law allowing police to notify residents if a convicted sex offender moves into the neighborhood. Two years later, a federal court made such notification mandatory.

Memphis. The southern city, famous for Beale Street, the W. C. Handy museum, and Elvis Presley's Graceland home, was founded by Andrew Jackson in 1819. It was named after its storied sister city, which was the capital of the Old Kingdom of ancient Egypt from ca. 3400 to ca. 2445 *b.c.,* at the apex of the Nile delta 12 miles above Cairo.

Men seldom make passes / at girls who wear glasses. Author Dorothy Parker's celebrated couplet was originally published in her friend Franklin Pierce Adams's "The Conning Tower" column under the title "News Item." One of the great wits of all time, Parker had the sharpest tongue of anyone at New York's celebrated Algonquin Round Table, a luncheon group that met at the Algonquin Hotel in the 1920s and included Adams, Robert Benchley, Heywood Broun, George S. Kaufman, Alexander Woollcott, and others from time to time. Later, an anonymous wit qualified Parker's famous couplet, writing: "Whether men will make passes at girls who wear glasses / Depends quite a bit on the shape of the chassis."

merry widow. Late in the 19th century Merry Widow was a U.S. trade name for a brand of condoms. Within 30 years or so, however, *merry widow* had become a synonym for any kind of condom and remained so until the firm making Merry Widows went out of business in the 1940s. The product preceded Franz Lehar's operetta of that title, which was first produced in 1905. *Merry* does figure in several British slang expressions, all obsolete, including *merry-legs,* a harlot; *merry-maker,* the penis; *merry bout,* sexual intercourse; *merry bit,* a willing wench; and, merriest of all, a *merry-arsed Christian,* a whore.

message to Garcia. In his inspirational *A Message to Garcia* (1899), Elbert Hubbard dramatized the true adventure of Lt. Andrew Summers Rowan, U.S. Bureau of Naval Intelligence, who during the Spanish-American War was sent by the U.S. chief of staff to communicate with General Calixto Garda, leader of the Cuban insurgent forces. No one knew just where the elusive Garda might be, but Rowan made his way through the Spanish blockade in a small boat, landing near Turquino Peak on April 24, 1898, where he contacted local patriots, who directed him to Garda far inland, and returned to Washington with information regarding the insurgent forces. The brave and resourceful Rowan became a hero, but Hubbard transformed him into an almost Arthurian figure and it was his essay that made *carry a message to Garcia* a byword.

mess hall. Since Civil War days the colorful name for a tent or Quonset, or any place where meals are served to soldiers and sailors. But the military has recently decreed that such place should properly be called the more eloquent dining facilities.

metrosexual. *Newsweek* (November 10, 2003) says presidential hopeful Howard Dean proclaims during his campaign that he's a metrosexual, "a word used to describe a straight man in touch with his feminine side." I can't find metrosexual recorded anywhere else, though the metro in the word may suggest the relative sophistication of men living in metropolitan areas.

Micah Rood's apple. An apple with streaks of red running through the white flesh. The tale is that on a spring day in 1693 a jewelry peddler visited old Micah Rood's farm at Franklin, Pennsylvania. Shortly afterward the peddler was found murdered under an apple tree in Rood's orchard, but his jewelry was never recovered and the farmer never was convicted of the crime. According to legend, though, all the apples harvested from the tree that autumn had streaks of blood inside. Rood died of fright after seeing them, the "damned" spot or streaks called "Micah Rood's curse" from that day on. When recounting this one, don't ruin a good story by quibbling that apples with red running through the flesh were common before Rood's time, that they are simply a "sport," like the famous golden delicious variety and many others. There seems to be no record of a farmer named Micah Rood, but two other peddlers were involved in sensational murders at the time he was allegedly murdered; perhaps these cases inspired the story.

Michigan. Our 26th state, admitted to the Union in 1837, takes its name from *Michigaman,* both the name of an Indian tribe and a place, translating as "great water." The Wolverine State had first been the Michigan Territory. The Indians thought it "the first batch of earth the Great Spirit made."

Mickey Mouse. Mickey Mouse only began to lose popularity when he was streamlined for later films, his tail cut off and his bare chest covered, among other "modernizations." He looked as if he had come off an assembly line of drawing boards, and this commercial slickness was reflected in phrases like *Mickey Mouse music.* In the armed forces during World War II and the Korean conflict *Mickey Mouse* meant anything childish or silly, such as white-glove inspections. "Mickey Mouse movie" was a humorous term G.I.'s gave the frightening films servicemen were shown that gruesomely detailed the effects of gonorrhea and syphilis and that caused many men to swear off sex—for a few days. Mickey Mouse was of course invented by the late Walt Disney (1901–66) in 1923. Disney called his creation Mortimer Mouse at first, but changed the name when his wife suggested Mickey Mouse instead. The cartoonist was Mickey's voice in the early Mickey Mouse cartoons. In Disney's words, "He was my firstborn and the means by which I ultimately achieved all the other things I ever did—from Snow White to Disneyland."

Mickey Mouse rules. One theory holds that World War II U.S. Navy Military Indoctrination Centers, or M.I.C.'s, where undisciplined sailors were restrained, gave their initials to this expression for petty rules. The term has been around since early in World War II and probably can be explained by the fact that such rules seem silly and childish, like MICKEY MOUSE cartoons. Mickey Mouse was better honored when his name became the password chosen by intelligence officers in planning the greatest invasion in the history of warfare—Normandy, 1944. Mickey Mouse diagrams were maps made for plotting positions of convoys and bombarding forces at Normandy.

Middle America. Capital columnist Joseph Kraft (1925–86) coined *Middle America* in the mid-1960s as a term for "the middle-class America whose views were often overlooked by the opinion-molders on the two coasts," according to one of his editors.

midnight ride of Paul Revere. A literary reference to the ride of Paul Revere from Charlestown to Lexington and Concord to warn Americans of the approach of British troops at the beginning of the Revolutionary War. It comes from Henry Wadsworth Longfellow's poem *PaulRevere's Ride* (1861).

mighty small potatoes and few to a hill. This old Americanism is heard more often today in its abbreviated form *small potatoes*. Both expressions mean someone or something of little consequence, insignificant, and were first recorded in 1831. A variation is *small potatoes and few in a hill.*

milkshake. In most of America a milkshake is a thick sweet drink made of milk, syrup, and ice cream. An exception is Rhode Island where such a drink is called a cabinet, after the wooden cabinet in which the mixer used to be encased; a *milkshake* in Rhode Island is just milk and syrup shaken up together. In northern New England the drink most Americans call a *milkshake* is often called a *velvet* or a *frappé*.

Milk Street. A Boston street so named because "country slickers" used to water their milk at a stream there before bringing it into market and selling it to city bumpkins.

million-dollar wound. A war wound, suffered in combat or self-inflicted, that is bad enough to send a soldier home or at least behind the lines out of the combat zone. The term *million-dollar wound* dates back to World War II, while the practice of self-inflicted wounds is as old as the "art of war." In the American Civil War, for example, minor self-inflicted wounds were common, and the reaction to them was often harsh. One Union soldier at Cold Harbor shot himself in the foot. Sure by the powder burn that the wound was self-inflicted, a surgeon chloroformed the soldier and sawed off his leg. "I shall never forget the look of horror that fastened on his face when he found his leg was cut off," an observer wrote.

million-footed Manhattan. A phrase used by Walt Whitman in his poem "A Broadway Pageant" (1883). In it he also called the borough "Superb-faced Manhattan." It might more accurately be called twenty-million footed Manhattan today, counting visitors.

Minnesota. No one is sure exactly what *Minnesota* means, for the Sioux word translates as either "sky-blue water" or "cloudy water." The Gopher State had been called the Minnesota Territory before being admitted to the Union in 1858 as our 32nd state.

minor league. *See* MAJOR LEAGUE.

mint julep. An alcoholic drink, associated with Kentucky since the early 19th century, made with bourbon, sugar, and finely cracked ice and garnished with sprigs of mint, all served in a tall, frosted glass. *Julep* comes ultimately from the Persian *gul,* rose, and *ab,* water, indicating that it was originally some kind of rose water drink.

the miracle of Coogan's Bluff. *See* THE SHOT HEARD ROUND THE WORLD.

Miss America. The winner of the annual national beauty contest held in the U.S. every year since 1921, though it wasn't called the Miss America contest until the following year. The winner is crowned as the most beautiful young woman in the nation. *Miss America* is also used to describe any pretty American girl. Since the Miss America contest debuted, there have been many spinoffs, including a Mrs. America, Miss Universe, and Miss World contest.

missing man formation. One plane, the missing man, from a formation of fighter planes heads up and away from the others, disappearing into the clouds or "the wild blue yonder." A relatively recent way in which the U.S. Air Force honors deceased American heroes and leaders at a funeral, such as that of President Ronald Reagan on June 10, 2004.

Mississippi. The Chippewa called the river for which the state is named the *mice sipi,* the "big river," which white men spelled *Mississippi.* The Magnolia State was admitted to the Union in 1817 as our 20th state.

Missouri. *Missouri* is either from the name of a Sioux tribe, "people of the big canoes," living in the region, or from an Algonquian word adapted by the French meaning "muddy water," in reference to the Missouri River. The Show Me State was admitted to the Union in 1821 as our 24th state, having previously been the Missouri Territory.

miss the boat. To miss a chance or opportunity because one is too late, as a person might be for a ship set to sail at a specific time. This American expression dates back to the early 1900s. *Miss the bus* or *train* are variations on the phrase.

moaningestfullest. American mountain folk like to use comparative and superlative suffixes, which can be attached to any part of speech, as in "He was the moaningestfullest hound I ever did see." *Beautifulest, curiousest,* and *workingest* are also good examples.

mom and pop stores. Mom and pop stores are an ole American institution; there were, for example, thousands of candy stores run by a husband and wife team in New York City from the 1920s through the 1950s. But the term *mom and pop store* is first recorded in 1962. It is occasionally used today to describe any small business with a few employees.

Monday-morning quarterback. Someone who plans strategies or criticizes the actions of others with the benefit of hindsight and not in the heat of battle is a Monday-morning quarterback. The Americanism is from football, dating back to the early 1940s, and originally referred to the fervid fan who tells anyone who will listen on Monday morning just what the quarterback in Saturday's or Sunday's game should have done.

Monitor; Merrimack; Virginia. Though the Civil War battle of the *Monitor* and *Merrimack,* the first ironclad action at sea, is a familiar one, there is usually some confusion about the name of the Southern vessel. Actually, she was launched as the *Merrimack* in 1855 at the Boston Navy Yard and was originally a wooden steam frigate. She was then seized by the Confederacy in 1861, encased while in dry dock with double layered railroad iron, renamed the *Virginia,* and then launched again in 1862. After that time she was called both the *Merrimack* and the *Virginia,* even though only the last name was correct. In fact, she was most often referred to as the *Merrimac* (without the terminal *k*) over the years, a spelling that is totally unjustified. A nickname for the *Monitor* was the *tin can on a shingle.* She was the forerunner of today's battleship.

monkeyshines; monkey business. "You may have barefooted boys cutting up 'monkeyshines' on trees with entire safety to themselves," observes one of the earliest writers to use *monkey-shines,* monkey-like antics, which is first recorded in 1828. *Monkey business* was recorded a little earlier, at the beginning of the century, both words suggested by the increasing numbe of monkeys imported by America's growing circuses and zoos

Monroe Doctrine. Something else named for our fifth U.S iresident, James Monroe (1758–1831). Monroe Doctrine was the name others gave to his speech before Congress on December 2, 1823, in which he warned European powers not to interfere in affairs of the American continent.

Monrovia. Monrovia, the seaport capital of Liberia, was named for U.S. president James Monroe in 1822 when the American Colonization Society founded it as a haven for exslaves from the United States. Mencken quotes a Liberian diplomat who says that the descendants of these American slaves, now Liberia's ruling class, "prefer to be called . . . Monrovian Liberians to distinguish themselves from the natives of the hinterland, who are generally called by their tribal names." Monrovia is the only world capital, except Washington, D.C., that is named for an American president.

Montana. Montana, previously the Montana Territory, takes its name from the Spanish word for "mountainous." The Treasure State was admitted to the Union in 1889 as our 41st state.

Monterey Jack. A mild American cheddar cheese said to have been named about 1945 after its inventor, David Jack, and Monterey County, California.

moonshine. Liquor made illicitly by individuals with no distilling license; in this sense, *moonshine* dates back to the late 19th century. The name reflects the fact that the liquor was made surreptitiously, at night under the light of the moon. It was first used in this sense in America, although the British previously used the term to mean any smuggled liquor. Colorful synonyms are angel teat, Kentucky fire, squirrel whiskey, swamps dew, white lightning, and white mule.

moon shot; moon ball. *Moon shot* refers to a rocket launching aimed at sending a spacecraft to the Moon, the term first recorded in 1958, before the U.S. made a successful moon shot. In baseball *moon shot* or *moon ball* is a long, lofty home run hit far up toward the Moon. Paul Dickson, in *The Dickson Baseball Dictionary* (1989), calls *moon shot* "a space age term," adding that "it took on new meaning in 1986 when a statistician determined that slugger Mike Schmidt hit best under a full moon."

Morgan horse. The Morgan is one of the first horse breeds developed in the United States. A bay stallion named Figure was foaled in 1789 in Springfield, Massachusetts. He belonged to Justin Morgan (1747–98), a Vermont schoolteacher. The horse bearing Morgan's name was probably a blend of thoroughbred and Arabian with other elements, fairly small at 14 hands high and 800 pounds. Morgan, an aspiring musician, bought his colt in Massachusetts, naming him Figure and training him so well that he won trotting races against much larger thoroughbreds. Eventually, Figure came to be called after his master. After his owner died, the horse was bought and sold many times in the 28 years of his life. One of those unusual horses whose dominant traits persist despite centuries of inbreeding, his individual characteristics remain essentially unchanged in the Morgan breed of horses he sired. Morgans are still compact, virile horses noted for their intelligence, docility, and longevity, many of them active when 30 years of age or more. Heavy-shouldered, with a short neck but delicate head, they are noted for their airy carriage and naturally pure gait and speed. Morgans were long the favorite breed for American trotters until the Hambletonian strain replaced them.

Mormon. The name of members of the Church of Jesus Christ of Latter-day Saints, which is centered in Salt Lake City, Utah. *Mormon* derives from the name of the fourth-century prophet said to be the author of writings found by Joseph Smith and published in 1830 as the *Book of Mormon.* "Mormon Church" is a common but unofficial name for the Church of Jesus Christ of Latter-day Saints.

Mormon City. An old name for Salt Lake City, Utah.

Mormon crickets. Early Mormon settlers knew of no way to fight the wingless locustid *(Analrus simplex)* and were left to rely on their prayers. (See GULL). The Mormon cricket remains a formidable problem in Utah today, destroying over $25 million in crops in 2001. These "eating machines" will eat anything, even themselves, according to the U.S. Agriculture Department. They have been plaguing Utah farmers for over a century and a half, and there is no end in sight.

Mormon State. A popular nickname for Utah, which was of course settled by Mormons. Utah calls itself the Beehive State and its state seal depicts a beehive and bees representing the industry of its people. It is also called the Deseret State *(deseret* is a word in the *Book of Mormon* signifying a honeybee), the Land of the Mormons, the Land of the Saints, and the Salt Lake State. *See* UTAH.

moron; amp. It is often noted that *moron,* as a scientific designation for a feebleminded person, was the only word ever voted into the language. It was adopted in 1910 by the American Association for the Study of the Feeble Minded from the name of a foolish character in Molière's play *La Princesse d'Élide.* This claim overlooks the fact that the unit of electric current called an *ampere,* or *amp,* was adopted at the International Electrical Congress held in Paris 29 years earlier. The ampere, the unit by which the strength and rate of flow of an electric current can be measured, was named for the brilliant French scientist Andre-Marie Ampere (1775–1836). His name also gives us such technical terms as *amperehour, Ampère's law, ampereturn,* and *amperometric titration.*

mossback. A very conservative person, a reactionary. The term is said to have been coined to describe draft-dodging southerners who hid out in the swamps so long that moss grew on their backs. These mossybacks weren't forgotten after the Civil War, for by the early 1880s their derogatory name began to be used as an epithet for extremely conservative political factions.

motel. Most sources credit West Coast motor lodge owner Oscar T. Tomerlin with coining the word *motel* in 1930, Tomerlin welding it together from *motor hotel,* which he had previously called his place. But in her book *Palaces of the Public, A History of American Hotels* (1983) Doris E. King says that the word originated in 1925 with a

San Luis Obispo, California establishment that offered a garage with its roadside cottages and called itself a *Motel Inn.*

Mother of States. Usually applied to Virginia, because it was the first state settled by the English, this nickname has also occasionally been given to Connecticut.

Motown. A much-used nickname for Detroit, Michigan, a shortening of *Motor Town,* referring to all the cars made in America's automobile capital. Since the 1950s *Motown* has also described the upbeat, pop-influenced music made by such black artists as Stevie Wonder, the Supremes, and Marvin Gaye that was first produced on records by the black-owned Tamla Motown label in Detroit. This music is often called the "Motown sound."

mountain lion. The North American panther or cougar. The name originated in the Colorado Rocky Mountains over a century ago.

mountain man. Men, much celebrated in song and story, who had great skills for living off the land in the mountains. Usually a guide, trapper, or trader in the Far West before the region was settled.

Mount Rushmore. The colossal busts of Presidents Washington, Jefferson, Lincoln, and Theodore Roosevelt are carved on the face of the Mount Rushmore National Memorial in South Dakota, but the mountain itself is named for an obscure New York lawyer who was sent to the area by businessmen eager to know if mineral rights would be a good investment there. Young Charles Rushmore, traveling all over the Black Hills, was well liked by miners thereabouts, and one story has it that when a stranger inquired about the name of a local hill, a worker jokingly replied, "Why that's Mount Rushmore." The name stuck. The story, which may be apocryphal, is from a letter to the *New York Times Book Review* (12/22/02).

mourning dove. The American bird gets its name from both its often incessant mournful cry and its dull grayish blue plummage. It is also called the turtledove, wild dove, old-field dove, and Carolina dove or pigeon.

movie; film. The most popular name for American motion pictures is *movies,* a word first recorded in 1906. At first the motion picture industry regarded this term as undignified, but by the 1930s all opposition had faded. Many designations were used before *movies,* including *motion pictures* (1891), *picture show* (1896), and *moving pictures* (1898). *Films, cinema,* and *flicks* are also heard though these are primarily British variations. The word *ilm* itself was not recorded until 1905.

movie sexperts. "Goodness, where did you get that necklace?" a friend asked Mae West.

"Never mind," Miss West responded, "but you can take it from me that goodness had nothing to do with it." This became the title of her autobiography.

"How did you get to know so much about men?" gossip columnist Hedda Hopper once asked the irrepressible Miss West.

"Baby," Mae replied, "I went to night school."

Told about a certain promiscuous actress, Dorothy Parker observed, "That woman speaks 18 languages and she can't say 'no' in any of them."

"What do you wear when you go to bed?" a reporter asked Marilyn Monroe.

"Chanel No. 5," she answered. (Another version has her saying she put on nothing but the radio).

moxie. The rather bitter, tart, unsweetened flavor of Moxie, a popular New England soft drink, or tonic, as soda pop is often called in the area, has been suggested as the reason it yielded the slang word *moxie,* for "courage, nerve, or guts." Or maybe, Moxie braced up a lot of people, giving them courage. These are only guesses, but the tonic, a favorite since at least 1927, is definitely responsible for *a lot of moxie* and other phrases, which, however, aren't recorded until about 1939. But Moxie was originally made in 1884 as a patent medicine nerve tonic said to cure "brain and nervous exhaustion, loss of manhood, softening of the brain, and mental imbecility." This goes far in explaining *moxie,* "nerve or courage," if earlier uses for the term could be found. In any event, Moxie's Lowell, Massachusetts makers fizzed up their product toward the turn of the century when the government began cracking down on their health claims and Moxie became America's first mass-market soft drink, the company even selling their product in "Moxie-mobiles," car-shaped bottles.

Mr. Clean. Someone very clean, untouched by scandal or corruption; someone obsessively clean. The eponymn here is the liquid cleaner Mr. Clean introduced in the late 1950s. The Mr. Clean pictured on the bottle and in ads was a bald muscular man who inspired a rash of bad jokes ("He found his wife on the floor with Mr. Clean").

Mr. Watson, come here: I want you. This was the first complete sentence transmitted over the telephone, by American inventor Alexander Graham Bell to his assistant Thomas A. Watson on March 10, 1876.

muckraker. Teddy Roosevelt used the expression *man with the muckrake,* taken from *Pilgrims Progress,* as a derogatory term for those who indiscriminately and irresponsibly charged others with corruption. Lincoln Steffens and other reformers, however, gladly wore the epithet *muckraker* as a badge of honor.

mug; mugging; mugger. Mugging seems first to have been New York City slang for what was called "yoking" in other parts of the country, that is, robbery committed by two holdup men, one clasping the victim around the neck from behind while the other ransacks his pockets. The term either derives from the "mugs" who commit such crimes or from the expression on the victim's face as he is brutally yoked, which can appear as if he is mugging, grimacing, or making a funny face. The term is now well-known throughout the country. As often as not the *mugger* acts alone today, and *mugging* has become a synonym for holding someone up. The spelling "mugg" seems to be yielding to *mug.* The word *mug,* for "a grimace" was introduced to England by the Gypsies and may derive from the Sanskrit word *mukka,* "face." *Mug* was used as slang for "face" in Britain as early as

1840. *Mug* for a heavy cup may come from the Swedish *mugg* meaning the same.

Muhammad Ali. The chosen name of Cassius Clay, which many African Americans considered a "slave name." Ali, born in 1942, was a U.S. boxer who held the Olympic light-heavyweight championship in 1960 and became the world professional champion four years later. He was a true boxer complete with fancy footwork and stinging punches, although he had a knockout punch as well. The only man to regain the title twice, he was noted for his quick wit and little poems, such as:

> "You don't want no pie in the sky when you die,
> You want something here on the ground
> While you're still around."

Murder, Inc. Spelled this way, but always pronounced "Murder Incorporated." This enforcement agency of the organized crime syndicate during the 1930s is believed responsible for between 400 and 500 deaths. Murder, Inc., was controlled by top crime bosses such as Meyer Lansky, Lucky Luciano, and Frank Costello and led by Lord High Executioner Albert Anastasia, a notoriously violent killer. The group provided the mob with a ready pool of paid assassins to be used around the country. Killings were considered strictly business and carried out to protect the interests of the growing syndicate. Members of the group headquartered at Midnight Rose's, a 24-hour candy store in Brownsville, Brooklyn, where they traded tips on killing techniques and waited for assignments. Most prominent among the assassins was Pittsburgh Phil Strauss, target of 58 murder investigations but believed responsible for twice that many deaths. In 1940 law enforcement authorities arrested a number of mob members, including Abe Reles, a Murder, Inc., lieutenant. Reles, fearing others would talk to the police before him, turned informer to save himself, providing details on hundreds of murders and sending many of his colleagues to the electric chair. Before completing his testimony against the highest-ranking mob bosses, Reles fell to his death from the window of a Coney Island hotel where he was under police protection. He was thereafter called "the canary who couldn't fly."

Murderers' Row. Still a popular nickname for the batting order of the 1927 New York Yankees, one of the greatest teams in baseball history. The lineup, which "murdered" opposing pitchers, included Babe Ruth, who hit his famous 60 home runs that year; Lou Gehrig (47), Earl Combs; Bob Meusel; and Tony Lazerri. The Bronx Bombers won 110 games in 1927. The phrase *Murderers' Row* was, however, coined way back in 1858, according to historian Bill Bryson, who traced it to a sportswriter's account of a baseball game, his use of the term suggested by "the isolated row of cells containing dangerous criminals in the Tombs prison in New York." The words have been used generally to describe any group of dangerous people.

Murphy bed. A Murphy bed is a space-saving bed that can be folded or swung into a closet or cabinet; it is named after American inventor William Lawrence Murphy (1876–1950).

mushroom cloud. This image for the explosion of an atomic bomb was first used by *New York Times* reporter William L. Laurence in reporting the initial test of the bomb on July 16, 1945, near Alamogordo, New Mexico. Laurence called the cloud a "supramundane mushroom:" "At first it was a giant column that soon took the form of a supramundane mushroom. For a fleeting instant it took the form of the Statue of Liberty magnified many times."

mutual admiration society. An Americanism that was first recorded in Oliver Wendell Holmes's *Autocrat of the Breakfast Table* (1858) but was coined by Thomas Gold Appleton, Longfellow's brother-in-law. The *OED* defines the phrase as "a satiric designation for a coterie of persons who are accused of over-estimating each other's merits," though it also can be used in a lighthearted, humorous way, as between two friends. Called "the first (best) conversationalist in America" by Emerson, the rich, worldly Appleton was according to Van Wyck Brooks in *New England: Indian Summer* (1940) "the only man who could ride over Holmes and Lowell and talk them down." He also coined the humorous *all good Americans go to Paris when they die,* which is often attributed to Holmes or Oscar Wilde. Holmes, in fact, quoted the remark in *The Autocrat of the Breakfast Table. See* FROZEN YANKEE DOODLE; ALL GOOD AMERICANS GO TO PARIS WHEN THEY DIE.

Muzak. This trademarked name has been around since the late 1930s, when, so the story goes, it was coined as a blend of *mus*ic and the popular Kod*ak*. Since then Muzak has been the light, serene music piped into elevators, restaurants, stores, and even offices and factories. The word is often used disparagingly for light or overly sentimental music.

my back teeth are floating. "I have to urinate—badly." This U.S. expression, still heard, originated in the early 1900s and is used in England as well.

"My Country 'Tis of Thee" *See* AMERICA THE BEAUTIFUL; AMERICA.

my foot! An American expression of extreme disagreement or strong skepticism about something another person has said. First recorded as *your foot!* in the Roaring Twenties, it is almost always heard as *my foot!* today.

my way or the highway. Follow my rules or leave; a coinage probably dating back to the late 20th century. Heard mostly in the United States.

N

nail a lie to the counter. Early country store proprietors often protected themselves against the many types of bogus money in circulation by keeping a copy of *Day's New York Bank Note List and Counterfeit Detector* (1826) on the shelf by the cashbox. They have also been said to have nailed all counterfeit coins they had accepted to the counter as an aide against clerks being cheated in the future and as a warning to would-be sharpies trying to pass bad money in the store. Some say that this practice was the inspiration for the Americanism *to nail a lie to the counter,* "to expose anything false."

naked bear. *Hush or the naked bear will get you!* was an expression mothers stilled their crying children with a century ago. First recorded in 1818, the words refer to an American Indian legend of "a very ferocious kind of bear, which they say once existed, but was totally destroyed by their ancestors." Longfellow mentions the naked bear in one of his poems.

names for both sexes. Linguist Mario Pei says in *What's in a Word* (1968) that in the American South a greater number of first names can be both female and male than in any other area of the country. Such names include Pearl, Marion, Leslie, Beverly, Kim, and Dana. Although these names are all used for both males and females in other sections as well, they are so used with more frequency in the South.

Nantucket. There is a hoary tale, probably untrue, that an old seaman owned an island group off Massachusetts. To his oldest daughter he gave his most productive island, which he named Martha's Vineyard; to his next, he gave the island closest to home, Elizabeth's Island; and to his last daughter, Nan, he just offered what remained, and Nan-tuck-it. No one is sure of *Nantucket*'s real derivation.

Nantucket sleigh-ride. This old expression refers to a whaleboat fastened to a whale, which runs off furiously, towing the boat behind it. Such Nantucket sleigh-rides, often lasting for miles, are described in Herman Melville's *Moby-Dick* (1850) and other great books of the sea.

Nashville, Tennessee. The capital of Tennessee (qv), founded in 1779 as Fort Nashborough, is named for General Richard Nash, who was the ancestor of 20th-century humorous poet Ogden Nash (1902–71). Nashville is known for its country music industry.

nassau. In a golf game, a nassau is an 18-hole match in which one point is given to each of the players having the lowest scores for the first nine holes, the second nine holes, and the entire round. The scoring and betting system is not named for the seaport capital of Nassau in the Bahamas, as is often said. It is actually named after the Nassau County Golf Course at Glen Cove in Nassau County, Long Island, New York, where it was developed in 1901 by players who didn't want to lose by embarrassingly high scores.

National Dictionary Day. An American holiday that falls on October 16th of every year, honoring the great U.S. lexicographer Noah Webster (1758–1843).

national pastime. Baseball was becoming a truly national game in about 1856, when the expression is first recorded, but at that time the term really meant baseball as played by a new code of rules introduced by the New York Knickerbocker Ball Club in 1845. As the game grew even more popular, people assumed that the expression *the national game* implied that baseball was the nation's favorite sport, and they used it this way; the variation *the national pastime* was introduced in the 1920s.

Native American. In the last decade *Native American* has been much used as a synonym for Indian, American Indian, or Amerindian. It is preferred by some, though far from all, "aboriginal people of the Western Hemisphere." *Indian* itself is of course a misnomer used since Columbus, believing he had found India on his first voyage, applied the name to the people he found living in the Americas. A Native American, however, can be anyone born in America, and the first people known to have settled in America weren't Native Americans, they were Asians who crossed the Bering Strait sometime during the late glacial epoch. The term *Native American* was first applied not to Amerindians but to white Anglo-Saxon Protestants in about 1837 when the Native American Association was formed as an anti-Catholic and antiforeign movement. Thus, though the term *Native American* does avoid offensive stereotypes associated with the word "Indian" throughout American history, it has a certain negative connotation of its own.

Native American place-names. "Mississippi," Walt Whitman wrote, "the word winds with chutes—it rolls a stream three thousand miles long. . . . Monongahela, it rolls with venison richness upon the palate." Thousands of charming place-names deriving from American Indian languages adorn the map of the United States. These include, to mention just a few of the most notable, Chicago, Niagara, Allegheny, Saratoga, Susquen-hanna, Potomac, Tallahassee, Manhattan, and Tacoma. Fully 24 of the 50 states bear American Indian names.

nattering nabobs of negativism. Spiro Agnew (1918–96), U.S. vice president under Richard Nixon, coined this phrase in 1969. *Natter* means to talk incessantly, its origin unknown, and *nabob* is used here in its sense of "an influential person." Agnew resigned in 1973 in a plea deal after being charged with accepting bribes. He was the first vice president in U.S. history to resign because of criminal charges. The quote refers to liberals, who liked him as much as he liked them. The whole quote is: "In the United States today we have more than our fair share of the nattering nabobs of negativism. They have formed their own Four H Club: the hopeless, hysterical hypochondriacs of history." As for President Nixon, he became the only U.S. president to resign from office, thanks to his part in the Watergate scandal.

Nebraska. Nebraska, previously the Territory of Nebraska, takes its name from the Omaha Indian *ni-bthaska,* "river in the flatness," for the Platte River. The Cornhusker State was admitted to the Union in 1867 as our 37th state.

necessity mess. An American dish made of thinly sliced potatoes and onions fried in the grease of salt pork. Also called "very poor man's dinner."

Neilsen Ratings; Q rating. Neilsen ratings are a survey conducted by the A. C. Neilsen Company since about 1960 to measure television viewership of various programs. The ratings are based on meters placed in TV sets and viewer diaries of a preselected sample of viewers. A. C. Nielsen had been measuring radio audiences since 1922. The ratings, especially the Sweeps, taken in the months of February, May, July, and November, determine what the networks charge sponsors. The Q rating is a poll that tries to measure the familiarity of actors, products, etc., to the television viewing audience. It is named for its devisor, the TVQ/Marketing Evaluations Co.

nene. Hawaii's official state bird, also called the Hawaiian goose (*Nesochen sandvicensis*). The official name of the barred, gray-brown wild goose is pronounced "neigh-neigh."

nerd. The storyteller-artist Dr. Seuss (the pen name of the late Theodor Seuss Geisel) apparently invented the word *nerd* in his children's book *If I Ran the Zoo* (1950): "And then, just to show them, I'll sail to Ka-Troo And Bring Back an It-Kutch a Preep and a Proo a Nerkle a Nerd and a Seersucker, too!" The nerd is pictured by Dr. Seuss as a thin, cross, humanoid creature. His word and illustration were picked up by small kids and within 10 years became a term for a socially inept, though often intelligent, person.

nervous Nellie. Any very cautious, worried person, often fearful and jittery. Sometimes capitalized, the expression is said to come from the nickname of Frank Billings Kellogg (1856–1937), U.S. secretary of state, who won the Nobel Peace Prize in 1929 largely for his successful negotiating of the 1927 Kellogg-Briand Pact, sometimes called the Pact of Paris, which condemned "recourse to war for the solution of international controversies." Briand was Aristide Briand, foreign minister of France, one of the 62 nations that ultimately ratified the agreement, which failed to provide enforcement measures. The name *Nervous Nellie* seems to have attached itself to Kellogg when he served as a U.S. senator from Minnesota (1917–23), but he was always a nervous man.

Nevada. The Spanish for "snowed upon" or "snowy" is the basis for *Nevada*. The Silver State, which had first been part of the Washoe Territory, was admitted to the Union in 1864 as our 36th state.

Nevaeh. A girl's name, mostly in the United States. There were only eight Nevaehs in 1999, but there are fully 4,457 as of 2006, according to the *New York Times* and the Social Security Administration. How come? Mainly because Christian rock star Sonny Sandorval so named his infant daughter in 2000. Why did he do so? Because *Nevaeh* is *Heaven* spelled backward.

New Amsterdam. The Dutch name for what is now New York City. New Amsterdam, named after the city of Amsterdam in the Netherlands in about 1626, was originally one of the Dutch trading posts in New Netherland. Among other firsts during the New Amsterdam period of the city, the first murder occurred in 1638, the first lottery was held in 1665, and the first "welfare" assistance was given in 1661.

New Deal. *New Deal* comes from Franklin Delano Rooserelt's acceptance speech at the Democratic National Convention on July 2, 1932: "I pledge you, I pledge myself, to a new deal for the American people." Coined by Roosevelt's speech-writers, Raymond Moley and Judge Samuel Rosenman, the phrase incorporated elements of Woodrow Wilson's New Freedom and Teddy Roosevelt's Square Deal.

New England. Captain John Smith thought that the area called New England in North America greatly resembled England. He was the first to record the name, on a map he made in 1616: "That part we call New England . . . betwixt the degree 41. and 45."

New England boiled dinner. Meat, often corned beef, boiled with vegetables such as potatoes, carrots, turnips, and onions.

New England clam chowder. *See* CHOWDER.

New England conscience. This expression is often illustrated with a story about William Ellery of Rhode Island, signer of the Declaration of Independence. When Ellery was a collector of customs in 1790, his grandson dropped into the office. Casually taking a sheet of paper off his grandfather's desk to write a letter, he felt Ellery's hand restraining him. "My boy," the old man said, "if you want paper, I'll give you some, but this is Government paper." However, a cynical definition of *New England Conscience* advises that having one doesn't keep you from doing anything, it just keeps you from enjoying it.

New England weather. An old term for very varied, unpredictable weather. Mark Twain had this to say about it at a dinner of the New England Society in 1876: "There is a sumptuous variety about the New England weather that compels the stranger's admiration—and regret. The weather is always doing something there; always attending strictly to business; always getting up new designs and trying them out on people to see how they will go. But it gets through more business in Spring than in any other season. In the Spring I have counted one hundred and thirty-six different kinds of weather inside of twenty-four hours."

New Hampshire. When Captain John Mason was granted the land including this state in 1622 he named it after his homeland—England's Hampshire County. The Granite State was admitted to the Union in 1788 as our ninth state.

New Jersey. Though it doesn't look like it at first glance, the state's name is another that has to be credited to the Caesars. *New Jersey* was named after *Jersey,* the largest of England's Channel Islands, in honor of Sir George Carteret, who had been governor of the Isle of Jersey and successfully defended it against Cromwell's forces. In 1664 Charles II had granted all lands between the Delaware River and Connecticut to his brother, the duke of York, who in turn granted the New Jersey portion to Carteret and Lord Berkeley. England's Isle of Jersey (a corruption of *Caesaria*) had been named for the Caesars when the Romans added it to their possessions, and so *New Jersey* also bears the immortal name. The relationship can be best seen in New Jersey's official Latin name, *Nova Caesaria*.

New Mexico. Spanish explorers from Mexico named this area Nuevo Mexico, "New Mexico," in 1562. The Land of Enchantment became our 47th state in 1912, previously having been called the New Mexico Territory.

New York. New York is named for James, duke of York and Albany, who in 1664 was granted the patent to all lands between the Delaware River and Connecticut by his older brother, King Charles II. The duke gave away the Jersey portion, but held on to what was then the Dutch colony of New Netherlands. York became the patron of Col. Richard Nicholls, who that same year set sail for the New World, captured New Amsterdam from the Dutch and named both the city of New Amsterdam (New York City) and the colony of New Netherlands (New York State) after the duke. New York State's capital, Albany, is also named for the duke of York and Albany.

New York alligators. There are many stories about New Yorkers flushing baby pet alligators down the toilet and the alligators growing to full size in the sewer pipes beneath the city streets. There were, in fact, several stories about alligator sightings in the local papers during the 1930s, and Smelly Kelly, a noted city worker who sniffed out gas leaks in the underground tunnels, claimed he had encountered one. True or not, the tales are part of New York City folklore. So are New York "rats as big as cats" in the subway tunnels, but these could simply be raccoons, hundreds of which commute on foot in the tunnels every day along with the 4 million people who prefer to use the train.

New York Times. The eminent daily newspaper was founded in 1851 by journalist Henry J. Raymond and former banker George Jones as the *New-York Daily Times*. Its goal was to oppose the distorted news reporting of the day. The name became the *New York Times* in 1857. In the 1890s it went through a period of decline and then was bought by Adolph Ochs who brought it back to prominence under the slogan "All the News That's Fit to Print" and whose family has maintained the paper's reputation since. The slogan remains on the paper's masthead.

n.g.; n.n. The expression *n.g.* has been an abbreviation for "no good" since at least 1839 in America, and it meant "no go," "completely unacceptable," some five years before this. The term *n.n.* is a British one dating back to the beginning of this century and means "a necessary nuisance," especially a husband.

nice guys finish last. This cynical proverb has been attributed by *Bartlett's* to former Brooklyn Dodger manager Leo Durocher, who wrote a book using it as the title. Back in the 1940s Leo was sitting on the bench before a game with the New York Giants and saw opposing manager Mel Ott across the field. "Look at Ott," he said to a group of sportswriters. "He's such a nice guy and they'll finish last for him." One of the writers probably coined the phrase *nice guys finish last* from this remark, but the credit still goes to The Lip.

nice Nelly. Someone so prudish he or she is ridiculous. American humorist Franklin Pierce Adams (he usually signed his work with his initials FPA) is responsible for this term. A prudish woman called Nice Nelly was a character in his newspaper column "The Conning Tower" and her name passed into the language from there.

nice work if you can get it. Common in the U.S. since at least the late 1930s, this phrase—which means "a favorable or agreeable arrangement"—is in Noel Coward's *Peace in Our Time* (1947). A musical comedy song of the same title popularized the expression in America (in *A Damsel in Distress,* 1937).

nickel curve. In baseball a nickel curve is a curve that doesn't break much. The term has been traced to William Arthur (Candy) Cummings (1848–1924), a Hall of Famer who is credited with inventing the curveball over 120 years ago. Cummings's curve was inspired by the half clam shells that he skimmed across a Brooklyn beach as a youngster, but he perfected it by experimenting with a baseball that cost a nickel.

nifty. *Nifty* for "smart, stylish, fine, or clever" may have originated as American theatrical slang. It is first recorded in an 1865 poem by Bret Harte, the author claiming that the word derived from *magnificent.* Another possible source is the older *snifty,* "having a pleasant smell."

nimby. An American acronym that has been common since the late 1980s. It appears to have been coined by American scientist Walter Rodger and means "*n*ot *i*n *m*y *b*ack *y*ard," referring to objection by residents to the establishment in their neighborhoods of dangerous, unsightly, or other undesirable projects, such as shelters for the homeless, prisons, landfills, and incinerators. The people often don't mind if such projects are built elsewhere.

9/11 war. It seems safe to say that the war resulting from the terrorist attack on the World Trade Center in New York on September 11, 2001, will always be remembered by most Americans as the 9/11 war. The only real rival for this designation is the *war on terrorism.*

nine months winter and three months late in the fall. An old one-liner describing, often accurately, New England weather. The saying dates back well over a century.

19th hole. Mencken calls *the 19th hole* "the one American contribution to the argot of golf." While this isn't quite true (*par, birdie, eagle, chip,* and *sudden death* are among U.S.- invented golf terms) the expression has been with us at least since the early 1920s and means "a convivial gathering place," such as a locker room or bar, after a game of golf.

nitwit. This Americanism, first recorded in 1926, may be a combination of the German *nicht,* "not," and the English *wit—nichtwit,* "not with wits, without wits"—corrupted in speech to *nitwit.* Another theory has *nitwit* deriving from "a scornful English imitation" of Dutchmen who answered questions asked in English with the Dutch expression *Ik niet* *wiet,* "I don't know." This, however, would date *nitwit* to Dutch days in New York and there are thus far no examples of the word's use that far back.

Nixon's resignation. Sure that he would be impeached and found guilty in the Senate for his Watergate cover-up, Richard M. Nixon decided to resign from office. It came as a very brief 12-word letter addressed to Secretary of State Henry Kissinger on August 7, 1974, reading:

I hereby resign the office of the President of the United States.

Nixon's the one! This political slogan was turned against Richard Nixon in 1968 when he ran for the presidency—the button with the slogan was sometimes worn by pregnant women (Democrats, of course). In any case, Nixon won, perhaps more because of his slogan "Let's Get America Going Again."

noble experiment. President Herbert Hoover did not coin the expression *noble experiment* for Prohibition, nor even repeat the words. While seeking the presidency in 1928, Hoover answered a question about prohibition in a questionnaire Idaho senator William E. Borah sent to several candidates. What Hoover actually replied in part was: "Our country has deliberately undertaken a great social and economic experiment, noble in motive and far-reaching in purpose."

nobody but nobody undersells Gimbels. This slogan of the now defunct Gimbels department store, often used by other stores today, was invented by the irrepressible Bernice Fitz-Gibbon, an English teacher who became Macy's star copywriter before Gimbels shoplifted her from them. (She had coined Macy's famous *It's Smart to Be Thrifty* slogan, not to mention a legendary ad featuring a voluptuous woman in a strapless evening gown that was captioned "How do you keep it up night after night?") Gimbels' slogan became world famous, Winston Churchill once asking his friend Bernard Baruch if it was "really true that nobody, but nobody, undersells, Gimbels?"

nobody loves Goliath. A saying of the seven-foot-tall Philadelphia Warrior basketball star Wilton "Wilt the Stilt" Chamberlain (1936–1999), whose play dominated the NBA for many years. Called the greatest offensive player in basketball history, Chamberlain was also known as The Dipper, because he dipped so many shots into the basket from above. On March 2, 1962, against the New York Knicks, he scored 100 points, the most ever scored in a single pro game.

nobody never hit nobody. Famous triple negative words of Yankee catcher Yogi Berra when he testified in a lawsuit about a fight in a nightclub.

no bucks, no Buck Rogers. A recent U.S. space agency saying advising or threatening that there will be no exciting manned space probes unless Congress appropriates money needed by the agency for many purposes.

no can do; can do. The negative phrase, and its opposite, are not contemporary expressions, as many people believe. They date back about a century and a half to England, where they probably originated in the Royal Navy.

no cheese, no bees, no trees. American astronaut Neil A. Armstrong's humorous reply back on Earth to those who asked, just as jocularly, if the Moon was made of green cheese. On July 20, 1969, Armstrong had become the first man to walk on the Moon.

no comment. This common expression used by people hounded by reporters is an Americanism dating back no earlier than the beginning of the century. The original journalists given "no comments" may have been Hollywood gossip columnists in the 1920s. In his *On Language* column (March 5, 2006), William Safire says that in 1946 Winston Churchill told reporters: "I think *no comment* is a splendid expression. I got it from Sumner Welles." Though Churchill made the phrase famous, it has never been a favorite of reporters.

no dice. *No dice,* for "no" or "absolutely not," derives from the game of dice, where *no dice* means "a throw that doesn't count." *No dice* can also mean "worthless and completely unsuccessful," all of these meanings apparently dating back to the late 1920s in the U.S.

no hits, no runs, no errors. Dating back to at least the 1930s and deriving from literal use in reports of baseball games, *no hits, no runs, no errors* has come to mean either complete failure (like the team shut out with no hits, no runs, no errors), perfection (like the pitcher who pitches a perfect game with no hits, no runs, no errors), and even something uneventful or without hitches (as in a game where there were no hits, no runs, no errors).

nohow. Anyhow. An Americanism dating back to the early 19th century. In one of Solomon Franklin Smith's books set in the Southwest in the 1850s, he tells of a woman who was offered condolences on the death of her husband. "Warn't of much account, no how!" she replied.

No more free lunch! When he was elected in 1934, New York's reform mayor Fiorello La Guardia invented the slogan "No More Free Lunch!" (No more graft). The words are a translation of the Italian "E finite la cuccagna!" said to have been shouted by the Little Flower while he angrily shook his fist at City Hall.

no more use for them than Meader's teeth. A saying, only historical now, that derives from the old story about a man named Nick Meader, who at about the time of the War of 1812 borrowed a hammer to knock out all his teeth, claiming, "I have no need of them, for I can get nothing to eat."

nondenial denial. Government or any official evasion. The expression was made famous by the words and phrases of President Richard Nixon's chief spokesman, Ronald L. Ziegler (1940–2003) known as *Zig-Zag* to reporters. When Ziegler was asked if U.S. troops were planning to invade Laos in 1971, he advised: "The president is aware of what is going on in Southeast Asia. That is not to say anything is going on in Southeast Asia." The youngest press secretary in U.S. history at 29, he coined the phrases *photo-op* and *third-rate burglary* (for Watergate), among other inventions.

noogie. No one is sure where noogie comes from, though the word is first recorded among U.S. college students in the early 1970s. A *noogie* is a blow to the head with the knuckles, but it can also mean rubbing someone's head with the knuckles.

no problem. Don't worry about it, no trouble to replace or fix it. As in "I'm sorry I broke the plate." "That's O.K., don't worry about it; no problem." A very common American expression.

no more use for them than Meader had for his teeth. A historical saying that derives from an old story about a man named Nick Meader who at about the time of the War of 1812 borrowed a hammer to knock out all his teeth, claiming "I have no need of them, for I can get nothing to eat."

North Carolina; South Carolina. Both states really honor three kings—deriving from the Latin *Carolus,* meaning "Charles." Originally dedicated to France's Charles XI in the 16th century, the territory now comprising North and South Carolina was next named for England's Charles I. Charles I granted the patent for the Carolinas to Sir Robert Heath in 1629, Heath calling the territory Carolana in his honor. This it remained until 1663, when Charles II granted a new patent and the colony was called Carolina in *his* honor.

North Dakota; South Dakota. These states are named for the Dakota tribes in the area, *Dakota* meaning roughly, "allies" from *da,* "to think of as," and *koda,* "friend."

northeast, southwest, northwest, southeast. In parts of Kansas settled along the geographical grids suggested by Thomas Jefferson, the appropriate burners on gas and electrical stoves are still called northeast, southeast, northwest, southwest. Nowhere else is this nomenclature used.

northern fox grape. A wild grape ranging from New England to Illinois and south to Georgia that is so named because it suposedly "smelleth and tasteth like unto a foxe." It is the source f the Concord and other cultivated grape varieties

North Star State. *See* GOPHER STATE.

no skin off my back. Originally *no skin off my nose* was the form of this Americanism, which dates back 75 years or so. It means "it is no concern to me, not my business, doesn't hurt me one bit." Perhaps *nose* better fits the phrase than *back*—if you don't stick your nose into someone else's business, you won't get it punched. But the phrase is also heard as "no skin off my tail," "no skin off my ass," and "no skin off my butt," all of these often preceded by it's or that's.

No-tel Motel. Over the last decade or so "hot pillow joints" (the pillows are still warm from the last occupants when you get the room, so rapid is the turnover) have sprung up all over America. These swingers' motels usually offer rooms with porno films on closed-circuit TV, water beds, mirrored ceilings, etc. They often advertise on billboards ("Special Two-Hour Rates $11.95 Only") and are of course usually places of sexual assignation for businessmen and housewives, which is why they have been humorously dubbed *No-tel Motels. See also* MOTEL.

nothing is certain but death and taxes. The widely quoted saying is attributed to Benjamin Franklin, who wrote in an 1789 letter: ". . . in this world nothing is certain but death and taxes."

nothing on the ball. A baseball pitcher who is pitching poorly (giving up hits) is said to have *nothing on the ball,* the expression dating back to at least 1912, when it is first recorded. Conversely, a pitcher with *something* or *a lot on the ball* is pitching well. The first expression is used generally to describe someone who is incompetent, while the latter means someone who has the ability to succeed.

not in the same league with. Not nearly comparable with, nowhere near as good as someone or something else. This American expression comes from baseball, in which someone in the major leagues is generally a far better player than someone in the minor leagues. The British use the phrase *not in the same street with* to mean the same thing. Said San Francisco Giant's first baseman J. T. Snow recently (4/3/02) of his teammate home run king Barry Bonds: "The guy's in another league. . . . I think the rest of us feel like we're Little Leaguers. . . . He does things others can't do."

not to know beans. The nationally used not to know beans may initially have been a Boston expression, suggesting that anyone who didn't know how to make baked beans in Boston, "the home of the bean and the cod," would have to be incredibly ignorant.

not to know if one is coming or going. Used to describe a very confused, ignorant, or stupid person, this American expression dates back to at least the early 1920s.

not what it's cracked up to be. Martin Van Buren, not a very popular president, though he gave us the expression O.K., was once disparaged by Davy Crockett, who said he "is not the man he is cracked up to be." The expression, meaning "not what he is generally believed to be," is apparently an Americanism dating back to the 1830s, but it may have British roots that go back much further, for *cracked* here has the old meaning of to boast or brag, a usage that dates back to at least the 16th century.

not worth a continental. Before the U.S. Constitution was adopted, the Continental Congress had no power of taxation to raise revenue. The Congress issued bills of credit called continentals, the dollar bills of the time, printing bills with a face value of more than $250 million though there was virtually no bullion or specie in the treasury with which to redeem them. To make matters worse, the British and Tories circulated immense amounts of counterfeit continentals, selling them for the price of the paper they were printed on and sending the fake currency out of New York City by the cartload with persons going into other colonies. By 1790 continental dollars were worth so little that it took 40 paper dollars to buy a dollar in silver and the expression *not worth a continental*—worthless—had become part of the language.

not worth a red cent. American pennies—once made with more copper, and thus redder—were formerly called reds, which is what a Californian describing a card game in 1849 meant when he observed, "Silver is not plenty . . . on the tables and anybody can . . . bet a red on any card he chuses." This accounts for the expression *not worth a red cent*, which has roots in the British "not worth a brass farthing" and which remains a good descriptive phrase because the penny still has enough copper in it to appear reddish.

Now I lay me down to sleep. . . . . The first line of a prayer known to millions of Americans through its inclusion for centuries in the *New England Primer*, though the first verse of the prayer is the *Enchiridion Leonis* (1160). The full prayer goes:

> Now I lay me down to sleep,
> I pray the Lord my soul to keep
> If I should die before I wake,
> I pray the Lord my soul to take.

Ernest Hemingway used part of the first line as the title for his short story "Now I Lay Me," in which the wounded narrator (based on the author) feared that "if I ever shut my eyes in the dark and let myself go, my soul would go out of my body . . . and [I] said my prayers over and over and tried to pray for all the people I had ever known."

nuke. *Nuke* is relatively new American slang for a nuclear weapon, being first recorded in 1964 in a *Time* magazine article, which discussed the possibility of using nuclear bombs to dig a new canal in Panama. *Nuke* as a verb, "to attack with nuclear weapons," is first recorded in a July 4, 1970 *New Yorker* interview with Eugene V. Rostow.

number, please. Telephone operators had been advised by Thomas Edison to greet callers with *ahoy* instead of *hello,* but operators fell into the habit of opening with a curt "What number?" However, according to Stuart Berg Flexner's *Listening to America* (1982), by 1895 the city manager of the Chicago Telephone Company, one J. W. Thompson, issued the following instructions to the company's chief operator in a memorandum: "In answering calls the query 'Number Please?' spoken in a pleasant tone of voice and with rising inflection must be invariably employed." Within 10 years all of the Bell System followed suit.

Nutmeg State. A nickname for Connecticut (*see* DON'T TAKE ANY WOODEN NICKELS). Also called the Wooden Nutmeg State, the Land of the Wooden Nutmegs, the Blue Law State, the Mother of States, the Constitution State, the Brownstone State, the Freestone State, and the Land of Steady Habits.

Nutmeg Stater. A resident of Connecticut, the Nutmeg State. As John Updike put it in *The Afterlife* (1994): "Driving down Route 86 into the blinding splinters of a sunset. He heard the disc jockey crow, 'Get your long johns out of the mothballs, Nutmeg Staters, we're going to flirt with zero tonight!' "

NYSE; AMEX. *NYSE* is the abbreviation for the *New York Stock Exchange*, which was originally named the New York Stock and Exchange Board (1817), taking its present name in 1863. The American Stock Exchange (AMEX), which took its present name in 1963, was formed as the New York Curb Exchange in 1842, because it was composed of curbstone brokers who were not members of any exchange and conducted business outside on the curb.

O

o. The popular name for the humuhumunukunukuakuaa, "the world's littlest fish with the longest name." The fish won fame in the 1930s song "My Little Grass Shack in Lkealakekua," which has a verse that mentions it. By popular vote the little creature became Hawaii's official state fish in 1984.

O-be-joyful. A humorous American historical term for hard liquor dating back to the 1860s.

Obies. Since 1955 the New York weekly *Village Voice* has presented Off-Broadway awards, popularly called Obies, honoring the best Off-Broadway productions. A different panel of judges each year is picked to select the best play, playwright, actor, director, composer, designer, etc. Other annual awards for outstanding Off-Broadway achievement include the Lucille Lortel awards.

ode on tooth diseases. Not many, and probably not any poets have published an *Ode on Tooth Diseases*. But in 1840, New York dentist Solyman Brown wrote and published a long ode, *Dentologia: A Poem on Diseases of the Teeth in Five Cantos*. One of the strangest of literary works, it gives after the poem a list of 300 qualified American dentists of the time.

oesophagus. When Mark Twain wrote his satire on Sherlock Holmes's stories called "A Double-Barrelled Detective Story," he began the tale as follows:

> "It was a crisp and spicy morning in early October. The lilacs and laburnums, lit with the glory-fires of autumn, hung burning and flashing in the upper air, a fairy bridge provided by kind Nature for the wingless wild things that have their homes in the tree-tops and would visit together; the larch and the pomegranate flung their purple and yellow flames in brilliant broad splashes along the slanting sweep of the woodland; the sensuous fragrance of innumerable deciduous flowers rose upon the swooning atmosphere; far in the empty sky a solitary oesophagus slept upon motionless wing; everywhere brooded stillness, serenity, and the peace of God."

The "solitary oesophagus" in the passage was solitary all right, for it never existed outside of Twain's teeming imagination. He had of course invented the bird—which know-it-alls were quick to describe to friends—and later remarked that few readers ever questioned him about it.

off base. Someone off base in today's slang is wrong or badly mistaken. The term refers to a runner in baseball taking a lead so far off the base that he is caught and tagged out. *See* OFF ONE'S BASE.

off one's base. To be off one's base is to be crazy, mentally unbalanced. Americans have been using this slang term since at least 1912. It has its origins in baseball, suggesting a base runner blithely hanging far off base without any thought of being picked off. *See* OFF BASE.

O. Henry. An immensely prolific author, O. Henry wrote tales characterized by ironic, surprise endings, "twists," "stingers," or "snappers" which while they aren't supposed to be fashionable anymore are still widely used by authors and known as O. Henry endings. O. Henry was the pen name of American writer William Sydney Porter. While working as a bank teller in Austin, Texas, Porter was indicted for the embezzlement (really mismanagement) of a small amount of money and fled the country to South America. On returning to his dying wife, he was imprisoned for three years and adopted the pseudonym O. Henry to conceal his real identity when he began writing and selling the stories that would make him famous. Released from prison he pursued his literary career in New York, where he published at least 15 books of short stories, including such perennial favorites as the "Gift of the Magi," before he died when only 48. O. Henry suffered from hypoglycemia, the opposite of diabetes, his classic summary of the condition being "I was born eight drinks below par." His famous last words, quoting a popular song, could have ended one of his stories: "Turn up the lights, I don't want to go home in the dark."

Another story about the O. Henry pen name claims that the author was imprisoned for embezzlement and was employed in the prison pharmacy. There he used the medical reference work U.S. *Dispensatory,* which listed in its pages the name of French pharmacist Étienne-Ossian Henry. From this name he took the pseudonym O. Henry that he used to conceal his true identity when he began writing his first stories.

Oh Henry! According to the official story about the name of this popular candy bar, the Oh Henry! was named after a freshmouthed boy who teased the girls on the production line at the candy factory where it was made. Reacting to his taunts or jokes, the girls would so often cry out "Oh, Henry!" that the manufacturer adopted the name.

Ohio. In Iroquois *Oheo* means "beautiful water," referring to the Ohio River for which this state is named. The Buckeye State (so called for its buckeye or horse chestnut trees) was admitted to the Union in 1803 as our 17th state.

O.K. Many word authorities believe that *O.K.* comes from the nickname of Martin Van Buren (1782–1862), who rose from potboy in a tavern to president of the United States. A colorful character (as vice president he presided over the Senate with dueling pistols on his desk), Van Buren was elected president in 1836. He became an eponym, however, during the campaign of 1840, when he ran for reelection in a tight race against "Tippecanoe and Tyler, too," General William Henry Harrison, legendary hero who fought against the Indians at Tippecanoe, and Virginian John Tyler. The election of 1840 brought with it the first modern political campaign—mostly to President Van Buren's disadvantage. One popular advertising stunt was "to keep the ball rolling for Harrison"—10-foot "victory balls," made of tin and leather and imprinted with the candidate's name, were rolled from city to city for as far as 300 miles. Harrison's followers, trying to identify Van Buren with the aristocracy, christened the general the "log cabin and hard cider candidate," and tagged Van Buren "Little Van the Used Up Man," "King Martin the First," "The Enchanter," "The Red Fox," "The Kinderhook Fox," "Little Magician," and several other of the derogatory nicknames he had earned over the years. But "Old Kinderhook," a title bestowed upon the president from the name of his birthplace in Kinderhook, N.Y., sounded better to his supporters, better even than "the Sage, Magician, or Wizard of Kinderhook." In order to stem the tide, a group in New York formed the Democratic O.K. Club, taking their initials from "Old Kinderhook." These mystifying initials, appealing to man's love of being on the inside of events, became a sort of rallying cry for the Democrats. One contemporary newspaper account reported "how about 500 stout, strapping men" of the O.K. Club marched to break up a rival Whig meeting where "they passed the word O.K. . . . from mouth to mouth, a cheer was given, and they rushed into the hall like a torrent." The mysterious battle cry spread rapidly and soon acquired the meaning "all right, all correct," probably because "Old Kinder-hook" or O.K. was all right, all correct to his supporters. But neither mystification, ruffians, nor new words did Van Buren any good, because voters remembered the panic of 1837, and Harrison defeated him in his bid for reelection. Not that victory was any blessing to Harrison; the old general contracted pneumonia on the day of his inauguration and died shortly thereafter. Scores of interesting theories had been offered on the origin of *O.K.* before Columbia Professor Allen Walker Read supposedly laid the ghost to rest with his *Saturday Review* article (July 19, 1941), tracing the word to the president who was O.K. Most etymologists accept Read's explanation but fail to mention an important qualification. Read established an earlier date than the campaign of 1840 for the first use of *O.K.* He showed that the expression was used in the Boston *Morning Post,* March 23, 1839, in the same sense—all correct—by editor Charles Gordon Greene but claims that the word got a second *independent* start in the 1840 campaign and really owes its popularity to Old Kinderhook's candidacy. No earlier reliable date than Read's for the use of *O.K.* has been found, and so the matter is apparently settled for all time—although other scholars have recently come up with entirely different explanations that etymologists are still debating. It will prove difficult, however, to take the credit for *O.K.* away from President Van Buren. The word honoring his name is undoubtedly the best known of American expressions. International in use and what H. L. Mencken calls "the most shining and successful Americanism ever invented," *O.K.* does service as almost any part of speech. Surprisingly, the effort to give it an antonym *(nokay)* has failed, but the expression *A-O.K.* has gained currency from space flights, and the older *oke-doke,* from an abbreviation of one of its forms, *okey,* is still heard in everyday speech. *O.K.* is used more often than *salud* in Spain, has displaced English *right-o,* and is spelled *o-ke* in the Djabo dialect of Liberia. The most universally used of all eponyms in any language since World War II, it is inscribed almost everywhere, from the town of Okay, Oklahoma, to the pieces of equipment marked with *O.K.*s that are possibly on the Moon. However, the useful little word may become even smaller and more useful. To this writer it sounds like *k* with more frequency every year, and perhaps someday that will be the spelling.

Okies. The migrant farm workers of the Great Depression called the Okies took their name from Oklahoma, where many of them originally lived before they left the Dust Bowl and began their journey west searching in vain for a golden land. They were of course immortalized in John Steinbeck's *The Grapes of Wrath*.

Oklahoma. Oklahoma takes its name from a Choctaw word meaning "red people," for the Indians who lived in the region. The Sooner State (so called after those "sooners" who "jumped the gun sooner" and grabbed choice land there before they legally should have) was admitted to the Union in 1907 as our 46th state.

Old Abe. A nickname for Abraham Lincoln, not when he was a great wrestler and rail splitter, but when he was stooped, frail, and depressed from a Civil War that seemed never to end.

Old Brains. Only one person in American history has the honor of being called Old Brains and he probably didn't deserve it. Union General Henry Wager Halleck (1815–72) was a fortifications expert and able organizer, but the prestige he enjoyed for the victories of U.S. Grant and others under his command were unwarranted—he wasn't the "old brains" behind them, as many believed, contributing little to Union strategy.

Old Dominion State. A nickname for Virginia and the oldest of state nicknames, dating back to 1778 when first recorded Virginia has also been called the Cavalier State, the Mother of Presidents, and Mother of States.

old fuddy-duddy. A stuffy, fussy, old-fashioned person, either old or young, who often fusses over minor details. The expression was first recorded in 1904 and was mainly confined to Maine and other parts of New England, but is now heard nationally. The term's origin is not certain, but some suggest that it derives from the English dialect word *fud* for buttocks, *old fuddy-duddy* (*duddy* added for rhyme) referring to someone who sits around on his duff doing very little, fussing with details, etc.

Old Glory. The many paintings that show the Stars and Stripes flying at Valley Forge and in major battles of the Revolution are all in error, for no official stars-and-stripes flags were used by the Army until 1783. *Old Glory* was named by Captain William Driver of the brig *Charles Doggett* on August 10, 1831. Captain Driver had brought back the British mutineers of the H.M.S. *Bounty* from Tahiti to their home on Pitcairn Island, and some say that in recognition of this humane service a band of women presented him with a large American flag. Others claim that friends gave him the flag as a present. In any case, as he hoisted the flag to the masthead, he proclaimed, "I name thee Old Glory." His ship's flag became famous and by 1850 its name became common for the flag in general.

Old Ironsides. Built six months after the *Constellation,* the *Constitution* is America's oldest warship still afloat and in commission. A national historic monument today, she is moored in Boston Harbor flying the flag of the commandant of the First Naval District. The high point of her illustrious career came on August 19, 1812, when she engaged and defeated the British frigate *Guerrière* off Nova Scotia. During the battle an American sailor, watching British shots fall into the sea, cried: "Huzza! Her sides are made of iron!" and *Old Ironsides* she has been since that day. In 1830 Oliver Wendell Holmes, hearing that she was to be sold by the Navy, wrote his famous poem "Old Ironsides" in protest and she was saved.

Old Line State. A nickname for Maryland recalling the Maryland Line of fine soldiers in the Continental Army. Maryland has also been called the Terrapin State, the Monumental State (Baltimore, Maryland, is the Monumental City), and the Oyster State.

Old Muddy. A nickname used for both the Missouri and the Mississippi rivers since the mid 19th century.

Old Ned. The Americanism to *raise Old Ned* means "to raise hell or start a row," *Old Ned* being recorded as a name for the devil, along with *Old Splitfoot* and *Old Scratch* as early as 1859.

Old Philadelphia Lady. One of the most famous letters to an editor in newspaper history is one an anonymous "Old Philadelphia Lady" sent James Gordon Bennett, the publisher and editor of the *New York Herald:* "I am anxious to find out the way to figure the temperature from centigrade to Fahrenheit and vice versa. In other words, I want to know, whenever I see the temperature designated on the centigrade thermometer, how to find out what it would be on Fahrenheit's thermometer— Old Philadelphia Lady, Paris, December 24, 1899." The letter became famous after it was unintentionally reprinted the next day, a mishap that made the famously eccentric Bennett so mad that he published it every day until he died in 1918. Readers cancelled their subscriptions, even threatened to kill the old woman, but Bennett nevertheless ran her letter for the next 18 years and five months, for a total of 6,718 continuous days in all.

Old Probabilities. Americans have been having fun with the weatherman for several centuries now. Knowing that weather forecasters always hedge their bets with a "probability" ("There is a probability of rain tomorrow"), they dubbed such prognosticators Old Probabilities in the late 19th century. The term is first recorded in 1873 for the superintendent of the weather bureau in Washington, D.C. *Old Probs* was the nickname of Cleveland Abbe (b. 1838), the first American to make daily weather predictions. Today, weather forecasters are even vaguer, generally saying "there is a possibility."

Old Public Functionary; OPF; Old Pennsylvania Fossil; Harriet Lane. James Buchanan (1791–1868), a compromise candidate and a minority president, called himself Old Public Functionary or OPF. Buchanan served one term, from 1857 to 1861. Among the most indecisive and ineffective of presidents, he was called Old Pennsylvania Fossil by many. Another of his nicknames was Ten-Cent Jimmy, because he supported low tariffs. The only bachelor to serve a full term as president, his niece Harriet Lane served as his hostess. This golden-haired girl was immensely popular compared to her uncle—a gown, a racehorse, a flower, and even the warship *Harriet Lane* were named after her, and the song "Listen to the Mockingbird" dedicated to her. One wit observed, "There is no power behind the throne, either."

old stamping grounds. An interesting theory connects this Americanism, used before the Revolution, with the mating behavior of male prairie chickens, who congregated in spring on hills and performed elaborate courtship dances, stamping the hills bare. Another guess is that the stamping of stallions while they covered mares suggested the phrase. All that's known is that *stamping grounds* were first referred to as places where horses or other animals customarily gathered. It wasn't too long (1836) before the term became a place where people customarily gathered. The British definition of *stamping ground* as "a place for amorous dalliance," like a lover's lane, gives some support to the prairie chicken or stallion theories. The expression is generally used by or about males.

one-armed bandit. A U.S. phrase that became popular in the 1930s Great Depression. Slot machines offered a player the chance of winning a lot for a little, but more often robbed those who could least afford playing them. The machine is so named for the handle at its side.

one for Ripley. Cartoonist Robert Leroy Ripley traveled widely from his California home to gather bits of odd information for his "Believe It or Not" newspaper series, books, and radio program, though much of the material he used was library researched. His name became as well known as "Believe It or Not" itself, the phrase *one for Ripley* used to describe any strange, almost unbelievable happening. Though he died in 1949, aged 56, Ripley's series still runs in newspapers throughout the world today, along with a host of imitators. There was a Ripley "Odditorium" at the Chicago World's Fair of 1933–34 and today seven

"Believe It or Not" wax museums are doing a thriving business in the United States and England.

one man's meat. The complete saying is one man's meat is another's poison; that is, what is good for one person can be bad for another. A slight variation is one man's meat is another man's poison. American humorist E. B. White wrote the One Man's Meat Department for *Harper's* magazine from 1938 to 1943 and also wrote the *New Yorker's* Talk of the Town essay columns.

one-man tango. Someone supremely self-confident, who looks like he could dance the grand tango all alone. In his autobiography *One Man Tango* (1955), actor Anthony Quinn claims Orson Welles gave him this nickname. Whether Welles invented the words or not isn't established, but the expression does deserve to be recorded.

One perry and one porter were too much for John Bull to swallow! A popular American slogan after the War of 1812, this punning expression refers to American naval hero Oliver Perry, whose last name means a hard cider made of pears, and David Porter, whose last name means a strong, dark beer. John Bull, of course, is the national nickname for England.

One small step for a man, one giant leap for mankind. These were the words of American astronaut Neil Armstrong when he became the first man to step on the moon on July 20, 1969. Unfortunately, in Armstrong's transmission of the words, the indefinite article *a* was inaudible and thus the words are often given incorrectly today as *That's one small step for man, one giant leap for mankind,* which makes little sense.

on the ball. Depending on how it is used, the expression has two different origins. *To be on the ball,* "to be alert, knowledgeable, on top of things," probably refers to close and clever following of the ball by players in British soccer or American basketball. The phrase may have arisen independently in each sport, or it may have originated in the 1940s with the "bop and cool" jazz musicians and fans as the *American Dictionary of Slang* suggests. There is no hard evidence for any theory, but the sports analogy seems more logical. To *have something on the ball,* "to be talented or effective in some way," is surely of American origin, a baseball term referring to the various "stuff"— curves, spin, etc.—a good pitcher can put on the ball to frustrate a batter.

on the cuff. *On the cuff* apparently arose at the turn of the century. Since bartenders commonly wore starched white cuffs at the time, the theory that our term for "on credit" derives from bartenders jotting down the debts of patrons on their cuffs during the rush of business is an appealing one. *On the arm* probably derives from *on the cuff,* while *off the cuff,* unrehearsed or extemporaneous, may come from impromptu notes early Hollywood directors jotted down on their cuffs while shooting a difficult scene in a movie. These ideas, not in the script, were conveyed to the actors when the scene was reshot.

on the make. In mid-19th-century America, *on the make* meant only to be out for money, to be ruthlessly ambitious. During the Great Depression, interests shifted outwardly from money to sex, there being more of the latter around then than the former, and the expression acquired its second meaning of to be "out for love." The words probably are the source of to *make it with* someone, "succeed in having sexual intercourse"; *make time*, "have relations," *make out* and *make-out artist*. The earlier meaning remains primarily in *to make it*, "to succeed in any endeavor, to rise to the top."

on the pad. Since the late 19th century this Americanism has referred to policemen who accept bribes, the *pad* meaning the account book in which the bagman recorded the bribes paid and the officers sharing in the split.

on the ropes. The allusion here is to a weary, exhausted boxer who is pinned against the ropes in a prizefight and just a punch or two away from being knocked out. The expression dates back long before Muhammad Ali's "rope-a-doping," in which he used the ropes to his advantage, and figuratively means to be on the edge of ruin. It is first recorded in 1924 but may be much older, for boxing rings have officially been enclosed by ropes since about 1840.

on the same sheet of music with. In agreement with. U.S. Secretary of Defense Donald Rumsfeld recently used and defined the expression: "I know that the interim [Afghanistan] government is right on the same sheet of music with us. They want the Taliban caught. They agree with us. They want the Al Qaeda the dickens out of their country."

on the wagon. The original version of this expression, *on the water wagon* or *water cart,* which isn't heard anymore, best explains the phrase. During the late 19th century, water carts drawn by horses wet down dusty roads in the summer. At the height of the Prohibition crusade in the 1890s men who vowed to stop drinking would say that they were thirsty indeed but would rather climb aboard the water cart to get a drink than break their pledges. From this sentiment came the expression *I'm on the water cart,* I'm trying to stop drinking, which is first recorded in, of all places, Alice Caldwell Rice's *Mrs. Wiggs of the Cabbage Patch* (1901), where the consumptive Mr. Dick says it to old Mrs. Wiggs. The more alliterative *wagon* soon replaced cart in the expression and it was eventually shortened to *on the wagon. Fall off the (water) wagon* made its entry into the language almost immediately after its abstinent sister.

oomph. Movie actress Ann Sheridan (1915–67) was dubbed the "Oomph Girl" for publicity purposes in 1939, making this word for sex appeal familiar to millions of Americans. But *oomph* goes back at least 40 years, first recorded by poet Paul Laurence Dunbar in *Gideon* (1900). The word is an echoic coinage that, according to Dr. Robert Chapman, suggests "the gasp of someone hit hard by . . . a transport of desire."

op-ed page. *Op-ed page* means "opposite the editorial page." The term was coined by Herbert Bayard Swope, editor of *The New York World* in the 1920s, to describe the page in a newspaper opposite the editorial page, where columnists and other contributors can present their own views, often different from the newspaper's editorial policy.

Oprah. *Oprah* has almost become a synonym for a television talk show host, referring to Emmy Award-winning Oprah Winfrey (b. 1954),

American talk show host, actress, and producer, whose show has become a most influential entertainment. The actress also received a best supporting actress Oscar nomination for her performance in the film *The Color Purple* (1985).

Oregon. *Oregon* may come from the Spanish *oregones,* meaning "big-eared men" and referring to Indians who lived there. Other possibilities are the Algonquian *Wauregan,* "beautiful water," for the Colorado River, and an unclear Indian name possibly meaning "place of the beaver" that was misspelled on an early French map. The Beaver State was admitted to the Union in 1850 as our 33rd state.

Oregon Trail. A 2,000-mile-long route from Missouri to Oregon much used during the 1840–60 westward migrations and called "the longest unpaved highway in the world." Over half a million pioneers used it.

organize! Short for the last words of Swedish immigrant Joe Hill (1879–1915), a member of the Industrial Workers of the World—the Wobblies. Joe Hill was executed by a firing squad in Utah for a grocery store stickup and killing, a crime his supporters claimed he was framed for. His last words were to labor legend Big Bill Hayward and the full quote was "I will die like a true-blue rebel. Don't waste any time in mourning. Organize!"

Orlando, Florida. The site of Disney World in Florida has an interesting etymology. It was originally named for its first settler, Aaron

Jernigan, but rechristened Orlando in 1857 in memory of Orlando Reeves, who had been killed in a skirmish with Indians.

Oscar. Hollywood's gold-plated Oscars remained nameless for years after the Academy of Motion Picture Arts and Sciences first awarded them in 1927. Called simply the Statuette, the 10-inch-high trophy was designed by Cedric Gibbons, weighed about seven pounds, was bronze on the inside, and originally cost about $100. The statuette quickly became a symbol of film fame, but not until 1931 did it get a name. At that time Mrs. Margaret Herrick, librarian of the Academy, was shown one of the trophies and observed, "He reminds me of my uncle Oscar." As fate would have it, a newspaper columnist happened to be in the room and soon reported to his readers that "Employees of the Academy have affectionately dubbed their famous statuette 'Oscar.'" The name stuck. Mrs. Herrick's uncle Oscar was in reality Oscar Pierce, a wealthy Texan from a pioneer family who had made his fortune in wheat and fruit and migrated to California, where he could now bask in glory as well as the sunshine. Did any real Oscar ever *win* an Oscar? The answer is: Oskar Homolka, Oscar Brodney, Oscar Werner, and Oscar Hammerstein II were all nominated for Oscars, but the only Oscar ever to win an Oscar was Hammerstein. In fact, Oscar Hammerstein II won two Oscars for best song. In 1941 he and composer Jerome Kern won for "The Last Time I Saw Paris" from *Lady Be Good*. In 1945 he and composer Richard Rodgers won an Oscar for "It Might As Well Be Spring" from *State Fair*.

ought to be bored for the hollow horn. Said of a seemingly feeble-minded person. This Americanism was suggested by the hollow horn disease in cattle, which made cattle ill and feeble and was supposedly cured by drilling a hole in the horns.

our country right or wrong. At an 1816 dinner honoring him in Virginia, U.S. naval hero Stephen Decatur gave the toast: "Our Country! In her intercourse with foreign nations may she always be in the right; but our country, right or wrong." This seems to be the origin of the saying *our country right or wrong,* which is also heard as *my country right or wrong.* U.S. Senator Carl Schurz paraphrased the expression in an 1872 speech: "Our country right or wrong! When right, to be kept right; when wrong, to be put right."

Our Perry and our Porter were too much for John Bull to swallow! A popular Yankee slogan after the War of 1812, this punning expression refers to American naval heroes Oliver Perry, whose last name means a hard cider made of pears, and David Porter, whose last name means a strong, dark beer. John Bull, of course, is the national nickname for England.

out. According to American historian Frederic D. Allen (1890–1954): "Along the [New England] seaboard, the wind is 'out' or 'has got out' when it blows from the sea. The expression is known in Portsmouth, Salem, and Plymouth. I do not think it is common in Boston."

out of left field. Since left field is not any more odd or less active a position than right or center field in baseball, it is hard to understand why it is featured in this common slang expression meaning "very unorthodox and wrong, weirdly unconventional, even crazy." In fact, anyone who has ever played sandlot baseball knows that the most inept (and therefore a little odd, to kids) fielders were relegated to *right* field, because there were fewer left-handed hitters to pull the ball to right field. It has been suggested that the phrase refers to the left field seats in Yankee Stadium that are far away from the coveted seats near Babe

Ruth's right field position. Another suggestion links the phrase to the Neuropsychiatric Institute flanking left field in Chicago's 19th-century West Side Park, though there are no references to the expression at that time. I would suspect that the words simply refer to the relative remoteness of left field compared to all other positions except center field and that left field is used instead of center field in the expression because *center* by definition means in the middle (of things) and *left* has long had negative associations of clumsiness, awkwardness, and radical or eccentric behavior. The expression *from out of left field,* meaning from out of nowhere unexpectedly, lends credence to this remoteness theory. The term *left field* itself was in use by the mid-1860s, along with the names for the other outfield positions, following by 20 years the first recordings of the names for the infield positions.

over a barrel. Here the person over the barrel is in the other person's power or at his mercy. In the days before mouth-to-mouth resuscitation and other modern methods of lifesaving, lifeguards placed drowning victims over a barrel, which was rolled back and forth while the lifeguard tried to revive them. Victims were certainly in the lifeguard's power, and the process is probably the origin of the Americanism *to have someone over a barrel.*

overcoat. A U.S. term for a long, warm winter coat. Someone wrote of Gogol's story "The Overcoat:" "All of modern Russian literature came out of Gogol's 'Overcoat.'"

over the top. A very popular expression in the U.S. lately, when reality itself often seems over the top. It means "excessive, exaggerated, even gross," and may come from the name of the British television series *Over the Top,* which premiered in 1982. It apparently has no connection with the World War I expression over the top, meaning "to climb out of trenches and attack the enemy." Rather, it seems to refer to a container that is filled to overflowing. In just one instance of the wartime *over the top*—on the first day of the battle of the Somme in World War I over 21,000 men were slaughtered by machine gun fire as they charged out of the trenches.

Oysters Rockefeller. Oysters broiled with a puree of spinach and seasonings on a bed of rock salt probably originated in 1899 at Antoine's, the famous New Orleans restaurant still in business. The first customer to taste the fabulous dish is supposed to have said, "It's as rich as Rockefeller," the name appearing on the menu shortly afterward.

Ozarks. The Ozark Mountains in Missouri, Arkansas, and Oklahoma, ranging up to 2,300 feet high, cover an area of 50,000 square miles, and are noted more for their beautiful scenery and mineral springs, which make them a resort area, than their rich deposits of lead and zinc. The Ozarks are named for a local band of Quapaw Indians who lived in the Missouri and Arkansas region of the mountains. "The French were in the habit of shortening the long Indian names by using only their first syllables," an article in the *St. Louis Globe-Democrat* explains. "There are frequent references in their records to hunting or trading expeditions 'aux Kans,' or 'aux Os,' or 'aux Arcs,' meaning 'up into' the territory of the Kansas, Osage, or Arkansas tribes." This *aux Arcs* seems to be the more likely explanation for *Ozarks*, although the local Arkansas band may have been named from the French *aux Arcs*, meaning "with bows," which could also have been corrupted to *Ozarks* and later applied to the mountains where the Indians lived.

P

paddleball. A fast-growing amateur sport today, paddleball is played with the same basic rules as handball but with short-handled, perforated paddles, and a tennis-like ball. The sport was invented in 1930 by University of Michigan physical education teacher Earl Riskey. Riskey even invented the ball and paddle for the game, and along with James Naismith (of basketball fame), William Morgan (the inventor of volleyball), and the Reverend Frank P. Beal (who invented paddle tennis), is one of the four people who are known to have invented a popular sport.

pain in the ass. An Americanism of the 20th century which has several euphemisms that often have slightly different meanings. A *pain* is a person who is mildly annoying, while *a pain in the neck* is more so and *a pain in the ass* is someone really obnoxious.

paint the town red. If Indians burning down a town suggested this phrase meaning to go on wild sprees, to make "whoopee," no one has been able to find the actual culprits. More than one scholar does nominate the flames Indians on the warpath often left behind for the "red" in the phrase, and the expression did originate in the American West, where it was first applied to the wild partying of cowboys in about 1880. Another good guess suggests a link with the older expression *to paint*, meaning "to drink," which, coupled with the way a drunk's nose lights up red, may have resulted in the phrase. Or *red*, a color commonly associated with violence, could have derived from the way the "painters" did violence to the town or to themselves.

paleface. Various American Indian tribes did use *paleface* as a general term for whites, but they also employed more specific insulting words, including *pale-colored-and-scrawny,* and *spirit-white-and-thin,* this last term comparing whites to ghosts. Some writers claim, however, that the word was invented by James Fenimore Cooper (1789–1851), who certainly did popularize the term in his novels. *Paleface* has also been applied to whites by blacks, and The Palefaces was an organization similar to the Ku Klux Klan that thrived during Reconstruction.

Palmetto State. A nickname for South Carolina, after the palm tree called a palmetto that commonly grows there. South Carolina has also been called the Gamecock State (in honor of fiery Revolutionary War general Thomas "Gamecock" Sumter, after whom historic Fort Sumter is named), the Rice State, and the Swamp State. It is called the Sand-lapper or Sand-hiller State after poor people in its sandy regions who ate aluminous earth to fill their stomachs.

to pan. Apparently the parent of this is the expression *it didn't pan out.* American prospectors long before the California gold rush were expert at using metal mining pans to separate gold from the sand and gravel they scooped from a stream bed. When gold wasn't found after the pan was shaken, miners would say that it hadn't panned out. Similarly, when any effort, say a stage play, didn't pan out, it didn't succeed. After enough literary critics had said plays or books didn't pan out, to criticize a production severely came to be known as panning it. Another suggestion is that *to pan* derives from the head, or "pan," of a tamping bar, which receives the blows of a sledgehammer, but the first recorded use of the word in this sense contains several allusions to mining processes, including panning.

Panhandle State. A nickname for West Virginia, after its long "panhandle" of land between Ohio and Pennsylvania. West Virginia is also called the Mountain State, the Switzerland of America (like four other states) and, by its proud residents, West by God Virginia.

panic doors. Panic doors in today's theaters that open outward from slight pressure on a bar were inspired by the loss of life in Chicago's Iroquois Theater tragedy in 1903, America's worst theater fire. Panic resulted when it was found that all the exit doors were locked and opened inward so that they were blocked by the people around them. No one succumbed to the flames; all of those who died were trampled to death by the stampeding crowd. It took only eight minutes for 589 people to die.

par for the course. *Par* is an American golfing term dating back to 1898 and deriving from the Latin *par*, "equal." It means the score an expert is expected to make on a hole or course, playing in ordinary weather without errors. The expression *par for the course,* meaning just about normal or what one might have expected, owes its life to the golfing term and dates back to about 1920.

parking meter. This expression became common only after July 16, 1935, when the world's first parking meter was installed in Oklahoma City, Oklahoma. However, two Oklahoma State University professors developed the first Park-O-Meter in 1933 and it had been suggested by journalist Carl C. Magee a year or so before that. Park-O-Meter No. 1 is now on display in the Oklahoma Historical Society. It originally cost five cents for one hour's use and the first person to be arrested for a meter violation was a minister.

parlay. *Parlay* is an Americanism first recorded in 1828, but probably used before then, that means to wager money on a horse race, cards or other sports event, and continue to bet the original stake plus all winnings on the next race, hand, or the like. The word derives from the Italian *paro*, meaning equal. It has since been extended to mean to use one's money, talent, or other assets to achieve a desired objective, such as spectacular wealth or success: "He parlayed his small inheritance into a great fortune."

passel. *Parcel* has been pronounced "passel," without the r, since at least the late 15th century. But the use of *passel* as a collective noun indicating an indefinite number dates back to 19th-century America. Wrote Mark Twain in *Adventures of Huckleberry Finn* (1884): "[They] just kept a-smiling and bobbing their heads like a passel of sapheads."

passion for anonymity. Not a man who liked to be upstaged by his staff, Franklin D. Roosevelt announced midway through his first term in office that he was going to appoint several new assistants "with a passion for anonymity." Possibly he was weary of all the newspaper coverage given his "brain trust." Anyway, he did manage to appoint several assistants so self-effacing that nobody remembers them today— and contributed a new phrase to the language as well.

pastrami; pistol. Pastrami is a highly seasoned, smoked shoulder cut of beef, its name deriving from the Rumanian *pastrama*. U.S. deli workers may call pastrami pistol ("Pistol-shoot it all the way!") because, as the *New Dictionary of American Slang* humorously suggests, the eater of a hot pastrami sandwich "feels as if shot in the stomach soon after eating it."

pathfinder. A person who makes a path for others to follow, one who finds a way. The word derives from the name of a fictional character created by American novelist James Fenimore Cooper, not the other way around. *Pathfinder* is the name Cooper coined for his colorful character Natty Bumppo in his novel *The Pathfinder* (1840), because of Bumppo's skill in finding his way through the wilderness. Before long the word was being used generally.

Patriots Day. The third Monday in April. A legal holiday marking the anniversary of the battle of Lexington on April 16, 1775; celebrated in Massachusetts and Maine since 1894.

patsy. *Patsy*, American slang for a dupe or sucker since at least 1909, may derive from the Italian *pazzo*, "foolish or crazy," brought to America by Italian immigrants. *Pazzo*, in turn, could derive from the Italian expression *uno dei pazzi*, "one of the fools or crazies," which may come from the name of the much ridiculed Pazzi family of 15th-century Florence, who were foolish enough to oppose the powerful Medici and were slaughtered.

Paul Bunyan. A legendary giant lumberjack in many folk tales, an American folk hero of the Pacific Northwest. Originally, the tales described a French Canadian, Bon Jean. Among the prodigious feats credited to Paul Bunyan are the creation of the Grand Canyon, and the invention of the double-bitted ax. When his crews and his huge blue ox Babe logged winters on the Big Onion River it was "so cold that cuss words froze in the air, thawing out the next Fourth of July with a din."

Paul Jones dance. A popular square dance featuring promenades and numerous changes of partners that was named for American naval hero John Paul Jones during the Revolutionary War, one of the few honors awarded his name at the time.

paydirt. One authority traces this expression to the Chinese *pei* (to give) used by Chinese miners in California, *pay dirt* thus meaning "dirt that gives gold." However, it more likely derives from the fact that it is dirt containing enough gold dust to pay for working it. The expression is first recorded in 1856.

payola. Entering the American lexicon in 1960, when it was found that disc jockeys in New York, Chicago, and other cities accepted payments from record companies in return for airing their records, the coinage *payola* is a contraction of *pay* and Victr*ola*. The word came into the news again in 1974 and 1985 with similar scandals in the record business, but *payola* is also used to mean bribes paid to anyone.

pay the fiddler. This is an American expression that apparently arose in the early 19th century, based on the old English expression "to pay the piper," which dates back to 1681: "After all this Dance he has led the Nation, he must at least come to pay the Piper himself"—Thomas Flatman, *Heraclitus ridens*.

PB & J; peanut butter; jelly. PB & J is recent shorthand, written and verbal, for a peanut butter and jelly sandwich. *Peanut butter* itself is first recorded in about 1890 as the health food invention of a St. Louis dentist, while the word *jelly* dates back to the 14th century.

P.D.Q. *P.D.Q.* stands for "pretty damn quick," as in "you'd better get started P.D.Q." Its origin hasn't been established beyond doubt, though it has been attributed to Dan Maguinnis, a Boston comedian appearing about 1867–89.

Peace Corps. A government organization formed in 1961 during the Kennedy administration under the Peace Corps Act. Initially about a thousand volunteers were chosen to teach their skills in 15 foreign countries, living like the people they help. Today Peace Corps volunteers work in about 100 countries.

the peacemaker. This was the nickname of one of the most famous weapons in American history, the Colt Revolver Model 1873, the name being adopted because it helped lawmen keep the peace in the American West. As an extra benefit, its .44 ammunition could be used in the 1873 Winchester rifle.

Peanuts, Cracker Jack! Vendors have been crying "Peanuts, Cracker Jack!" in ballparks (and at circuses and carnivals) at least since the early 1900s. Cracker Jack, now a trademark of the Borden Co., was first sold, under another name, in 1893. The cry is often heard as "Peanuts, popcorn, Cracker Jax" [Jacks]!" The words have been inextricably linked with baseball since 1908, when the song "Take Me Out to the Ball Game" was published, its lyrics including the line "Buy me some peanuts and Cracker Jacks; I don't care if I never get back." Over 250 million boxes of Cracker Jacks are sold every year.

pearls before swine. This famous modern-day quip wouldn't have been possible without a biblical injunction over four centuries ago. One version of the origin of this quip has Clare Boothe Brokow, who later became Clare Boothe Luce, encountering Dorothy Parker in the lobby of *Vanity Fair* headquarters one morning. "Age before beauty," said the sharp-tongued Clare, holding the door open. "Pearls before swine," said the sharper-tongued Mrs. Parker, entering first. Luce later denied this story, and a similar quip was used in one of Alexander Woollcott's pieces, but it has nevertheless become part of the Parker legend. It may be true, though. Recalled Mrs. Robert Benchley when she was 80 years old: "I was right there, the time in the Algonquin [hotel] when some little chorus girl and Dottie were going into the dining room and the girl stepped back and said, 'Age before beauty,' and Dottie said very quickly, 'Pearls before swine.' I was right there when she said it."

Peck's bad boy. This expression for a boy, or any person who annoys or embarrasses other people, is still heard today, if infrequently. It is the creation of American humorist George Wilbur Peck (1840–1916) who, among many writings, published very popular newspaper sketches about a mischievous boy who played pranks on his father, these published in book form as *Peck's Bad Boy and His Pa* (1883). Peck later was elected governor of Wisconsin, making him one of the few authors to hold public office (among them Dante, Yeats, Sir Thomas Malory, Victor Hugo, Ignatius Donnelly, John Greenleaf Whittier, Richard Sheridan, Hilaire Belloc, John Buchan, and Vaclav Havel).

Peekskill. New York's city of Peekskill on the east bank of the Hudson is named for the nearby Peeks Kill Creek, which would strictly be Peeks Creek Creek if translated completely, as *kill* is from the Dutch *kil,* meaning "creek." The word *Peek* in Peeks Kill Creek is from the name of trader Jan Peek, who discovered the creek in 1685.

Pelican State. A nickname of Louisiana, after the pelicans plentiful on its Gulf Coast and the pelican that appears on the state seal. Louisiana has also been called the Creole State.

pencil pusher; pencil-necked. Both of these are Americanisms. The common *pencil pusher,* usually a contemptuous term for an office worker, is first recorded in 1890. *Pencil-necked* is of very recent origin, and recorded here because I have heard it several times and can find it listed in no dictionary of slang or standard English. *Pencil-necked* is a contemptuous reference to relatively genteel men made by the boisterous and bullnecked. I heard it last from a huge professional wrestler with bulging muscles in his neck who declared that only "pencil-necked geeks" don't like to watch professional wrestling.

Pennsylvania. *Silvania* is the Latin for woodland, and *Pennsylvania,* formed on the analogy of Transylvania (that home of monsters and werewolves in fiction), means "Penn's woodland." The name does not honor the Quaker William Penn, as is generally believed, but his father, Admiral Sir William Penn (1621–70). Admiral Penn, a naval hero who helped frame the first code of tactics for the British navy, had been imprisoned in the Tower in 1655 for political reasons still unknown, and the author Samuel Pepys speaks bitingly of him in his diary. The crown, however, had become indebted to the admiral, Penn having loaned Charles II 16,000 pounds. On June 24, 1680, the younger Penn petitioned Charles for repayment of this debt, asking for a 300-by-160-mile "tract of land in America. . . ." The tract was to become a colony for Protestant Quakers suffering religious persecution, and Charles repaid his debt with a charter. Penn's account tells us that he suggested the names Sylvania and New Wales. When Charles II added the "Penn" in honor of his father, he strongly objected since Quakers are opposed to such use of personal names.

Penn Yan, New York. This old New York town, settled by New Englanders, is said to have been named from the first four letters of *Penn*sylvania plus the first three letters of *Yan*kee.

penny-ante. *Penny-ante* for anything or anyone of small importance is a figurative use of the poker term *penny-ante* meaning a poker game in which the ante, the first bet in the pot, is only a penny. The term dates back to mid-19th-century America.

Pepsi generation. The *Pepsi generation* is used, sometimes sarcastically, to mean the now, "with-it" generation. The term comes from the Pepsi-Cola slogan *Come alive, you're in the Pepsi generation.* Recently Pepsi-Cola moved into the Thailand soft drink market and had their slogan translated. It later developed that the Thai translation it was using said: "Pepsi brings back your ancestors from the dead." Incidentally, the word *Pepsi* in Pepsi-Cola is there because the drink's inventor, North Carolinian drugstore proprietor Caleb D. Bradham, first marketed his invention as an elixir to relieve dys*pepsi*a.

the perfect word. Mark Twain said that in writing "the difference bet ween a perfect word and a near-perfect word is like the difference between lightning and a lightning bug."

peter out. It seems unlikely that disappointed American miners during the '49 gold rush derived the expression *to peter out,* "to taper off or come to an end," from the French *peter,* "to break wind." This would indeed have been an expression of their disappointment when a mine failed to yield more gold, but there were ample American words available to express the same sentiment. Another guess is that the *peter* here refers to the apostle Peter, who first rushed to Christ's defense in the Garden of Gethsemane, sword in hand, and then before the cock crowed thrice denied that he even knew Him. Most likely the expression springs from the fact that veins of ore in mines frequently petered out, or turned to stone. The gunpowder mixture of saltpeter, sulfur, and charcoal, commonly called peter by miners, was used as an explosive in mining operations and when a vein of gold was exhausted it was said to have been petered out.

peverly bird. A name in New England for what is more commonly called the Peabody bird and white-throated sparrow elsewhere. The little sparrow is said to sound like it's singing, "Old Sam Peabody, Peabody, Peabody," hence *Peabody bird.* As for *peverly bird,* an old story has it that a Mr. Peverly, a New England farmer, was walking his fields one early spring day trying to decide whether he should plant his wheat yet. A little sparrow in the adjacent woods seemed to sing, "Sow wheat, Peverly, Peverly, Peverly!" so Mr. Peverly went ahead and did so, reaping an abundant harvest that fall. Ever after the little sparrow was called the *peverly bird* in New England.

phat. The expression *phat*, first recorded in 1992, means excellent, which is fast becoming a common slang expression for great itself. A number of origins have been suggested for *phat*, most of them sexual in nature (such as the first letter of *p*ussy, *h*ips, *a*ss, and *t*its), but the word *emphatic* is probably the father or mother of the term, *emphatic* here being the decidedly emphatic appearance of a very sexy woman.

Phi Beta Kappa. A U.S. national honor society whose lifetime members, both college undergraduates and graduates, are chosen on the basis of high academic achievement. The letters constituting the society's name are from Greek *philosophia biou kubernetes:* philosophy the guide of life. Founded in 1776 at the College of William and Mary in Virginia, Phi Beta Kappa is the oldest Greek-letter society. It was originally a secret social society at the college but soon became a scholarship honorary society.

Philadelphia lawyer. Folklore has it that when Andrew Hamilton successfully defended New York printer John Peter Zenger against libel charges in 1735, establishing the right of freedom of the press in America, observers noted that it took a *Philadelphia lawyer* to get the printer off. But the term is first recorded more than 50 years later, in 1788, in the form of "It would puzzle a Philadelphia lawyer." Another theory claims the words come from the New England saying "any three Philadelphia lawyers are a match for the devil." Philadelphia at the time was the intellectual and literary center of America, and it was only fitting that a very clever lawyer, versed in the fine points of the law, should be named for the city.

pho. A new word, unrecorded in any dictionary, that entered the language with Vietnamese immigrants to the U.S., pho is a noodle soup with beef that is becoming more popular every year. It is said that along Garden Grove Boulevard in Orange County, California, "it is easier to lunch on pho . . . than on a hamburger."

phony as a three-dollar bill. Very false, far from genuine, there never having been a U.S. three-dollar bill. A humorous exaggeration of this (heard in the movie *The Eiger Sanction*, 1970) is "He looks like he could change a nine-dollar bill in threes."

Pickle Factory. A little-known nickname of the CIA, among its members, in the Central Intelligence Agency's early days of the late 1940s and 1950s. The CIA is also called the Company.

a pier six brawl. A pier is a platform built over the water and supported by pillars. It can be used for shipping or for entertainment of various kinds. Where the *six* in the American phrase comes from is unknown, but a *pier brawl* can do a lot of damage to both ships and men.

pinch a loaf. A euphemism for the euphemism *to have a bowel movement*. It is used in the film *The Shawshank Redemption* (1994), based on Stephen King's story of the same name, but I haven't seen it recorded elsewhere in any slang

pinch an inch. A term used by American runners since the beginning of the running craze, starting in about 1975, for the amount of flesh that should be on a runner's frame. Anyone who can pinch more than an inch of flesh in any one place on his/her body, according to this extreme formula, is not in good condition.

pinch hitter. An old story has the 1905 New York Giants manager John J. McGraw using one Sammy Strang as baseball's first *pinch hitter* and apparently inventing the term himself. However, this phrase—for a player who bats in a pinch for someone else—had been recorded three years earlier. The expression has wide general use for any substitute or understudy in any endeavor.

Pine State. A nickname for Georgia first recorded in 1843. Georgia has also been called the Cracker State, the Buzzard State, the Goober State (after its peanut crop), the Peach State, and the Empire State of the South.

Pine Tree State. A nickname for Maine dating back beyond ts first recorded use in 1860. Maine, also called the Lumber State, has a pine tree on its state seal.

Pinkerton. When he came to America from Glasgow in 1842, Allan Pinkerton opened a cooper's shop in West Dundee, Illinois, his shop becoming a station in the underground railroad smuggling slaves north. Later he captured a ring of counterfeiters, this leading to his appointment in 1850 as the first city detective on Chicago's police force— a one-man detective squad. In Chicago Pinkerton also organized a detective agency to capture railway thieves, which became Pinkerton's

National Detective Agency in 1852. But he achieved national prominence in February 1861, upon foiling a plot to assassinate President-elect Lincoln when his train stopped in Baltimore on the way to his inauguration in Washington. Pinkerton died in 1884, aged 65, but his sons Robert and William continued the agency. It is from this period on that Pinkerton's was chiefly engaged by industry as spies and strike-breakers, earning the bitter condemnation of labor, especially for its role in suppressing the Homestead Strike in 1892. A *Pinkerton* or *Pinkerton man* came to mean either a private detective or, in the opinion of many working men, something lower than a fink. In 1937 the agency was subjected to congressional investigation during industrial disputes over the redecognition of unions.

pinstriper. There is no truth to the old story that the New York Yankees adopted their pinstriped uniform because it made the big-bellied Babe Ruth look thinner. The team was actually wearing pinstripes years before Ruth had his problems with hot dogs, soda pop, and beer. The Yankees are sometimes referred to as the Pinstripers, though nowhere nearly so often as they are called the Yankees, Yanks, Bronx Bombers, and even the Bronx Zoo. In baseball's early days they were first called the Highlanders and then the Hilltoppers.

pinup girl. During World War II, U.S. servicemen commonly decorated barracks walls with pictures of scantily clad film stars, the most popular of which showed Betty Grable wearing a one-piece bathing suit. This practice led to the term *pinup girl*, which is still occasionally used for any attractive woman, while *pinup* alone can refer to an attractive woman or man.

pipsqueak. By 1900 American hoboes were contemptuously calling young punk hoboes pip-squeaks, perhaps from the little pips on playing cards, or the pips that were small seeds, and *squeak* for their squeaky adolescent voices. Although these derivations are only guesses, *pipsqueak* did mean a little, worthless, insignificant person in hobo talk, whence it passed into general use. The term passed into British English by 1910, and during World War I, British soldiers called a small, high-velocity German artillery shell a pipsqueak. Use of *pipsqueak* for the shell reinforced the earlier meaning, which became a common expression on both sides of "the big pond," as the Atlantic still was called at the time.

pistol-whip. This was not originally a gangster expression. *Pistol-whip* is first recorded in the U.S. West in 1940 where it meant to beat someone with the barrel, not the butt, of a gun—it took too long to get a grip on the barrel in a fight.

Pittsburghese. Pittsburgh, often called Pixburgh and D'burg, doesn't seem the ideal place for an extensive regional vocabulary, but the Steel City has one of the most colorful. For example, *yinz* is the Pittsburgh way to say *y'all*, and a *yinzer* is a *Pixburger* with a strong local accent. Among others, *neb* means to stick one's nose in somebody else's business, a *poke* is a bag, *gum band* is a rubber band, *sputzie* is a sparrow, a *roller* is a ruler, and *Mon* is the Monongahela River.

Pittsburgh Pirates. The baseball team takes its name from the nickname of its first president, J. Palmer "Pirate" O'Neill, who was so called because he signed a player from another club, pirating him away rather unscrupulously.

pixilated. Although the British have used the term *pixy-led* for "enchanted by a pixie or fairy," *pixilated* is an Americanism dating back to about the mid-19th century. A combination of *pix(ie)* and *(tit) illated,* it means slightly eccentric, or amusingly whimsical, silly. The word also has the meaning of "drunk" in American slang.

plain brown wrapper. The designation *plain brown wrapper,* often used to describe how sexually explicit material will be sent through the mail, has its origins in the mail-order wars of the 1890s and at first had nothing at all to do with sex. Mailorder companies like Montgomery Ward (the beloved "Monkey Ward" of rural dwellers) and Sears, Roebuck sent their catalogs and goods in unmarked "plain brown wrappers" to protect customers from the wrath of local merchants and their allies, who wanted to see the mail-order firms go out of business from the time Aaron Montgomery Ward founded the first great national mail-order company in 1872.

play both ends against the middle. In faro, America's favorite game after poker in the 19th century, *playing both ends against the middle* described the way the dealer provided for a double bet by a player. The phrase came into general use soon after, meaning to use each of two sides for your own purpose.

playboy. A man, usually rich, devoted to the pursuit of pleasure. The term was not invented by Hugh Hefner with his magazine of that name. *Playboy* actually dates back to about 1620 in England. The word fell into disuse for a long period of time and was revived in New York City in about 1900 as a synonym for a bon vivant, a man about town.

play-by-play account. A detailed, sequential account of any event is called a play-by-play account or just a play-by-play. The term has been traced back to 1912 in baseball where it originated; radio play-by-play broadcasts of baseball games popularized the phrase.

play hardball. Baseball was popularly called hardball in the early days of the game. A change in the rules—so that runners were tagged to be declared out rather than being hit with the ball—prompted a change from the soft ball formerly used to a hard one. There was never an official game called hardball, but, at least from the 1930s to 1960s, the term was common among kids in the Northeast and other areas to distinguish baseball from the game called softball. Softball is played with a larger ball (not nearly as hard on the hands for kids catching barehanded) that can't be hit as far; it is also officially played on a smaller field and the ball is pitched underhanded. Perhaps the term *hardball* we now use was born in the sandlots, but that is not certain. In any case, it gave birth in about 1944 to the expression *play hardball*, which means to act or work aggressively, competitively, or ruthlessly. Demeaning as it is to softball players, who can be just as serious and competitive as their "hardball" compatriots, the phrase lives on.

play hooky. There is no widely accepted explanation for the word *hookey*, or *hooky*. An Americanism that arose in the late 19th century, when compulsory attendance laws became the rule in public schools, *hooky* may be a compression of the older expression *hook it,* "to escape or make off," formed by dropping the t in the phrase. Or it could be related to the old slang word *hook*, meaning "to steal": kids stealing a day off from school. *Hooky* has so often been associated with going fishing that it may even owe its life to *getting off the hook* the way a fish can; anyway, school is often as insufferable as a hook to schoolchildren and many kids squirming in their seats all day look like they are on a hook.

playing the air guitar. Miming the joyous playing of an imaginary guitar while listening to rock music. The first print use of the phrase appeared in the June 6, 1982, *Washington Post*, but it is certainly older. In the movie *Risky Business,* according to *Newsweek* (6/9/86), Tom Cruise famously "played air guitar in his underwear to 'Old Time Rock & Roll.'"

play penny pool. Anyone who deals in petty, trivial matters can be said to play penny pool, like a pool player who gambles for pennies on the outcome of the game or on a shot in the game. The expression is an Americanism dating back 50 years or so.

play possum. Opossum is one of the earliest of Americanisms. Borrowed from Indian language, it made its first appearance as *appossoun* in 1610, was changed to *opassom* a few years later and within a century was being written as *opossum* and its abbreviated form *possum.* The animal, which Captain John Smith described as having "an head like a swine, a taile like a rat, and is of the bigness of a cat," was known from the earliest days for the way it feigned death when threatened with capture. Trapped possums close their eyes and lay completely insufferable limp and no matter how much abuse they are subjected to, will only become active when thrown into water. Hunters knew this from the earliest days and so although the expression *play possum,* "pretend or deceive," was first recorded in 1822 the phrase is probably much older.

play the dozens. To insult one another in a rapid exchange of insults, a phrase used by both whites and blacks, though it seems to have originated with blacks in the American South toward the end of the 19th century.

play the market. This expression originated in the Roaring Twenties, or the Golden Twenties as they were known on Wall Street. Other expressions that were born in the 1920s include *moneybags* for a rich person, *good times,* and finally *Black Thursday,* October 29, 1929, the day of the stock market crash, and the start of the Great Depression.

plaza. A word widely used throughout the United States for a public square or open space; first recorded in the Southwest, it is an American borrowing of a Spanish word meaning the same.

pleased as a basketful of possum heads. Why does this Southern expression mean "very pleased indeed"? Apparently the words capitalize on the possum's proverbial grin, or what seems to us a grin—a basketful of which would seem exceedingly pleased.

Plot hound. For over a century the Plotts of western North Carolina bred this bear-hunting dog named after their family. The courageous, fierce dog is said "to have bear blood in him."

plug ugly. *Plug ugly* describes "a city ruffian or rowdy" or any such disreputable character. First recorded as an Americanism in 1856, the word is of unknown origin, although one early source says "it derived in Baltimore . . . from a short spike fastened in the toe of [such rowdies'] boots, with which they kicked their opponents in a dense crowd, or as they elegantly expressed it, 'plugged them ugly.'"

Pocahontas. Everyone knows one or another story about Pocahontas, among the most famous Native American women in history. But few know that Pocahontas was not her real name. Some American Indians at the time believed that knowing a person's real name gave one great power over that person. Therefore, her father Powhatan told the white settlers in Jamestown that his daughter's name was Pocahontas, when her real name was Matoaka, her parents having named her so from a word meaning "to play" because of her playful nature as a little girl. Powhatan himself was really named Wahunsonacock.

Podunk. *Podunk* means "a neck or corner of land" in the Mohegan dialect of Algonquian. Originally an Indian place name used by settlers in Connecticut and Massachusetts, it came to be a derisive name for any small or insignificant, out-of-the-way place. (Peoria and Hooterville are other names generations of comedians have used for the home of the rube and the boob.)

Poes of Princeton. Edgar Allan Poe is arguably America's best-known poet. Few are aware, however, that he was an excellent athlete as well. Poe, who would hardly suggest anything but an emaciated aesthete today, long jumped 21 feet while at West Point. He was as good a swimmer as Lord Byron (who swam the Hellespont), and once swam 7 1/2 miles from Richmond to Warwick, Virginia, "against a tide running two to three miles an hour." Another time he boxed the ears of and horsewhipped a scurrilous critic. He is also remembered for the *Poes of Princeton*, football players famous in their time if now all but forgotten. They were six members of the 1899 Princeton College football team, each named Poe and each a great-nephew of the poet. All of them apparently inherited Uncle Edgar's athletic prowess, but none his poetic genius off the field.

poker; poker face. *Poker* takes its name from the French *poque,* for a similar card game, though the rules of the Persian game *As Nas* (played with five cards) and *poque* (played with three cards) were combined to make America's characteristic gambling game. The game is mentioned as early as 1834 and probably dates back at least 10 years earlier. *A poker face,* a face that conceals all emotions, also comes from the card game, in which bluffing is an important tactic.

Polar Bear Club. An organization of winter swimmers based in Coney Island whose New Year's Day dip is traditionally televised every year. But the most famous of New York's coldwater swimmers didn't belong to the Coney Island group; it was playwright Eugene O'Neill, who when he lived in Rockaway Beach swam every day through the winter.

political plum. When a delighted Matthew S. Quay was elected U.S. senator from Pennsylvania in 1887, he assured his supporters that he would "shake the plum tree" for them. From this promise came our expression a *political plum*, an excellent or desirable thing, a fine job. The Little Jack Horner who pulled out a plum from the pie may have contributed to the term's popularity.

political slogans. Even before "Tippecanoe and Tyler Too" swept William Henry Harrison and John Tyler into office (*see* CIDER), slogans played an important part in politics. Like all slogans, good political slogans are usually short and simple, with rhyme or rhythm, and say what the electorate feels but is unable to express. Yet some great slogans have had few or none of these qualities. For example, Herbert Hoover's backers used the negative scare slogan "Rum, Romanism and Rebellion" to defeat Al Smith in 1928. The Democrats' slogan against Grover Cleveland's opponent in 1884 was: "James G. Blaine, James G. Blaine / Continental liar from the State of Maine!" Humorous slogans have also been effective, such as the Democrats' gem: "In Hoover we trusted, now we are busted." There is no space here for a complete accounting of political slogans, but below are some famous ones that may or may not have succeeded:

> "We Polked You in '44; "We Shall Pierce You in '52!"—
> Franklin Pierce (1852)
> "A Square Deal"—Theodore Roosevelt (1912)
> "He Kept Us Out Of War"—Woodrow Wilson (1916)
> "A Chicken in Every Pot"—Herbert Hoover (1928)
> "A New Deal"—Franklin Roosevelt (1932)
> "A Fair Deal"—Harry Truman (1948)
> "I Like Ike"—Dwight Eisenhower (1956)
> "The New Frontier"—John F. Kennedy (1960)
> "All the Way with L.B.J."—Lyndon Johnson (1964)
> "In Your Heart You Know He's Right—Barry Goldwater (1964)
> "Nixon's the One"—Richard Nixon (1968)
> "We Can't Stand Pat"—Pat Paulsen (1972)

politicians, whores, and buildings all get respectable after they get old. Heard in the movie *Chinatown* (1974).

politics stop at the water's edge. An old American maxim meaning Americans of all parties should join together when dealing with foreign powers.

Pontiac. The one American car named after an Indian, in this case Chief Pontiac of the Ottawa tribe, who waged Pontiac's War against the British in 1763. Though his tribe lost the war, Pontiac's name became legend in Michigan, and two centuries later Detroit's General Motors Corporation gave his name to the car and mounted his head on the hood.

Pony Express. The Pony Express, more often called simply the Pony at the time, was the common designation for the Central Overland Pony Express Company, which lasted only from April 3, 1860 to October 24, 1861, but is still operating in Western novels and films. It had 190 stations along its route between Missouri and California, riders, including "Buffalo Bill" Cody, changing swift Indian ponies at each station and riding on with the mail—often through bad weather and Indian ambushes. The record for its 2,000-mile run was seven days, 17 hours, but it couldn't beat the telegraph that connected East and West in 1861, and the Pony Express went out of business that year.

pony up. Since the early 1800s *pony up*, or *poney up*, has been American slang for "to pay up." These words may derive from the German *poniren*, "to pay," but *pony* was British slang for a small amount of money in the early 19th century, probably because a pony is a small horse (not over 14 hands high), and the term to *pony up* probably derived from this expression. Other uses of *pony* to indicate smallness include the *pony* that is a small glass or bottle of alcoholic beverage and the *pony* meaning a trot or crib—a translation used by students.

popcorn. Certainly known to the Aztecs, popcorn was so named by American settlers on the frontier in the early 19th century. It is a variety of small-eared corn (*Zea mays everta*), the kernels of which pop open when subjected to dry heat and has also been called "parching corn," "popped corn," "pot corn," "cup corn," "dry corn," and "buckshot" over the years. The great quantities of it sold in movie theaters prompted some early movie house corporations to grow thousands of acres of popcorn.

poppie. *Poppie* or *poppy* is American slang for a father or a grandfather. In South African English it is a slang term for a woman of any age.

poppycock. *Poppycock* means nonsense, the Americanism first recorded in 1865 and deriving from the Dutch *pappekak*, which means "soft dung" and owes its life, in turn, to the Latin *pappa*, "soft food," and *cacare*, "to defecate."

porterhouse steak. Martin Morrison's Porterhouse in New York City introduced the porterhouse steak in about 1814, according to the *Dictionary of Americanisms.* The tender steak taken from the loin next to the sirloin is an even more succulent cut than its neighbor, but has a lot of waste. In England, there is generally no distinction between it and sirloin. A porterhouse was a tavern serving the dark brown beer or ale called porter, once favored by porters and other laborers.

potato chip. George Crum, a Saratoga, New York cook of partial American Indian descent, is said to have invented potato chips in 1853 when a patron in the restaurant where he worked complained that the potatoes he had been served were too thick and undercooked. Crum sliced some potatoes paper thin, soaked them in ice-water and fried them in a kettle of boiling oil. According to the old story, the customer raved about them, they became a specialty of the restaurant and were soon dubbed potato chips.

pot head. In Maine this term has nothing to do with habitual users of marijuana, meaning instead someone of very limited intelligence, with a head like an empty pot.

pot likker. The rich liquid left after boiling vegetables like turnip greens with fatty meat, especially ham or fatback. Southern U.S. tradition insists it should be eaten with corn *pone dipped* or crumbled in it.

POTUS. *President Of The United States.* A new word coined only a few years ago, possibly by the U.S. Secret Service.

pound for pound. For many years Sugar Ray Robinson has been popularly called the greatest fighter in the world pound for pound. But boxing historian Bert Randolph Sugar, in his *The Greatest Fighters of All Time,* ranks welterweight champion Jimmy McLarnin 22nd and claims he was called the best fighter pound for pound years before Robinson. Jimmy "Baby Face" McLarnin beat 13 world champions over the course of a long career. He died in 2004, age 96.

power breakfast. A term thought to be coined by billionaire Preston Robert Tish (1926–2005) to describe the breakfast he hosted at his Regency Hotel on Park Avenue in Manhattan. There, beginning in the 1970s, famous and powerful people such as Henry Kissinger, David Dinkins, and investment broker Felix Rohatyn came to eat and socialize and often solve city and national problems.

power is the ultimate aphrodisiac. A saying that has been credited to former U.S. Secretary of State Henry Kissinger (b. 1923) in the 1970s.

power lunch. A lunch attended by at least two powerful people, often movers and shakers of society, people who can get things done. The power lunch is said to have been born in the Grill Room of the Four Seasons restaurant in New York City, or at least to have been so named there. The Four Seasons, designed by Philip Johnson, opened in 1959 and is considered an "interior landmark" of New York City.

prairie dog. *Prairie dog* was one of some 1,528 names given to animals, plants, and places observed on the Lewis and Clark Expedition into the Louisiana Territory in 1803—this said to be a record in vocabulary making. Captain Meriwether Lewis had first called the animal a barking squirrel, but this probably more accurate description was changed to *prairie dog* by his friend William Clark.

prairie dogging. What happens when somebody yells or drops something loudly in an office full of cubicles and worker's heads pop over the walls to see what's going on. (Thanks to Michael J. Gelb for this humorous corporate buzzword.)

Prairie State. A nickaname for Illinois first recorded in 1842 Illinois has also been called the Garden of the West, the Corn State and the Sucker State (probably because land speculators often cheated the early settlers, but possibly after the catfish of the genus *Catostomus* common in the state's rivers).

president. The first Senate of the United States selected "His Highness" as the title of the president of the U.S., the full title decided upon being "His Highness the President of the United States of America and the Protector of the Rights of the Same." However, the House of Representatives voted the title down and the president was referred to as the more democratic *Mr. President.* The first president's wife, however, was called Lady Washington during his terms in office. President Washington himself objected to terms like "Your Majesty." The word *president,* also deriving from the Latin *praesidere,* to preside, govern, was used as the title of the highest officer in an American colony, a practice that began in Jamestown. William Howard Taft, a president handpicked for the position by his predecessor Theodore Roosevelt, once said that whenever he heard someone say "Mr. President" while he was in office, he looked around for Teddy.

presidential daily brief. A little-known report that is delivered every morning to the U.S. president and is usually abbreviated to PDB.

presidential nicknames. George Washington was of course the *Father of His Country*; John Adams, who loved to eat, was called *His Rotundity*; while tough old Andy Jackson was known as *Old Hickory*; Abraham Lincoln was widely called *Honest Abe,* and *the Great Emancipator*; Calvin Coolidge was *Silent Cal*; *Ike* was Dwight Eisenhower; and *the Great Communicator* was Ronald Reagan. Among other less famous nicknames were *Long Tom*—Thomas Jefferson, *Old Veto*—John Tyler, *Old Rough and Ready*—Zachary Taylor, *Lemonade Lucy*—Rutherford Hayes (he didn't drink the hard stuff), *Ten Cent Jimmy*—James Buchanan (because of his small stature and terrible bearing), *the Beast of Buffalo*—Grover Cleveland (he was rumored to beat his wife), *George W.* (or *"W"*)—George W. Bush (humorous, or to distinguish him from his father, George Bush, who served as president eight years before him). The president with the most nicknames, virtually all of them derogatory, was Martin Van Buren, who was called, among other nasty things: *Little Van the Used Up Man, the American Tallyrand, Motley Van, Old Kinderhook* (his birthplace was Kinderhook, New York), *the Sage* or *Wizard of Kinderhook, the Little Magician, the Red Fox, the Enchanter, Petticoat Pet* (for his foppish dress), and *Martin Van Ruin* (for the depression he helped cause). It should be noted that two women married to presidents (Abigail Adams and Woodrow Wilson's wife) were called *Mrs. President.* Wilson's wife was also called *Presidentress of the United States.*

profile. Like many innovations, this word in its recent usage is first recorded in *The New Yorker*. It derives from the Italian *profile*, which is composed of the Latin *pro* (forward) and *filau* (draw a line). The light, often entertaining, profile is now found in many magazines.

prospector. Someone who explores an area for gold, silver, oil, or other valuables. Though *to prospect* for minerals is recorded as early as 1400 in England, *prospector* is an Americanism dating back to about 1846.

P-town. A nickname for Provincetown used on Cape Cod Someone called it a hardworking town where a lot of people seemed to be playing all the time.

public be damned. In 1882 a reporter asked William Henry Vanderbilt why the New York Central Railroad had continued to run a high-speed train from New York City to Chicago despite the fact that it was losing money. Commodore Vanderbilt told him he did it to compete with a similar Pennsylvania Railroad train. Wouldn't you run it just for the benefit of the public, competition aside, the reporter continued, and Vanderbilt roared the classic reply that has unfortunately become associated with big business ever since: "The public be damned! Railroads are not run on sentiment but on business principles."

public enemy number one. Al Capone was the original Public Enemy Number One, that is, the most dangerous criminal in the United

States. The term was first recorded in reference to him in the *Chicago Tribune* (February 22, 1931).

public relations. American publicity writer Eddie Bernays (1891–1960), a nephew of Sigmund Freud, is said to have coined the name *public relations* in May 1920 as a respectable way to describe his profession—in the wedding announcements heralding his marriage. Bernays had previously established the first firm doing such work, though the term *public relations* had been recorded as far back as the early 19th century. Since about 1942 PR has been used as an abbreviation of *public relations.*

Pulitzer Prize. Hungarian-born Joseph Pulitzer was persuaded to immigrate to America by an agent who recruited him for the Union Army in 1864. After serving until his discharge a year later, he settled in St. Louis, where he founded the *St. Louis Post-Dispatch* in 1878. But when his chief editorial aide, Col. John A. Cockerell, shot and killed Col. Alonzo Slayback during a bitter political quarrel, Pulitzer left his paper and moved to New York, where he founded the *New York World* in 1883. He proceeded to become a congressman and make his paper among the best in the world, despite the fact that he went blind at age 40. A liberal, crusading newspaper, the *World* did much to raise the standards of American journalism, employing many of the greatest reporters and columnists of the day. Absorbed by the Scripps-Howard chain in 1931, it was eventually merged out of existence. When Pulitzer died in 1911, aged 64, his will provided a fund to Columbia University, where he had established and endowed the school of journalism, which has been used since 1917 to give annual monetary awards for writing. Prizes in journalism for local, national, and international reporting; editorial writing; news photography; cartooning; and meritorious public service performed by an individual newspaper. There are also prizes for music and theater, and four traveling scholarships.

pulling a Crater. On August 6, 1930, colorful, well-known New York Supreme Court Judge Joseph Crater vanished from the face of the earth, never to be found again, despite countless theories of what became of him. Judge Crater (1889–?) was even said to have been killed by the mob and buried under the Coney Island boardwalk. In any event, he ranks along with labor leader Jimmy Hoffa as America's best-known missing person, his name a synonym for *vanishing*. Another famous missing person is aviation pioneer Amelia Earhart, the first woman to make a solo flight across the Atlantic, who disappeared on July 18, 1937, while trying to circle the globe.

Pullman car. Abraham Lincoln's assassination made the Pullman sleeping car a reality. George Mortimer Pullman (1831–97), a cabinetmaker, had experimented in building much-needed railway sleeping cars just before the Civil War but couldn't sell his idea, even though he had made a successful test run with two converted coaches. In 1863 he invested $20,000, every penny he had, in a luxurious sleeping car called the Pioneer that he and his friend Ben Field built on the site of the present-day Chicago Union Station. But the Pioneer, unfortunately, was too wide to pass through existing stations and too high to pass under bridges. For two years it lay on a siding, a well-appointed waste, until President Lincoln was assassinated in 1865. Every area through which Lincoln's black-creped funeral train passed brought out its finest equipment, and Illinois, the Rail Splitter's birthplace, could be no exception. The Pullman Pioneer was the best that the state had, and Illinois spared no expense in promptly cutting down station platforms and raising bridges so that the luxurious car could join the presidential funeral train in its run from Chicago to Springfield. The funeral party traveling in the Pioneer was greatly impressed by the car. As a result, the Michigan Central cleared the line for the big car and other railroads around the country began to follow suit. Pullman soon went into partnership with Andrew Carnegie in the Pullman Palace Car Company and his sleeping cars, or Pullmans, eventually made him a millionaire many times over.

pump priming. Just as a pump is primed with water to increase its water production, the U.S. economy was stimulated by U.S. spending, this tactic the brainchild of Franklin D. Roosevelt and his advisers during the Great Depression.

punching bag. Someone who takes much abuse and punishment is said to be a punching bag. The term is American and comes from boxing; it is first recorded in 1897, although boxers practiced on heavy bags filled with sand long before then.

Purple Heart. George Washington originated the medal called the Purple Heart during the Revolutionary War. His order in 1782 explained that "the General, ever desirous to cherish virtuous ambition in his soldiers, as well as to foster and encourage every species of military merit, directs that whenever any singularly meritorious action is performed, the author of it shall be permitted to wear over the left breast, the figure of a heart in purple cloth, or silk, edged with narrow lace or binding." Originally given for "meritorious action," and awarded to three or four Revolutionary War soldiers, it is now granted for battle wounds.

purse. A New Hampshire pronunciation of "pierce," as in Franklin Pierce (1804–69), the New Hampshire-born 14th president of the United States. "She [New Hampshire] had one president. Pronounce him Purse," Robert Frost wrote, "and make the most of it for better or worse."

pussyfoot. Teddy Roosevelt seems to have either coined or popularized *pussyfoot* in about 1905. Meaning crafty, cunning, or moving in a cautious manner, it refers to the way cats can walk stealthily by drawing in their claws and walking on the pads of their feet. It's very unlikely that the redoubtable William Eugene "Pussyfoot" Johnson, a crusading American do-gooder, has anything to do with the expression. Johnson was nicknamed "Pussyfoot" because "of his catlike policies in pursuing lawbreakers" when he served as chief special officer in the Indian Territory. Later his nickname, in the form of *pussyfooters,* was applied to all advocates of Prohibition. While crusading in England, fresh from his triumph of securing the passing of Prohibition in the U.S., Johnson was blinded by a stone thrown by a crusading drunk.

put a sock in it. Seldom heard anymore, this phrase goes back to the days of early phonographs, first invented by Thomas Edison in 1877. The first phonographs had no form of volume control and in order to hold the volume down, teenagers were told to put a sock in the horn to mute the sound. *To put a sock in it* came generally to mean "to stop anyone from talking too much or too loudly."

put on nothing but the radio. To be naked. When a reporter asked Marilyn Monroe what she wore when she went to bed, she supposedly replied, "I put on nothing but the radio." An other version of the tale has her answering that she put on nothing but Chanel No. 5.

put on the dog. Lap dogs were all the rage among the new rich in America shortly after the Civil War, especially King Charles and Blenheim spaniels, rather imperious-looking dogs to the common man and certainly very distant relatives sociologically of the average American mutt, who had to work or scrounge for his supper. These snooty dogs being pampered by their snooty owners probably inspired the expression *putting on the dog*, "showing off," which apparently arose in the 1860s as college slang at Yale University. Attempts to derive *put on the dog* from the older *put on side* all seem strained. The reasoning behind the latter is that dogs "show off" by arching out one side while moving their feet in intricate maneuvers.

put the pedal to the metal. To drive a car as fast as it can be driven, drive!, floor it! This Americanism has nothing to do with soft pedal, which means to deemphasize and comes from the pedal on a piano that softens notes.

Q

Quantrill. Any fabled gunfighter or guerrilla; after William Clark Quantrill (1837–65), who formed a pro-Confederate guerrilla band during the Civil War, more to serve his penchant for cruel bush whacking, bloodletting, and looting than out of any sympathy for the Confederacy. In 1863 he led 448 men into Lawrence, Kansas, where they slaughtered 142 Jayhawkers, or pro-Union, citizens. Quantrill died two years later after being shot in the back while trying to escape from a detachment of Union soldiers.

quarterback. Football's *quarterback*, the backfield player who directs the offensive play of a team on the field, suggested this general verb meaning "to lead, direct, or manage anything." The term has been in use for a good 70 years.

quarter horses. Quarter horses are named for their ability to run well in quarter-mile races, not because of their size or lineage. The term is an Americanism, first recorded in 1834, though quarter races are mentioned a good 50 years earlier as being very popular in the South. Quarter horses, usually smaller than Thoroughbred racehorses, were also called quarter nags.

quarter section. The Americanism *quarter section* of land was popularized by the Homestead Act of 1862, which said that any settler on the frontier could have 160 acres of public land free if he could raise a crop on at least 40 acres of it for five years. The 160 acres equaled a quarter of a square mile and was commonly called a *quarter section* or *quarter*. The former term, however, had been used as early as 1804, and the latter as early as 1640.

queen's taste. *To the queens taste* means completely, thoroughly, utterly. The queen's taste, the most discriminating in the land, would demand the best, something completely or thoroughly done. No one has been able to connect any specific queen with this phrase, which is, oddly, an Americanism and not British in origin, dating back to the late 19th century.

quick as greased lightning. *Quick as greased lightning* is an Americanism dating from about the 1840s, but is a typical western exaggeration of the British *quick as lightning*, first recorded 100 years earlier. *Quicker than hell can scorch a feather* is a similar Americanism from the mid-19th century.

quick draw. A contest in which the winner is the quickest contestant to draw a gun from a holster, fire it, and hit a target. The Western term is now used throughout the United States.

quicker'n a snake goin' through a holler log. An old U.S. phrase describing any rapid movement made by someone.

Quick time, march! A familiar U.S. Army command dating from the 19th century. It specifically means marching 120 paces of 30 inches per minute, but has come to mean any fast march in general use.

quirly. This odd Americanism had some currency into the early 20th century. It was originally a cigarette rolled in a corn shuck instead of paper, but came to be a cowboy word for any cigarette. Its origins are unknown.

R

radio. *Radio* is an Americanism that came into the language in about 1910, as a shortening of *radiotelegraph*. The *radio* in radiotelegraph derives from the Latin *radius*, beam, ray.

to railroad. Americans built railroads in a hurry in the 19th century, and the mountains, rivers, and forests that stood in their way as they crisscrossed the continent were unfortunately regarded as mere obstacles blocking the right of way. The speed with which lines were built and the railroad builders' disregard for anything that stood in the way of "progress" inspired the term *to railroad* by the 1870s. At first it meant to send a person speedily to jail without a fair trial, or by framing him, and then it took on the additional meaning of rushing important legislation through Congress without regard for opposition to it and in disregard of regular procedures.

Rainbow Division. A celebrated army division commanded by Douglas MacArthur during World War I and so named because it consisted of troops from 26 U.S. states.

rat cheese. An American term for a cheap cheese, first recorded c. 1935, fit only for rattraps.

rat pack. The term *rat pack,* referring to humans, was first applied to singer Frank Sinatra (1915–98) and his close friends (Dean Martin, Peter Lawford, Sammy Davis, Jr., etc.) by Republicans angry at Sinatra for the help he gave John F. Kennedy in the 1960 presidential campaign. Later, angry at Kennedy, Sinatra supported Nixon, Reagan, and the Republicans. Sinatra ("Chairman of the Board," "The Voice," "Frankie Boy," "Old Blue Eyes") was a legend in his own time. The singer won an Oscar for his portrayal of Maggio in *From Here to Eternity.* Sinatra himself called the rat pack his "pallies."

Rattlesnake Buttes. A landmark in Colorado infested with myriad poisonous snakes. "Rattlesnake Buttes!" James Michener wrote in *Centennial* (1974): "A thousand westward travelers would remark about them in their diaries: 'Yesterday from a grate distance we seen the Rattlesnake Butes they was like everybody said tall like castels in Yurope and you could see them all day and wundered who will be bit by the snakes like them folks from Missuri?'"

razorback. A wild hog common in the southern U.S. that people often tamed and let roam free to forage for its food. The Americanism, traced back to about 1815, was inspired by the hog's ridge-like back. It was an argument over the ownership of a razorback hog that initiated the bloody Hatfield-McCoy feud that lasted from about 1873 to 1890 in the mountains of Kentucky and West Virginia. A *Hatfield-McCoy feud* itself became a synonym still occasionally used for any feud between families or neighbors. In fact, the Hatfields and McCoys are still feuding, though in a less violent way. A recent news item (12/23/01) advises that "In Pikesville, Ky., descendants of the Hatfield and McCoy clans, which battled each other in a famous, bloody feud from 1878 to 1890, are apparently still sore. In a lawsuit, the McCoys claim the Hatfields control access to a cemetery and won't let them get in." Like many Americans, they're getting more litigious.

read 'em and weep. A common cry of a cardplayer or crap shooter after a good hand or roll of the dice. The American expression is now used generally to mean "here's some very unwelcome information for you, information that will benefit me."

Reaganomics. A term coined in 1980 describing the economic theories and plans of Ronald Reagan, who served as U.S. president from 1981 to 1989. Reaganomics was marked by tax cuts and free market policies. The word construction Nixonomics preceded it and Clintonomics came after it.

real McCoy. Kid McCoy happened to hear a barroom braggart claim that he could lick any of the McCoys around—any time, any place. The Kid, then at the top of his boxing division, promptly delivered his Sunday punch in person. When the challenger came to, he qualified his statement by saying that he had only meant that he could beat any of the other fighters around who were using the Kid's name, not the real McCoy himself. In another version of the story, which also takes place in a saloon, a heckler sneers that if the Kid was the real McCoy, he'd put up his dukes and prove it. McCoy does so and the heckler, rubbing his jaw from his seat in the sawdust, exclaims, "That's the real McCoy, all right." But there have been numerous, unproved explanations for the origin of *the real McCoy* for "the genuine, the real thing." Still another is that advertisements of Kid McCoy's fights proclaimed that the real McCoy, and not some imitation, would appear. The fabulous Kid McCoy won the welterweight title in 1896, but outgrew his class; he was once ranked by *Ring Magazine* as the greatest light heavyweight of all time, though he never held this title. It is possible that the cachet of his name may have been strengthened by the ring exploits of Al McCoy, who held the middleweight title from 1917 to 1919. Certainly there were a lot of McCoys around in the early days of boxing, among the myriad Mysterious Billy Smiths, Dixie Kids, Honey Melodys and Philadelphia Jack O'Briens. But which McCoy is the real McCoy remains open to debate; he may not even have been a boxer. For example, another tale has it that the real McCoy was African-American inventor Elijah McCoy, whose machine for lubricating the parts of a steam train engine was widely popular and inspired many inferior knock-offs.

rebel yell; Texas yell. A leading expert believes that the *rebel yell,* or *yalo,* originally used in combat in the Civil War and intended to strike terror into the hearts of the enemy, came from the Creek Indians, loosely combining "the turkey gobbler's cry with a series of yelps." The high-pitched, blood-chilling yell was borrowed by Texans and adopted for their *Texas yell.* But others say the Texans got their yell from the Comanche Indians. In any case, everyone agrees that the "Yah-hoo" or "Yaaaaaheee" of fiction writers sounds nothing like the rebel yell. Several experts believe it is a corruption of the old English foxhunting cry *tallyho!*

Red Cross Banner. The Confederate battle flag is the most familiar symbol of the American South but was not the official flag of the Confederacy, an honor that goes to the STARS AND BARS. The familiar Red Cross Banner was designed by General P.G.T. Beauregard following the first battle of Bull Run, after Southern troops in the confusion of battle mistook the Stars and Bars for the Union flag, which it resembled. The flag that most southerners fly today is this Red Cross Banner or battle flag, not the Stars and Bars.

red dog. Linebackers "hound" or "dog" the passer in a football red dog, crashing through the line to try to break up a play. When the tactic was invented in the 1960s, "red dog" was the signal if one linebacker was to try cracking the line, "blue dog" if two were to be used, and "green dog" if all three linebackers were to charge. Football fans, however, misused the terms and applied *red dog* to any rush through the offensive line, made by linebackers or linemen, and that is what the term means today. I've also heard it used outside of football for any rush on one person by a group of men.

red-light district. Brothels once advertised their presence by burning electric lights covered with red shades or glass in their windows. This led to the Americanism *red-light district* for an area known for its houses of prostitution, the term first recorded in the late 19th century.

redneck. A poor, white, often rowdy southerner, usually one from a rural area. The word, which is sometimes derogatory, has its origins in the sunburned necks of farmers and outdoor laborers, and originally meant a poor farmer. "A redneck is by no means to be confused with 'po' whites," wrote Jonathan Daniels in *A Southerner Discusses the South* (1938): "Poor white men in the South are by no means all po' white even in the hills. Lincoln and Jackson came from a southern folk the back of whose necks were ridged and red from labor in the sun." Another source claims that in the 1930s striking West Virginia coal miners wore red bandanas around their necks and were called "The Redneck Army."

refrigerator. The first refrigerator was named by its inventor, Maryland farmer Thomas Moore, in 1803. Moore coined the word from the Latin re-, "thoroughly," plus *frigerare,* "to cool." His invention was actually an icebox and such devices were usually called that until the first electric refrigerator was invented in 1916. It wasn't until the 1930s that refrigerators became inexpensive enough to begin replacing iceboxes in American homes.

relocation centers. Places to which U.S. Japanese-American citizens on the West Coast were unjustly removed by the U.S. government during World War II because they were thought at the time to be security risks, a charge totally unfounded.

Remember the Alamo! *See* ALAMO.

reports of my death are greatly exaggerated. A traditional story has it that in 1897 an American newspaper bannered Mark Twain's death. When another paper sent a reporter to check the story Twain came to the door of his Connecticut home and gave him the following statement: "James Ross Clemens, a cousin of mine, was seriously ill two or three weeks ago, but is well now. The reports of my illness grew out of his illness. The reports of my death are greatly exaggerated." Nothing any scholar says will change this tale, which is by now part of American folklore, but the true story is that a reporter from the *New York Journal* called on Twain while the author was staying in England—to check out a rumor that Twain was either dead or dying in poverty. Twain explained to the reporter that his cousin had been seriously ill in London and that reports of his own illness grew out of his cousin's illness, that "the report of my death was an exaggeration." But then maybe Twain had the facts wrong. "When I was younger," he confided toward the end of his life, "I could remember anything, whether it had happened or not; but my faculties are decaying now and soon I shall be so I cannot remember any but the things that never happened. It is sad to go to pieces like this, but we all have to do it."

Reuben. No one is sure who invented this grilled sandwich of corned beef, Swiss cheese, sauerkraut, and Russian dressing on rye bread. The best guess is that it was first concocted at Reuben's Delicatessen in Manhattan during the early 1900s.

rich as Rockefeller. *Rich as Rockefeller* refers to the family fortune amassed by John Davison Rockefeller (1839–1937). The oil refinery that became the Standard Oil Company made Rockefeller a billionaire before it was dissolved by the Supreme Court in 1911. Variations on the phrase above include *he's a regular Rockefeller,* and *Rockefeller* itself is the American equivalent of *Croesus.* John D. may have given only dimes to beggars, but his philanthropies included the founding of the University of Chicago, the Rockefeller Institute for Medical Research (1901), and the Rockefeller Foundation (1913) for worldwide humanitarian purposes, in all worth about half a billion dollars. John D. Rockefeller, Jr., built New York's Rockefeller Center, with Radio City completed in 1940. There is no popular saying "as rich as Bill Gates," despite a 2002 study by *New York Times* business editor Allen R. Myerson that concluded that Gates's fortune amounted to $46 billion compared with Rockefeller's $25.6 billion when both fortunes were adjusted for inflation.

ride. To kid, to ridicule or harass. Both this word and the American underworld phrase *take someone for a ride* are first recorded at about the same time, around 1915. It has been suggested that the facetious *ride* derives from the sinister gangster expression meaning to force or entice someone into a car, take him to a lonely place, kill him, and dump him.

To ride a person is of course not nearly so brutal as to take someone for a ride, but it isn't especially pleasant, either.

to ride off into the sunset. So many Hollywood Western movies ended with the hero riding his horse off happily into the sunset that the phrase became a synonym for a happy ending.

ride shotgun. To act as a guard, or to ride in the front seat of a car. The expression was suggested by the armed guard with a shotgun who often rode beside the driver on stagecoaches in the old American West.

right smart. In parts of New England and the South right smart can mean a large or considerable amount, as in "We have right smart of those Jonagold apples." The words can also mean talented or accomplished.

ring the bell; ring a bell. *To ring the bell,* "to succeed at something," is an Americanism that has its origins in either amusement park shooting galleries, where the marksman rings a bell when he hits the target, or in those familiar carnival strength-testing machines, where a person tries to sledgehammer a wooden ball hard and high enough up a board to ring a bell. *Ring the bell* is common in the spiels, or pitches, for both games. *To ring a bell*—"to strike a familiar chord, to evoke a memory"—on the other hand, may refer to memories evoked by ringing church bells or school bells.

rising tide lifts all boats. This American proverbial saying may have originated in Cape Cod, as President Kennedy implied in a speech he made. The words seem to date back to the early 20th century and mean that in good times everybody prospers. A variation is *on a rising tide all boats are lifted.*

roadhog. Surprisingly, this term for a driver who doesn't keep to a lane, who takes more than a share of the road, was first applied to bicycle riders, not motorists. The term is an Americanism first recorded in 1891, according to the *OED,* but recorded two years later according to *A Dictionary of Americanisms.* At the time there were roughly 10 million bicycles on U.S. roads but no more than *two dozen* cars.

rock 'n' roll. The best guess is that *rock 'n' roll* "reflects a sexual metaphor," as one writer puts it, quoting the lyrics "My baby rocks me with one steady roll." *Rock and roll* music, an outgrowth of black culture in America, of course dates back much earlier than the first recorded use of the term in the early 1950s, deriving from black "rhythm and blues." The first major film to use rock and roll music was *Blackboard Jungle* (1955). Director Richard Brooks bought the rights to use the song "Rock Around the Clock" in the film for $4,000. He could have bought the song outright for another $1,000, but the studio refused to pay. "Rock Around the Clock" went on to sell 1.5 million records that year, becoming one of the biggest hits of all time.

Rocky Mountains. North America's chief mountain system, ranging from central New Mexico to northern Alaska with its highest peak being Mount McKinley (Alaska) at 20,300 feet. Also called the Rockies. The Rocky Mountain states are those states in the Rocky Mountain region, traditionally Arizona, Colorado, Idaho, Montana, Nevada,

New Mexico, Utah, and Wyoming. The Rocky Mountain goat is a long-haired, shorthorned, white antelope-like animal *(Oreamnos montanus)* of mountainous regions, especially the Rocky Mountains, while the Rocky Mountain canary is a humorous term for a burro coined by early prospectors in the American West. Rocky Mountain spotted fever is an infectious disease transmitted by ticks that was first reported in the Rocky Mountain area.

rocky road. The variety of ice cream, consisting of chunks of chocolate ice cream, marshmallows, and almonds, was originally the name of a candy bar in the Great Depression years. Both the candy and the ice cream that took its name were meant to symbolize the rocky road people had before them in hard times, making the hard times easier by joking about them.

rode hard and put up wet. Someone who says he's been "rode hard and put up wet" feels he has been treated badly, abused. The analogy in this Americanism is to a horse that is sweaty from having been worked hard and is not properly cared for.

roscoe. A pistol or revolver. This old American slang word was first recorded at the end of the 19th century, but its origin is unknown. Maybe a criminal named Roscoe is involved, but I haven't found him. The male name Roscoe comes from the Germanic words meaning "swift horse." One Roscoe with something named after him is William Roscoe (1753–1831), a British philanthropist and historian who has the American bird *Roscoe's Yellowthroat* honoring his patronym.

Rough Riders. Teddy Roosevelt named his Spanish-American War cavalry unit the Rough Riders, after the American cowboy bronco-busters called roughriders, many of whom were part of his regiment.

rubber chicken. An unappetizing dish invariably on the menu at dinners, banquets, and other large gatherings in the U.S.

rubberneck. Who invented *rubberneck* for a gawking tourist is unknown, but the Americanism dates back to the 1890s in New York City. In the words of H. L. Mencken (*The American Language,* 1948) *rubberneck* "is almost a complete treatise on American psychology . . . one of the best words ever coined . . . It may be homely, but it is nevertheless superb, and whoever invented it, if he could be discovered, would be worthy of a Harvard LL.D., but also the thanks of both Rotary and Congress, half a bushel of medals, and 30 days as the husband of Miss America."

rub out. To *rub someone out,* "to kill him," isn't gangster talk from the Prohibition era, as is so often assumed. The term dates back to the early 19th-century American Far West and has its origins in Plains Indian sign language, which expresses *to kill* with a rubbing motion. The term is first recorded in George Ruxton's *Life in the Far West* (1848) and it is he who gives the sign language source.

Rum Row. During Prohibition, Rum Row was a line of ships anchored off New York City outside the three-mile coastal limit, waiting for smaller boats to speed out to buy their contraband liquor and bring the bootleg booze ashore. Fully one-third of all the illegal liquor that came into the country came in via this Rum Row.

run the gamut of emotions from A to B. Sometimes said of unaccomplished actors and actresses, this expression has its origin in a witticism of American author Dorothy Parker. "Kate's wonderful, isn't she?" a friend said of Katharine Hepburn's Broadway performance in *The Lake,* between acts at the Martin Beck Theater. "Oh, yes," Miss Parker agreed. "She runs the gamut of emotions all the way from A to B." These words became as celebrated as any of her ripostes, but years later Miss Parker told Garson Kanin that she didn't think there was a finer actress anywhere than Katharine Hepburn; she had made the remark for the same reason she said many things—because it was funny, a joke. Miss Hepburn, however, agreed with her assessment of *The Lake.*

run wild as outhouse rats. Kansas wheat farmers appear to have coined this Americanism a century or so ago. It was often used to describe unsupervised, unruly kids.

rush hour. The term *rush hour* came into the language long before the first cars clogged American streets. It dates back to 1883, when the Brooklyn Bridge was completed, releasing more traffic into Manhattan and Brooklyn. The subway expression *rush hour express* was first recorded in 1928. In Japan rush hour workers called "fanny pushers" (a euphemistic translation) are employed to pack people into rush hour trains.

rustler. A cattle thief. This usage is first recorded in the American West in 1882. At first *rustler* meant an energetic person, one who rustled up stray cattle for his boss. The word appears to have evolved from "hustler," as this quote from Owen Wister's *The Virginian* (1902) indicates: "It [*rustler*] was not in any dictionary, and current translations of it were inconsistent. A man at Hossie Falls said that he had passed through Cheyenne, and heard the term applied in a complimentary way to people who were alive and pushing. Another man had always supposed it meant some kind of horse. But the most alarming version of all was that a rustler was a cattle thief. Now the truth is that all these meanings were right. The word ran a sort of progress in the cattle country, gathering many meanings as it went." Of course, the common meaning of the word came to be "a cattle or horse thief." As a matter of fact, a Texas state legislator was convicted of cattle rustling as recently as 1983.

S

Sadie Hawkins Day. In 1939 cartoonist Al Capp's comic strip *Li'l Abner* featured a race held on "Sadie Hawkins Day," in which single women chased bachelors, trying to win their love. The fictional day soon inspired real Sadie Hawkins Days all over America. Usually held in November, these Sadie Hawkins Days are days on which girls escort boys to dances and parties, or ask boys to escort them.

Sagebrush State. A popular nickname for Nevada, along with the Silver State. Nevada is called the Battle-Born State because it came into the Union during the Civil War, and, jocularly, the Divorce State because of Reno and Las Vegas, famous for quickie divorces.

sand in my shoes. Said by or of people who have spent their lives in a seaside community. The expression dates back to at least the late 19th century in the U.S. and is usually heard as *I've got sand in my shoes.*

sandman. The U.S. personification of sleepiness, especially for children, a mythical man who puts sand in the eyes of youngsters to make them sleepy. Often parents tell kids, "The sandman is coming." The term originated in the mid-19th century; counterparts in other countries include Olaf Shuteye, Scandanavian, and Wee Willie Winkie, Scottish.

Satchmo. The nickname of Louis Armstrong (1900–71), American jazz trumpeter, gravelly voiced singer, and virtuoso musician. He was first known as *Satchel-mouth*, which means someone with a big mouth, a very talkative person, and a jazz musician who plays a horn. Later on, it is said, a British admirer compressed *satchel-mouth* into *Satchmo*, a word used for the one and only Louis.

say it ain't so, Joe. They said "Shoeless Joe" Jackson, a poor boy from South Carolina, played ball without shoes down home, but he put on spikes when he made the majors and became a great star, his lifetime average of .356 the third highest in the history of baseball. Shoeless Joe never made Coopers-town's Hall of Fame, though, and never will. Jackson was one of the eight Chicago White Sox players who conspired with gamblers to throw the 1919 World Series, after which he was banished from baseball for life. After confessing his role in the affair on September 28, 1920, Jackson walked down the steps of the Cook County Courthouse through a crowd of reporters and a ragged little boy grabbed his sleeve and said "Say it ain't so, Joe." The phrase is still used in reference to any hero who has betrayed his trust, though Jackson denied that the boy said it.

scalawag. Undersized, lean, undeveloped cattle that were of little use were called scalawags by American ranchers and farmers in the West toward the middle of the 18th century. The term then came to be applied to disreputable people, rogues, scoundrels, rascals, those who refused to work, and had a special use in the South after the Civil War to describe anyone willing to accept Reconstruction. As for *scalawag* itself, the word remains something of a mystery. It may derive from the Gaelic *sgalag*, for "a lowly servant or rustic," but more likely comes from *Scalloway*, one of the Shetland Islands that is known for its dwarf ponies and cattle, which could have been considered worthless. Other suggestions are the Scottish *scurryvaig*, "a vagabond"; the Latin *scurra vagas,* "a wandering buffoon"; and the English dialect *scall,* "skin-disease." No one seems to know why the word, with so many possible British derivations, is first recorded in America.

scarcer than hen's teeth. Nothing is scarcer because not even Ripley has found a hen with even a single tooth. The Americanism, which also means nonexistent, probably goes back to Colonial days, though it was first recorded in 1862.

schlep. This Yiddish word has become part of the American vocabulary, meaning either "to lug around" (He schlepped the package all the way from Jersey), or "to move in a slow, awkward, or tedious manner."

schmuck. One wouldn't think *schmuck* is an obscene word, judging by its common use in America. *Schmuck* is Yiddish for "penis," deriving somehow from a German word meaning "ornament," and has come to mean a stupid, obnoxious person, of whom there are apparently enough to make *schmuck* one of the best-known Yiddish expressions.

schnozzola. This word for the nose, especially a large nose, was popularized by American comedian Jimmy Durante, who was called the Schnozzola or the Schnoz after his considerable proboscis, the most famous nose on the stage since that of Cyrano de Bergerac. The word comes from Yiddish *shnoz,* which derives from the German word for "snout."

sci-fi. A term invented and financed by Forrest J. Ackerman, "one of science fiction's greatest fans."

scow. *Scow* is another word born in America; its parent is the Dutch *schouw,* "a large flat-bottomed pole boat or river boat," which, through a mispronunciation, became *scow.* Usually serving as a ferryboat or lighter in the beginning, the scow first entered the language in the mid 17th century and is first recorded in 1669. *To scow* meant to cross a river by scow and America has since known cattle, dumping, ferry, mud, oyster, snag, sand, steam, stone-trading, and garbage scows.

Scrabble. The word game's name was coined by unemployed architect Alfred Mosher Butts when he invented the game in 1931. *Scrabble* he said, stood for players "digging" for letters, part of game strategy. Two to four players in this popular game use counters of letters with various point value to build words on a playing board. The highest competition score in the game is 1,049, a record set in 1989.

screwball; screw loose. "King Carl!" Hubbell's famous screwball, which he introduced in the early 1930s, is probably responsible for this expression meaning an eccentric person. The New York Giant pitcher used his screwball in winning 24 games in a row, pitching 46 consecutive scoreless innings, and, most amazing of all, striking out in order the greatest concentration of slugging power ever assembled—Babe Ruth, Lou Gehrig, and Jimmy Foxx—in the 1934 All-Star game. Hubbell's erratic pitch obviously got a lot of publicity in the sports pages. Since it corkscrewed crazily as it approached the batter and you never knew how it was going to break, it was inevitably compared with an unpredictable, erratic, eccentric person, helped by the expression *he has a screw loose* ("is a little unhinged"), common since the 1860s.

scuzzy; scuz. *Disgusting* gives us this relatively recent adjective, which was first recorded in 1969 and means "dirty, grimy, disgusting, awful." A scuz is simply someone who is scuzzy. Another theory states this Americanism is a blend of *scummy* and *fuzzy*.

secede. In the sense of "to secede from the United States," *secede* appears to have first been used by Thomas Jefferson in 1825: "Possibly their colonies might secede from the Union."

Seeing Eye dog. Dogs used to guide blind people are called *Seeing Eye dogs,* after the Seeing Eye organization in Morristown, New Jersey, where such dogs have been trained for over half a century.

See Spot run! Many millions of Americans read this and similar memorable lines as their first effort at reading. The words are from the Dick and Jane elementary textbooks that were written by Zerna Sharp, a first grade teacher in Las Porte, Indiana, and were used from the 1940s through the 1970s. The characters in the stories included Mother, Father, Dick, Jane, Spot the dog, and Puff the cat.

see you later. This widespread good-bye is an Americanism first recorded in the early 1870s. There have since been a number of variations on it, such as SEE YOU LATER, ALLIGATOR.

see you later, alligator. British rhyming slang spread to California in the 1850s, and one result was the word *alligator,* which rhymed with and meant "see you later." Rhyming slang never really caught on in America, and *alligator* in this sense didn't last long, but the full expression *see you later, alligator* remains with us. There are several variations on the 1960s phrase, including *on the Nile, crocodile* and *in a while, crocodile.*

self-made man. This expression seems like it would be an Americanism, and it is, the *O.E.D* tracing it back to an 1832 speech by a Kentucky congressman. One time a politician collared American editor Horace Greeley at a convention and proudly confided to him that he was a "self-made man." "That, sir," Greeley replied, "relieves the Almighty of a terrible responsibility." But then author Henry Class said Greeley himself "was a self-made man who worshipped his creator."

self-starter. *Self-starter* has come to mean "someone who doesn't need much help in performing a task," who has a remarkable amount of initiative. It is an Americanism dating back to 1894 and originally referred to an attachment for starting a car's engine without hand cranking.

sell like hot cakes. Hot cakes cooked in bear grease or pork lard were popular from earliest times in America. First made of cornmeal, the griddle cakes or pancakes were of course best when served piping hot and were often sold at church benefits, fairs, and other functions. So popular were they that by the beginning of the 19th century *to sell like hot cakes* was a familiar expression for anything that sold very quickly, effortlessly, and in quantity.

sent up the river. To be sent to prison. First recorded in the 1930s, this term must be much older. *The river* referred to is the Hudson in New York City and *up* it, at Ossining, is Sing Sing Penitentiary, which was founded in 1830.

Seven Cities. Ancient towns in New Mexico that inspired the Spaniards to explore the Southwest because of their reputed wealth; now thought to be Zuni pueblos, they are also known as the Seven Cities of Cibola.

Seventh-Day Adventists. In 1831 New York farmer and preacher William Miller (1782–1849) founded the Protestant sect of Second Adventists, often called Millerites. Convinced from his reading of the Bible that the second coming of Christ would occur 12 years later in 1843, he spread his belief throughout America, attracting many followers who prepared for the end of the world and Judgment Day. When 1843 and then 1844 passed without his prophecy coming true, Miller founded the Adventist Church, whose name was changed to the Seventh-Day Adventists 15 years later. Numbering well over a million members today, their church observes Saturday as the Sabbath (as do Seventh-Day Baptists) and forbids the use of alcohol and tobacco.

sexist. A relative newcomer, based on *racist* and coined in an 11/18/65 speech by Paulette M. Leet, director of special programs at Franklin and Marshall College. *Sexist* refers to a person whose attitude or behavior is based on traditional stereotypes of sexual roles. Said Ms. Leet in her speech: "When you argue . . . that since fewer women write good poetry this justifies their total exclusion [from taking English courses], you are taking a position analogous to that of the racist—I might call you in this case a 'sexist.' . . ."

sgnik sdneirf. Early Americans liked to spell backwards things that they detested, as in the case of O-GRAB-ME. This was also the case with the expression *king's friends,* which the Tories called themselves, contemptuous patriots calling them by the derogatory name *sgnik sdneirf.* As for the Loyalists, they called the patriots "rabble."

shanty; shantytown. *Shanty,* for "shack or rough cabin," is an Americanism first recorded in 1820 that probably derives from the Gaelic *sean tig,* "old house," though the French Canadian *chantier,* "log hut," is also a strong possibility. *Shantytown,* recorded in 1845, first meant a cluster of shacks near a railyard where railroad construction workers lived. Because many Irish lived in such shantytowns the term soon meant a poor Irish district, *shanty Irish* (1925) coming to mean poor Irish people who lived in such districts.

Shea Stadium. The New York Mets home field in Flushing Meadows, Queens. Completed in 1964, it is named for attorney William Shea, who was instrumental in getting the stadium built. A new home field for the Mets will open in 2009.

shell out. From the actual "shelling out" of peas and corn—removing the first from their pods and removing corn from the cob—came the figurative use of *to shell out,* "to pay out." Removing a seed from the pod, etc., is like taking money out of a purse or pocket and, furthermore, dried shelled peas and "shelled corn," as it was called in America, were often a medium of exchange in the past. The phrase is first recorded in 1825.

shenanigans. Though now it is always used in the plural, this Americanism for "mischief" or "trickery" was first recorded as *shenanigan* in 1855, in California. There have been several suggestions as to its ancestors, including the Spanish *chanada,* "trick," and the argot German *schinaglen,* meaning the same. More likely it comes from the Irish *sionnachuighim,* "I play the fox," or "I play tricks."

shirtsleeves to shirtsleeves in three generations. "There's no' but three generations atween clog and clog," says the old Lancashire proverb that is probably the ancestor of this expression, but American multimillionaire Andrew Carnegie (1835–1919) is credited with the exact words *shirtsleeves to shirtsleeves in three generations,* meaning that family wealth is not long-lasting. The words don't apply to the Rockefeller, Du Pont, Rothschild, and Ford families, to name but a few that come quickly to mind.

shit. From the Indo-European root *skei,* "to divide," comes the Old English *scitan,* "to defecate," that is the ancestor of our word *shit. To shit* thus means strictly to divide or cut (wastes) from the body. *Shit,* as slang for nonsense or lies, is an Americanism probably first used by soldiers during the Civil War as a shortening of *bullshit,* another

Americanism that probably goes back 30 years or more earlier, though it is first recorded, in the form of its euphemism *bull,* in about 1850.

shoddy. Civil War suppliers cheated the Union Army with a cheap uniform cloth called "shoddy," which literally unraveled on the wearer's back—and added a new adjective to the language.

shootin' iron. A handgun. This term dates back to 18th-century America and did not originate in the West, despite its constant use in Hollywood westerns.

shoots. As far as I know, there is no real synonym for OK in the American language unless one counts the long so-called stretch form of OK, such as okeydoke, or the okie dokie used in a popular 1947 song. Several sources, however, say that the Hawaiian shoots or shootz can also serve as an OK substitute, meaning satisfactory, all right, etc. In my own brief travels in Hawaii I didn't come across this word. *See* OK.

shoot the works. A western Americanism meaning to spend everything, get whatever you want.

short story. The name, though not the form, was invented in the U.S., its first mention in *Harper's Magazine* in 1887 in the form of "short story writing." A short story, briefly, is usually a prose work of fiction under 10,000 words, "differing from a novel in being shorter and less elaborate," according to the *O.E.D.* A short short story is even more condensed, perhaps of up to 1,200 words. Edgar Allan Poe is regarded as the originator of the modern short story, which Americans have excelled in. An old joke has an English teacher telling a class that the five requisites to a good short story are "brevity, a religious reference, a sexual reference, some association with society and an illustration of modesty." The next day a student handed in a story that read in full: "My God!" said the duchess. 'Take your hand off my knee!'"

shotgun wedding. Any wedding where the father or other member of the family, pointing a gun at his head, forces the groom to marry the bride, who has been made pregnant by or lost her virginity to the man. It is doubtful that many real shotguns were used in such weddings, but since 1925 or so, when first recorded, the Americanism has meant "a wedding made by pregnancy."

shot heard round the world. Baseball fans ascribe a different meaning to this Ralph Waldo Emerson line describing the opening of the American Revolution. For half a century now they have remembered the words as a name for the home run New York Giant slugger Bobby Thomson hit in the ninth inning of the last game of the 1951 playoffs against the Dodgers to win the National League pennant. The "Jints" victory was dubbed "The Miracle of Coogan's Bluff" after the hill behind the Giant's Polo Grounds stadium.

shot in the dark. A random conjecture, a wild guess, and most likely a guess that will fail. This Americanism refers to a gun shot in the dark at a target or anything else, a shot that would rarely succeed.

Show-Me State. A nickname for Missouri (see I'M FROM MISSOURI). It has also been called the Ozark State, the Lead State, the Bullion State, (after Senator Thomas Hart Benton, "Old Bullion," an advocate of metallic currency), and the Pennsylvania of the West. Obsolete is the nickname the Puke State, possibly so named as a misprint for Pike County, Missouri, or after a word describing a backward yokel.

shut your face. Stop talking. This Americanism is first recorded by Upton Sinclair in *King Coal* (1917): "The marshall bade him 'shut his face,' and emphasized the command by a twist at his coat collar."

since the hogs et grandma. This humorous expression from the U.S. Ozark mountains means a long time ago, as in "I haven't had so much good fun since the hogs et grandma." A variation is *since the hogs et little brother.*

sink one's teeth into. *To sink one's teeth into something* means to eat it, usually with great enjoyment, or to get into the spirit of anything. The Americanism was first recorded in 1892 as *sink tooth into:* "Only a favored few of the millions of feasters on Thanksgiving Day will sink tooth into genuine wild turkey meat."

sin to Davy Crockett. A historical expression meaning something exceptional or extraordinary, as in "The way we used 'em up [killed them] was a sin to Davy Crockett." It refers, of course, to Davy

Crockett (1786–1836), legendary frontiersman and hero at the Alamo.

Sioux State. A nickname of North Dakota, where the Sioux Indians once ruled. North Dakota has also been called the Land of the Dakotas and the Great Central State. It is called the Flickertailed State after a ground squirrel called the flickertail found only in the state.

sippin' whiskey. An old name in the South and elsewhere for the best quality BOURBON.

$64 question. On the radio quiz program "Take It or Leave It," which premiered in 1941 and was emceed by Bob Hawk, topics were chosen by contestants from the studio audience and questions on these topics answered by each contestant on seven levels. The easiest question was worth two dollars and the questions progressed in difficulty until the ultimate $64 Question was reached. The popularity of the show added to the language the expression *the $64 question,* "any question difficult to answer," and inspired a slew of similar quiz shows. A decade later came television's "$64,000 Question" with its plateaus instead of levels, its isolation booth, and its scandals involving prominent contestants who cheated in cahoots with the producers. Then, after a long hiatus, there was the "$128,000 Question," but despite these programs with their inflated prizes, *$64 question* retains its place in the national vocabulary.

skate on thin ice. The allusion here is to skating over ice so thin that it hardly bears the skater's weight. This was actually once a sport called tickledybendo in New England. The metaphor *skating on thin ice* means that someone is taking chances, or behaving in a questionable, dangerous, or indelicate manner.

skedaddle. *Skedaddle* is often thought of as an Americanism for "to retreat, flee, clear out, depart hurriedly." But the expression probably comes from Scottish and English dialect, possibly deriving from the Greek *skedannunai,* "to split up." First used in America during the 1820s it became popular among Northern troops during the Civil War as a word describing Rebels fleeing the battlefield after a loss.

skid row. The expression, common throughout the United States, originated in the Northwest, where roads were made of debarked small logs called skids. Skid row then came to mean a town with these skid rows and finally a disreputable part of town.

skinny dipping. Dipping has been used by Americans for swimming since early Colonial days, and skinny dipping, "swimming naked," has been popular just as long. While dipping is not much used by itself anymore, it is still found in the expression let's take a dip.

skulduggery. *Skulduggery,* for "dishonesty or trickery," has no connection with heads or skulls. It does have something to do with adultery. *Skulduggery* is the American variant of the Scottish *skulduddery,* which means illicit sexual intercourse or obscenity, the Scottish word originally coined as a euphemism for *adultery (duddery,* "adultery"). Thus the word is doubly euphemistic: *skulduddery* itself and the American *skulduggery* fashioned from it that is first recorded in 1856. In America the word has never suggested any sexual hijinks, usually meaning political trickery.

skyscraper. The world's first skyscraper office building was the 10-story Chicago office of the Home Insurance Company built in 1883 by architect William Le Baron Jenney. The fitting name *skyscraper* was given to this first building to employ steel skeleton construction, a building much higher than any other building of its time, but journalists had borrowed the word from the triangular sails that had long been used high on the masts of sailing vessels, scraping against the sky. Novelist Henry James wrote that Manhattan skyscrapers looked "like extravagant pins in a cushion already overplanted, and stuck in as in the dark, anywhere and anyhow."

slam dunk. *Dunk* simply meant to shoot a basketball through the goal in the 1930s when the term is first recorded. But in the mid-1960s tall players developed what is known as the dunk shot by leaping above the basket and stuffing the ball in. The slam dunk came soon after, this a more theatrical version of the dunk shot in which the ball is slammed down through the hoop. *Slam dunk* has come to mean any "sure thing," as in, "We'll win tomorrow, it's a slam dunk."

slice. Often used by Americans instead of a piece of pizza when ordering pizza in a pizzeria or pizza parlor: "Gimme a slice anna small coke." When a whole pizza pie is ordered it's "Gimme a pie." This word is first recorded in the United States in the early 1930s, when slices weren't widely sold as they are today and pies prevailed, these usually eaten at a table in an Italian restaurant. It should be noted that while thinner pie-slice-shaped Neopolitan pizza can be asked for by ordering a slice, a square cut of thick Sicilian pizza shouldn't be: "Gimme a piece of Sicilian." Chicago pizza is a deep-dish pizza popular in the Midwest.

slow bear. A humorous Civil War term that foragers used for farmers' pigs that they stole, killed, and ate. Humorous, that is, so long as you weren't the farmer.

slumgullion. By the end of the 19th century *slumgullion* meant a meat and vegetable stew in America, but the word started out meaning "slime." *Slum,* a mispronunciation of slime, had first meant the scummy liquid left over in the tryworks after blubber was processed aboard whaling ships. By midcentury *slum* came to mean a stew. Then miners in the 1849 gold rush borrowed *slum,* for "soup," added *gullion,* an English dialect word meaning "mud," and used *slumgullion* to mean the soupy liquid resulting from sluicing. *Slumgullions,* in turn, seemed to make a funny word for soup to some miners and this became its primary meaning.

smart cookie. "He's a real smart cookie," a doctor recently told me (2003) of another diagnostician, proving that the expression is still used. The *cookie* in the phrase is American slang for a person and is first recorded in this sense about 1917 in the form of "He's a hardboiled cookie," by hardboiled cookie President Harry S. Truman in his book *Dear Bess.* The expression *smart cookie* in its entirety didn't find its way into print until 1955. *Tough cookie* and *rough cookie* are also heard.

snail mail. A humorous synonym for postal mail coined in the early 1980s by some anonymous e-mail user. Electronic e-mail is of course much faster than regular mail. The expression was born in the U.S. but is widely used today.

snollygoster. One very rarely hears this word today, but in the 19th century it was a common Americanism for "a pretentious boaster." The word is probably a fanciful formation coined by some folk poet who liked its appropriate sound; it is first recorded in 1862. A Georgia editor defined a snollygoster as a "fellow who wants office regardless of party, platform or principles, and who, whenever he wins, gets there by the sheer force of monumental talknophical assumacy." The type is still common, even if the word isn't.

snowbirds. Southwesterners use this term today for northerners who come south for the winter, but it originated in the U.S. Army in the late 19th century as a name for men who enlisted for food and quarters during the winter and deserted in the spring.

soap opera. *Newsweek* seems to have used *soap opera* first in an 11/13/39 article, putting the expression in quotes as if it were new. Earlier a writer in the *Christian Century* (8/24/39) came very close to coining the term, however: "These fifteen minute tragedies . . . I call the 'soap tragedies' . . . because it is by the grace of soap I am allowed to shed tears for these characters who suffer so much from life." He was referring, of course, to the soap manufacturers who sponsored many of the early radio serials characterized by melodrama and sentimentality that are now called *soap operas,* or simply *soaps* (an abbreviated form that is 20 years or so old).

so fun. Americans, especially young Americans, have recently taken to saying so fun, in conversation, as in "That was *so fun* at the club last night," instead of, say, "That was so much at the club last night." When this usage first appeared is not known.

Solid South. A political term much used from the Civil War to the late 1950s, when the South's electoral votes could be counted upon by the Democratic party. Political realignments have made the term purely historical today.

someone stole his rudder. We find this expression, for "a helpless drunk," first recorded in the American West during the 19th century, but it is obviously a borrowing from nautical language, of the sea or the inland waterways of America.

something on the ball. A baseball pitcher with *something on the ball* has the ability to throw a variety of pitches that are usually effective. Since the early 1900s the phrase has been extended to mean anyone with skill or ability.

Sooner; sooner. *Sooner,* capitalized, refers to a native of Oklahoma, the Sooner State. Uncapitalized, the word has several meanings: 1) someone who settles on government land before it's opened to settlers; 2) any person who unfairly gets ahead of another; and, most interesting of all 3) a child born fewer than nine months after his or her parents were married, one who came out sooner than he or she should have. The last is an expression used mainly in the Appalachian Mountains.

Sooner State. A nickname for Oklahoma, after the "sooners" who "jumped the gun sooner" and sneaked over the border before the lands there were thrown open to settlement by U.S. citizens at noontime on April 22, 1889. Many of the 20,000 people who came to claim land on that day found that "sooners" had gotten there before them. Indians, of course, were there sooner than anyone, for all the good it did them. Today residents of Oklahoma are called Sooners.

so ugly that when he was a little boy momma had to tie a pork chop around his neck so the dog would play with him. A saying heard in Texas, probably of recent origin.

soul brother, etc. As a term for blacks used by blacks, *soul brothers* has been around since at least the 1950s. Today it is often abbreviated, by blacks, as *the brothers* (or *sisters*) and further shortened to *bro* when used in a greeting. The meaning here is that blacks are alike in the soul, but in earlier combinations *soul* is used in many ways. *Soul sharks* were rapacious preachers, black or white, usually without a pulpit, and *soul butter* was a term for moralizing drivel, black or white, that Mark Twain popularized. *Soul mate* can be someone much loved, or even a mistress. *Soul music* and *soul food* (food like collard greens, black-eyed peas, hog maw, etc., associated with southern blacks) are also black terms dating back at least to the 1950s.

soup. Nitroglycerin was dubbed *soup* by safecrackers because the liquid can be obtained by *very very very* gently simmering dynamite in water. The Americanism is first recorded in about 1905.

soup and fish. Dating back to 19th-century America, this term for formal white-tie dinner clothes probably derives from the obsolete American term *soup and fish,* for a lavish dinner of many courses. *Soup and fish* for an elaborate dinner, in turn, is apparently related to the still common expression *from soup to nuts,* but this last term seems to have been first recorded in the 1920s.

Soup Nazi. A phrase used on the New York-inspired television comedy *Seinfeld* to refer to a real-life soup merchant located in midtown Manhattan. The impatient Soup Nazi is known for supposedly badgering disorganized patrons and for not including the customary piece of bread with an order of soup for customers who take too long to decide what they want. People tolerate his attitude because he reportedly serves outstanding soup.

soup up. To soup up a car is to improve its capacity for speed by enriching its fuel and/or adjusting the engine. This use of the words was first recorded in about 1940. Soup itself is American slang for car or airplane fuel, while to soup up a horse is to inject dope into the animal to make it run faster.

sourdough bread. Now known in commercial forms throughout the United States, sourdough bread, made from sour or fermented dough, was first a mainstay of miners in the early West, who were in fact *sourdoughs* because they carried some of the fermented dough with them from place to place to start new batches of bread.

South Carolina. See NORTH CAROLINA.

South Dakota. See NORTH DAKOTA.

Southern chivalry. Though rarely, if ever, heard today, this historical term was common up until the end of the Civil War. According to the *Magazine of American History* (vol. 3, 1885), "It was claimed as a proud title by Southerners and their friends, but has always been heard and used by the North with a shade of contempt."

southerner. Often capitalized, this common word for a resident of the American South may have been coined between 1820 and 1830. The term first appeared in *Western Monthly Magazine* in 1828. *Southern gentleman* was recorded about half a century earlier.

southern fried chicken. Originally chicken fried in bacon grease, southern fried chicken has been popular in the American South since before 1711, when the term *fried chicken* is first recorded there. It became popular throughout the country in the 1930s, when it was first widely sold at roadside restaurants.

southern gentleman. This term for a courtly, well-bred southerner dates back at least to the late 18th century. Clare Booth Luce, in *Kiss the Boys Goodbye,* offered this definition: "If you can shoot like a South Carolinian, ride like a Virginian, make love like a Georgian, and be proud of it like an Episcopalian, you're a Southern gentleman." But an anonymous infidel Yankee defined the chivalrous species as "one who rises to his feet when his wife comes in bearing the firewood."

southern hospitality. The words *southern hospitality,* the hospitality characteristic of southern people and sometimes considered the epitome of sectional hospitality, have been traced back to 1819, when a traveler from the North wrote in his journal, "The mistress . . . treated us to milk in the true spirit of Southern hospitality." But the South was famous for its hospitality long before this, as it still is today, and the much-used phrase is surely older.

Spalding; Spaldeen. Alfred Goodwill Spalding (1850–1915) deserves his place in baseball's Hall of Fame as much as any man. He may not be "the Father of Baseball," but is certainly "Father of the Baseball," and it was only when he came upon the scene with his uniform manufacturing methods that what had been a chaotic minor sport was fashioned into the national pastime. Lively balls were once so rubbery that baseball scores like 201–11 were not uncommon, and others so dead that the phrase "fell with a dull thud" found its way into the language. The former Chicago White Sox manager did not invent the hard ball when he founded his company in 1880, but the rigid manufacturing standards he maintained made it possible for the newly formed National League of Professional Baseball to survive. Such careful preparations over the years have made the Spalding trademark synonymous for a baseball. Other sporting equipment manufactured by the firm includes a red rubber ball called the Spaldeen (spelled *Spalding),* which has been known by that name to several generations of American youngsters.

Spam. People all over the world have eaten some 5 billion cans of Spam since the Hormel Foods Corporation began selling it under this name. At first Hormel sold the mixture of pork shoulder, ham, salt, sugar, and sodium nitrate as *special ham.* When other meatpackers began selling the same product, the company in 1936 sponsored a nationwide contest to create a memorable brand name. Actor Kenneth Daigneau, the brother of a Hormel executive, won a mere $100 for *Spam,* which Judith Stone in an exhaustive July 3, 1994, article in the *New York Times Magazine* ("Five Million Cans And Counting") called "arguably the planet's most recognizable portmanteau word" (a combination of the s from *shoulder,* the p from *pork* and the *am* from *ham).* However, *chortle* (from *chuckle* and *snort)* may be better known.

spark. Americans were "sparking" at least as far back as 1787, when the expression was first recorded. *To spark,* an old-fashioned term meaning "to make love, to court," especially by a young woman's sweetheart or "feller," may be of Scandinavian origin.

speakeasy. The word goes back 30 years or more before its use during Prohibition, to at least the 1880s. Samuel Hudson, a newspaperman of the day, said he first heard it in Pittsburgh, used by an old Irish woman who sold liquor without a license and told her clients to "spake asy" when they came to buy it. Over a century before this there were Irish *spake-aisy* shops or smugglers' dens. Speakeasies were also called speaks during Prohibition. The original "spake-aisy" places may have been so named because patrons had to speak quietly when entering them to avoid alerting police and neighbors.

speculator. The first speculators in the U.S. to be called speculators did business during the Revolutionary War boom, though there was no formal stock exchange at the time and wheeling and dealing was done in coffeehouses along Wall Street in downtown Manhattan, or outside. The word *speculator* has its roots in the Latin *speculatus,* observed, watched.

spiel. This Americanism, for "sales talk or a line," has been used at least since 1870. It derives from the German *spielen,* "to play a musical instrument." In its American usage the word meant "to talk in a high-flown, grandiloquent manner" before it was used to describe the voluble talk of the carnival barker and then the salesman.

spizorinkum. Born on the American frontier, *spizorinkum* was originally used during the 1850s as the term for "good" hard money, as opposed to greenbacks or paper currency, but soon came to have many diverse meanings, including "tireless energy." It was possibly used so much because people liked the sound of the word! In any case, *spizorinkum* is "an impossible combination" of the Latin *specie* ("kind") and *rectum* ("right"), "the right kind." The word is sometimes spelled with two z's.

splendid little war. A name President William McKinley's secretary of state, John Hay, invented for the U.S. war against Spain, best known as the Spanish-American War (1898). The war only lasted from late April until mid-August, and the U.S. was victorious.

the Splendid Splinter. The nickname of slugger Ted Williams, the best-known baseball player to play for the Boston Red Sox since Babe Ruth. Often shortened to *the Splinter*. Among the best hitters in the history of baseball.

spoils system. Often attributed to Andrew Jackson, this phrase did arise during his presidency, when the practice of giving appointive offices to loyal members of the party in power was first adopted on a large scale. However, the phrase was suggested by New York senator William Learned Marcy, who defended Jackson's 1829 policy in a speech a year later. Marcy, a member of the Albany Regency, a political group controlled by "The Little Fox," Martin Van Buren, rose in the Senate to defend the appointment of Van Buren as minister to England, his public defense of this political patronage being "the rule that to the victor belong the spoils of war." This remark led to the anonymous coining of *spoils system,* the phrase first recorded in 1838. The political atmosphere of an era can often be seen in the expressions born in that period and during the Jackson and Van Buren administrations we find the following first used in a political sense: *dyed in the wool* (1830), *party line* (1834), *picayune* (1837), *party machinery* (1829), *wirepuller* (1832), and even *expose* (1830), among others. *See also* o.k.

Spokane. Settled on the site of a trading fort in 1810, this city in eastern Washington State is named after the Spokane Indian tribe, whose name means "children of the sun," or "sun warrior," or "sun."

spondulix. Where this old American word for money came from is anybody's guess, but *spondulix* is recorded as early as 1856. It's another word that can only be guessed to be of fanciful origin, a funny word that caught on because people liked its sound. Mark Twain used it in *Huckleberry Finn.*

spunky. *Spunky* means "courageous, spirited, plucky." Among early American colonists *spunk* (from Scottish Gaelic *spong)* meant "tinder" and to *spunk up a fire* meant "to kindle it up, throw more wood on it." Soon *getting one's spunk up* meant "to become fired with courage," the term first recorded in 1834, *spunky* coming along a few years later.

Stars and Stripes; Star-Spangled Banner. Though the Continental Congress resolved in 1777 that the U.S. flag be composed of 13 stripes and 13 stars, the term *Stars and Stripes* for the flag isn't recorded until five years later. *Star-Spangled Banner,* for the flag, was of course inspired by the national anthem, whose lyrics Francis Scott Key wrote in 1814, but the song didn't become our official national anthem until 1931 (though it had for almost a century been called our "national ballad"). The Greek lyric poet Anacreon (fl. 6th century B.C.) wrote light bright poems praising wine and love that were imitated by Jonson, Herrick, and other early English bards. A drinking club in London used his name, and its club song, "Anacreon in Heaven," provided the music for Francis Scott Key's "Star-Spangled Banner," the American national anthem.

State of Franklin. *See* TENNESSEE.

State of the Union message. George Washington delivered the first State of the Union message to Congress, though it was called the

Annual Address at the time. It reports on the state of the nation and is also called the State of the Union address. The speech is required of the president by the U.S. Constitution (Article II, Section 3). It was not called the State of the Union message until 1945.

stateside. *Stateside* may have been invented by G.I.'s in World War II for "to, toward or in the continental U.S." At least the word is first recorded at about that time when many soldiers were far from home. In the U.S. itself today the term is only used by Alaskans (it is rare in Hawaii) for the mainland. Alaskans also call the 48 contiguous states the Lower 48, the lower states, the Outside, and even the South!

States'-Rights Democrat. A designation, not frequently heard anymore, for southern Democrats espousing the doctrine of states' rights. It was apparently coined just after the Civil War.

Statue of Liberty. The statue of Liberty Enlightening the World, better known as the Statue of Liberty, is, of course, as much a symbol of the United States as Uncle Sam. The colossal 152-foot statue of a woman with uplifted arm holding a burning torch stands at the entrance to New York Harbor. It was a gift from France to the United States, designed by French sculptor Frederic Auguste Barthold; its steel framework was designed by Gustav Eiffel, designer of the Eiffel Tower. French citizens contributed the $250,000 for the statue itself, and Americans gave $250,000 for its pedestal on Bedloes Island, whose name was changed in 1956 to Liberty Island. Dedicated in the statue is now under the protection of the National Park Service, which administrates it along with Ellis Island, a former detention center for immigrants entering America, as part of the Statue of Liberty National Memorial. In the statue's left arm is a tablet with the date July 4, 1776, engraved upon it. At its feet are the broken shackles of tyranny.

Statue of Liberty play. Named for its resemblance to the uplifted arm of the Statue of Liberty, this football play has a passer faking a pass, and another back coming behind him, taking the ball from his upraised hand and either passing it himself or running toward the goal with it. Outdated today, it was the pride of every kid's sandlot team a generation ago.

Steadi Cam. Short for *steady camera,* a traditional device that holds a camera steady to the cameraman's body, enabling him to take smooth shots without any jerking or shaking. The first Steadi Cams were used in the Oscar-winning film *Rocky* (1976).

steamboat. *Steamboat* is an Americanism dating back to at least 1785, when John Fitch invented the first workable one. Fitch was not able to secure the financial aid necessary to promote his invention after his fourth ship was destroyed, and he died a broken man, leaving a request that he be buried on the banks of the Ohio River so that he might rest "where the song of the boatman would enliven the stillness of my resting place and the music of the steam engine soothe my spirit." His dream became a reality in 1807, nine years after he died, when Robert Fulton's steamboat *Clermont,* which had been called "Fulton's Folly," proved a great success.

Stepin Fetchit. American vaudevillian Lincoln Theodore Monroe Andrew Perry took his stage name, Stepin Fetchit, from a racehorse he had won money on, hoping that the nag's name would continue bringing him good luck. It didn't, in the long run. *Stepin Fetchit* instead became the synonym for a servile, silly black man when Hollywood typecast the talented actor in such roles throughout the 1940s. By the time of the civil rights movement, the actor was completely out of favor and out of work.

the sticks. *The sticks* is an Americanism for the country, or the backwoods. First recorded in 1905, it derives from the use of *sticks* by lumbermen for "timberlands."

stone crab. This delicious crab *(Menippe mercenaria)* of the southern United States is named from the rocky shores it inhabits. Usually the crab's meaty claws are broken off to be eaten and the rest of the crab is discarded to grow new claws.

stonewaller. One who obstructs or blocks anything with stubborn, stonewall-like resistance. The term may come from the nickname of Civil War Confederate general Thomas Jonathan Jackson (1824–63), who got the name Stonewall at the first battle of Bull Run when a fellow officer told of seeing Jackson "standing like a stone wall." Stonewall Jackson was accidentally killed by his own troops at the battle of Chancellors-ville. "I have lost my right arm," Robert E. Lee, commander of the Confederate armies, said on hearing of his death.

straphanger. A term for a subway commuter popular at least since the first U.S. subways were built early in the 20th century and which may even date back to the days of horsedrawn trolleys.

strawberry friend. This oldtime rural Americanism describes people who visit from the city when strawberries are in season to get free berries (and other produce) from their rural friends or relatives.

stumped. *To be stumped* for "to be baffled" has its origins in the stumps that American settlers had to pull from the earth after felling trees— some stumps were so big and deep-rooted that they perplexed the pioneers. The expression is first recorded in 1812: "John Bull was a little stumped when he saw [Brother] Jonathan's challenge."

Sugar Bowl. A college football end-of-season game held in New Orleans since 1936 and so named because the annual trophy is an antique sugar bowl. Also a nickname for Louisiana, famous for its output of sugar.

Suicide Six. A nickname for highway route 6 on Cape Cod. As novelist William Martin put it in 1991: "Nervous damn stretch—two lanes runnin' straight and flat through pine woods for thirteen miles, speed limit fifty and damn-you-straight-to- hell if you were an old man who didn't go over forty. Somebody always itchin' to pass. Tourists comin' the other way. No wonder they called it Suicide Six."

sundae. Wisconsin ice-cream-parlor owner George Giffy probably first called this concoction, which he did not invent, a *Sunday* back in the early 1890s because he regarded it as a special dish only to be sold on Sundays. No one knows exactly why or when *Sunday* was changed to *sundae.*

Sunshine State. This is Florida's official nickname (at least it is on state license plates), but its nicknames the Everglade State and the Peninsula State are a century older. New Mexico shares the nickname the Sunshine State with Florida and adopted it in 1926. New Mexico has also been called the Cactus State, the Land of the Cactus, the Spanish State, the Land of the Montezumas, the Land of the Delight Makers, the Land of Opportunity, the Land of Enchantment, and the Land of Heart's Desire.

superman. George Bernard Shaw, not Friedrich Nietzsche, coined *superman,* never expecting a movie to be made of him. The German philosopher's word for a dominant man above good or evil, introduced in *Thus Spake Zarathustra* (1883–91), was *Übermensch,* "overman" or "beyondman." Shaw didn't like the sound of Nietzsche's word and so translated its German prefix *über* into the Latin *super-* then added to it the English *man,* translated from the German *Mensch.* Shaw used the new word for the first time in his play *Man and Superman* (1903). The term was widely popularized by an American comic book character of the same name who made his debut in the 1930s.

sweet talk; sweet mouth. Sweet talk is smooth, unctuous flattery designed to win over a person. There is no proof of it, but this southern Americanism possibly comes from Krio, an English-based Creole of Sierra Leone, specifically from the expression *swit mot,* sweet mouth, for "flattery." To *sweet mouth* someone is the opposite of to *bad-mouth* him.

T

Tabasco. The condiment sauce's name, which is a trademark, was apparently first applied to a potent liquor once popular in the American Southwest. The liquor, in turn, took its name from the state of Tabasco in Mexico.

take a bath. American slang meaning "to take a great financial loss," to lose everything or close to everything in a business venture. Someone who takes a bath financially is stripped of everything, as a person taking a bath is stripped of his clothes. The expression dates back only to the 1930s, when someone who took such a bath was said to be "in the tub." More recently, *take a bath* has come to be applied to any complete failure. The older phrase TAKE TO THE CLEANERS is similar but has the sense of fraudulent means being used to effect the loss.

take a cab. U.S. mob slang for to be killed. Comedian Alan King on the Arts & Entertainment channel's "Las Vegas" program (December 1996) said he was told of Bugsy Siegel's killing this way: "Bugsy took a cab."

take a long walk on a short pier. Get lost, don't bother me, you're not wanted here. Apparently an American slang expression dating back a century or so.

take a stab at it! A 20th-century Americanism meaning to take a try at, as in: "That's a tough question, but I'll take a stab at it."

take it on the chin. To endure anything, especially pain, is the meaning of to *take it*, an American expression from boxing, where someone who can take it can endure anything an opponent can dish out. The same thought is behind the expression *take it on the chin*, also from boxing. Both of the phrases now generally mean to take punishment or adversity with courage and not let it defeat you.

take to the cleaners. A person defrauded or bilked in a business deal or a confidence game is said to have been *taken to the cleaners*. A relatively recent phrase, probably dating back no later than the early 1900s, the words are related to *to be cleaned out*, an early 19th-century saying that sometimes meant "to be duped of all one's money" (usually in a card game), but today always means to lose all one's money.

talk a blue streak. This American expressions refers to lightning bolts and has been traced back to about the middle of the 19th century, though it is probably much older. Similarly, *a bolt from the blue,* "something unexpected and startling," draws the picture of a lightning bolt striking from a cloudless blue sky, without any warning at all. *Blue streak* refers to a blue streak of lightning flashing through the sky and was used to describe the rapidity of horses and coaches that "left blue streaks behind them" before it became part of the expression *talk a blue streak,* "to talk rapidly and interminably, to talk someone's ear off."

talkie. A synonym for a motion picture with sound that was first recorded in 1910 (at least *talking motion picture* was). Movie myth insists that Al Jolson's The *Jazz Singer* (1927) was the first sound film ever made, but in truth sound had been used in movies long before this, ever since Edison's first Kinetoscopes in the late 19th century. Many short sound films at the time featured great actors and actresses speaking their parts, as when Sarah Bernhardt spoke in the dueling scene from a 1900 version of *Hamlet*. What held back talking pictures was the huge investment needed to convert Hollywood studios and movie theaters across the country to sound systems. Toward the middle of the 1920s Warner Bros. realized that they had fallen far behind the other major studios and decided as a last-chance gamble to produce synchronized sound movies. Warners built its own huge Hollywood theater, bought the old Vita-graph company with its 15 houses, and converted its studio stages to sound. On August 6, 1926, it premiered its first synchronized sound film, a lavish Vitaphone production of *Don Juan* starring John Barrymore. A year later, it had its first big hit with The *Jazz Singer*.

Tarheel; Tarheel State. A nickname for a North Carolinian. According to the *Overland Monthly* (V.3, 1869): "A brigade of North Carolinians . . . failed to hold a certain hill [in a Civil War battle] and were laughed at by Mississippians for having forgotten to tar their heels that morning. Hence originated their cant name, 'Tar heels.' " The state of North Carolina has been called the Tar and Turpentine State. Other North Carolina nicknames have included the Old North State and the Land of the Sky, in reference to its beautiful western mountain country. In putting down their older, once more sophisticated neighbors Virginia and South Carolina, North Carolinians have called their state the Valley of Humility Between Two Mountains of Conceit.

Ten-cent Jimmy. The original was President James Buchanan, elected in 1856. The term was applied to Bachelor Buchanan because he advocated low tariffs and low wages (ten cents a day).

the tenderloin. In New York City, where the expression originated in the 1870s, the tenderloin was the area from 23rd to 42nd Streets west of Broadway. Gambling and prostitution flourished in this district, giving police officers "luscious opportunities" for graft. In fact, one cop named Williams was so happy to be assigned to the old 29th precinct covering the area in about 1890 that he said he had always eaten chuck steak but from now on he'd "be eating tenderloin." His remark led to the area being dubbed *the tenderloin,* that name eventually transferred to similar places throughout the country.

10-gallon hat. Although the hat's name is usually thought to be an indication of its liquid holding capacity, the Americanism *10-gallon hat* has its origins in the Spanish word for braid, *galón.* The wide-brimmed hats worn by cowboys were originally decorated with a number of braids at the base of the crown.. Actually, a ten-gallon hat holds about a gallon of liquid.

Tennessee. Admitted to the Union in 1796 as our 16th state, Tennessee's name derives from the name of a Cherokee settlement in the area that is of unknown origin. It had been called Tenaqui by the Spanish in the 16th century and went by the name State of Franklin, after Ben Franklin, from 1784–88.

Texas. Texas takes its name from a Caddo Indian word meaning "friends or allies" (written "texas," "texios," "tejas," "teyas") applied to the Caddos by the Spanish in eastern Texas, who regarded them as friends and allies against the Apaches.

Texas leaguer. A cheap hit that falls between the infield and the outfield in baseball is called a Texas leaguer because back in 1886 three players who had been traded up to the majors from a Texas league team enabled Toledo to beat Syracuse by repeatedly getting such hits. After the game, the disgusted Syracuse pitcher described the hits as just "little old dinky Texas leaguers," and the name stuck.

Texas longhorn. A once-common breed of southwestern beef cattle developed from cattle introduced from Spain and noted for their fecundity and resistance to disease. Also called coasters, these cattle have horns that can measure over 77 inches.

Texas mouse. A euphemism for a rat, or rather a failed euphemism. Back in February 1983, American Airlines captain Karl Burrell reported a big rat foraging aboard his plane in the first-class cabin as he prepared for takeoff to New York from Dallas. "The stewardesses prevailed on the captain to turn the plane around, and we sat on the ground for 45 minutes," said an eyewitness. "Finally, Captain Burrell polled all the first- class passengers and they decided we should go on with the rat. It was at least six inches long. We heard the captain say to the control tower, 'Let them take care of the problem in New York.' " The airline's public relations director euphemistically called the rodent a "Texas mouse," but a local exterminator said, "Smells like a rat to me—we don't get six-inch mice even in Texas." The rat was killed once the plane landed at La Guardia.

Texas T-shirt. William Safire's "On Language" column in the *New York Times* (March 27, 1991) defined this as a humorous derogatory term for "one of those disposable [toilet] seat bibs that are found in interstate roadside bathrooms."

Tex-Mex. This word, dating back to about 1945, means of or pertaining to aspects of culture developed in Texas but based on or strongly influenced by Mexican elements, such as Tex-Mex cooking.

Thanksgiving Day. A national holiday in the United States that some say was inaugurated by Abraham Lincoln but was actually first celebrated by George Washington in 1789 and before this by the Pilgrim colonists and neighboring Indians an 1621.

thank-ye-ma'am. An American courtship term that dates back to 19th-century New England. Roads at the time had diagonal earthen ridges running across them that channeled off rainwater from the high to the low side and prevented washouts. Rural Casanovas driving their carriages along these rude roads made sure that they hit these ridges hard so that their female companions would bounce up in the air and bump into them. With the head of his sweetheart so close, the gentleman could steal a kiss, and usually expressed his gratitude with a *Thank-ye-ma'am,* that expression becoming synonymous with a quick kiss or any hole in the road that caused riders to bump up and down.

that rings the bell. That's perfect, just what we wanted. This Americanism, first recorded in 1904, is almost certainly from the carnival game where one tests his strength by driving a weight up a pole with a mallet and wins if he rings the bell at the top.

that's life; that's the way it goes; that's the way the ball bounces. *That's life,* meaning "that's fate, that's the fortunes of life, the way things happen," probably dates back at least to the turn of the century. It is thought to be a loan translation of the French *c'est la vie.* The American expression *That's the way the ball bounces,* meaning the same, appears to have originated with U.S. forces in Korea, while the synonymous *that's the way it goes* came into the language a little later.

there's a sucker born every minute. Showman P. T. Barnum lived by this principle, but he probably didn't invent the phrase so often attributed to him. Since there is no recorded instance of Barnum uttering the words, they must be credited to "Anonymous," like another famous American cynicism, *Never give a sucker an even break,* which was the title of a W. C. Fields movie. Terms that Barnum did coin or help popularize include JUMBO, the Bearded Lady, the Wild Man of Borneo, Swedish Nightingale, Tom Thumb, Three-Ring Circus, and the Greatest Show on Earth.

thinks one hung the moon and stars. Someone who loves somebody madly, and blindly, as if that person were a god. According to Professor Frederick Cassidy, who is in the process of compiling a monumental study of American regionalisms, this expression is a southernism. It has been around since at least early in this century and by now, deservedly, has spread to other regions of the country.

30-something. Used to describe someone between 30 and 40 years old, *30-something* was popularized by the U.S. T.V. show of the same name in the late 1980s. Unlike the earlier term *29-plus,* which people once used to hide their age, *30-something* is not an attempt at such concealment.

Thomas Jefferson still survives. These famous last words are famous all right, but they are false, despite being widely believed. Former American presidents John Adams and Thomas Jefferson both died on July 4, 1826, 50 years after the founding of the United States, but Adams's last words were not "Thomas Jefferson still survives." Jefferson actually died a few hours before Adams and Adams's last words were "Independence forever." Jefferson's last words were "I resign my spirit to God, my daughter to my country."

three bricks shy of a load. An Americanism dating back to the 1960s, which is also heard as "a few bricks shy of a load." It describes someone simple-minded, or a little crazy or eccentric. The Australian version is *a few snags* (sausages) shy of a *Barbie* (barbecue). Americans also say half a bubble off of plumb.

three-fifths compromise. Under the U.S. Constitution, slaves were considered property and had no vote, but in order to redress the imbalance of representation between the populous North and the sparsely settled South, the southern states were allowed by the Founding Fathers to count each slave as three-fifths of a person for their congressional apportionment. This meant in practice that the more slaves there were, the less power they had and the more power the slaveholders enjoyed.

threepeat. A relatively new word, based on *repeat* and meaning to do something three times in a row, this expression may have been coined by New York Knicks coach Pat Riley in 1993, when the Chicago Bulls won the National Basketball Association title for the third straight year. There is already some controversy about the word's first use. After the previous edition of this book was published, San Francisco running back Roger Craig claimed he used the word in 1990.

thrown for a loss. Born as a football expression, *thrown for a loss* refers to a ball carrier who is thrown back for a loss by the opposing line on trying to penetrate its defense and gain yardage. Common in football, the words began to be used in postWorld War II years to describe someone's loss in any endeavor.

The Thug. He's been shot to pieces by police hundreds of thousands of times over the last 40 years, but this paper target, first used in New York City, has become the best-known in the United States. Officially, his name is Advanced Silhouette SP-83A, but no one calls him that. Some say he was named after various police officers he bore a resemblance to when the targets were adopted (namely New York officers Fred V. Worell and Bruno Fulginiti). Others opt for the actor Ernest Borgnine, very popular at the time and still working, but the target is usually called *The Thug* among lawmen at firing ranges. According to one account *(New York Times,* February 17, 2005), The Thug has hardly changed over all these years, a husky, crouching tough guy, a gun in his right hand, "maybe a little German, maybe a little Italian, some Irish, with his pug nose and his thick head of dark wavy hair."

ticker tape. The tape emanating from the first stock ticker installed in the New York Stock Exchange in 1867 was called ribbon. Ticker tape didn't come into use until the turn of the century.

tick-tock. Journalists use this recent U.S. term to mean "the time sequence of events," as in "What's the tick-tock on this?" when does it happen, how long will it last?, etc.

Times Square. Part of New York City's midtown Manhattan surrounding the intersection of Broadway and Seventh Avenue. Originally known as Long Acre Square, it was an important commercial center and home to William Vanderbilt's Horse Exchange, as well as to an exclusive neighborhood built by the Astor family between 1830 and 1860. It was renamed Times Square around the turn of the century in honor of the newly built *New York Times* building on 43rd Street, and the newspaper's publisher, Adolph Ochs, sponsored what has since become Times Square's most famous event—an annual New Year's Eve celebration that is still observed today. Following World War I, the district became a major center for the theater and entertainment industries and a popular tourist attraction.

tinhorn gambler. In chuck-a-luck, an ancient dice game very popular during the Gold Rush, gamblers bet against the house that all three dice used would read the same when rolled, or that the sum of all three dice would equal a certain number, or that one of the three dice would turn up a specified number. It is a monotonous game and was looked down upon by players of faro, a more complicated and costly pastime. Faro operators coined the name *tinhorn gamblers* for *chuck-a-luck* players, giving us the expression for any cheap gambler. Pulitzer Prize winner George Williston explained how in his book *Here They Found Gold* (1931): "Chuck-a-luck operators shake their dice in a 'small churn-like affair of metal'—hence the expression 'tinhorn gambler,' for the game is rather looked down upon as one for 'chubbers' [fools] and chuck-a-luck gamblers are never admitted within the aristocratic circles of faro dealers."

Tin Pan Alley. The original Tin Pan Alley was and is located between 48th and 52nd Streets on Seventh Avenue in New York City, an area where many music publishers, recording studios, composers, and arrangers have offices. The place was probably named for the tinny sound of the cheap, much-abused pianos in music publishers' offices there, or for the constant noise emanating from the area, which sounded like the banging of tin pans to some. *Tin Pan Alley,* the term first recorded in 1914, today means any place where popular music is published, and can even stand for popular music itself.

Tinseltown. "Strip the phony tinsel off Hollywood," musician and wit Oscar Levant said in the early 1940s, "and you'll find the real tinsel underneath." This sardonic remark allegedly led to the cynical name "Tinseltown" for Hollywood.

Today I consider myself the luckiest man on the face of the earth.
The words of New York Yankee hero Lou Gehrig on July 4, 1939, at a
ceremony honoring him at Yankee Stadium. Gehrig, the "Iron Man" or
the "Iron Horse," had been forced to retire two months earlier by the
insidious Amyotrophic lateral sclerosis, which came to be called Lou
Gehrig's disease after him.

toilet. In America, the term refers to what the British call the water
closet. The word comes from the French *toilette,* which originally
meant a "little cloth." This became the British name for the cloth
used to cover a dressing table, then meant the table itself, and was
finally used for the dressing room in which the dressing table was
located. It took over four centuries, but Americans ultimately used
toilet for the *john* in the room most often used for dressing or making
one's toilet.

Toll House cookie. Perhaps America's favorite pastry, or at least cookie,
this chocolate chip delicacy was invented in 1930 by pastry chef Ruth
Wakefield of the Toll House Inn in Whitman, Massachusetts.

Tomb of the Unknown Soldier. The first American unknown soldier, whose body was chosen from four unknowns, in 1921 placed in
the Tomb of the Unknown Soldier in Arlington National Cemetery.
Its inscription reads: *Here Rests in Honored Glory an American Soldier
Known but to God.* Unknowns from three other wars were added over
the years.

tommygun. The infamous *chopper* so often hidden in violin cases in gangster movies, takes its name from the patronym of one of its inventors, American army officer John T. Thompson (1860–1940). Thompson and Navy Comm. John N. Blish invented the .45 caliber portable automatic weapon during World War I and much improved it in later years. Gangsters and reporters popularized the nickname *tommygun* in the Prohibition era along with colorful expressions like *torpedo, triggerman, bathtub gin, hideout, hijacker, to muscle in,* and *to take for a ride.* Although *tommygun* originally identified the Thompson machine gun, with its pistol grip and shoulder stock, the term is now used to describe any similar lightweight weapon with a drum-type magazine.

Tom Thumb. This term, often applied to a "little person," as many "dwarfs" prefer to be called, and to little children as well, has its origins in fairy tales of old, in which Tom Thumb was the size of a man's thumb. However, its modern use is due in great part to "General Tom Thumb" (Charles Sherwood Stratton, 1838–83), whom American showman P. T. Barnum exhibited in the mid-19th century.

tongue oil. In my continuing quest for synonyms for whiskey and other strong drink I've come upon *tongue oil* several times. It's a western U.S. expression dating back perhaps to the mid-19th century and obviously refers to the way spirits loosen one's tongue.

ton of cobblestone. A large quantity of anything ordinary or commonplace. American radio comedian Fred Allen (1894–1956) coined the expression. He bound all the scripts for his long-running radio show—39 a year—and stacked them on 10 feet of shelves beside a one-volume copy of Shakespeare's collected works, which occupied a mere 31/2 inches of space. "I did that as a corrective," he explained, "just in case I start thinking a ton of cobblestone is worth as much as a few diamonds."

too lazy to work and too nervous to steal. An Americanism describing any person regarded as a totally useless no-account.

too poor to paint and too proud to whitewash. A term describing any impoverished southern gentleman or lady. Whitewash is much cheaper than paint.

too thick to drink and too thin to plow. Muddy, unpalatable water, the expression probably first said by American pioneers over a century ago.

Tootsie Roll; Chunky. The still popular Tootsie Roll was invented by American candy maker Leo Hirschfield in 1896. He named the chewy chocolate for his daughter Clara, whose nickname was Tootsie. Another similar named candy is the square hunk of chocolate, cashews, brazil nuts, and raisins called the Chunky. Candy maker Philip Silverstein invented the confection and named it after his daughter, nicknamed Chunky.

top banana. A comic or comedian in American burlesque or vaude-ville. The expression derives from an old turn-of-the-century burlesque skit that involved the sharing of bananas.

top-drawer. Of the best or highest quality. This American term comes from the early 1900s British expression *out of the top drawer,* meaning "well-bred, gentlemanly, upper class, aristocratic." *Drawer* refers to a chest of drawers, one's valuables usually kept in the top drawer.

top of the heap. The biggest, or best, an American expression that goes back at least to the 1930s. *Heap* itself can mean a pile or large amount of money, that meaning a century older. I remember an old Mark Hellinger story about a gangster who vowed he'd wind up with more money and fame than anyone—on top of the heap. He was finally killed by rival gangsters and dumped on the top of a garbage heap.

To the babies! A toast made at an 1879 Chicago banquet for General Ulysses S. Grant. Mark Twain answered it: "We haven't all had the good fortune to be ladies; we haven't all been generals, or poets, or statesmen; but when the toast works down to babies, we stand on common ground."

tough it out. An Americanism meaning "to undergo hardship," as in "They toughed it out on that rocky soil for three years before they quit." The expression was first recorded in 1830 and is still heard today. *Rough it out* is also used.

trailblazer. A trailblazer isn't someone who blazes new paths by "setting the world on fire." To *blaze a trail* means to indicate a new path by notching trees with an ax or knife. *Blaze* in this sense is the white mark in the notch when the bark is removed. It originally meant the white spot on the forehead of a horse before American pioneers *trailblazed* the new use of the word.

Trail of Tears. The term is explained by Edna Ferber in *Cimarron* (1930): "Tears came to his own eyes when he spoke of that blot on southern civilization, The Trail of Tears, in which the Cherokees, a peaceful and home-loving Indian tribe, were torn (1838–39) from the land which a government had given them by sworn treaty to be sent far away on a march which, from cold, hunger, exposure, and heartbreak, was marked by bleaching bones from Georgia to Oklahoma."

Treasure State. A nickname for Montana, which once was called the Bonanza State. It has been called the Stub-Toe State because of its steep hills and mountains.

A Tree Grows in Brooklyn. Although never named in Betty Smith's novel *A Tree Grows in Brooklyn* (1943) nor the movies made from it, the tree in the book is *Ailanthus altissima,* also called the tree of heaven. No other tree withstands smoke and other city conditions so well, and the ailanthus seeds easily everywhere, often growing out of cracks in deserted sidewalks. Only female trees should be planted, however, as the odor of the male flower is obnoxious to many, which is why the ailanthus, a native of China, is also called the stink tree or stinkweed. The tree was brought to France by a missionary in 1751 and reached America 39 years later. Also called the backyard tree.

Tricky Dick. A sobriquet for former president Richard Nixon that may have its roots in an Irish-American nickname for another politician named Richard. My grandmother spoke of a New York ward heeler named Tricky Dick, but she may have meant Slippery Dick Connolly, comptroller for the Tweed Ring. In any case, James Joyce named a politician Tricky Dick Tierney in his short story "Ivy Day in the Committee Room" (1914), and it is not inconceivable that it was a felicitous Irish turn of speech, one of so many that came to New York with Irish immigration.

Tucson bed. A humorous expression from the western range that probably dates back to the late 19th century, a Tucson bed, after Tucson, Arizona, means "lying on your stomach and covering that with your back." Early cowboys apparently didn't think much of Tucson's accommodations.

tumbleweed. Any of several plants, including the *Amaran- thus* genus and the Russian thistle *(Salsola kali),* whose branching upper parts come loose from the roots and are driven by the wind across the prairie. The plant, like sagebrush, has become a symbol of the West, as in song lyrics such as "drifting along with the tumbling tumbleweed." One old belief has it that God put tumbleweed here to show cowboys which way the wind is blowing. The plant was originally imported to the U.S. as a border hedge!

turkey neck. A U.S. slang term for a person's neck similar to a turkey's: fleshy, bunched up, and full of depressions and swellings.

tuxedo. What do Indians have to do with tuxedos? In 1890, dress requirements at the local country club in Tuxedo Park, New York, 40 miles or so from Manhattan, called for men to wear a tailless dinner jacket at most nightly affairs. This was known as a *tuxedo coat* until matching pants were added to the outfit and it became known as a *tuxedo,* which inevitably was shortened to *tux.* The word *tuxedo* itself derives from the white settlers' pronunciation of the name of the Ptuksit Indians, a subtribe of Delaware Indians who lived in what is now Tuxedo Park. *Ptuksit* meant "roundfoot" or "wolf tribe" in allusion to the wolf, "he of the roundfoot."

TV dinner. Few people realize that the ubiquitous frozen TV dinner is a trademark name of the C. A. Swanson Company. It was coined in 1953, during the early days of television, when people first began to sit around their TV sets and eat prepared dinners that were easily heated in the oven. It should be added that Gerry Thomas (1922–2005), a Swanson salesman, invented the TV dinner, whose sales now total $30 billion a year. The first dinner was sold in 1954 and consisted of turkey, peas, sweet potatoes, and cornbread and was served in a compartmentalized tray similar to an army mess kit.

21-gun salute. Guns were fired as salutes in early times, but a 21-gun salute is an American expression. According to an official U.S. Navy publication: "Guns could not be loaded quickly then, so the act of firing one in a salute indicated that the saluter had disarmed himself in deference to the person being saluted. The larger the number of guns fired the greater degree of disarmament . . ." Since 21 guns was the greatest number found on one side of one of the larger ships of the line, firing all of them became the highest mark of respect, reserved for heads of state. Fewer numbers of guns were fired in salutes to people of lesser importance. But for any salute only odd numbers are used, reflecting the old seagoing superstition against even numbers. This form of saluting was first recognized in the U.S. in 1875. As commander in chief, the president is accorded the highest salute of 21 guns.

20 tailors around a buttonhole. An old American variation on the older 16th-century *too many cooks spoil the broth*.

23 skiddoo. For well over half a century no one has used this expression seriously, but it is still remembered today—mainly as a phrase representative of the Roaring Twenties, which it is *not*. Twenty-three skiddoo is important, too. It goes back to about 1900 and for 10 years enjoyed great popularity as America's first national fad expression, paving the way for thousands of other dispensables such as *Yes, we have no bananas, Shoo-fly, Hey, Abbott!, Coming, mother!* and *I dood it!* Twenty-three skiddoo practically lost its meaning of "scram" or "beat it" and just became the thing to say, anytime. As for its derivation, it is said to have been invented or popularized by that innovative early comic-strip artist "Tad" Dorgan, encountered frequently in these pages under *hot dog, yes man,* and other of his coinages. Regarding its composition, *skiddoo* may be a shortening of the earlier "skedaddle." *Twenty-three* is a mystery. Perhaps it was a code number used by telegraphers. There is even a theory that it "owes its existence to the fact that the most gripping and thrilling word in *A Tale of Two Cities* is twenty-three": Sydney Carton, the 23rd man to be executed on the 23rd of the month. Finally, there is the story that *twenty-three* referred to the address of New York City's Flatiron Building, on whose windy corner men liked to watch women's skirts blow upward, until cops told them to scram—"Twenty-three skiddo!"

twepping. Homicide was called by the acronym *twep,* "terminate with extreme prejudice," in C.I.A. circles during the Vietnam War, and may still be used today. *Twep* was used so frequently that it gave rise to the euphemistic verb *twepping*.

Twinkie defense. When former San Francisco supervisor Dan White was on trial in 1979 for killing Mayor George Moscone and supervisor Harvey Milk, the defense psychiatrist claimed White's lethal actions were caused by an overindulgence in junk food such as Twinkies. This came to be called the Twinkie defense. White was paroled after serving five years of his eight-year sentence, but committed suicide 19 months later.

Twin Towers. Until their tragic destruction by terrorists on September 11, 2001, the Twin Towers of the World Trade Center complex in downtown Manhattan were New York's tallest office buildings, surpassed only by the Petronas Towers in Malaysia and the Sears Tower in Chicago. Over 50,000 people worked in the World Trade Center complex, thousands of whom were killed in the terrorist attack on the Twin Towers.

twist. In American slang a *twist* is a woman, often a woman who associates with gangster types. But the Twist is also a dance very popular in the 1960s.

twofers. *Twofers* has meant "two theater tickets for the price of one" since about 1948 in America. Previously, since as early as 1890, *twofers* had referred to "two-for-a-nickel" cigars.

two whoops and a holler. In western U.S. parlance *two whoops and a holler* means a short distance, not far, "within spitting range." The phrase probably dates back to the late 19th century.

tycoon. *Tycoon* is just an American phonetic spelling of the Japanese *taikun,* for "great prince." The Japanese word, in turn, comes from the Chinese *ta,* "great," and *chun,* "prince." Americans encountered the *taikun,* whose military title was *shogun,* during Commodore Perry's expedition to Japan of 1852–54 and brought the word home, where it was applied to any powerful man, especially a wealthy businessman.

Tyler grippe. John Tyler (1790–1863) has the dubious honor of being the only U.S. President for whom an epidemic is named. The Tyler grippe was a virulent influenza that swept the country at the time he became President in 1841. In fact, Tyler, elected vice-president, assumed office when his running mate, old William Henry Harrison, died a month after being inaugurated as President. Harrison died of pneumonia or the Tyler grippe, or a combination of both.

typewriter. The word *typewriter* was coined by American Christopher Latham Sholes, who patented the first practical commercial typewriter in 1868 (slow, difficult machines, intended primarily for the blind, had been invented as early as 1714). Sholes's "type-writer" had only capital letters. Manufactured by Remington, it was owned by Henry James, Mark Twain, and Sigmund Freud, among other famous early experimenters. Mark Twain, in fact, typed *The Adventures of Tom Sawyer* on Sholes's machine in 1875, this being the first typewritten book manuscript (a fact that Twain kept secret in his lifetime because he didn't want to write testimonials or show the uninitiated how to use the machine).

typo. *Typo,* short for typographical error, is an Americanism dating back to the 1890s. Newspapers and magazines regularly run features pointing out the best or worst typographical errors in other newspapers and magazines. For example, a Clive Barnes review in the *New York Times* of *A Midsummer Night's Dream* found "David Waller's virile bottom (instead of 'Bottom') particularly splendid." Possibly the worst modern-day slip appeared in the *Washington Post* in 1915, where it was noted that President Wilson had taken his fiancee, Edith Galt, to the theater and rather than watching the play "spent most of his time entering Mrs. Galt," instead of "entertaining Mrs. Galt."

U

UFO. *UFO,* as a term, has been in use since the 1950s or earlier, but the first *u*nidentified *f*lying *o*bjects were reported in America in 1896. UFOs are often called flying saucers, but they have been reported in many different shapes. The first were said to resemble "cigar-shaped airships."

ugly as a mud fence. American pioneers often made fences of sod and dirt when stone and wood were in short supply on the prairie. These homely fences served their purpose but were eyesores, leading to the expression *ugly as a mud fence* for someone or something extremely ugly.

un-American. *Un-American* is a very American word, dating back to at least 1817, when it is first recorded, and not at all of recent vintage. It means contrary to U.S. values, even traitorous, and was most prominent recently in the name of the House [of Representatives] Un-American Activities Committee, active from 1938 to 1975, which critics claim was more un-American than many of the people it investigated. In 1945 HUAC's name became the Committee on Un-American Activities; in 1969 it was renamed the Committee on Internal Security; and it was finally abolished in 1975.

Uncle Sam. The original *Uncle Sam* was Samuel Wilson, the nephew of army contractor Elbert Anderson, who owned a store or slaughterhouse in Troy, New York and had a contract to supply the army with salt pork and beef during the War of 1812. Wilson and his uncle Ebenezer, Elbert's brother, worked as army inspectors and frequently inspected the meat Elbert Anderson packed in barrels with the initials

"E.A.—U.S." stamped on them. According to a popular version of the story, one soldier asked another what the initials E.A.—U.S. (Elbert Anderson United States) meant and his companion quipped that they stood for "*E*lbert *A*nderson's *U*ncle *S*am." Some scholars dispute this story, which was widely accepted during Wilson's lifetime, but no better explanation has been given. The term's first recorded use was in the *Troy Post* of September 7, 1813, which speaks well for the Samuel Wilson theory except that the article only says the words derive from the initials on government wagons. The name *Uncle Sam* caught on quickly as a symbol of the army and then as a national nickname to counteract that of England's John Bull.

Uncle Tom. Everyone knows that *Uncle Tom* comes from the character in Harriet Beecher's Stowe's *Uncle Tom's Cabin* (1852), the immensely popular American antislavery novel that caused President Lincoln to say on meeting Mrs. Stowe, "Is this the little woman whose book made such a great war?" Mrs. Stowe depicted Uncle Tom as simple, easygoing, and servile, willing to put up with anything, though it should be remembered that she intended him as a noble, high-minded, devout Christian and that he is flogged to death by the brutal overseer Simon Legree at the end of the book for bravely refusing to reveal the hiding place of Cassie and Emmaline, two female slaves. Few people know that Mrs. Stowe's model for Uncle Tom was a real-life slave named Josiah Henson, born in Maryland in 1789, who wrote a widely read autobiographical pamphlet. Henson was far from an *Uncle Tom* in the term's recent sense. Like many slaves, he served as the overseer, or manager, of a plantation before he escaped to Canada. Once free, he started a prosperous sawmill, founded a trade school for blacks, whites, and Indians and helped over 100 slaves escape to Canada. When he journeyed to England on business, the archbishop of Canterbury was so impressed with his speech and learning that he asked him what university he had studied at. "The University of Adversity," Henson replied.

Uncle Tomahawk. Recent slang for an American Indian who is accused of being servile to whites by other Indians; patterned on the older familiar term "Uncle Tom." Also *Uncle Taco (Tio Taco).*

unconditional surrender. "Unconditional Surrender" was the nickname of Union General U. S. (Ulysses Simpson) Grant, who would give "no terms but unconditional surrender" to the Confederates in 1862 when his forces captured Fort Donelson in Tennessee, the first major Union victory of the war. The term has been used in every war since, but got its start with "Old Unconditional."

United States of America. Thomas Paine, the author of *Common Sense,* a popular tract that attracted many to the side of the American Revolution in 1776, coined the name *United States of America* for his adopted country. The name was first used in the subtitle of the Declaration of Independence: "The Unanimous Declaration of the Thirteen United States of America." However, before the Articles of Confederation was ratified in 1781 the nation was known as The Congress. Under the Articles it was called The United States in Congress Assembled and under the Constitution was finally called Paine's United States of America. It should be added that from as early as 1617 to as late as 1769 the kingdom or republic of Holland was called the United States.

united we stand, divided we fall. The commonly-quoted words are originally from "The Liberty Song," by John Dick- man, first published in the *Boston Gazette,* July 18, 1768: "Then join hand in hand, have Americans all! / By uniting we stand, by dividing we fall."

unreconstructed southerner. A term applied to a southerner not reconciled to the results of the Civil War; first recorded in 1867, it is still used today. *Unreconstructed rebel* is a later variation. For a stanza of "A Good Old Rebel (Unreconstructed)" by Innes Randolph (1837–87), *see* GOOD OLE BOY.

until the last dog is hung. This colorful Americanism was appropriately first recorded in an old-fashioned western, Stuart Edward White's *The Blazed Trail* (1902), in which the hanged dogs referred to hanged men. Today the words are usually heard in reference to someone staying at a party, bar, event, etc., until the very last, as in "We were there until the last dog was hung.

U.S. Navy. America had a colonial navy until the Revolution, which was replaced by the 53-ship continental navy in 1776 after the break with Great Britain. Commodore Esek Hopkins was appointed its commander in chief (the only time a navy head has held that title except for presidents). This became the U.S. Navy in 1794.

Utah. Utah takes its name from the fierce proud tribe called the Utes that resided there and whose name meant "hill dwellers." In 1850 the area encompassing present-day Utah was constituted the Utah Territory, the colorful Mormon name for it, *Deseret*, or "honeybee," being rejected by Congress.

V

Vaseline. Among those flocking to America's first oil strike near Titusville, Pennsylvania in 1858, was Robert A. Chesebrough, a Brooklyn chemist, who noticed that workmen with cuts, bruises, and burns used as a soothing ointment a waxy substance from the pump rods bringing up the oil. Gathering some of the oily residue, Chesebrough took it back to Brooklyn and made a jelly-like product from it. This he patented at once, giving it the trademark *Vaseline,* a word he formed from the German *Wasser* (pronounced "vasser") "water" and the Greek *elaion,* "olive oil."

veep. From the common abbreviation V.P. for the vice president of the United States came the informal word *veep,* which was coined about 1949. The first person to be called a *veep* was Harry S Truman's vice president Allen William Barkley (1877–1956), who hold office from 1949–53. A variation on it is *vee-pee*

vending machine. The term *vending machine* seems to have been introduced either by the Adams' Gum Company (now part of American Chicle) in the 1880s to describe the machine the company used to sell tutti-fruitti gumballs on New York City elevated train platforms, or at about the same time by the Frank H. Fleer Gum Company. At that time Fleer's founder agreed to an experiment proposed by a young vending machine salesman. The salesman argued that vending machines were so great a sales gimmick that people would actually drop a penny in them for nothing. Frank Fleer agreed to buy several machines if the young man's pitch proved true, and the experiment was conducted at New York's Flatiron Building. The salesman set up a vending machine there, with printed instructions to "drop a penny in the slot and listen to the wind blow." He got Fleer's order when hundreds of people contributed their pennies and continued to do so until New York's Finest hauled the machine away.

verbicide. *Verbicide,* "word murder," the act of destroying the sense or value of words, or the perversion of a word from its proper meaning, has been applied in our time to political speechmaking and government gobbledygook or officialese. But the word seems to have been coined by Oliver Wendell Holmes, who patterned it on *homicide,* and applied it to punning in his *The Autocrat of the Breakfast-Table* (1858).

Vermont psalm. Psalm 121 from the Bible, a psalm often used to start funeral services in Vermont: "I lift my eyes unto the hills." This was noted in a *New York Times* news story on May 2, 1994, from Woodstock, Vermont: "Psalm 121 . . . They call it the Vermont Psalm here."

Verrazano-Narrows Bridge. This 1964 suspension bridge connects Brooklyn and Staten Island over New York Bay. Its 4,260-foot center span is the longest in North America. The Verrazano, as it is usually called by New Yorkers, is named for another Italian navigator and explorer, Giovanni da Verrazano (c. 1480–1529), who sailed in New York waters 85 years before Henry Hudson. Verrazano was later killed by Natives while exploring the West Indies.

very poor man's dinner. An appropriate name for this Maine dish made of thinly sliced potatoes and onions fried in the grease of salt pork. A similar dish made in Massachusetts is called "Necessity Mess."

Viagra. This drug for the treatment of male impotence by stimulating blood flow to the penis was introduced by the Pfizer Company in 1998. Its name is said to come from Niagara Falls, which is vital and powerful, like anyone who takes Viagra. Viagra's generic name is sildenafil citrate (its active ingredient). The drug's chief competitor is Levitra, which takes its name, most appropriately, from elevate.

victory garden. The victory garden was a home vegetable garden popular in the United States during World War II; such gardens were encouraged by the government to increase food production during a time of shortages. The idea helped revive the idea of home vegetable gardens, once known as kitchen gardens, among many Americans who had lost touch with the land.

vim. *Vim* is an Americanism first recorded in 1843 and usually regarded as the accusative singular of the Latin *vis,* "strength or energy," though it may possibly be, judging by some of its earliest uses, of imitative or interjectional origin ("He drove his spurs . . . *vim* in the hoss's flank," 1850). The word is usually heard in the alliterative expression *vim and vigor.*

V.I.P. dummy. The name given to the first automotive crash-test dummy in 1968 by U.S. inventor Samuel W. Alderson (1914–2005).

Such dummies have been used to test automotive safety features like seat belts and air bags, which are estimated to have saved over 329,000 lives to date. Before dummies were so employed, cadavers were used for the same purpose. Today, the far more sophisticated Hybrid III crash dummy has replaced V.I.P.

Virginia. That gallant of gallants, Sir Walter Raleigh, suggested that what became Virginia be named after England's Elizabeth I, the Virgin Queen, when in 1584 he founded his colony there, probably on what is now Roanoke Island. (The island, which is in North Carolina, was originally part of the great area from Florida to Newfoundland that Virginia encompassed.) Virginia, the Old Dominion state, was the site of the first permanent English settlement, at Jamestown in 1607, and the scene of the British surrender in the American Revolution at Yorktown. Called the Mother of Presidents, the state sent Washington, Jefferson, Monroe, Madison, Tyler, William Henry Harrison, Taylor, and Wilson to the White House, and is renowned for many historic shrines. As to the state's exact naming, one writer tells us that "Queen Elizabeth graciously accorded the privileges proposed by Raleigh, giving to this new land a name in honour of her maiden state, and it was called Virginia. Raleigh was knighted for his service and given the title of 'Lord and Governor of Virginia.'"

vitamin. American biochemist Casimir Funk coined the word *vitamin* (or, rather, *vitamine*) in 1912, at which time he was credited with the discovery of the existence of vitamins, organic substances necessary for normal health. Funk constructed the word from the Latin *vita*, "life," and *amine,* from the Greek *ammoniakon,* because he believed that an amino acid was present in vitamins. *Vitamine* was stripped of its e when it was found that amino acids were not involved.

voice mail. *Voice mail,* first recorded in 1980, was coined by American inventor and entrepreneur Gordon Matthews (1937–2002). According to his *New York Times* obituary (2/26/02), Matthews was inspired to invent the system when "he was stuck in heavy rain and noticed in a nearby dump a large bunch of pink 'While You Were Out' message slips. This gave him the idea that an apparatus permitting callers to record substantial messages in their own voices could help do away with the multitudes of message slips . . . that were burdening modern communications, notably in corporations." Today, over 8 percent of American corporations use voice mail.

Volunteer State. A nickname for Tennessee since the Mexican War in 1847, when 30,000 men from the state enlisted. It has also been called the Lion's Den (possibly after border ruffians nicknamed lions), the Hog and Hominy State, from the Tennesseans' reputed liking for fatback and cornmeal (grits), and the Big Bend State, after the big bends in the Tennessee River. At the time of the Scopes "Monkey Trial" there in 1925 Tennessee was called the Monkey State.

W

W. Several presidents have been called by their initials, including F.D.R. (Franklin Delano Roosevelt) and J.F.K. (John Fitzgerald Kennedy), but only one has been called by *one* initial: President George W. Bush (the *W* stands for Walker), who was dubbed W (pronounced Dubya) by the press.

Waa hoo! A cowboy yell that the prolific western writer Zane Grey (1872-1939) explained in *The Last of the Plainsmen:* "We'll use a signal I have tried and found far-reaching and easy to yell. Waa hoo!"

wake-up call. An expression that originated in U.S. hotels about 1835, long before the telephone. At the time clerks from the front desk would knock at your door, calling you whenever you wanted to be awakened in the morning. Over the years the telephone ring replaced the knock on the door, and the expression also took on the figurative meaning of waking a person or people up from lethargy or unpreparedness.

walk down the aisle. Americans have been using *walk down the aisle* as a synonym for "getting married" for almost a century now. A bride who literally "walked down the aisle," however, would be walking along either side of the church and might confuse everyone. The passageway the bride walks "down" to the altar is actually called the nave, though there is no chance that this will alter the expression in the slightest.

Wall Street. Wall Street, which is both a street and a term symbolizing the American financial world in general, is located in downtown Manhattan at the southern end of the island and takes its name from the wall that extended along the street in Dutch times. The principal financial institutions of the city have been located there since the early 19th century. *Wall Streeter, Wall Street broker, Wall Street plunger,* and *Wall Street shark* are among terms to which the street gave birth. We find *Wall Street broker* first used as early as 1836, and Wall Street being called *The Street* by 1863.

war correspondent. "Since the first gun discharged at Fort Sumter awoke the American world to arms, War Correspondence on this side of the Atlantic has been as much an avocation as practicing law or selling dry goods . . . The War Correspondent is the outgrowth of a very modern civilization." So wrote the first observer to record *war correspondent,* in 1861, when the term, if not the profession, came into being.

ward heeler. A *ward heeler* is a political hanger-on of a ward boss in American politics, the *heeler,* coming from the comparison of such a man to a dog that "heels" for its master, that is, follows behind submissively in its master's footsteps. The term is first recorded in 1888.

war is hell. Union general William Tecumseh Sherman said this in an 1880 Columbus, Ohio, speech after the Civil War: "There is many a boy here who looks on war as all glory, but, boys, it is all hell." "Red" Sherman (red-haired and red-bearded) had however said the equivalent throughout the war. "War is cruelty and you cannot refine it," he said of his destruction of Atlanta, and "You might as well appeal against the thunderstorm as against these terrible hardships of war." "Cump" or "Uncle Billy," as his "Yankee Bummers" often called him, was called the "Hun," the "Burner," the "Killer," and "Human Fungus" by Southerners as he marched through Georgia to the sea. For more Sherman coinages.

Warren Commission. An inquiry into the assassination of John F. Kennedy (1917-63), 35th president of the United States. The Warren Commission (1964) found that only one assassin, Lee Harvey Oswald, killed J.F.K. but the U.S. House of Representatives Assassinations Committee (1979) claimed more than one gunman conspired to kill the president.

watered stock. To water a stock is to increase its number of shares without increasing the value of its assets; it is thus diluted or watered down. According to one old story, the expression originated with Wall Street speculator Daniel Drew, who was a cattle dealer after the Civil War. Drew sold his cattle by weight, of course, and did so immediately after they finished drinking a large quantity of water.

we-all. Early during World War II, Thomas J. Watson, the president of I.B.M., borrowed this expression from southern mountain talk to use in full-page newspaper advertisements throughout the country. He proclaimed: " 'I' represents only one person. 'We' may mean only two or a few persons. Our slogan now is WE ALL. . . . President Roosevelt, our Commander-in-Chief, can be certain that WE-ALL are back of him."

weasel words. "Weasel words are words that suck all of the life out of the words next to them just as a weasel sucks an egg and leaves the shell," a writer explained in the June 1900 issue of the *Century Magazine*. The writer then gives an example: " 'The public should be protected.' 'Duly protected,' said Gamage, 'that's always a good weasel word.' " The term was applied to politicians in this first recorded use and has often been associated with politicians since then.

well, back to the old drawing board. Few would suppose that this very common expression for a resigned unruffled reaction to the failure of plans of any kind derives from a cartoon caption. It almost certainly does: from a 1941 Peter Arno cartoon in *The New Yorker* which shows an airplane crash, the plane mangled, rescue squads working frantically, and the plane's designer, plans under his arm, musing aloud, "Well, back to the old drawing board." Partridge says it's used "when one has to make an agonizing re-appraisal" and traces it "probably" to World War II aircraft designers.

Well, if that don't take the rag off the bush! A southern Americanism originating in the late 19th century, this expression refers to outrageous behavior, as lowdown as stealing the rags or clothes someone in the swimmin' hole has left spread out on a bush.

well-heeled. Before *well-heeled* meant "well provided with money" in American slang, it meant "well provided with weapons." Back in frontier days men who went "heeled" carried a gun, the expression apparently deriving from a cockfighting term meaning to provide a fighting cock with an artificial spur before he went into the pit. *Well-heeled* is recorded in this sense as early as 1867 and it wasn't until over a decade later that it took on the meaning it has today, perhaps because men found that it was easier and safer to protect themselves with money than with guns. In any case, *well-heeled* is not simply the opposite of *down at the heels,* someone so hard pressed for money that his shoes are run down at the heels. *Down at the heels* may even be traced back to Shakespeare, who wrote in *King Lear* (1600): "A good man's fortune may grow out at the heels."

West. Generally used in the United States today to mean the region west of the Mississippi River. The term *westerner* for someone who lives in the region west of the Mississippi is first recorded in 1835.

West-by-God-Virginia. This humorous name for West Virginia is said to have been coined by an irate native when it was said that he came from Virginia. Replied the man: "Not Virginia, but *West* by God!, Virginia!"

western sandwich. A sandwich made of an omelet with onions, green peppers, and chopped ham between slices of bread or toast; also called a *Denver sandwich.*

Westinghoused. To be put to death in the electric chair. Thomas Edison championed DC (direct current) over the AC (alternating current) that his competitors preferred to use in converting the world to electricity. AC eventually triumphed, but not before Edison campaigned stubbornly against it over the years. The Wizard of Menlo Park even went so far as to coin *Westinghoused* (after the name of his rival the Westinghouse Company) as a replacement for the word *electrocuted,* in reference to criminals put to death in the

(AC) electric chair. The coinage didn't live long but did have some currency.

West Virginia. West Virginia is composed of 40 western mountain counties that seceded from Virginia at the outbreak of the Civil War, these counties voting not to secede from the Union and forming their own state government. After rejecting New Virginia, Kanawha, and Alleghany, the new state settled on West Virginia for a name, an ironic choice since Virginia extends 95 miles farther west than it does. West Virginia had considered seceding from Virginia several times, due to unequal taxation and representation, and the Civil War provided an excellent excuse. Its constitution was amended to abolish slavery and President Lincoln proclaimed *West Virginia* the 35th state in 1862, justifying his action as a war measure. Called the Panhandle State, it has an odd outline, leading to the saying that it's "a good state for the shape it's in."

wetback. A disparaging term for an illegal Mexican immigrant or worker who crosses the Rio Grande into the United States, sometimes swimming to get across. The term is a relatively recent one, first recorded in 1948.

wet behind the ears. *He's still wet behind the ears* would refer to someone as innocent in the ways of the world as a newborn baby. The American expression goes back at least a century and refers to the traditional belief, which may be true, that the last place to dry on newborn animals such as calves and colts is the small indentation behind each ear.

We the people of the United States, in order to form a more perfect Union. . . . These words that begin the preamble of the U.S. Constitution were, appropriately enough, taken from a Native American document, a 1520 treaty that established the Iroquois Confederacy, which begins, "We, the people, to form a union . . ."

we wuz robbed. When Jack Sharkey won a decision over Max Schmeling in 1932 to take the world heavyweight championship, Schmeling's manager Joe Jacobs grabbed the radio fight announcer's mike and shouted "We wuz robbed!" to a million Americans, his words still a comic protest heard from losers in any endeavor. Jacobs's *I should of stood in bed* is even more commonly used in fun. He said it after leaving his sickbed to watch the 1935 World Series in Detroit. According to John Lardner's *Strong Cigars and Lovely Women* (1951), *Bartlett's* is wrong in saying Jacobs made the remark to sportswriters in New York after returning from Detroit, and it had nothing to do with his losing a bet that Detroit would win the Series. Jacobs made the remark, Lardner says, in the press box during the opening game of the Series, when "an icy wind was curdling his blood" at the coldest ball game anyone could remember.

wham bam (thank-ye-ma'am). *Thank-ye-ma'am* is an American courtship term that dates back to the 19th century. Roads at the time had diagonal earthen ridges running across them that channeled off rainwater from the high to the low side and prevented washouts. Rural Casanovas driving their carriages along these rude roads made sure that they hit these ridges hard so that their female companions would bounce up in the air and bump into them. With the head of his sweetheart so close, the gentleman could steal a kiss and usually express his gratitude with a *Thank-ye-ma'am,* that expression becoming synonymous for a quick kiss or for any hole in the road that caused riders to bump up and down. It wasn't long before some wit took this innocent phrase to bed, or to the side of the road somewhere, and elaborated on it, for in 1895 we find recorded the related expression *wham bam (thank-ye-ma'am)* for quick coitus. As a matter of fact, the first recorded use of both expressions occurs in that year.

What a way to run a railroad. A U.S. saying dating back to the late 19th century. Said of any poorly managed business. Eric Partridge tells of a 1932 *Ballyhoo* magazine cartoon "showing a railway signalman watching two trains about to collide head-on and saying 'Tch-tch—what a way to run a railway.' "

whatcheer. In John Bartlett's *Dictionary of Americanisms* (1848), he defines this term as "the shibboleth of the people of the State of Rhode Island." He goes on to say that "when Roger Williams, the founder of the ancient colony, pushed his way from Salem, Massachusetts, in the year 1636, through the wilderness, he embarked in a canoe with five others, on Sekonk river, and landed near the present site of the city of Providence. As the party approached the shore, they were saluted by a company of Indians with the friendly interrogation of 'What cheer?' a common English phrase which they had learned from the colonists, equivalent to the modern How do you do? and meant by the natives as Welcome! The cove where the party landed is called *Whatcheer Cove,* which term is also applied to the lands adjacent; besides which there is in Providence a *Whatcheer Bank, a Whatcheer Church, Whatcheer hotels, a Whatcheer Insurance Company,* and, last of all a *Whatcheer Lager Beer Saloon!"* (John Bartlett, *Dictionary of Americanisms,* 1848).

What do you know about that? An Americanism meaning "isn't that amazing, I would never have believed it," etc. Sometimes heard as "Well, what do you know," or "How about that!" The earliest appearance of the expression in print was the 1914 novel *Perch of the Devil* by American author Gertrude Atherton.

What goes around comes around. A U.S. proverb from the late 20th century.

What goes up must come down. A U.S. catchphrase that seems to have entered the language in about 1870.

what's good for General Motors is good for the country. Former head of General Motors Charles E. Wilson didn't say this when testifying before a Senate committee in 1953 when nominated for secretary of defense. The words have become proverbial, but what Wilson said was less arrogant: "I thought that what was good for our country was good for General Motors, and vice versa."

What's new?; What's with you? The greeting *What's new?* has been traced back to 1880s New York. It is thought to be a translation of the *was ist los?* ("what's the matter?") of German immigrants, as is the similar expression *what's with you?*

What's up, Doc? Bugs Bunny first said this to Elmer Fudd in his famous cartoon series launched in 1937, though it may be an old western expression suggested by Tex Avery, one of the cartoon's animators. It is said that when Mel Blanc, the voice of Bugs Bunny in the cartoons, emerged from a coma in 1983, he looked at his physician and asked, "Er, what's up, Doc?"

what the hey. A popular catchphrase invented by comedian Milton Berle on his television variety program in the 1950s.

wheeler dealer. In gaming houses of the 18th-century American West a big wheeler and dealer was a heavy bettor at cards and the roulette wheels. Through this tradition, and the association of a *big wheel* as the man (or wheel) who makes the vehi cle (things) run, the expression came to mean a big-time operator by the early 1940s, usually with an unsavory connotation, the *wheeler dealer* being the type who runs over anything in his path with no regard for rules of the road.

when a dog bites a man . . . Crusty old *New York Sun* editor John B. Bogart (1845–1921) is said to have originated in conversation the old saw "When a dog bites a man, that is not news, because it happens so often; but if a man bites a dog, that is news." However, the adage may be based on an old story.

when chickens have teeth. A 19th century Americanism meaning "never, it won't happen," as in "She'll be on time when chickens have teeth." Chickens, of course, have no teeth.

when it hits the fan. This expression "indicative of grave consequences" is of course an expurgated version of *when the shit hits the fan.* Common in the U.S. since about 1930, it is traced by some to the punch line of an old joke. Partridge, however, says the original reference is to "an agricultural muck- spreader," without further elaboration.

When the going gets tough, the tough get going. A favorite saying of American president John F. Kennedy, who learned it at the knee of his tough-minded industrialist father Joseph P. Kennedy (1888–1969), who, in turn, may have coined the expression—or at least believed he had.

Where's the beef? Actress Clara Peller delivered this line hundreds of times in a 1984 television ad campaign for the Wendy's hamburger chain comparing the beef content of its burgers with that of its competitors. The words soon became a catchphrase meaning "where's the real substance of a plan, or an idea, or an issue." It is still heard, often in political circles, as when Walter Mondale used it in his unsuccessful run for president in 1984.

Where's the fire? "What's your rush?" this phrase inquires when directed at a rather busy person or someone hurrying along. The Americanism is first recorded in the 1920s, but must have been in use before this. *Where's the fire?* may even date back before the invention of the gasoline fire engine in the 1890s, to the days of horse-drawn "fire engines."

"Where's the rest of me?" The famous line future U.S. president Ronald Reagan, playing a small-town playboy, cried out on awaking from surgery in the film *King's Row,* during which a sadistic doctor amputated his legs.

Whip City. An old nickname for Westfield, Massachusetts, which in 1900 had 40 whip factories that turned out 90 percent of the world's supply of horse whips. Its days of glory are now over.

white-collar worker; blue-collar worker. *White-collar worker,* dating back to about 1920, means anyone who performs nonmanual labor; it especially indicates salaried office workers and lesser executives who haven't been unionized. His or her opposite in America is the *blue-collar worker,* anyone who works with his or her hands, is usually unionized, and often works for an hourly wage. The *white-collar worker's* counterpart in Britain is called a "black coat." All of these designations were obviously suggested by working attire, just as a "hard-hat," a construction worker, takes his or her name from the protective helmets such workers wear.

white hats and black hats. Early western silent movies dressed the hero in a white hat and the villain in a black hat to make it easier for the audience to follow the plot. Observed Louis L'Amour in a 1982 interview: "They joke about the black hats and the white hats, but there were very few grays in the West . . . There were a few men who shifted from one side of the law to the other, but by and large that was not true, they were just what they seemed to be."

White House. Designated the palace by its architect, the Washington, D.C., residence of U.S. presidents was painted white after being gutted by a fire that darkened its gray Virginia limestone.

The designation *White House* is first recorded in 1811, but Teddy Roosevelt made the term an official title by using it on his stationery. Today, of course, it is also a synonym for the presidency and the U.S. executive branch.

whole ball of wax. Everything sticks to wax and leaves an impression on touching it. Therefore, *whole ball of wax* (sometimes *ball of wax*) has come to mean "everything, the whole lot, the whole kit and caboodle." That is possibly the origin of this common Americanism, first recorded in 1953 and still common on Madison Avenue, although several more complicated explanations have been suggested by word and phrase Hawk- shaws. One such guess involves wax balls used in a complicated drawing for the distribution of estates; another claims *whole ball of wax* is a corruption of *whole bailiwick*. No one is sure.

whole kit and caboodle. The *caboodle* in this American expression meaning "the whole lot," is the same as the word *boodle*, for "a pile of money," deriving from the Dutch *boedal*, "property." The *whole kit*, of course, means entire outfit. The phrase doesn't read "the whole kit and boodle" because Americans like alliteration in speech and added a "k" sound before *boodle* in the phrase.

whole shebang. The earliest recorded use of *shebang* is by Walt Whitman in *Specimen Days* (1862), and Mark Twain used it several times as well. Meaning a poor, temporary dwelling, a shack, this Americanism possibly derives from the Anglo-Irish *shebeen,* "a low illegal drinking establishment," older than it by a century or so. In the expression *the whole shebang,* first recorded in 1879, *shebang* means not just a shack but anything at all, that is, any present concern, thing, business—as in "You can take the whole shebang," you can take all of it.

whole shooting match. Large crowds gathered at frontier shooting matches in America to watch marksmen compete in hitting targets, snuffing out candles, etc. *The whole shooting match* thus came to mean "the whole crowd in attendance" and, by extension, "the totality, everything, the whole thing." An earlier British phrase *the whole shoot,* meaning the same but with a different origin, may have strengthened the usage.

whoopi; whoopi cushion. Comedian Whoopi Goldberg (her name is Caryn Johnson, Whoopi is her stage name) got the pseudonym Whoopi because she often "got a little gassy" when performing on stage and had to "let it go," there being no other alternative. People took to saying she sounded like a whoopi cushion, hence the nickname Whoopi. See the New York Times, August 20, 2006.

Who's afraid of the big bad wolf? One British critic claimed that "This is the song that helped Americans lick the depression of the early 1930s." It was written by songwriter Ann Ron- nell for Walt Disney's *Three Little Pigs* (1933) and its title became a catchphrase of courageous defiance.

wide place in the road. Truckers popularized this synonym for a very small town. But the phrase was born over a century ago in the American West, where there were many towns so small they were not even on the map.

widow and orphan makers. A name given to the famed Pennsylvania rifles that American backwoodsmen used in the Battle of New Orleans (1815) in the War of 1812. The accurate rifle and these sharpshooters were a lethal combination.

wild and wooly West. First came *wild West,* recorded in 1851 and so called because the American West was relatively lawless compared with the "civilized" East. Some 30 years passed before the more alliterative *wild and wooly West* was invented by some unknown poet, the *wooly* in the phrase perhaps referring to uncurried wild horses or the sheepskin chaps some cowboys wore, or perhaps to the bragging of cowboys in a popular song:

> I'm a wooly wolf and full of fleas,
> I never been curried below the knees—
> And this is my night to howl!

The first use of the expression, in an 1885 book called *Texas Cow Boy,* has *wild and wooly* referring to a herd of steers.

Wild Bill Hickok. Any fabled gunfighter; after James Butler "Wild Bill" Hickok (1837–76), army scout, gambler, and town marshall of Abilene, Kansas. Though a handsome dandy, with long blond hair hanging over his shoulders, Hickok was first called "Duck Bill" after his long nose and protruding lip. He met his violent end at the hands of a paranoid rival who shot him in the back of the head while he was playing poker.

wild man of Borneo. P. T. Barnum coined the name of this sideshow attraction, as he did many others. In the mid-19th century, Barnum displayed the Wild Man in his Brooklyn-based American Museum of Curios. The name holds on today as a humorous description of someone unkempt and disheveled, as in "Is that what you're going to wear—you look like the Wild Man of Borneo!"

Wild West show. A circus of cowboys and Indians performing various feats ranging from riding to shooting, the words first applied to William F. (Buffalo Bill) Cody's Wild West Show, which opened at Omaha, Nebraska May 17, 1883.

window; window of opportunity. A period of time favorable for beginning or completing something: "I'd say you have a window of about three more months to invest before interest rates rise." Also window of opportunity and period of opportunity. The expression dates back to 1965, when it was first used in the U.S. space program.

win one for the Gipper. This one is so well known, of course, because President Ronald Reagan played George Gipp, or the Gipper, in a movie about Knute Rockne and his football team at Notre Dame (*Knute Rockne, All American,* 1940). Rockne urged his team to go out and "win this game for the Gipper," who on his deathbed had requested that the team win a game in his honor—and Notre Dame proceeded to do it. Actually, Gipp had made this request of Rockne in 1920 when dying of pneumonia and the coach had used the same appeal several other times before the 1928 game with heavily favored Army that is depicted in the film.

Wisconsin. Wisconsin takes its name from the Algonquian name for a river within its boundaries that translates as either "place of the beaver" or "grassy place." The Badger State was admitted to the Union in 1848 as our 30th state.

wish book. A rural name a century ago for the Montgomery Ward and Sears catalogs, both no longer published to the regret of many.

wisteria. A spelling error made by Thomas Nuttal, curator of Harvard's Botanical Garden, led to the accepted misspelling of this beautiful flowering plant—*wisteria* being the common spelling today even though *wistaria* is correct. Nuttal, who named the plant after Dr. Caspar Wistar, had meant to write "wistaria," but his slip of the pen was perpetuated by later writers, and *wisteria* has become accepted. All attempts to remedy the situation have failed, even Joshua Logan's play *The Wistaria Trees,* in which the author purposely spelled the word with an *a.* A Philadelphia Quaker, Caspar Wistar (1761–1818) taught "anatomy, mid-wifery, and surgery" at what was then the College of Pennsylvania. The son of a noted colonial glassmaker, Dr. Wistar wrote America's first anatomy textbook, succeeded Jefferson as head of the American Philosophical Society, and his home became the Sunday afternoon meeting place of many notable Philadelphians. Anyone in the vicinity of Sierra Madre, California in the late springtime should see the giant Chinese wisteria near the Los Angeles State and County Arboretum. During its five-week blooming period this giant species becomes a vast field filled with over one and a half million blossoms, the largest flowering plant in the world. Planted in 1892 the fabulous vine covers almost an acre, has branches surpassing 500 feet in length, and weighs over 252 tons.

Witch City. A nickname for Salem, Massachusetts, where in 1692 a wave of hysterical witch-hunting led to the hanging of 19 innocent people. This was the beginning of witch-hunting in America, but the practice had been common elsewhere since ancient times. Thousands were executed worldwide from 1450 to 1650. In England "Witch-Finder General" Matthew Hopkins (1621–47), as he named himself, hanged more than 100 people in one year. Since about 1920 *witch-hunting* has been applied to any effort to expose subversion or disloyalty, usually based on little evidence.

Wolverine State. A nickname for Michigan since the 1830s, though no one knows why since there were no wolverines in what was Michigan at the time. Michigan has also been called the Lake State because it borders on the Great Lakes.

Wonder State. A nickname for Arkansas officially adopted by the state in 1923. Arkansas is sometimes called the Bear State and the Hot Water State (after Hot Springs, Arkansas). Residents of Arkansas are called *Arkansawyers. See also* BOWIE KNIFE.

won hands down. Won effortlessly, easily, as in "She won the race hands down." An Americanism familiar to horse-racing enthusiasts, dating back to about 1870.

woodchuck. A New England name for the groundhog (*Marmota monax*), *woodchuck* probably derives from a New England Algonquian Indian word meaning the same. "A boy always had woodchuck holes to explore after the leaves were down in the fall . . . ," Mayden Pearson wrote in *New England Flavor,* 1961.

Woolworth's. The great American retailer Frank W. Woolworth's death in 1919 was an ironic one, for the same W. H. Moore who had given him his start was indirectly responsible for his death. Moore had had all his teeth removed by a dentist late in life and died in the dentist's office of a stroke. Woolworth refused all dental care from that day on and subsequently died of septic poisoning.

workaholic. American pastoral counselor Wayne Oates coined the word *workaholic* for "an uncontrollable need to work incessantly," in 1971, from *work* and *alcoholic.* Himself a workaholic who discovered his sickness only when his "five- year-old son asked for an appointment to see him," Oates published his *Confessions of a Workaholic* in 1972. There have since been many similar but less popular constructions, including *bookaholic* (1977), *wordaholic* (1978), and *hashaholic* (1973), someone who uses a lot of marijuana or hashish.

World Series. This term is, of course, still used in baseball and has been extended to cover any highest-level contest, from the *world series* of poker to the *world series* of go-cart racing. The first World Series in baseball called the *World Series* was held in 1889, the term a shortening of the World Championship Series. This was a series of post-season games held each year between the pennant winners of the National League and the American Association beginning in 1884. But the first World Series between two major league teams came in 1903, when the American League was recognized as a bona fide major league. The American League's Boston Pilgrims (later the Boston Red Sox) beat the National League's Pittsburgh Pirates in this best-of-nine game series, which fans paid one dollar a game to see. *See also* MAJOR LEAGUE.

World's Largest Store. The slogan of New York's Macy's, and it is no hype. Macy's Herald Square store covers a full 55.5 acres, containing 2.2 million square feet of floor space. A good-size house has 2,000 square feet, so you could put 10,000 houses in Macy's. The store opened in 1902 on a site that had been occupied by, among other enterprises, a few quality brothels and a music hall where Thomas Edison first projected a movie. Harrods, the largest store in the United Kingdom, is only half as big as Macy's.

World Trade Center. *See* TWIN TOWERS.

World Trade Center cough. A general hacking and congestion that workers suffered after working at the World Trade Center site after the 9/11 terrorist attack. New, even more serious disorders are now being discovered among workers and visitors.

wouldn't touch it with a 10-foot pole. This expression may have been suggested by the 10-foot poles that river boatmen used to pole their boats along in shallow waters. Possibly the expression was first something like *I wouldn't touch that with the 10-foot pole of a riverman* and that this shortened with the passing of pole boats from the American scene. However, the image first appears in the Nantucketism *can't touch him with a 10-foot,* meaning "he is distant, proud, reserved." In the sense of not wanting to get involved in a project or having a strong distaste for something, the words aren't recorded until the late 19th century.

wrong side of the tracks. This American expression arose in the 19th century when railroad tracks, which sometimes split a town in two, provided a clear social demarcation—well-to-do people living on the right side of the tracks and the poor living on the wrong side, in the slums or seedy area of town. Today the expression *to be born on the wrong side of the tracks,* "to be born poor and disadvantaged," hangs on despite the fact that the physical distance between rich and poor has increased and that they now tend to live in different towns or counties altogether.

Wrong-Way Corrigan. Douglas "Wrong-Way" Corrigan *may* have gone the wrong way unintentionally. The 31-year-old pilot flew from California to New York in a record time of less than 28 hours and took off the next day in his battered plane to return to California. His plane had no radio, beam finder, or safety devices, and had failed safety inspections, which would indicate that he had no plans for a publicity stunt. But even though extra gas tanks blocked his view, it is hard to explain how, after he took off in a westerly direction over Jamaica Bay, near the present Kennedy International Airport in New York, he swung his plane in a wide arc and crossed the Rockaway Peninsula, heading out over the Atlantic Ocean. Presumably, he flew through a thick fog, convinced he was California-bound until the fog lifted that fine morning of July 18, 1938, and he looked down at the grass roofs and cobblestoned streets of Ireland! Corrigan told officials at Dublin's Baldonnel Airport that he had accidentally flown the wrong way, and he promptly b ecame known as *Wrong-Way Corrigan.* As a result he became a hero, made close to $100,000, and even played himself in *The Flying Irishman,* a movie based on his "mistake." When asked recently if he had really meant to fly to California, Corrigan replied,

"Sure . . . well, at least I've told that story so many times that I believe it myself now."

Wyatt Earp. A fabled gunfighter; after Wyatt Barry Stapp Earp (1848–1929), most famous for his part in the 1879 gun- fight at the O.K. Corral in Tombstone, Arizona. Considered quick on the draw (from a leather-lined, waxed coat pocket), Earp was never bested and died quietly in his sleep, one of the two legendary western gunfighters who definitely didn't meet a violent end (Bat Masterson was the other).

Wyoming. *Wyoming* comes from the Algonquian *Mache-weaming*, meaning "place of the big flats," actually a west Pennsylvania valley where a pre-Revolutionary Indian massacre had occurred that was celebrated in the popular sentimental poem "Gertrude of Wyoming." It became the name of several U.S. counties and in 1890 that great name-giver Congressman James M. Ashlet bestowed it upon our 44th state ("The Equality State") because it was "a beautiful name," never thinking that "place of the big flats" hardly suited this mountainous western state.

X

x as a baseball symbol. The letter *x* is used as an English language symbol in many ways, including baseball scoring. When an unusual or extraordinary play occurs in a baseball game, the scorer marks it on his scorecard with an *x*.

Xerox. U.S. inventor Chester Carlson invented the Xerox machine in 1938 and *Xerox* remains a trademark of the company that makes it, its name deriving from *xero,* a learned borrowing from the Greek for "dry," and *graph,* an element from the Greek meaning "drawn, written." Inventor Carlson became a multimillionaire from royalties on his dry copier, the rights to which he sold to what is now the Xerox Corporation in 1947.

X rated. In 1968 the Motion Picture Association of America began to rate films as a guide for moviegoers. Their system ranged from *G,* "general, all ages permitted," to *X,* "restricted, no one under 17 admitted." The *X* rating referred to explicit sex and violence in a movie and became so common that *x-rated* almost immediately became a term for anything pornographic or sexy, from a film to a book or even a person!

Y

yada, yada, yada. A catchphrase (qv) popularized by the television show *Seinfeld*. Yada, yada, yada is akin to blah, blah, blah in meaning and usage: "We exchanged greetings, *went* to lunch, yada, yada, yada, and signed the deal."

Yale blue; Yale lock. Yale blue, a reddish blue, takes its name from the Yale University colors. It is the royal blue of the Egyptian Rameses dynasty, also called Rameses. *Yale lock* has no connection with the school. American inventor Linnus Yale (1821–68) invented numerous locks, including the trademarked key type with a revolving barrel that bears his name. Linnus founded a company to manufacture locks at Stamford, Connecticut the same year that he died.

Yale University. Yale University, ranking after Harvard and William and Mary as the third oldest institution of higher education in the United States, is named for English merchant Elihu Yale (1649–1721). Founded in 1701 as the Collegiate School of Saybrook, Connecticut, the school was named Yale College at its 1718 Commencement, held in the first college building at New Haven. It became a university in 1887. Yale might have been called Mather University, for Cotton Mather suggested naming it so in return for his financial support, but Elihu Yale won out when he donated a cargo of gifts, books, and various goods that brought about 562 pounds when sold. Yale had been born in Boston in 1649, but returned with his family to England three years later. He served with the British East India Company, and as governor of Fort St. George in India until scandals in his administration led to his removal in 1692.

yank. *Yank,* to pull abruptly or vigorously, is of uncertain origin. A U.S. invention, probably originating in New England early in the 19th century and much used since then, it has nothing to do with the word YANKEE for a New Englander. It may be akin to the English dialect word *yerk,* a variant of *jerk,* but there is no proof of this.

Yankee. The source of *Yankee* has long been disputed and its origin is still uncertain, despite all the research devoted to it. Candidates, among many, have included a slave named Yankee offered for sale in 1725, a Dutch sea captain named Yanky, the Yankos Indians, the Dutch name Janke ("Johnny"), which the Dutch applied to the English, and an Indian mispronunciation *(Yengees)* of the word *English.* The most popular explanation, also unproved, is that Yankee comes from *Jan Kees,* a contemptuous Flemish and German nickname for the Dutch that the English first applied to the Dutch in the New World. In any case, *Yankee* seems to have been first applied to Americans by British soldiers serving under General James Wolfe in the French and Indian War prior to 1758. A letter written by Wolfe himself in that year uses the word as a contemptuous nickname for Americans: "My posts are not so fortified that I can afford you two companies of Yankees, and the more as they are better for ranging and scouting than either work or vigilance . . . [they] are in general the dirtiest most contemptible cowardly dogs that you can conceive. There is no depending on them in action. They fall down dead in their own dirt and desert by battalions, officers and all. Such rascals as those are rather an encumberance than any real strength to an army." Wolfe's low opinion of the Americans and further contemptuous use of *Yankee* is seen in a 1775 chronicle, which is also notable as an early description of the practice of "mooning": "They [British soldiers] abused the watch-men on duty, and the young children of Boston by the wayside, making mouths at them, calling them Yankeys, shewing their posteriors, and clapping their hands thereon."

It wasn't until the Battle of Lexington, the first battle of the Revolution in 1775, that Americans began applying the nickname *Yankee* to themselves and making it respectable. Soon after, the process of dignification began and the story about the Yankos Indians was invented. In this tale a mythical tribe of Massachusetts Indians are said to have been defeated by a band of valorous New Englanders, the defeated Yankos so admiring the bravery of their victorious adversaries that they gave them their name, *Yankos,* which meant "Invincibles" and was soon corrupted to *Yankees! Yankee* has been an admirable or contemptuous nickname for Americans ever since, depending by whom and in what context it is used. At any rate, *Yankee* described a New Englander by the middle 18th century and was used by the British to designate any American during the Revolution, the most notable example found in the derisive song *Yankee Doodle.* Nowadays the British still use the word for an American, southerners use it for northerners (see DAMN YANKEE) and northerners use it for New Englanders, who, despite its early history, remain proud of the designation.

Yankee cheesebox on a raft. A widespread derisive description of the U.S. armored warship the *Monitor,* which fought the famous Civil War battle against the Confederate *Merrimac.* The *Monitor* was also called a cheesebox upon a plank.

Yankee Clipper. One of sport's best-known nicknames, *Yankee Clipper* honors New York Yankee centerfielder Joe DiMaggio, one of baseball's greatest players, who hit safely in 56 consecutive games, a record that still stands. The popular song "Joltin' Joe DiMaggio" was written in his honor. DiMaggio was also called the Yankee Clipper both for the way he "clipped" the ball and for his grace as a fielder, moving as effortlessly as a clipper ship (or possibly the popular Yankee Clipper plane of the 1930s) across the field to make even the hard catches seem easy.

Yankee Doodle. Legend has it that during the French and Indian War, the shabbily dressed troops of Colonel Thomas Fitch of Norfolk,

Connecticut, inspired a British army surgeon with musical talents, a Dr. Sheckburgh or Shackburg, to write the derisive song "Yankee Doodle." The story is recounted in the *Federal Writer's Project Connecticut* (1938): "According to local tradition, Elizabeth Fitch, on leaving the house to bid goodbye to her brother [Colonel Fitch], was dismayed by the ill-sorted costumes of the 'cavalry.' Exclaiming, 'You must have uniforms of some kind,' she ran into the chicken yard, and returned with a handful of feathers announcing, 'Soldiers should wear plumes,' and directed each soldier to put a feather in his cap. When Sheckburgh saw Fitch's men arriving at Fort Crailo, Rensselaer, New York, he is reputed to have exclaimed, 'Now stab my vitals, they're macaronis!' sarcastically applying the slang of the day for fop, or dandy, and proceeded to write the song, which instantly caught popular fancy." There is no firm proof of this theory about the origin of the song, which ironically came to be a popular song of patriot troops during the Revolutionary War. There are said to be hundreds of verses to the song. Before the Civil War, the tune, identified with New England, was often hissed off the stage in the South.

"Yankee Doodle Dandy"; "Over There." These patriotic songs were both written by George M. Cohan (1878–1942) to support America and her allies in World War I. Both the "Over There" lyrics ("The Yanks are coming, the Yanks are coming") and "Yankee Doodle Dandy" lyrics ("a real live nephew of my Uncle Sam, born on the Fourth of July . . .") have been used as titles for novels and movies, most recently the film *Born on the Fourth of July.* Enrico Caruso lent his great tenor voice to an early recording of "Over There." For more patriotic songs *see* GOD BLESS AMERICA.

Yankee Notion State. See quote from the *Hartford Courant* (October 29, 1904): "The Yankee Notion State, as Connecticut has often been called, earned its title in the early part of the 19th century, when there was a great impetus given to the manufacture of almost all sorts of implements for the farm and the household."

Yankee peddler. "The whole race of Yankee Peddlers," wrote a British observer of American character in 1833, "are proverbial for dishonesty. They go forth annually in the thousands to lie, cog, cheat, swindle; in short to get possession of their neighbor's property in any manner it can be done with impunity." In fact, the name "damn Yankee," coined long before the Civil War, probably came from Yankee peddlers who worked the rural South. Yankee peddlers were known as far away as Europe for their trickery and sharpness, especially for their wooden nutmegs (it took an expert wood carver a full day to make just *one* in a recent experiment) when these kernals of an evergreen tree cultivated in the Spice Islands sold for less than a penny apiece. But whether carved wooden nutmegs ever existed (no one has yet turned up an authentic one), many country people did believe that Yankee peddlers sold them, along with carved wooden hams painted pink ("Basswood Hams"), carved cigars, and wooden pumpkin seeds. Connecticut is still called the Nutmeg State for this reason, and the warning *don't take any wooden nutmegs* probably influenced the coining of the still current phrase DON'T TAKE ANY WOODEN NICKELS. An old rhyme went: "There is in Yankeeland / a class of men called tin-peddlers, / A shrewd, sarcastic band / Of busy meddlers." And an old joke went: "Know how to revive a Yankee peddler when he drowns?" "Just turn out his pockets!" But though they were well-versed in chicanery and the Yankee art of giving people "a steer in the wrong direction," as P. T. Barnum put it, Yankee peddlers helped settle America, carrying the materials of civilization to sparsely inhabited regions. Wherever a man swung an ax in the wilderness, an old saying went, a Yankee peddler would show up in the clearing the next day.

yap. *Yap* is an echoic word that first meant only the barking of a small dog. The word is first recorded in this sense in 1603, and it apparently took over two centuries before *yapping* was applied to a person who yaps as well as a dog that yaps. In the process *yap* also became American slang for the mouth, as in *shut your yap,* recorded in about 1900, and American slang for a stupid person. The Yap Islands in the West Pacific, noted for the stone money long used by the Micronesians there, are not named from the English *yap,* taking their name instead from a native language.

yellow-dog contract. The yellow dog, generally considered to be a cowardly common cur or mongrel, has long been a symbol of utter worthlessness in America. The term *yellow dog* has been used in expressions of contempt since at least 1833, when it is first so recorded, and toward the late 19th century it began to be heard in the term *yellow-dog contract,* a contract in which company employees do not or cannot join the union. Though outlawed by the Wagner Act in 1935, yellow-dog contracts still persist.

yellow-dog Democrat. A term applied to loyal Democrats, so named, according to the old story, because they would vote for a yellow dog before voting for any Republican. The designation dates back to post-Civil War days.

yellow journalism. *Yellow* has been used to describe sensational books and newspapers in the U.S. since 1846, the "yellow" referring to the cheap yellow covers some sensational books were wrapped in. *Yellow journalism* was first used in 1898, when the phrase was applied to the sensational stories that appeared in Hearst's *New York Evening*

Journal and Pulitzer's *New York World* about Spanish atrocities in Cuba. Hearst's cartoon character the "Yellow Kid" could also have figured in the coining.

yellow rose of Texas. The yellow rose of Texas, which is part of the state's folklore and even has a famous song written about it, actually originated in the 1830s on a farm in New York City near the present-day Pennsylvania Station. There a lawyer named George Harrison found it as a seedling growing among other roses on his property and began cultivating it. Settlers soon took the yellow rose west with them, and legend has it that Texans finally claimed it as their own when Mexican general Santa Anna, the villain of the Alamo, "was distracted by a beautiful woman with yellow roses in her hair." We have this nice story on the authority of Stephen Scanniello, rosarian of the Crawford Rose Garden in the New York Botanical Garden, who told it to the *New York Times* (6/19/92).

Yerba Buena. An old name for San Francisco; so named from the Spanish for "good grass" because the area had excellent pasturage for animals.

yes, we have no bananas. Originally, this was the title of a song written by Americans Frank Silver and Irving Cohen in 1923. One story has the team borrowing the first line from wordsmith Tad Dorgan and creating the song with the refrain "Yes, we have no bananas, / We have no bananas today." Another more dramatic account has Silver getting the idea for the song when he heard a Greek fruit peddler yell up to a woman at a New York City tenement window, "Yes, we have no bananas!" Whatever the case, the song became immensely popular, and, according to H. L. Mencken, *yes, we have no bananas* became the most widely used catchphrase of the 1920s, even spreading across the sea to England. In his book *The Illiterate Digest* (1924) Will Rogers wrote, "I would rather have been the Author of that Banana Masterpiece than the author of the Constitution of the United States."

You ain't heard (seen) nothin' yet! No one has had much luck finding the source of this phrase still commonly used today. It is an Americanism and the title of a 1919 popular song; but probably dates back 50 years or more before that. It was popularized in Al Jolson's movie *The Jazz Singer* (1927) and again in the 1940s in two film biographies of Jolson's life.

you are my sunshine. The phrase is from the long-popular song of that name written by Louisiana governor Jimmie Davis, who died at the age of 101 in 2000. According to the *New York Times* (March 22, 2004), Davis "wrote 'You Are My Sunshine' [and] had five Top Five country singles during his first term as Louisiana's governor from 1944 to 1948." The song by now enjoys the status of a folk song.

You bet!; You betcha!, etc. *You bet!* means "surely, without a doubt, certainly" and has been a popular-American expression of affirmation since the mid-19th century, the variants *you betcha!, bet your sweet ass!* and *you bet your sweet life!* being not much younger. The expression arose with the gambling-pioneering spirit in 19th-century America. Wrote Mark Twain in "Buck Fanshaw's Funeral" (1872): "Slang was the language of Nevada . . . Such phrases as 'You bet!' . . . and a hundred others, became so common as to fall from the lips of a speaker unconsciously." *You bet your bippy!* is a comical play on the expression dating back to the 1960s, with the nonsense word "bippy" probably a euphemism for "ass." I believe the expression was invented for, or popularized by, Rowan and Martin's *Laugh In*—a television comedy show.

you can play with my dog, you can play with my wife, but you'd better leave my gun alone. A humorous Texas saying, possibly of recent vintage.

You can say that again! An emphatic agreement with what a previous speaker has said. Originally a U.S. expression probably originating in the early 20th century, it is now heard in Britain, Australia, and New Zealand as well, In *Strong Cigars and Lovely Women* (1951), John Lardner wrote: "This year's drought has got real significance, and don't tell me I can say that again. I know I can. It has got real significance."

you can't judge a book by its cover. An early 1900s American saying meaning "not to judge things from surface appearances." In writing a review of Stephen King's *Everything's Eventual: 14 Dark Tales* (2002), *New York Times* critic Janet Maslin praised the jacket illustration by artist Mark Stutzman and turned the old saying around: ". . . a tranquil restaurant scene on the front cover with just a wee trace of blood in one water glass. But turn to the back, and all hell has broken loose. You *can* tell the book by its cover."

You Gotta Believe. A New York Mets slogan coined by relief pitcher Frank "Tug" McGraw, who helped the underdog Amazin' Mets win their first World Series in 1969. McGraw's parents gave him the nickname *Tug* after the way he tugged at things around the house.

you have money, give money; you don't have money, give yourself (volunteer). *Heard in New York's Chinatown, said to be an old Chinese saying.*

you have the words, but you don't have the music. You don't have the essence of something. The phrase can be traced back to Mark Twain. In a foul mood one morning and unable to find a clean shirt fit to wear, he unleashed a string of expletives only he could have strung together. His wife, Livy, standing in the doorway, decided to teach him a lesson and slowly repeated each curse he had uttered. But when she was done, Twain simply sighed and said, "My dear, you have the words, but you don't have the music."

yucca. Any plant of the genus *Yucca* native to the Southwest. Yucca, the state flower of New Mexico, has pointed sword-shaped leaves and bears clusters of white waxy flowers on tall stalks. Weekley says that according to a *Notes & Queries* correspondent, yucca (Spanish, from the native language of Haiti) "is among the very earliest native American words on record. It is quoted by Amerigo Vespucci in his famous 'First Letter' dated 1497."

yuppie. A slang term that has been around for over a decade and threatens to stay longer. It is generally a disparaging term meaning

Young Urban Professional, especially one who puts getting ahead ahead of everything, and was first recorded in 1983 by syndicated columnist Bob Greene, who overheard it in a bar. As Green explained the word's origin: "While [Gerry Rubin] and Abbie Hoffman once led the Yippies—the Youth International Party—one social commentator has ventured that Rubin is now attempting to become the leader of the Yuppies—Young Urban Professionals."

Z

zap. The exact origin of *zap* is unknown, but the term possibly arose during World War II, as an onomatopoetic word imitating the sound of a rifle shot hitting someone. According to the *New Dictionary of American Slang* (1986), the word began life as an exclamation deriving from "the sound of a ray gun in the old comic strip Buck Rogers in the Twenty-fifth Century." Since then the word has taken on wider meanings. As slang for "to kill or strike violently," *zap* probably dates back to the Vietnam War. It is also used for "to cook" when food is being prepared in a microwave oven (a common synonym of this is *to nuke).*

zep. Short for *zeppelin* and one of the many names for the Italian hero sandwich or hero in America. These names include *hoagies* (in Philadelphia), *submarines* or *subs* (in Pittsburgh and elsewhere), *torpedos* (Los Angeles), *wedgies* (Rhode Island), *Garibaldis* (Wisconsin), *bomber* (upstate New York), *wedge* (downstate New York), *Cuban sandwich* (Miami), *Italian sandwich* (Maine), *an Italian* (Midwest), *grinder* (New England), *rocket* (New York State), and *poor boy* (New Orleans), though this last one is made with French instead of Italian bread. *Blimpie,* though it's a tradename and is on a shorter roll, might also qualify, as might *Dagwood sandwich,* for any large sandwich—after *Blondie* comic strip character Dagwood Bumstead's midnight snack creations. That's 20 in all—and there must be more. Is the *Italian hero* possibly the most numerous-named thing in English?

zilch. *Zilch,* "nothing," is an Americanism that has been traced back to the 1920s when a *Joe Zilch* meant a good for nothing college boy. Other sources, however, trace the expression to a character called Mr. Zilch in a *Ballyhoo* magazine cartoon series of the 1930s, in which

Mr. Zilch was never seen but scantily clad, wide-eyed girls, reacting to things he had obviously done, cried "Oh, Mr. Zilch!" Since Mr. Zilch wasn't depicted, according to this theory, he came to represent nothing, or *zilch.*

zip; zipper. *Zip* is common American slang for zero, nothing, and probably derives in part from the z sound in *zero.* The story that American soldiers in Vietnam named Vietnamese Zips from an acronym for *Z*ero *I*ntelligence *P*otential is unlikely—it probably derived from the earlier *zip.* *Zip* for zero is not related to *zipper;* this slide device for fastening clothing, once a trademark, takes its name from *zip* for fast, which is first recorded in about 1855 and is imitative of the sound *zip.* The zipper was invented in 1893 by Whitman L. Judson, who called it the Universal Fastener. An anonymous executive at the B.F. Goodrich Company changed the name to Zipper, but Goodrich did not protect its trademark and the word is not capitalized today.

zip code; zip. The *zip* in *zip-code* is an acronym for *z*one *i*mprovement *p*lan, an acronym that was invented to convey the idea of speed—zip! The system and name for it were introduced by the U.S. Post Office in 1963. The actual inventor of the code was postal employee Robert A. Moon (1918–2000), who first submitted his idea in 1944 but waited almost 20 years to see it accepted. Mr. Moon's contribution consisted of the first three digits of the zip code—those referring to the general regions of the U.S. The last two digits—identifying smaller delivery areas—are credited to others. At the time of his death Mr. Moon was said to be working on a zip code plan for interplanetary mail.

zoot suit. A men's clothing style of the 1930s and early 1940s featuring peg trousers, jacket with padded shoulders, wide-brimmed hat and wide tie, among other flamboyant items of apparel, all in bright colors. A good example of the style can be seen in the film *Malcolm X* (1993). *Zoot suit* is probably a rhyming phrase, *zoot* an alteration (!) of suit.

z's. *Z's* is American slang for sleep. Originating within the last 35 years or so, the term probably derives from the *Z's* indicating snoring in comic strip and cartoon captions, which themselves represent the sound of snoring.